Free Trade in the Americas

NEW HORIZONS IN INTERNATIONAL BUSINESS

Series Editor: Peter J. Buckley
Centre for International Business,
University of Leeds (CIBUL), UK

The New Horizons in International Business series has established itself as the world's leading forum for the presentation of new ideas in international business research. It offers pre-eminent contributions in the areas of multinational enterprise – including foreign direct investment, business strategy and corporate alliances, global competitive strategies, and entrepreneurship. In short, this series constitutes essential reading for academics, business strategists and policy makers alike.

Titles in the series include:

Network Knowledge in International Business
Edited by Sarianna M. Lundan

Business Strategy and National Culture
US and Asia Pacific Microcomputer Multinationals in Europe
Denise Tsang

Learning in the Internationalisation Process of Firms
Edited by Anders Blomstermo and D. Deo Sharma

Alliance Capitalism and Corporate Management
Entrepreneurial Cooperation in Knowledge Based Economies
Edited by John H. Dunning and Gavin Boyd

The New Economic Analysis of Multinationals
An Agenda for Management, Policy and Research
Edited by Thomas L. Brewer, Stephen Young and Stephen E. Guisinger

Transnational Corporations, Technology and Economic Development
Backward Linkages and Knowledge Transfer in South East Asia
Axèle Giroud

Alliance Capitalism for the New American Economy
Edited by Alan M. Rugman and Gavin Boyd

The Structural Foundations of International Finance
Problems of Growth and Stability
Edited by Pier Carlo Padoan, Paul A. Brenton and Gavin Boyd

The New Competition for Inward Investment
Companies, Institutions and Territorial Development
Edited by Nicholas Phelps and Phil Raines

Multinational Enterprises, Innovative Strategies and Systems of Innovation
Edited by John Cantwell and José Molero

Multinational Firms' Location and the New Economic Geography
Edited by Jean-Louis Mucchielli and Thierry Mayer

Free Trade in the Americas
Economic and Political Issues for Governments and Firms
Edited by Sidney Weintraub, Alan M. Rugman and Gavin Boyd

Free Trade in the Americas

Economic and Political Issues for Governments and Firms

Edited by

Sidney Weintraub

William E. Simon Chair in Political Economy, Center for Strategic and International Studies, Washington, DC, US

Alan M. Rugman

L. Leslie Waters Chair in International Business, Kelley School of Business, Indiana University, US

Gavin Boyd

Honorary Professor, Political Science Department, Rutgers University, US and Adjunct Professor, Management Faculty, Saint Mary's University, Canada

NEW HORIZONS IN INTERNATIONAL BUSINESS

Edward Elgar

Cheltenham, UK • Northampton, MA, USA

Published by
Edward Elgar Publishing Limited
Glensanda House
Montpellier Parade
Cheltenham
Glos GL50 1UA
UK

Edward Elgar Publishing, Inc.
136 West Street
Suite 202
Northampton
Massachusetts 01060
USA

A catalogue record for this book
is available from the British Library

Library of Congress Cataloguing in Publication Data
Free trade in the Americas : economic and political issues for governments and firms / edited by Sidney Weintraub, Alan M. Rugman, Gavin Boyd.
p. cm.— (New horizons in international business)
"This volume is the result of a conference on trade liberalization in the Western Hemisphere sponsored by Saint Mary's University, Halifax, in the Autumn of 2002"—Foreword.
1. Free trade—America—Congresses. 2. America—Economic integration—Congresses. I. Weintraub, Sidney, 1922– II. Rugman, Alan M. III. Boyd, Gavin. IV. Series.

HF1745.F738 2004
382'71'097—dc22

20030677447

ISBN 1 84376 667 1

Printed and bound in Great Britain by MPG Books Ltd, Bodmin, Cornwall

Contents

Figures

Tables

Contributors

Louis Bélanger is a Professor of Political Science at Laval University, Quebec, Canada

Gavin Boyd was an Honorary Professor of Political Science at Rutgers University, Newark, New Jersey, USA, and an Adjunct Professor in Management at Saint Mary's University, Halifax, Canada

Paul Brenton is in the Poverty Relief and Economic Management Department at the World Bank, Washington, DC, USA

Walid Hejazi is a Professor in the Rotman School of Management, University of Toronto, and the Division of Management, University of Toronto at Scarborough, Toronto, Canada

Gordon Mace is a Professor of Political Science at Laval University, Quebec, Canada

Miriam Manchin is at the Centre for European Policy Studies, Brussels, Belgium

Heinz G. Preusse is Professor of Economics at Eberhard Karls University, Tubingen, Germany

Stephen J. Randall is Dean of Social Sciences at the University of Calgary, Calgary, Alberta, Canada

Alan M. Rugman is L. Leslie Waters Chair in International Business, Kelley School of Business, Indiana University, Bloomington, Indiana, US

Jose M. Salazar-Xirinachs is Director of the Trade Unit at the Organization of American States, Washington, DC, USA

Sidney Weintraub is William E. Simon Chair in Political Economy at the Center for Strategic and International Studies, Washington, DC, USA

Foreword

This volume is the result of a conference on Trade Liberalization in the Western Hemisphere sponsored by Saint Mary's University, Halifax, in the autumn of 2002. The conference was planned in anticipation of reductions of trade barriers that could lead to the formation of a Free Trade Area of the Americas – a virtual expansion of the North America Free Trade Area. In the world economy the hemispheric area of liberalized commerce would potentially balance and complement the role of the European Union as it enlarges with the admission in 2004 of several East and Central European countries. Although there has not been an emerging consensus for the formation of a hemispheric economic community, it was clear before our conference, and even clearer during our discussions, that the structural and policy interdependencies which would become larger and more complex in the proposed free trade area would cause interest groups and policy communities to become very active across borders in the Southern and Northern parts of the hemisphere.

Our conference brought together a coordinated group of specialists, and I wish to thank them for their very valuable contributions. The event was associated with the 2002 Annual General Assembly of World Trade Centres, held at the Halifax World Trade Centre, with excellent support from its management, for which I was very grateful. Our discussions were very fruitful, in part because the lead editor of this volume, Professor Sidney Weintraub, William E. Simon Chair in Political Economy at the Center for Strategic and International Studies in Washington, DC, is a well-recognized expert on Latin America. Several participants in the project, including Alan M. Rugman, L. Leslie Waters Chair in International Business at Indiana University, Bloomington, Indiana, had been involved in previous conferences sponsored by Saint Mary's University including one on the Structural Foundations of International Finance, in spring 2002. The volume which came out of that conference was edited by Pier Carlo Padoan, Executive Director, International Monetary Fund, Paul A. Brenton, Senior Economist, International Trade Department, World Bank, and the late Gavin Boyd, who was an Honorary Professor, Political Science Department, Rutgers University, Newark, New Jersey and Adjunct Professor in Management at Saint Mary's University, Halifax.

The linkages among national economies, which must be expected to grow more rapidly if hemispheric trade is liberalized, can be seen to set requirements for planning by policymakers and corporate managements. Issues of cooperation in the treatment of foreign direct investment demand attention; competition policy issues will also have to be taken up. There will be questions about coordinating monetary policies, regulating financial markets and ensuring the expansion of infrastructure network industries. This volume, I believe, will contribute substantially to sound orientations for engagement with the necessary planning tasks. It will also, I hope, prepare the way for our forthcoming project on Alliance Capitalism for the New Atlantic Economy – a study of structural linkages between North America and the European Union, which commenced with a conference at Saint Mary's in September 2003 and will be published later this year.

J. Colin Dodds, Ph.D.
President and Professor of Finance
Saint Mary's University

Postscript

As this volume was being prepared for publication, in December 2003, Gavin Boyd died. His energy, knowledge of, and contributions to the trade and investment literature will be sorely missed.

Preface

A Free Trade Area of the Americas will constitute a new regional economy, new because of its size, diversity, and potential, with a central member that is already new in terms of being knowledge intensive, achieving advances in applied frontier technology ahead of other major industrialized states. The USA's status as the central member will tend to become more significant, through growth generated by entrepreneurial dynamism, and through contributions to regional policy learning and the learning of corporate managements, as well as through assertions of interests on issues of trade and investment cooperation. Difficult macromanagement problems will have to be overcome in the USA, however, for highly constructive involvement in the vast new regional economy. Efforts to reform corporate governance will have to continue, fiscal prudence will be required, and the current account will have to be brought into balance, while the financial sector will have to provide more productive funding for the real economy, with much less destabilizing speculation. Consideration of these imperatives in the regional context is necessary because of the persistence of serious macromanagement problems in Latin America.

In this volume we have been privileged to have contributions by distinguished area specialists. They have recognized, from differing perspectives, the relevance of the European Union's experience of regional economic integration, its slow processes of policy learning and its low overall growth rates. Hopes of forming a more vigorous regional economy in the hemisphere have been indicated, with understandings of the efficiencies of widely coordinated entrepreneurship, active across national boundaries without impediments, but with bonds conducive to the building of trust and goodwill.

The details of regional market opening can be engrossing, and can occasion intensive bargaining by aggressive interest groups. There is a clear requirement for superior statecraft and corporate magnanimity. Pursuit of hard and precise agreements can lead to wrangling that generates distrust and hinders friendly adjustment to problems and opportunities that cannot be foreseen. The natural development of entrepreneurship in economies that are becoming more knowledge based is distinguished by alliances, which are likely to be more and more technology based; if they are sustained by relational bonds their orderly development can ensure stability, without restricting the scope for new ventures.

Critics of globalization and of regional market integration have roused concerns about deindustrialization and employment losses associated with increases in economic openness. These should not be dismissed with affirmations of naive faith in the efficiencies of market forces. Capitalist systems becoming more knowledge intensive and more interdependent have to develop with extensive corporate cooperation, with sensitivities to issues of fairness, reciprocity, and social justice that have been stressed by Joseph Stiglitz in his work on behavioural macroeconomics. His observations have become especially meaningful because of the numerous well-publicized cases of corporate fraud that have affected public confidence and investor confidence in the USA in recent years.

We have hopes for knowledge-intensive and high-principled engagement with the issues of trade liberalization in the Americas. Market efficiencies and failures, and government efficiencies and failures, all tending to become internationalized, demand attention in policy communities and corporate associations. The attention that has the most practical significance is likely to be that given by managements of international firms to the development of their transnational production systems. This has strongly influenced our perspectives on the prospects for hemispheric market integration.

Sidney Weintraub
Alan M. Rugman
Gavin Boyd

1. Potential for hemispheric regional cooperation

Sidney Weintraub

INTRODUCTION

The focus of this chapter will be on trade cooperation. The reason for this emphasis is the conviction that without largely unimpeded access to the US market for their goods and services, most countries in the hemisphere would have little incentive to cooperate with the United States in other ways, such as joining the global struggle against terrorism, impeding the financing of terrorism, and eroding the shipment of narcotics. Hemispheric summit meetings devote much time to the promotion of democracy and combating corruption, but there is clear recognition that the centerpiece of these meetings is open trade. US promotion of other issues is likely to be seen as empty rhetoric if, at the same time, the United States is unable to deliver on the 'centerpiece'.

There is a related aspect of cooperation, namely, among the Latin American and Caribbean (LAC) countries themselves. MERCOSUR, the common market of the South, made up of Argentina, Brazil, Paraguay, and Uruguay, remained more of a shell than a vibrant economic integration agreement because of the weak cooperation between Brazil and Argentina for many years. The cooperation was more rhetorical than actual for most of the 1990s. The two current presidents, Luis Inacio 'Lula' da Silva of Brazil and Néstor Kirchner of Argentina, have renewed the talk about cooperation, but it is too early to tell how this will translate into action. One of the virtues of the free-trade negotiations between the United States and the five countries of the Central American Common Market (CACM) is that this is forcing a modicum of cooperation among the five.

The main reason for the development policy adopted by almost all the countries in Latin America and the Caribbean (LAC) starting in the mid-1980s was the realization that exports mattered and should be promoted, in contrast with the earlier ingrained view of export pessimism.[1] Import substitution was discarded in favor of more liberal economic policies – involving, among other things, substantially lower import barriers, export promotion, a search for foreign investment, and open as opposed to protective regional integration. It may have been coincidence, but the shift to more democratic regimes occurred at roughly the same time, in the midst of LAC's lost decade of the 1980s. Many analysts have pointed out that simultaneity does not signify cause and effect, but I think there is some relationship.[2]

There have been substantial impediments to trade cooperation – as well as to joint activities in other areas – coming both from the United States and other hemispheric countries. The principal US impediment is protectionism, in direct and indirect forms. The direct form is the reluctance to open the US market to competitive products from low-wage countries, particularly in sectors that employ large numbers of workers. One important indirect form is the subsidization of US agriculture, particularly for products upon which other hemispheric countries rely heavily for export earnings.

The main LAC impediment is the growing belief that liberal economic policy (or neoliberal, to use the word preferred by the opponents of this policy) has not benefited the majority of their populations. This is potentially correctible by transfers to poor families or to deprived regions, as is done in the European Union. The United States, from which external transfers would have to come, has shown no willingness to do this. A second impediment is the inability to achieve cooperation among the LAC countries as a whole, where interests and capacities differ sharply. There is no extensive cooperation among the four main regions of what is commonly referred to as Latin America – that is, between the countries from South America, Central America, the Caribbean (which is only partly Latin), and Mexico. Indeed, the differences among countries in the sub-regions are significant.

Despite the existence of NAFTA, there are major lapses in cooperation between the United States, Canada, and Mexico and this has led to much soul-searching in the latter two countries about how to strengthen their relations with the United States.[3]

The next section will deal with the hemispheric development policies as they emerged in the 1980s and since – in LAC countries, the United States, and Canada. This will be followed by a discussion of the efforts at cooperation, in trade as well as in other areas, and on the progress and failures of these efforts. The final section will further develop the analysis of the centrality of trade, and the closely related theme of investment, and conclude with recommendations to encourage hemispheric cooperation – primarily between the United States and the LAC countries. The task is a formidable one.

An overview of the contents of the entire book is provided at the end of this chapter. Many of the issues discussed in this opening chapter are dealt with in greater detail by other authors, as are related themes necessary to construct a community of the Americas.

EFFORTS AT COOPERATION

Chile started the path to liberal economic policies in the 1970s under the dictatorship of Augusto Pinochet, but the original structure led to a sharp collapse of the economy in 1982 and Chilean policy was reconstituted shortly after that.[4] Between 1985 and 1997, following the modifications in policy, Chile's gross domestic product grew at an annual average rate of 7 percent, which was more than double the Latin American average over that period.[5] This example was noted in other LAC countries, but there was no rush to emulate the policy because Chile is a small country and is seen as an outlier – or as one colleague put it, as a 'boutique' country.

The shift in Mexican policy also started in the early 1980s, after the onset of the country's debt crisis in 1982, but the changes there were instituted more gradually than they had been in Chile; and, beyond that, Mexico's GDP growth in the 1980s was modest. Nevertheless, tariffs and other border barriers were reduced sharply, the country joined the General Agreement on Tariffs and Trade (GATT) in 1986, and the overall policy thrust was to promote exports. Mexico succeeded spectacularly in this effort, aided largely by the North American Free Trade Agreement (NAFTA), which gave the country assured access to the US market. These, too – both the trade opening and the free-trade agreement – were noted elsewhere in the hemisphere. The major shortcoming of Mexico's export growth is that it benefited mainly the northern part of the country that was physically close to the United States and this, consequently, widened pre-existing regional inequalities.[6]

By the mid-1990s, the trade policy change was nearly universal in the hemisphere, namely, to lower import barriers in order to increase the competitiveness of exports. The precise measures varied by country, but the role of trade as a potential engine of growth – rather than using trade protection as a device to develop domestic industry – has dominated development policy ever since. Mexico had the most spectacular success in increasing the export of manufactured products, many with a high technological content, but more modest increases took place elsewhere as well, particularly in Brazil.[7]

Another trade tendency took root during the same period. This was a shift from economic integration among hemispheric countries as a way to expand the scope for import substitution – what can be called protective integration – into what the Economic Commission for Latin America and the Caribbean (ECLAC) called 'open' integration.[8]

North American Integration

Canada entered into free trade with the United States in 1989 after several failed attempts to move in that direction over the course of a century. The opposition to free trade with the United States was powerful and it took an election focused on this issue in 1987, which the Conservative Party won, to permit the Canada–US Free Trade Agreement (CUSFTA) to go into effect. The main argument against CUSFTA, as articulated by the Liberal candidate for prime minister (John Turner) was that free trade would erode Canada's sovereignty. The Liberal Party logic was essentially that one thing leads to another, first the loss of trade policy freedom and then the loss of other sovereignty attributes in the political arena. This nationalistic argument against free trade with the United States has lost its vigor in Canada in the years since CUSFTA came into existence.[9] Attitudes on the connection between free trade (open markets) and sovereignty have altered substantially throughout the hemisphere during the last 15 years, although the manifestations of these altered viewpoints have varied by country.

Mexico's decision in the early 1990s to seek free trade with the United States represented a profound change in attitude, one that would have been unthinkable to most analysts of the Mexican scene ten years, or even five years, earlier. Based on historical grievances, Mexico assiduously kept its distance from the United States and this showed up in extreme import protection, toleration of US investment as long as it remained modest, and indifference to exploiting the country's location advantage to penetrate the US market. The Mexican mantra of non-interference in the internal affairs of other countries was directed primarily at the United States: keep your distance from our internal affairs and we will behave correctly in like manner in yours.

Entry into NAFTA, however, was a logical extension of Mexico's earlier shift in development policy.[10] This agreement was probably the most important treaty for Mexico since the Treaty of Guadalupe Hidalgo of 1848, under which Mexico confirmed US title to Texas and ceded the territories of California and New Mexico. In effect, entry into NAFTA sealed the operational, even if not emotional, closure of Guadalupe Hidalgo. It signified that defensive Mexican nationalism aimed at the United States would take a back seat to development aspirations.

The trade policy shifts of CUSFTA and NAFTA were important for the United States as well, although they involved less emotional soul-searching than was required for Canada and Mexico. The United States had long opposed bilateral agreements, especially preferential ones, and was perhaps the most important advocate of the unconditional most-favored-nation clause in the GATT. The United States did enter into bilateral agreements – non-preferential – with East European countries to set quantitative targets for US exports in order to bypass the reality that state trading eliminated much of the relevance of tariffs. In addition, the United States entered into free trade with Israel in 1985, but this was seen as a political and not an economic agreement. Entering into CUSFTA was the real change because this embraced bilateral preferences with the largest US trading partner.

The entry of Mexico into NAFTA solidified this change, but at a tremendous cost. Free trade with Canada was largely a non-event to the American public at large. Free trade with a low-wage country like Mexico, whose exports to the United States have grown immensely ever since, was a different story and it aroused all the latent protectionist sentiments among US labor unions and their supporters. It has been hard for the US government to obtain fast-track approval for other trade negotiations ever since, as witnessed by the many years it took until President George W. Bush achieved this in 2002. Even this accomplishment was marred by the many protectionist concessions to domestic interests required to achieve it.

When CUSFTA was negotiated, the sovereignty issue was raised by Canada. When NAFTA was under negotiation, the expectation was that Mexico would raise the sovereignty issues that had been the hallmark of that country's foreign policy for 150 years. The reality is that there has been more defensive nationalism on the part of the United States than of its two NAFTA partners. This is an issue that will surely affect the freedom of US negotiators in the hemispheric free-trade effort and in the needed final approval of any agreement by the US congress.

LAC Integration

LAC countries have a rich history of integration efforts dating back to the aspirations of Simon Bolívar for a united Latin America. The economic integration efforts of the past 50 years have been manifold, starting with the Treaty of Montevideo in 1960 which created the Latin American Free Trade Association (LAFTA). This was an ambitious effort at protective integration and it failed. LAFTA was replaced by the Latin American Integration Association (known best by its Spanish initials, ALADI), a less ambitious endeavor. Under the aegis of ALADI, however, the Treaty of Asuncion was signed in 1991 creating MERCOSUR. This is a good place to enter into the modern LAC open integration efforts in that MERCOSUR is potentially the most important of the sub-regional LAC integration efforts.[11]

MERCOSUR had considerable initial success in stimulating trade among the four member countries. One measure of this is that, after the agreement was signed, intra-MERCOSUR trade grew from 9 percent of total trade of the member countries to about 26 percent in 1998.[12] In 1996, Argentina sent 28 percent of its exports to Brazil (a proportion that later rose to well above 30 percent), while Paraguay sent 50 percent, and Uruguay 35 percent.[13] There were problems, however, in that even in these successful years extra-MERCOSUR exports were relatively stagnant. Then, in 1999, Brazil devalued its currency, the *real,* and this affected the other members, especially Argentina, which then had a convertibility system under which the Argentine peso traded at one-to-one with the US dollar. This new exchange rate alignment made Argentina's exports less competitive in the Brazilian market until Argentina discarded its convertibility system and devalued its currency in January 2002.

Almost from the outset, however, commitments made in MERCOSUR were delayed. Brazil and Argentina each raised protective duties in contravention of the treaty. The two countries knew well before 1999, when the Brazilian devaluation took place, that their exchange rates were inconsistent and constituted a calamity waiting to happen – yet they did nothing. The common refrain now among Brazilian and Argentine economists is that the necessary ingredient for future success is macroeconomic coordination (or cooperation).[14] They are preaching the self-evident based on past failure.

The other sub-regional integration agreements in the LAC countries, much as was the case in MERCOSUR, had difficulty in carrying out measures to make the integration effective. The others are the Andean Community (AC), the Central America Common Market, and the Caribbean Community (CARICOM). Beyond these, both Mexico and Chile have concluded free-trade agreements (FTAs) with other hemispheric and non-hemispheric countries. Perhaps the most significant of these non-hemispheric agreements is that between Mexico and the EU, which was signed in March 2000. The EU is also negotiating an FTA with MERCOSUR, but this may be more difficult to conclude than the agreement with Mexico because of the importance of competing agricultural production in the two regional groupings. The issue of competing US and EU preferential agreements will be addressed again later in the chapter. Canada and Chile concluded an FTA agreement modeled on NAFTA in the expectation that the United States would later have the authority to bring Chile into that agreement. In the event, after many false starts, the United States and Chile completed their own bilateral FTA negotiation early in 2003. If this is approved by the US Congress, each of the three NAFTA countries will have bilateral FTAs with Chile. This is surely a complicated way to achieve quadrilateral free trade.

A Synthesis of the Current Hemispheric Trade Structure

More than 20 bilateral and plurilateral preferential economic integration agreements have been launched within the hemisphere since 1990.[15] In addition, there are many FTAs between hemispheric and non-hemispheric countries (Mexico–EU, the United States–Jordan and Singapore (the latter still needs congressional approval at the time of writing), EU preferences to Caribbean countries under the Cotonou EU–Asia, Caribbean, Pacific agreement, plus others under negotiation). A former US trade negotiator once described the situation of FTAs within the Americas as 'spaghetti'.[16]

These agreements have had some effect on intra-hemispheric trade, but not as much as might have been the case if the original intentions had been carried out. MERCOSUR was described even by its supporters as an imperfect customs union. Intra-MERCOSUR disputes frequently had to be pushed up to the presidential level for resolution, to the extent that they were resolved at all.[17] Much the same can be said for the other sub-regional agreements. Differences among member countries persisted, compromising the integration intentions.

Each agreement has its own dispute-settlement arrangement. Rules of origin vary among the many FTAs, generating considerable confusion. There are cross preferences, and for corporations that can produce in more than one country, the actual place of production is often determined not by economic criteria, but by the preferences that prevail. 'To hell with efficiency' is what this preferential mishmash often signifies. This has been documented for shipment of goods to Chile, where the locus of production was shifted from the United States to Canada because Canadian firms could ship to Chile free of duty. The rules of origin theoretically can prevent transshipment from a non-preferential partner to an intermediary location where there is a preferential agreement with the country of destination, but it is hard to believe that this is not frequently violated in light of the great complexity.

MERCOSUR, as will be noted below, added a democracy clause after an attempted government overthrow in Paraguay, but such clauses do not exist in all the agreements. Democracy clauses may be desirable in a political-economy context, but combining two objectives in a single agreement does confuse which objective should be given primacy in any given situation. A democracy clause may find its way into the Free Trade Area of the Americas (FTAA) as well.[18]

On top of all of this, the markets involved in most of the agreements are modest. There are potential advantages for augmenting trade among the members of the CACM, for example, but not if this is at the expense of shipping to the United States, which is a far more important market for these countries. The natural market for shipment of goods from Paraguay and Uruguay is Brazil and this, as much as the trade preferences, explains Paraguay and Uruguay's high dependence on that country. Argentina, however, if it is able to develop a competitive export sector, could diversify its exports more broadly.[19] Lack of diversification had a high cost when Brazil devalued its currency in 1999. Mexico, which ships upwards of 80 percent of its exports to the United States, paid a high price for this dependence as the US economy slowed in 2001–2002. This problem is recognized and explains Mexico's policy of expanding its network of FTAs in the hope of one day reducing its great reliance on the US market. Mexico, like Chile, seeks market diversification by means of complicating its trading arrangements by having many FTAs with varying conditions. The policy, in the main, works but it surely does not benefit other hemispheric countries.

All of this suggests that the current network of trade agreements is surely not the optimal situation for the majority of hemispheric countries. Mexico enjoys a near monopoly in the hemisphere on preferential access to the US market – 'near' because Canada enjoys this as well, and so will Chile and presumably the CACM countries once agreements are negotiated and ratified – but this prejudices other hemispheric countries. This reality is the most persuasive logic of the proposed FTAA. The logic of the EU, even today as it prepares to expand to other European countries, is exactly this – to have a large preferential area with a single set of rules, with temporary derogations from these as needed, to fit particular country situations. The Americas, by contrast, are replete with inconsistent rules of origin, a pattern of cross discrimination, and a costly lack of cooperation between different regions of the hemisphere. The current US policy of signing more preferential bilateral agreements only complicates this structure. A single, overarching agreement could rationalize the trading architecture in the hemisphere.

AREAS OF POTENTIAL HEMISPHERIC COOPERATION

The heads of state and government of 32 LAC countries (that is, all of them except for Cuba), plus the United States and Canada, in their three summit meetings, have documented what they believe are the most important areas for cooperation among them.[20] In addition to trade, these include the defense of democracy, combating corruption, collective anti-narcotic efforts, protecting labor rights, fostering regional sustainable development (that is, environmental protection), upgrading women's rights, improving health care, fostering of education, altering the structure of the hemispheric institutions, and activating civil society. When a list lengthens at each new summit, it deserves the adjective 'laundry' list. The impression is that once the issues are raised, discussed, and approved at the summit meetings, most of them are forgotten until the next summit. One effort at evaluation, while supporting summitry, has stated outright that education 'flunks', sustainable development 'flounders', and civil society remains largely 'marginalized'.[21]

Are periodic summits useful in promoting hemispheric cooperation? The main argument in their favor is that they are forcing events that compel the summiteers themselves and the national institutions that support them to repeatedly study the pending issues. Many of the themes that arise at the summit meetings deal with internal matters – education, health care, participation of civil society, women's rights – whose sponsors believe that hemispheric support will reinforce the will of national governments to act. Other issues clearly require collective action, such as trade among them, combating terrorism, and cooperation in the fight against suppliers and users of narcotics. Still others fall in between, such as promotion of democracy, combating corruption in that there are corruptors from outside the countries and the corrupted inside the countries, and environmental protection because pollution does not respect boundaries. In a sense, all the items deal directly or indirectly with the overriding theme: how to foster national development in a democratic environment.

The US government tends to emphasize the following themes in its dealings with the hemisphere: freeing trade; stimulating foreign investment; encouraging development via market capitalism; safeguarding and promoting democracy; and invigorating anti-corruption measures. Since September 11, 2001, there is an additional item on the US agenda, namely, anti-terrorism cooperation. LAC countries have focused heavily on US protectionism (agricultural subsidies and high restrictions on their most competitive products) and what they consider to be shortcomings in the global development architecture which lead to systemic financial crises, sometimes regardless of their macroeconomic policies. Many of the issues stressed by either side are not solely hemispheric matters, but rather global ones.

In the following some key items are highlighted to shed light on the state of cooperation and to examine what more needs to be done.

Trade

There was tremendous LAC enthusiasm for hemispheric free trade when the idea was first enunciated by President George H.W. Bush in 1988, but this has been tempered by the inordinately 'deliberate' speed at which the process has moved forward. This modest pace of activity, coupled with the failure of President Clinton to obtain fast-track authority from the Congress, and the delay before George W. Bush obtained this authority, led to considerable doubt in the hemisphere that the United States was serious. Much of this skepticism, but by no means all, was erased when the Congress finally gave President George W. Bush this authority in July 2002.

The FTAA is a complex undertaking that involves free trade among a widely diverse set of participants, including some of the world's richest and poorest countries.[22] This heterogeneity also exists in the WTO, but there is more expectation there of differential treatment in favor of the least developed countries. There will surely have to be some special treatment of the poorer countries in the FTAA, probably in the transition arrangements.

The FTAA, looked at from the philosophical vantage point of those responsible for making US trade policy, would not only bring free trade onto a hemisphere-wide basis, thereby simplifying the current structure, but also would provide powerful pressure to lock this in. The trading arrangements that would be embodied in the FTAA also posit market economics. The quid pro quo that the LAC countries want is assurance of access to the US market as well as legal protection against wholesale backtracking by the United States. The prospective agreement, in other words, can meet the main trade objectives of the two sides. Much obviously depends on the negotiating dynamics: how much transitional leeway will be given to the poorest countries; the extent to which LAC countries will seek other permanent exceptions to free trade; and the degree to which the US negotiators can overcome powerful protectionist pressures, particularly but not exclusively in agriculture, and still assure approval from an apprehensive US Congress.

There has long been an asymmetry in the extent of import liberalization among the developed countries in contrast to the market opening afforded to developing countries. Levels of protection tend to be highest against products of great importance for developing countries, not just in the United States but also in developed countries generally.[23] This reality has been evident for quite some time, but has not been dealt with adequately in many rounds of trade negotiations. It will not be easy to deal with this problem in the FTAA either, but it must be accomplished – if not fully, at least significantly – if negotiations are to be meaningful to the LAC countries.

Brazil has acquiesced to the FTAA process and participated in the working and negotiating groups that have been meeting for several years now. In this sense, Brazil has been cooperating in the exercise – but with considerable reservations. There are many reasons for this hesitation, some nationalistic and others practical. Of all LAC countries, Brazil, because of its economic size, is the one country that believes it still has considerable scope for further import substitution in key sectors, such as telecommunications, electronics, automotive, and various kinds of machinery production. Second, Brazil is not convinced that the United States is prepared to open its market further to imports from Brazil, such as shoes, steel, concentrated orange juice, and especially other processed agricultural products. There is ample reason for this concern in the present structure of US import protection, which heavily prejudices Brazil's export sector. Third, Brazil considers itself a world trader and does not want to concentrate excessively on the US market. Finally, Brazil considers itself a leader in South America, especially in MERCOSUR, and is not fully prepared to cede this authority to the United States.

The United States and Brazil are the co-chairs of the FTAA negotiations in its current, presumably final one and a half crucial years, which may provide an incentive to cooperate. The cooperation seems to be taking the form of slimming down the substance of the FTAA. Brazil argued that if the United States removed a key Brazilian objective from the FTAA negotiations in favor of negotiating in the WTO, namely, eliminating domestic and export subsidies in agriculture, it too should be permitted to remove a theme that it considers domestically sensitive, namely, intellectual property protection. Other hemispheric countries then suggested watering down other substantive areas, such as trade in services, investment protection and dispute resolution, and government procurement. The outcome, at the time of writing, may be a less comprehensive FTAA, focused mainly on market access, that is, lowering import barriers, primarily in industrial goods. This would not be a negligible achievement, but it would be far from the initial ambitions. However, this could lead to simplifying rules of origin and reducing cross discrimination if it led to the elimination of many existing bilateral FTAs – something that now seems doubtful.

It is not clear whether the FTAA can be completed by its deadline, the end of 2004. The chances for this are good if the substance is drastically reduced in scope. The argument in favor of a less comprehensive FTAA is that it is achievable and other disciplines can still be negotiated in the WTO. The argument against a partial FTAA is that it leaves many problems for resolution in a forum, the WTO, which is even more diverse and unfriendly than the hemispheric forum. The outcome may be either a slimmed-down FTAA or no FTAA, and it is unclear which is preferable from the viewpoint of hemispheric trade cooperation. Probably the slimmed-down version, if that is the best that is possible, is to be preferred because it can resolve some problems now.

Democracy

Hemispheric countries, meeting under the aegis of the Organization of American States (OAS), were completing an Inter-American Democratic Charter in Lima at the time (September 11, 2001) that terrorists struck the United States. Many of the democracies in the LAC countries are fragile, but there is no longer any question that this is the favored form of government throughout the hemisphere. Despite severe hardships suffered in Argentina in recent years, adherence to democratic norms has remained intact. An attempted coup against the government of Hugo Chávez in Venezuela was reversed in April 2002. Chávez came under attack again in late 2002 as strikes and protests shut down much of the country, particularly its oil operations, but the fact that he was elected democratically does put some restraint on the opposition. Brazil and other countries of MERCOSUR prevented a military takeover in Paraguay in 1996, and then added a democracy understanding to the agreement that would deny preferences to any member country in which the government was unconstitutionally overthrown.

There are ambiguities concerning changes in government. Presidents were twice ousted under pressure, but constitutionally, in Ecuador in 2000 and in Argentina in 2001. President Fujimori of Peru managed a fraudulent election in 2000, but was forced out of office only after other scandals erupted. Any attempt to codify when these ambiguities are contrary to the democratic process would almost surely be futile because each case depends on national circumstances.

The issue that arises now, as an add-on to the democratic charter concluded in the OAS, is whether the FTAA should have a democracy clause to punish countries when democracies are forcefully overthrown – as was done in the MERCOSUR case. There is much hemispheric sentiment supporting this, as well as much questioning of its desirability because it is a form of interfering in the domestic affairs of other countries. It seems likely that a democracy clause will find its way into the FTAA. Hemispheric countries have already agreed collectively to safeguard democracy.

Hemispheric countries, also under the auspices of the OAS, reached an Inter-American Convention Against Corruption in 1996. This shows recognition that hemispheric countries now accept that corruption reduces a country's growth prospects. It also reflects the impatience of national populations with continuing corruption. It would be hard, perhaps impossible, to fashion an anti-corruption clause for inclusion in the FTAA. The issue is not as clear-cut as the non-democratic overthrow of a government (which, as noted above, is not always clear-cut either), because there are degrees of corruption in all countries and it would be impossible to quantify the precise point at which punishment in the form of trade sanctions would be appropriate. What we have are perceptions of corruption, as compiled by Transparency International, but not accurate measures of actual corruption. Yet, it is important to recognize that corruption is now seen, at least at the rhetorical level, as anti-social throughout the hemisphere.

Hemispheric cooperation against terrorism exists mainly in the financial field in an effort to reduce money laundering. Problems of definition enter into the equation when it comes to combating acts of terrorism. The threats are not identical across the hemisphere and it not always possible to separate internal guerrilla warfare from acts of outside incitement because the two frequently overlap. Other than in the financial field, the type of cooperation that is most needed is to deal with terrorism in the movement of goods and people – in containers that carry goods around the hemisphere and at land borders, such as those of Mexico and Canada with the United States, where anti-terrorist vigilance can interfere with the lawful movement of goods, services, and people. Efforts at cooperative measures are being designed to deal with this problem.

Trade cooperation is the centerpiece of cooperative economic efforts not only because of its importance in fostering development, but also because it is concrete and measurable. If a government is overthrown by non-democratic means, trade sanctions can be a powerful corrective weapon. LAC countries generally have accepted limitations on their sovereign freedom of action in the trade field as they exchange obligations and benefits in trade agreements, whereas skittishness over violations of sovereignty remain strong in other areas

Financial Architecture

There have been many financial crises in Latin America in the 1980s and 1990s. The causation of these crises has varied, sometimes arising from macroeconomic policies in the affected countries themselves, but often the result of shocks inherent in the international financial system.[24] Brazil, for example, felt the effects of contagion from the tequila crisis in Mexico in 1994–1995 and then again from the Russian debt default of 1998 when investors removed funds from Brazil for liquidity purposes. Uruguay needed support from the IMF in 2002 when Argentinians, concerned about their own banking situation, withdrew large sums of money from banks in Uruguay. Contagion, the word used to describe the adverse financial consequences on bystanders from crises elsewhere in the world, is most severe in developing countries. This is because their internal economic situations are often weak to start with, leading investors to react defensively.

The international financial architecture has made it near impossible for LAC countries to pursue countercyclical macroeconomic policies. Public expenditures decline, forcing tax rates up, in a recession and vice versa during periods of expansion.[25] Portfolio investments into developing countries tend to flourish in good economic times and then flee during downturns. This was the Mexican experience pre- and post-1994. It was the basis for the Chilean controls on short-term capital movements; these are no longer in force. There is no internationally agreed technique to compel all international creditors to participate during a debt workout of developing countries. These are not exclusively Latin American problems, as is evident from IMF initiatives to devise better techniques for dealing with sovereign 'bankruptcies', but hemispheric countries do seek discussions to find techniques for greater international cooperation in these financial areas.

CONCLUSIONS

Despite its overwhelming military power and tremendous political influence in the Americas, the United States is discovering that it can elicit cooperation from the countries of the hemisphere only if it satisfies their trade needs. This is not precisely the 'soft' power that Joseph Nye has analyzed, but rather the need to be responsive to the region's development aspirations.[26] This assurance of access to the US market has been largely attained by Canada and Mexico, thanks to NAFTA, and potentially for Chile once its FTA with the United States receives final congressional approval, but is still tenuous for the other countries of the hemisphere. The effort to make it more solid is the purpose of the many free-trade negotiations under way, primarily the FTAA, but also the prospective US–Central America FTA negotiations.

These negotiations are taking place at a time of considerable economic turmoil in LAC countries, which both complicates the negotiations for these countries and makes them considerably more urgent. For the most part, the LAC countries have accepted the evidence that the countries at the forefront of economic growth are those that are important exporters in relation to their GDPs. Chile, Costa Rica, and the Dominican Republic all demonstrate this trade/economic growth relationship. Mexico was in a similar position in the latter 1990s, but its economic growth started to falter when US economic growth slowed.

In past trade negotiations, poor and small countries were left largely to fend for themselves despite the reality that many of them lacked both the expertise and technical ability to take full advantage of negotiating opportunities. This time, many international organizations have taken a particular interest in providing technical assistance to these countries. It remains to be seen how effective this will be, but there is some promise that technical assistance will be offered this time.

The FTAA is thus an important opportunity for both economic and political cohesion in the hemisphere and its failure, if that is how it ends, would inflict a heavy blow upon hemispheric cooperation across the board. Most LAC countries see the FTAA as most desirable, even if it is not as comprehensive as the United States envisaged when it proposed the hemispheric accord. The two exceptions are Venezuela, at least under its current leadership, and Brazil, which, for a variety of reasons expounded earlier, is an uncertain participant in anything other than a slimmed-down agreement. Mexico is surely lukewarm about the FTAA because it already enjoys preferential access to the US market, but it has not been obstructionist.

In the end, however, the success of the negotiation depends more on the United States than on other countries in the hemisphere. The prospects for the US economy for 2003 and beyond are uncertain and a failure to sustain reasonably high GDP growth of, say, at least 4 percent a year, will adversely affect the trade prospects of most Latin American countries. Raising the US growth rate and sustaining it is undoubtedly the most important deliverable the United States can provide to its Latin American neighbors.

The remainder of 2003 and 2004 will be the crucial time in the negotiation of the FTAA. This agreement will be meaningful for Latin America only if the United States takes significant steps to open its market to trade-sensitive goods, from shoes to textile products, to steel, and agricultural products. If the United States is unprepared to reduce drastically the farm subsidies that stimulate overproduction, thereby limiting access for LAC producers of these products both in the US and third markets, a comprehensive FTAA is unlikely. A less ambitious FTAA may be the best outcome in that case. The reduction of producer and export subsidies for agricultural products, if it is accomplished at all, will have to take place in the global WTO negotiations where all the subsidizing countries will participate. This requires close coordination between the hemispheric and global negotiations, something clearly recognized by all the trade players.

There is a downside to preferential hemispheric negotiations. If they are bilateral or plurilateral, but not all-encompassing for hemispheric countries, they add to the abundant cross discrimination that already exists. If all the countries in the hemisphere do participate, this pushes the burden of discrimination onto non-hemispheric nations. This last point underscores the importance of the simultaneous global negotiations that can at least reduce the degree of discrimination against non-hemispheric countries. The FTAA, if it comes into being, will not be the only region to discriminate against outsiders; the EU does this as well, both within Europe and with its network of FTAs outside Europe.

The existence of competing discriminatory groups is an unstable situation. The United States is pushing the FTAA in order to limit the extent of discrimination it faces from the many partial hemispheric integration agreements that already exist. As the EU lost market share in Mexico after NAFTA, it sought and concluded its own FTA with Mexico. Both the United States and the EU are negotiating with MERCOSUR, the United States in the framework of the FTAA and the EU directly, but whichever concludes an agreement first will provide an incentive for the other to reach its own accord.

The position taken in this chapter is that if the trade-cooperation objective is met, this will stimulate hemispheric cooperation in other areas – primarily investment, but also in such areas as the promotion of democracy, reducing corruption, and fighting terrorism.

Economically, the LAC region went through two successive difficult decades at the end of the 20th century. The economic situation in the hemisphere at the start of the 21st century is not promising. The trade agenda is the most important beacon of hope that things may improve. Increased trade will not solve all development problems, but it would help. A successful trade outcome would also act as a catalyst for cooperation in other areas – social, political, and security.

The trade imperatives, and recommendations for US policy, that flow from this analysis include the following:

- A successful negotiation will require meaningful concessions from the United States, both for labor-intensive products from other hemispheric countries and agricultural products.
- Some agreement on agricultural subsidies is possible in the WTO, which means that the hemispheric and global negotiations must be seen as chapters in a larger negotiating framework.

- The richer countries of the hemisphere, the United States and Canada, should consider resource transfers to backward regions as part of the hemispheric trade deal.
- Technical assistance to poor and small countries to assist them in the negotiating process and then in the implementation of the agreement is required from the richer countries and multilateral organizations.
- Some special trade treatment will be required for the small countries, but much of this can be transitional.
- A democracy clause should be included in the final text of the FTAA.
- And, finally, negotiating further FTAs one by one (beyond Chile and Central America) is a complicated way to achieve a hemisphere-wide agreement.

CHAPTER OVERVIEWS

Gavin Boyd (Chapter 2) traces the political and economic history of Latin America, thereby providing a valuable introduction to the chapters that follow. He touches on the region's past political failures, its great dependency on the US market, and the structural dependencies that exist among hemispheric countries and with the United States. These dependencies have been growing in the linked operations of foreign and national companies, and have made exchange rate issues much more important than in the years of import substitution, export pessimism, and isolation from much of the world's markets. Much attention is given to the study of regionalism, which has flourished ever since the region's economic model changed in the 1980s. Latin America, Boyd emphasizes, needs to build effective outward-oriented and knowledge-based economies, and much more solid institutions than have existed heretofore. Regionalism can play an important role in attaining these objectives.

Walid Hejazi, in Chapter 3, focuses primarily on the effects of US foreign direct investment (FDI) on trade between Latin America and the United States. This is a forcefully argued chapter whose conclusions derive from a carefully detailed gravity model over the period 1982–1998, covering 52 countries. The details of the model and why it was chosen are provided. Three hypotheses are tested: (1) FDI is a complement to trade, and the model seeks to determine to what extent; (2) there is substantial scope for increased US–Latin American trade, and an effort is made to measure the magnitude of this potential; and (3) there are tradeoffs between US trade with Latin America and East Asia, and the analysis seeks to measure these.

The conclusions, stated simply, are: over the period examined, outward US FDI increased both US exports to and imports from Latin America in a generally neutral manner with respect to the trade balance. From the US trade balance viewpoint, outward FDI in natural resources and manufacturing have a negative impact, whereas FDI in services increases US exports significantly and stimulates only modest US import increases. Hejazi concludes from his simulation of US trade with East Asia and Latin America that without an FTAA, East Asian–US trade will become relatively more important, but with free trade in the Western Hemisphere, Latin America's relative trade with the United States – both exports and imports – will increase relatively more substantially than with East Asia.

Alan Rugman, in Chapter 4, examines the nature of integration at both the aggregate and firm levels over the ten years of NAFTA's existence, and uses these observations to project what might happen in an FTAA. His emphasis is on trade and investment relations between the United States and Canada. US–Canada integration, he finds, is mostly via trade, although integration in services is dominated by FDI. Rugman estimates that roughly half of US–Canada bilateral trade is in or related to the automotive sector. The increase in the total FDI of the two countries – especially of the United States – has been more interregional than intraregional. Rugman surmises that, under free trade, less US FDI in Canada has been needed to access the market. On the other hand, Canada's FDI in the United States has increased during the NAFTA period, which leads to the conclusion that Canada's access to the US market relies heavily on FDI. Rugman touches on the regional tendencies of the world's largest 500 multinational enterprises and concludes that there is a proclivity for them to focus heavily on their home areas – in this case, Canada, the United States, and Mexico – and he points out that Canada's large multinationals are largely regional. These observations lead him to the conclusion that if an FTAA makes the entire hemisphere regional, this will lead as well to increases in hemispheric trade and FDI.

Gordon Mace and Louis Bélanger, in Chapter 5, describe the institutions of NAFTA, analyze why they were chosen, and speculate about future changes. Their discussion is most appropriate at this point when the FTAA is under negotiation and much work is in progress on what its institutional structure should be and how it might relate to NAFTA. The chapter contains a detailed comparison between NAFTA and the European Union (using six criteria: origin, membership, scope, centralization, control, and flexibility) and, as one might expect, this shows that the two institutional designs are fundamentally different. The authors make the point that the obligations spelled out in the NAFTA agreement are quite detailed, which leads them to conclude that the agreement's main feature is 'legalization'. The main motive of both Canada and Mexico for entering into NAFTA was to gain some assurance against US protectionism, while the US motive was to seize the opportunity and to move forward in North America as an inducement to spur progress in the global trade negotiations then in progress. None of the three countries had any wish to forge a political or social union.

The authors note that recent suggestions for institutional change have come from Canada and Mexico, and both have stressed bilateral relations with the United States. The Canadian suggestions involve some kind of 'grand bargain' between the United States and Canada, and the Mexican proposals are largely for more meaningful agreements on migration. The authors conclude that the times do not seem propitious for either type of modification.

Heinz Preusse, in Chapter 6, examines the birth and middle years of MERCOSUR, and then speculates about its future. MERCOSUR is a major agreement in the hemispheric context, second in importance only to NAFTA in trade terms. Its members include two major countries in the Southern Cone, Brazil and Argentina, and two smaller ones, Paraguay and Uruguay. Preusse approaches his analysis by asking four questions: What did the architects have in mind when MERCOSUR was created? What was done to accomplish this intent? What are MERCOSUR'S structural weaknesses? Finally, what can be done to overcome these?

The answers to the first two questions are straightforward. The initial intent was to forge a common market, or at least a customs union involving macroeconomic coordination. The customs union remains imperfect to this day and rather than macroeconomic coordination, the two major countries practiced national policies of protection during the turbulence that affected the region. The heart of Preusse's chapter deals with the latter two questions. He argues that effective integration of MERCOSUR requires not only an increase in intraregional trade among the member countries (which was accomplished for a time behind a protective wall), but rather growth in inter-industry trade, namely, the development of industries prepared to compete outside the protective walls of the integration.

Paul Brenton and Miriam Manchin, in Chapter 7, provide original and valuable insights on the European experience of economic integration. They do not make direct comparisons with the Western Hemisphere integration experience, but many of their observations about Europe have considerable relevance in Latin America. The chapter provides a brief description of the historical origins of European integration growing out of the experience of World War II, and abetted by the Marshall Plan during the Cold War. The authors cite three early lessons: partial forms of integration are unlikely to provide a good basis for sound integration; free-trade agreements can be considered merely a form of deepening of multilateral liberalization, but not a sound basis for deepening regional integration; and the context in which integration occurs is important for establishing the willingness of participants to take difficult measures. Both Canada and Mexico first proposed only sectoral free trade with the United States, and this failed in both cases. There was little intention in most hemispheric integration agreements to achieve deep regional integration. The situation in the Western Hemisphere has not been conducive to taking the kind of difficult measures taken in Europe.

In Europe, the authors note that supranationality was present from the outset; in the Western Hemisphere, supranationality was not really ever on the table. Early progress in Europe was in intra-industry trade, as it was in MERCOSUR, but trade never moved beyond that point in MERCOSUR, as Heinz Preusse points out. Brenton and Manchin note that protectionism granted to a particular sector can become entrenched; this took place in agriculture in Europe and in the automotive sector in MERCOSUR. Liberalization of services was significant in Europe; this liberalization was resisted in most hemispheric integration schemes. The Europeans realized by the late 1980s that they had to remove non-border barriers, like internal protective regulations; this has been hard to accomplish in Latin America.

Perhaps too much should not be made of these similarities and inherent differences between the integration arrangements in Europe and Latin America. European integration has a 50-year history, while the open integration process is, at most, only 15 years old in the Western Hemisphere.

Gavin Boyd in Chapter 8 states that cooperative dollarization with the United States would put Latin America on a fast track toward monetary unity, but that the best that can be expected now is a unilateral and non-cooperative monetary union. De facto dollarization, he points out, has been increasing with expanding commerce and transnational production systems. He therefore expects the problems to mount, making the issue of cooperative dollarization more urgent. The current challenge, Boyd says, is for Latin America to regain sufficient monetary sovereignty in order to conduct sound macromanagement. The chapter puts much stress on the need for enlightened US leadership in the management of hemispheric monetary and financial interdependence.

The main point that Stephen Randall makes in Chapter 9 is that energy security is a major US policy objective. This stems from the reality that US energy demand is much larger than US supply, and that this poses a threat to economic growth. US energy policy in the hemisphere must be seen, he says, in the context of the global energy environment. A key element of US energy policy is to seek collaboration in the Western Hemisphere, especially in North America. Randall provides material on energy resources in all the key Latin American countries. The difficulties that have arisen in fostering collaboration in much of the hemisphere concern not only energy policy as such, but also are affected by the hemisphere's political, economic, and social difficulties that hamper optimal energy production. On this score, Randall points particularly to the uncertain policies of President Hugo Chávez of Venezuela as a reasonable basis for concern for the United States.

In Chapter 10, Gavin Boyd returns to a theme – alliance capitalism – that he has expounded in other works and he does it here with great flourish. His essential argument is that liberal policies in an integration process replete with vast asymmetries could lead to concentration of firms, disruptions of economic structures, and multiple forms of failures. In addition to the words 'alliance capitalism', he uses other expressions that have a similar connotation: coordinated entrepreneurship; collegial capitalism; competition policy cooperation; a consensus of interdependent management; and dynamic linkages between firms in Latin America and between them and US firms. He refers to monetary policy interdependencies. All of this could happen, he argues, if US firms take the lead, because Latin American firms would be responsive to the opportunities. This could be done, he says, by groups of firms and be supported by official infrastructure projects. Much of the thinking is summarized in a sentence that Boyd stresses toward the end of the chapter: 'A grand design for hemispheric infrastructure development, supplementing the formation of a free trade area of the Americas, would greatly enhance growth prospects in Latin America, and could infuse new vitality into the US political economy, while contributing indirectly to a more functional balance between the domestic operations of US firms and their foreign activities.'

Chapter 11 by Salazar-Xirinachs, benefiting from his extensive experience as Director of the Trade Unit at the Organization of American States, is a very comprehensive examination of the most prominent market-opening issues in the negotiations for hemispheric trade liberalization. He gives much attention to the implications of these issues for economic development in Latin America, and relates them to items listed for the Doha round of multilateral trade negotiations under the World Trade Organization. As a contribution to North American understanding of the developmental aspects of hemispheric market integration, this chapter may well assist the evolution of the hemispheric negotiations as a learning process, across social distances that will have to be shortened, for the building of trust and goodwill.

Chapter 12 by Sidney Weintraub and Gavin Boyd is intended to pull together the gist of the previous chapters. Some of the thoughts set forth in this chapter are: the FTAA would be an elementary form of regional economic integration; however, it can prepare the way for a zone of stability and growth in the hemisphere. The United States would have to take the lead in instituting integrative cooperation. The technology and knowledge-based growth of the United States can be advanced in Latin America through investment and cooperation. Cooperation with the United States will be needed for the development of sound financial markets in Latin America. An important aspect of hemispheric growth can be greater Latin American involvement in economic relations across the Atlantic and the Pacific; and this, too, can be aided by US leadership.

NOTES

1. There are, to be sure, many criticisms of the economic policies adopted over the past 15 to 20 years. These criticisms in Latin America center on the modest economic growth since the mid-1990s, coupled with some deterioration in income inequality. A more theoretical criticism can be found in Ha-Joon Chang (2002), 'Breaking the mould: an institutionalist political economy alternative to the neo-liberal theory of the market and the state', *Cambridge Journal of Economics*, 26, 539–59.
2. Judith A. Teichman (2001), *The Politics of Freeing Markets in Latin America*, Chapel Hill, NC: University of North Carolina Press, p. 5, makes the point that there is controversy among scholars as to whether market reform contributed to strengthening of democracy.
3. C.D. Howe of the Canadian research center has an extensive project and many papers have been published already on what actions might be taken to improve Canada–US cooperation; some studies in this project are Wendy Dobson (2002), 'Shaping the Future of the North American Economic Space: A Framework for Action'; and Jeffrey Schott and Gary Hufbauer (forthcoming), 'Prospects for the North American Economic Integration: An American Perspective Post 9/11. Mexico's president has spoken much about 'NAFTA plus', which would involve such ideas as a migration agreement between the two countries and more financial aid from the United States to Mexico.
4. The Chilean shift after 1982 has been amply described. See Barry Bosworth, Rudiger Dornbusch, and Raúl Labán (eds) (1994), *The Chilean Economy: Policy Lessons and Challenges*, Washington, DC: Brookings Institution; and Hernán Büc Büchi (1993), *La transformación economómica de Chile: del estatismo al la libertad económica*, Bogotá: Editorial Norma.
5. Guillermo Perry and Danny M. Leipziger (eds) (1999), *Chile: Recent Policy Lessons and Emerging Challenges*, Washington, DC: World Bank, p. 1.
6. Gordon Hanson (1998), 'North American economic integration and industry location', *Oxford Review of Economic Policy*, **14** (2), 30–44.
7. See Sanjaya Lall (1998), 'Exports of manufactures by developing countries: emerging patterns of trade and location', *Oxford Review of Economic Policy*, **14** (2), 54–73.
8. The seminal document was United Nations Economic Commission for Latin America and the Caribbean (1994), *Open Regionalism in Latin America and the Caribbean: Economic Integration as a Contribution to Changing Production Patterns with Social Equity*, Santiago: ECLAC. The fact that this position came from ECLAC was significant in view of the earlier, adamant position of ECLA (the final C was added later) advocating import-substituting industrialization.
9. Denis Stairs (1996), 'The Canadian dilemma in North America', in Joyce Hoebing, Sidney Weintraub, and M. Delal Baer (eds), *NAFTA and Sovereignty: Trade-Offs for Canada, Mexico, and the United States*, Washington, DC: Center for Strategic and International Studies, pp. 1–38.
10. This is an argument I have made before in Sidney Weintraub (1984), *Free Trade between Mexico and the United States?*, Washington, DC: Brookings Institution.
11. Maria Claudia Drummond (1998), 'The history of the institutions of MERCOSUL', in *Parliaments, Estates, & Representation*, Aldershot: Ashgate, pp. 209–17, gives a brief history of Latin American economic integration efforts and then focuses on MERCOSUR (as MERCOSUL is written in Spanish).
12. Inter-American Development Bank (IDB) (1998), 'Integration and trade in the Americas: a preliminary estimate of 1998 trade', Integration, Trade and Hemispheric Issues Division.
13. IDB 1999 'Integration and trade in the Americas: special report', Integration, Trade and Hemispheric Division (February), p. 36.
14. Diana Tussie, Mercedes Botto, and Valentina Delich (2003), 'Las negociaciones comerciales internacionales: el contexto para la estrategia Argentina', paper presented at a seminar on La Argentina en la Economia Global: las Dimensiones Comerciales y Financieras, Buenos Aires, May 12, Buenos Aires: FLACSO.

15. Robert Devlin and Lucio Castro (2002), 'Regional banks and regionalism: a new frontier for development financing', background paper for a conference on Financing for Development: Regional Challenge and the Regional Development Banks, organized by the Center for Global Development and the Institute for International Economics, Washington, DC, February 19.
16. Figure 1 in Inter-American Development Bank (2002), 'Market access in the Americas: an unfinished agenda' (March), a background document prepared by the IDE's Integration and Regional Programs Department and the Research Department for the annual meeting of the Bank in Fortaleza, Brazil, shows trade agreements signed and under negotiation in the Americas and it looks like a tangled web of wires.
17. Thomas Andrew O'Keefe (2002), 'Dispute resolution in MERCOSUR', *Journal of World Investment*, **31**, 3 (June), 507–20, contains a useful analysis of MERCOSUR'S dispute resolution structure and practice.
18. For the record, despite this confusion of goals, I do support a democracy clause in the FTAA.
19. According to an article in the *Wall Street Journal* December 31, 2002, p. A8, Argentina had a trade surplus of more than $15 billion in the first 11 months of 2002 largely because its currency, the peso, depreciated by 70 percent in 2002.
20. The three summits were held in Miami in 1994, Santiago, Chile, in 1998, and in Quebec City in 2001.
21. Leadership Council for Inter-American Summitry (2001), 'Advancing Toward Quebec City and Beyond', University of Miami: North-South Center. The Leadership Council is sponsored by the North-South Center, the Institute for International Economics, Foundation for the Americas (FOCAL) in Ottawa, and the University of California at San Diego.
22. This point is made by Robert Devlin, Antoni Estevadeordal, and Luis Jorge Garay (1999), 'The FTAA: some longer term issues', Institute for the Integration of Latin America and the Caribbean (INTAL), occasional paper 5, (August), p. 10.
23. Jose Antonio Ocampo (2002), 'Rethinking the development agenda', *Cambridge Journal of Economics*, **26**, 396.
24. Max W. Corden (2002), *Too Sensational: On the Choice of Exchange Rate Regimes*, Cambridge, MA: MIT Press, is a discussion on the choice of exchange rate regimes globally, but contains several chapters dealing with Latin American countries. Corden points out that the cost of failed exchange rate regimes has been high in Mexico, Brazil, and Argentina, the hemisphere's three largest economies. These three countries, plus Chile, now have floating exchange rate regimes.
25. Ernesto Stein, Ernesto Talvi, and Alejandro Grisanti (1999), 'Institutional arrangements and fiscal performance: the Latin American experience', in James M. Poterba and Jürgen von Hagen (eds), *Fiscal Institutions and Fiscal Performance*, University of Chicago Press, pp. 103–33.
26. Joseph S. Nye (2002), *The Paradox of American Power: Why the World's Only Superpower Can't Go it Alone*, New York: Oxford University Press. See also Pedro-Pablo Kuczynski and John Williamson (eds) (2003), *After the Washington Consensus: Restarting Growth and Reform in Latin America*, Washington, DC: Institute for International Economics.

REFERENCES

Bosworth, Barry, Rudiger Dornbusch and Raul Labán (eds) (1994), *The Chilean Economy: Policy Lessons and Challenges*, Washington, DC: Brookings Institution.

Büchi, Hernán Büc (1993), *La transformatión economómica de Chile: del estatismo al la libertad económica*, Bogotá: Editorial Norma.

Chang, Ha-Joon (2002), 'Breaking the mould: an institutionalist political economy alternative to the neo-liberal theory of the market and the state', *Cambridge Journal of Economics*, **26**, 539–59.

Corden, W. Max (2002), *Too Sensational: On the Choice of Exchange Rate Regimes*, Cambridge, MA: MIT Press.

Devlin, Robert and Lucio Castro (2002), 'Regional banks and regionalism: a new frontier for development financing', background paper for a conference on 'Financing for Development: Regional Challenge and the Regional Development Banks', organized by the Center for Global Development and the Institute for International Economics, Washington, DC, February 19.

Devlin, Robert, Antoni Estevadeordal and Luis Jorge Garay (1999), 'The FTAA: some longer term issues', Institute for the Integration of Latin America and the Caribbean (INTAL) occasional paper 5, August.

Drummond, Maria Claudia (1998), 'The history of the institutions of MERCOSUL', in *Parliaments, Estates, & Representation*, Aldershot: Ashgate, pp. 209–17.

Hanson, Gordon (1998), 'North American economic integration and industry location', *Oxford Review of Economic Policy*, **14** (2), 30–44.

Inter-American Development Bank (IDE) (1998), 'Integration and trade in the Americas: a preliminary estimate of 1998 trade', Integration, Trade and Hemispheric Issues Division.

Inter-American Development Bank (IDB) (1999), 'Integration and trade in the Americas: special report', Integration, Trade and Hemispheric Division (February).

Inter-American Development Bank (2002), 'Market access in the Americas: an unfinished agenda', background document prepared by the IDB's Integration and Regional Programs Department and the Research Department for the annual meeting of the bank in Fortaleza, Brazil (March).

Kuczynski, Pedro-Pablo, and John Williamson (eds) (2003), *After the Washington Consensus: Restarting Growth and Reform in Latin America*, Washington, DC: Institute for International Economics.

Lall, Sanjaya (1998), 'Exports of manufactures by developing countries: emerging patterns of trade and location', *Oxford Review of Economic Policy*, **14** (2), 54–73.

Leadership Council for Inter-American Summitry (2001), 'Advancing toward Quebec City and Beyond', policy report prepared for the University of Miami North–South Center, March.

Nye, Joseph S. (2002), *The Paradox of American Power: Why the World's Only Superpower Can't Go it Alone*, New York: Oxford University Press.

Ocampo, Jose Antonio (2002), 'Rethinking the Development Agenda', *Cambridge Journal of Economics*, **26**.

O'Keefe, Thomas Andrew (2002), 'Dispute resolution in MERCOSUR', *Journal of World Investment*, **31**, 3 (June), 507–20.

Perry, Guillermo, and Danny M. Leipziger (eds) (1999), *Chile: Recent Policy Lessons and Emerging Challenges*, Washington, DC: World Bank.

Stairs, Denis (1996), 'The Canadian dilemma in North America', in Joyce Hoebing, Sidney Weintraub, and M. Delal Baer (eds), *NAFTA and Sovereignty: Trade-Offs for Canada, Mexico, and the United States*, Washington, DC: Center for Strategic and International Studies, pp. 1–38.

Stein, Ernesto, Ernesto Talvi and Alejandro Grisanti (1999), 'Institutional arrangements and fiscal performance: the Latin American experience', in James M. Poterba and Jürgen von Hagen (eds), *Fiscal Institutions and Fiscal Performance*, Chicago: University of Chicago Press, pp. 103–33.

Teichman, Judith A. (2001), *The Politics of Freeing Markets in Latin America*, Chapel Hill, NC: University of North Carolina Press.

Tussie, Diana, Mercedes Botto and Valentina Delich (2003), 'Las negociaciones comerciales internacionales: el contexto para la estrategia Argentina', Paper presented at a seminar on 'La Argentina en le Economia Global: Las Dimensiones Comerciales y Financieras', May 12, Buenos Aires: FLACSO.
United Nations Economic Commission for Latin America and the Caribbean (1994), *Open Regionalism in Latin America and the Caribbean: Economic Integration as a Contribution to Changing Production Patterns with Social Equity*, Santiago: ECLAC.
Weintraub, Sidney (1984), *Free Trade between Mexico and the United States?*, Washington, DC: Brookings Institution.

2. The political economy of development in Latin America

Gavin Boyd

Latin America has a history of failures in macromanagement and regional economic cooperation. These failures have been attributable primarily to problems at intermediate levels of political development, above the primitive forms of personal rule and the despotisms in other Third World areas. The failures have been sources of constraints on domestically based growth, and have contributed to increasing asymmetries in dependence on access to the US market and the attraction of US investment. Rivalries between Latin American administrations, moreover, have entailed weak bargaining strengths in interactions with US governments and firms, and these disadvantages have become more significant in exchanges about hemispheric trade and investment liberalization while the USA has been recovering from the recession which ended its 1990s boom. There are challenges to concert Latin American bargaining strategies, to ensure substantial reductions of US levels of protection against imports of primary products and low technology manufactures. The US interest is to secure lower Latin American barriers to virtually all imports: very large trade deficits threaten to become unsustainable for the American economy.

Degrees of dependence on the US market and on the attraction of US direct investment have been highest in Mexico, and as a member of the North America Free Trade Area this country has become a base for southern US corporate expansion. European economic links with Latin America are weaker, overall, than those of the USA, as European firms, operating out of their slower growing home economies, have been less active in world markets.

Economic development in Latin America is being assisted by the growth of linkages between US enterprises and host country firms, but depends to a considerable extent on the ways in which those linkages are managed. There can be problems of compatibility because of differences in technological capabilities, managerial competence, and organizational resources. Host country enterprises can be driven into declines. Structural and competition policy issues tend to become more challenging for host governments, but in investment bidding they are rivals, and are disadvantaged by weak bargaining positions. The competition policy challenges have structural policy implications, and have to be dealt with under pressures to implement liberal foreign direct investment policies. The structural issues, moreover, while assuming larger dimensions because of hemispheric cross investment, involve vulnerabilities associated with Latin America's main interdependencies, as these can be affected by strains in the US economy.

Latin American administrations and policy communities, while engaging with their own problems of political development, have to strive for the promotion of more balanced and more dynamic hemispheric structural interdependencies. The challenges are not just to work for successful bargaining outcomes in negotiations on regional market liberalization, but to combine progress in the development of knowledge-based economies with policy learning and corporate learning in wide ranging exchanges with US policy communities and industrial groups. Initiatives for such exchanges are clearly needed on each side, and they can be inspired in the USA as well as in Latin America by revisions of what has been called the Washington Consensus (Williamson 2003, Ocampo 2002).

ANALYSIS

Problems of political development become more closely linked with issues of economic development in Latin America as domestic and external structural interdependencies become larger and more complex because of the operations of national and foreign enterprises, influenced by policy environments with mixes of efficiencies and failures. Key governance processes depend on leadership and institutional capacities to build consensus and aggregate interests, and to promote coordinated entrepreneurship, supported by general progress in the development of knowledge based economies. Increases in growth and stability, with equity, can aid the evolution of supportive political cultures, and this must be stressed because the opportunism of populist leaders has been a major factor in the Southern hemisphere's macromanagement failures. A special reason for this emphasis is that, for the development of knowledge based economies, the necessary learning processes require moral qualities, trust, and civic virtues (Archibugi and Lundvall 2001). The critical imperative, then, can be seen to be extensive multilevel relational cooperation, enhancing social capital.

Much economic advice from US and European sources focuses on the efficiencies of competition, driving production specializations that can expand with increases in market openness. This logic, however, is understood in Latin America, as in the USA, with awareness that trade liberalization is typically an outcome of unequal bargaining, with benefits determined increasingly by expansions of transnational production, with extensive dispersals of manufacturing processes across borders (Arndt and Kierzkowski 2001) that can limit technology transfers and the scope for linkages between host country and foreign enterprises.

Growth theory, contributing to the economic advice, has significance with reference to trade policies, and for Latin America has to be related to the discriminatory treatment of Third World exports by industrialized states, and to their use of bargaining leverage to ensure asymmetries in import penetration, as well as the acceptance of structural change through direct investment. Associated with these factors, moreover, there are concentration trends, driven by intensifying competition, which change market strengths and the spread of gains from liberalized commerce. Competition policy issues have to be reckoned with in assessing the benefits of economic openness, but may not be significantly open to negotiation because of disparities in bargaining strengths.

The promotion of linkages between foreign producers and host country firms is an appropriate focus of growth theory (UNCTAD 2002), but US transnational enterprises have been placing more emphasis on structuring operations within their own organizations rather than through joint ventures with foreign partners. Partial ownership of foreign affiliates has been giving way to whole ownership, because of increased efficiencies and lower costs in coordinating global operations (Desai, Foley, and Hines 2002). This trend has implications regarding Latin American potentials for the development of higher levels of technological competence and of more advanced production capabilities. Technology gaps that need to be overcome become wider, while the expanding transnational enterprises restrict diffusion of their advanced innovation systems and increase their market strengths in host countries.

Growth theory also has to be open to insights from behavioural finance, which assists understanding of the vulnerabilities experienced by developing countries after liberalizing their financial sectors (Shiller 2003, Lukauskas and Rivera-Batiz 2001, Bank of International Settlements 2002). The consequences of destabilizing speculation have been evident in Latin American financial crises, and in the USA's slow recovery from the collapse of its 1990s boom, which had drawn investment from developing areas. With the internationalization of financial markets, large funds move across borders in pursuit of rapid gains from speculation, with often high risks, and can be greater than the funding of productive operations, while also endangering such operations through disruptive effects on economies with sound fundamentals. Economic recovery in the USA has import drawing effects, of benefit for Latin American exports, but attracting increased capital flight. The funding of domestically based growth can then be inadequate to contribute substantially to export led growth. The destabilizing consequences of speculative financial flows moreover can be mixed with those of large scale frauds by managements of international firms operating without effective regulatory surveillance. Latin American countries have to reduce the dangers of capital market liberalization, but are under pressure to become even more open, despite weaknesses in their own regulatory systems and the limited external reach of the USA's system of financial regulation.

Institutional economics has special relevance in this context, and also has links with growth theory in so far as this has to engage with problems in the coordination of production specializations (Hall and Soskice 2001, Williamson 2000). Institutions for such coordination have become vital for Latin American industrialization, but are difficult to establish. Acute deficiencies in institutions for all areas of administration have been evident in Latin American financial crises, and in the failures of attempts at Southern hemispheric regional economic cooperation. The deficiencies can be attributed mainly to the dysfunctional effects of populist forms of governance. Institutional development for the coordination of production specializations tends to become more and more necessary because of the widening of technological gaps between Latin America and the industrialized states, and because increasing foreign direct investment tends to restrict market opportunities for national firms, that is through changes in relative market strengths and the use of informal barriers to entry. Meanwhile institutional development for collaborative bargaining on issues of hemispheric trade liberalization also becomes more imperative, but, as noted, there is also a need to build institutions for broad policy level cooperation with the USA that can assist interdependent development of hemispheric knowledge based economies.[1]

Studies of regionalism give more meaning to the differing institutional requirements. Regional market integration, because of its growth potential, attracts members if its viability is demonstrated. Substantial community formation, as a basis for collective management, is a major factor in the attraction of the European Union for neighbouring countries. The USA, as a large economic union contributing to structural integration in the North American Free Trade Area, draws Latin American states into closer trade and investment relations because of its size and advanced industrialization. In this context degrees of hemispheric structural integration develop as US transnational enterprises build international production systems (UNCTAD 2002). These tend to become associated with Atlantic structural linkages as US firms increase their presence in the European Union. European multinationals also expand their operations in Latin America, but, in rivalries with US enterprises, are disadvantaged by generally weaker competitiveness and by the status of their Union as a distant and slower growing economic grouping.

Altogether, insights from relevant strands of economic thought of significance for growth theory indicate that macromanagement challenges for Latin American administrations are becoming more demanding, as levels of structural interdependence rise with increasing asymmetries. Necessary advances in political development however are not being made, and have become more difficult because of stresses resulting from financial crises that have revealed much incompetence and opportunism, while discouraging confidence in prospects for growth through outward oriented industrialization.

The asymmetries in hemispheric structural interdependence have more and more serious implications for Latin American policy makers because of intensifying competitive pressures in the main area of their foreign economic relations. US firms are gaining strength in world markets, while Japan remains in a deep financial crisis and the European Union continues to experience slow growth. US foreign trade policy, moreover, is made effective through negotiating strategies aimed at securing hard and precise agreements, as was evident in the Uruguay Round of multilateral trade interactions and in the establishment of the North America Free Trade Area (Abbott 2000). New thinking in behavioural macroeconomics emphasizing issues of fairness and reciprocity, rather than the efficiency effects of competition (Stiglitz 2002) has yet to have a substantial influence in the dynamics of interest representation shaping US trade policy.

OUTWARD ORIENTED TRADE POLICIES

Latin American countries, before their financial crises in the 1990s, had adopted open-economy growth strategies after unsuccessful attempts at import substitution industrialization that had begun in the 1950s. Those attempts could have been more effective if implemented with substantial advances toward regional economic integration, and with greater integrity and competence, but there were acute problems of political development. The production capabilities of Latin American firms did not increase sufficiently, during the period of protected industrialization, to cope with competitive challenges encountered as that period ended. Its termination was forced by balance of payments crises that had resulted primarily from heavy foreign borrowing. This had become unsustainable because of inadequate export earnings. Protected industrialization had not contributed to the development of internationally competitive enterprises.

Successful import substituting industrialization would have required highly dedicated and highly competent macromanagement, with the use of technocratic capabilities to induce widely coordinated entrepreneurship that would make domestically based growth contribute more and more to the development of outward oriented industrial capacity. Leadership deficiencies and institutional weaknesses, however, were not overcome, mainly because populist forms of personal rule were socially divisive, encouraging clientelism, generating uncertainties, and obscuring basic policy issues (Weyland 2001). General losses of confidence in protected industrialization were increased by financial crises, and open-economy growth policies were forcefully advocated by international lending agencies.

Elements of the rationale for protected industrialization remained valid, demanding recognition in the implementation of the open economy growth policies. Terms of trade for exports of primary products were still declining, while industrialized states were discriminating against such exports as well as against low and medium technology Third World manufactures. These were the original challenges motivating import substituting industrialization (Prebish 1970). Latin American countries had intended to make protected industrialization serve the development of export capabilities at rising technological levels, with the support of industrial subsidies. Corporate inefficiencies, however, became a key problem, while increasing demands for subsidies. The potential benefits of regional economic integration had thus become even more apparent, but, as noted, the necessary political will was lacking. Open-economy growth had to be promoted, while barriers to trade in the Southern hemisphere remained in place and while competitive pressures in world markets became more intense with further expansions of operations by transnational enterprises. Heavier foreign borrowing, moreover, had become more necessary because of large oil price increases in the 1970s. Hence the regional crises in the early 1980s had been severe.

The shifts to open-economy growth reduced industrial protection and subsidization, and were accompanied by financial market liberalization, entailing vulnerabilities.[2] Exports did increase substantially, but lagged behind the trade expansion records that had been achieved by industrializing East Asian states. The overall results were mixed, with Brazil, Argentina, Peru and Venezuela performing poorly (Moguillansky and Bielschowsky 2001).

Argentina experienced an extraordinary financial crisis (Calvo, Izquierdo, and Talvi 2002), further disrupting MERCOSUR, which had been under pressure because of exchange rate divergence between that country and Brazil. Growth collapsed in Argentina and slowed considerably in Brazil, Columbia, Venezuela, and Peru. Contagion was avoided only by Chile, some Central American countries, and Mexico.

Developmental problems were evident in the reoriented growth policies. Freeing market forces for efficiencies to be increased by domestic and foreign competition entailed exposing policies and corporate operations to more and more international market discipline, in which the strategies of multinationals based in the USA and Europe were increasingly active, while in international financial markets such discipline was really weakening, in conjunction with declines in the effectiveness of regulatory discipline. Administrative functions necessary for the development and regulation of liberal market economies in Latin America remained seriously deficient. While dependence on foreign borrowing increased, capital flight continued, and was made easier by financial market liberalization.

The developmental problems had sociological dimensions. Growth before import substitution has been based on an alliance between landowners and an urban commercial class gaining from the development of world markets for agricultural products and mineral resources. Foreign capital was attracted, and in partnership with domestic capital, sustained the political influence of landowners. Middle classes and immigrant workers benefited, while indigenous populations were marginalized. For import substituting industrialization, social and political loyalties had to be changed, and this was attempted under the brilliant leadership of Prebish (1950, 1970, 1976) and his colleagues at the Economic Commission for Latin America. An alliance was advocated between 'patriotic' national entrepreneurs, industrial workers, and reformist strata of the middle classes. Employment opportunities were to be provided for urban industrial workers while the political influence of conservative rural elites was to be weakened and the interests of domestic entrepreneurs were to be favoured by protection against imports, which would also benefit the expanding industrial labor force.

For social cohesion the new course had to ensure fast industrialization, with stability and rapid increases in employment: otherwise there was a risk that government spending to expand employment would grow, together with private sector rent seeking, instead of innovative entrepreneurship. About 1960 these dangers became apparent: the new industrialization lost momentum after initial successes, and public spending grew. This spending exhausted foreign exchange reserves and quickly exceeded capacities to increase revenue from exports of primary products, which were being partially displaced in world markets by other countries. Balance of payments problems and inflation levels increased, while currencies depreciated. Exports stagnated despite the currency depreciations, but import demand became strong, due especially to rises in government spending. Relatively little foreign direct investment was attracted. Little, Scitovsky, and Scott (1970) and Balassa (1971) were among the first to sound warnings about these dangerous trends.

Although the growth strategy was becoming unsustainable, governments endeavoured to maintain it by increasing public spending. This continued through the 1970s, while the external environment became harsher because of the oil shocks. Reliance on foreign borrowing increased, but debt service capacities decreased. The debt crises which resulted in the early 1980s were therefore acute.

Further foreign borrowing, for adjustment and recovery, thus became very clearly dependent on responsiveness to external economic advice urging changes to economic openness and to export-led growth. The rationale for such policy reorientations was very persuasive because of East Asian successes in export-led growth (Grilli and Riedel 1995); factor productivity needed to be enhanced by market-oriented policies, greater competition, and systematic knowledge absorption, while macroeconomic balance had to be attained and financial sectors had to provide more productive investment. Understanding of this rationale by Latin American elites however appears to have been superficial, and general acceptance of it lacked the enthusiasm that had been aroused earlier for import substitution. The demands of adjustment to and managing open economy growth were underestimated by Latin American and foreign policy makers and economists. Public confidence was eroded. There were only partial recoveries of income growth, and employment generally declined during the 1990s. Also there was contagious financial instability: the vulnerabilities of financial liberalization were dramatized, especially by the 1995 Mexican crisis.

The liberal growth policy could have been supported by export interests in agriculture, mining, and new outward oriented industrial sectors, and could have encouraged alliances between domestic firms and foreign enterprises. Macroeconomic failures and failures in financial administration, however, while causing overall confidence to decline, gave impetus to capital flight which had been growing because of political uncertainties and disillusion with the import substitution policy. High interest rates, in response to inflationary pressures and to capital flight, hindered outward-oriented industrialization. State enterprises were privatized to increase efficiencies and revenues,[3] and to attract foreign investment, but this went mainly into finance and infrastructure sectors rather then new manufacturing. Trade deficits meanwhile became large while capital inflows contributed to currency appreciations and strong internal demand. Policy level opportunism, relying on capital inflows, allowed the trade deficits and currency appreciations to become unsustainable. Prospective defaults on government external debts thus caused financial crises, while export-led growth became even more difficult, especially in the MERCOSUR countries.

Currency depreciations followed the financial crises but contributed little to export expansion. Further declines in domestic investor confidence meanwhile caused greater capital flight, and financing from international lending agencies became less available. High inflation and high interest rates persisted, and falls in the international prices of primary products during the 1990s further increased the difficulties of export-led growth. Altogether, requirements for more functional management of the liberal growth policies became increasingly urgent, but the macromanagement failures had divisive effects which made them all the more difficult to overcome, and which tended to activate more policy level opportunism.

NEW DEVELOPMENTAL IMPERATIVES

Broad support for open-economy growth because of complementarities of interest between primary, manufacturing, and financial sectors could have been sustained. Improvements in income and employment could have offset adjustment costs after the shifts away from import substitution, and general confidence could have been encouraged. Fiscal and financial reform efforts were however inadequate, as noted, and the export proportion of output in the late 1990s was lower than it had been, regionally, in 1945.

To build comprehensively more functional outward-oriented market economies, through sound macromanagement and internal coordination, Latin American countries must become more knowledge based and more integrated. Levels of technocratic and technological competence have to be raised, entrepreneurial capabilities have to be enhanced, and high levels of institutional development have to be attained. Intercorporate cooperation has to be promoted in networks and alliances, and general increases in social capital have become necessary. All these requirements are similar to those in the less industrialized Southern members of the European Union, but the necessary efforts will have to be made with greater self-reliance in Latin America, because of the cumulative effects of macromanagement failures and more demanding challenges of an intensely competitive hemispheric environment.

As an economy becomes more knowledge based, depending on discontinuities and degrees of stagnation caused by macromanagement failures, there is greater scope for systemic development through the logic of coordinating specializations, within firms, in intercorporate systems, and in relations between those systems and the administration. Requirements for knowledge-intensive liberal administrative guidance, as well as commonly recognized regulatory functions, become more evident. Meanwhile, external challenges tend to become more potent as competitive pressures increase in the world economy, in conjunction with concentration trends and the strains caused by destabilizing speculation in financial markets.

The extensive coordination of specializations for knowledge-based growth has to become relational, through trust and goodwill, with intensive sharing of information and of tacit as well as codified knowledge. Increasing technology-based production interdependencies between firms can then assume larger and more functional patterns, generating linked increases in innovations. For all the relational cooperation a spirit of collegial capitalism can be cultivated, with understandings that potentials for applications of frontier research often develop unevenly, at differing speeds, through interactive entrepreneurial discoveries, and that there are systemic imperatives to share these in solidarity, with collective risk taking. The efficiency effects of competition have to be recognized, but the rivalries *must* become relational for the diffusion and development of advanced technologies, for continuing increases in social capital, and for spontaneous improvements in social justice.[4]

The development of knowledge-based economies in Latin America, set back by very serious macromanagement failures, must now be accelerated to compensate for the lost decades and to make possible more balanced and more dynamic structural and policy interdependencies in a hemispheric free trade area. The immediate imperatives are evident from the convergence of insights drawn out of strands of behavioural economics, related especially to trade theory and growth theory. Behavioural finance has exceptional significance because the disruptive potential of speculative operations in world finance is increasing, with concentration trends, a weakening of regulatory and market discipline, and volatilities associated with business cycles, notably in the USA.[5] Behavioural macroeconomics has made the logic of coordination in a market economy more evident, especially in its efficiency and social justice aspects, as well as regarding the generation of social capital and the formation of relational assets by firms. The institutional requirements for intercorporate coordination have also become more apparent. Growth theory and trade theory, meanwhile, have had to become more open to understandings of structural competitiveness, and of structural interdependencies shaped by transnational enterprises building international production systems.

The accelerated transformations into more knowledge-based economies in Latin America, requiring political will and corporate will, will also need external inputs, especially from the USA, made effective in rising levels of reciprocal accountability. Highly constructive knowledge intensive policies and widely coordinated corporate operations have become necessary, with emphasis on forming dynamic innovation systems. These require clusters of frontier research activity, contributing to commercial applications by enterprising firms, and to the raising of overall levels of technological competence, especially among the lower social strata. Developmental efforts throughout the area have tended to be dysfunctional because of biases due to the influence of local elites lacking capacities for public spirited entrepreneurship and concerned with the preservation of their privileged status: the emergence of an entrepreneurial culture has thus been hindered (Lopez 2003).

Mexico, because of proximity to the USA, has been challenged strongly and very directly to develop vigorous national centres of innovation, but official and corporate responses have been weak. Government funding for science and technology has been low, corporate investment in innovation systems has also been low: the economy's learning potential remains undeveloped (Ramirez and Unger 1988). The proportions of engineers and scientists in the labor force have been about one-seventh of those in Japan, and those in Mexican enterprises have been very few, indicative of general inertia and heavy dependence on imported technologies. Sectors outside the resource industry have remained internationally uncompetitive. The automobile sector, however, while dominated by US and other foreign multinationals, is developing local supplier linkages with innovative potentials. This sector is becoming a base for expansion, especially by US enterprises, into the rest of Latin America.

Structural policy tasks in Mexico (Moguillansky and Bielschowsky 2001) reflect deficiencies in technology funding. Assembly type manufacturing by foreign firms along the northern border has to be linked more extensively with domestic enterprises, with the aid of technology enhancement measures. Import competing firms, exposed to strong foreign competition, will have to be aided by increased access to credit and by competition policy enforcement. The development of venture capital arrangements with government support would be desirable, but the financing and guidance of these is difficult even in industrialized states (Lerner 2002, Carpenter and Petersen 2002).

Brazil, ranking higher as a destination for US foreign direct investment, and advantaged by greater size, relatively higher industrial development, and stronger trade and investment links with the European Union, as well as more balanced trade in manufactures with the USA, is better placed to sponsor centres of innovation. National manufacturing firms, however, tend to remain focussed on the internal market, because of the persistent uncertainties caused by financial crises, and distress in Argentina (Moguillansky and Bielschowsky 2001). Investments in new technologies that can be expected to have benefits only after a few years are discouraged by the difficulties of calculating risks, possibly even more than in Mexico, despite greater overall levels of technological competence and the scope for diffusing high technology advances, related especially to the nation's aerospace industry. Improvements in macromanagement, while encouraging entrepreneurial confidence, could prepare the way for European as well as US participation in the development of Brazilian centres of innovation.

THEORY, POLICY LEARNING, AND CORPORATE LEARNING

Broadly comparative research on efficiencies in finance, production, and exchange has become more closely related to work on social justice issues through advances in behavioural macroeconomics of special significance for developing countries (Stiglitz 2002), while urgent questions have been raised about the performance and regulation of large international firms because of numerous cases of high risk corporate fraud, especially in the USA. The contributions of multinational enterprises to Third World growth have had to be reassessed, with understandings that the regulatory capabilities of governments in developing areas remain weak. At the same time studies of potentials for technological advances that have had special significance for industrializing countries have indicated the importance of trust and goodwill in the formation of innovation systems (Archibugi and Lundvall 2001).

New imperatives, for liberal administrative guidance stressing technology enhancement, with the promotion of relational intercorporate cooperation, can thus be seen for reform minded Latin American elites striving for export-led growth. The primary task for administrative guidance has to be the promotion of wide ranging entrepreneurial coordination, for the development of extensive complementarities in production, through technocratic–corporate consultations, in which interactive learning would make the industrializing economies more knowledge based. The guidance would be a public goods function, and, while an administrative responsibility, it would be liberal and constructive in the sense of facilitating discoveries of opportunities for corporate cooperation, especially in view of actual and expected advances in frontier technology.[6]

Literature on the development and application of advanced technology, the innovative use of knowledge (intangible) assets, has in some cases focussed on the management of industrial knowledge by competing firms striving to protect their innovations (Nonaka and Teece 2000). More holistic studies see general increases in technology-based production interdependencies between enterprises, and, accordingly, the significance of relational assets that are more and more likely to be knowledge assets (Dunning and Boyd 2003, Archibugi, Howells, and Michie 1999). For industrializing countries seeking to achieve comprehensive gains in levels of technological competence, then, the increasing importance of wide ranging intercorporate cooperation in the development and sharing of advanced innovations indicates a vital imperative, especially in cases where incoming foreign enterprises seek to ensure exclusive use of their advanced technologies.

The theoretical basis for coordinated entrepreneurship, sponsoring very active innovation systems, has to be grasped by Latin American policy makers and corporate leaders while discriminating between external advice emphasizing only competition as a driving force for growth and external advice stressing the efficiency effects of integrative knowledge-based cooperation – of applications of internalization logic in intercorporate governance as well as within firms, for the spontaneous management of intangible interdependencies between enterprises. It is also necessary to grasp extensions of this rationale in foreign economic relations, for the integrative management of structural interdependencies that will expand in a hemispheric free trade area. The dynamics of domestic intercorporate cooperation will have to assume larger dimensions in entrepreneurial collaboration with US and other foreign enterprises. Policy learning and corporate learning in this external context will have to develop with widening forms of mutual accountability and obligations of reciprocity, meeting regionalized requirements for public goods. Reductions of the vulnerabilities to speculative operations in world financial markets will be a major benefit attainable through all the domestic and external entrepreneurial cooperation.[7]

In prospect would be a transformation of class interests and cleavages, and clientelist interests and cleavages, as national economies becoming more knowledge based also become more advanced *as systems*, with higher overall productivity and greater social justice. Information asymmetries and knowledge asymmetries hindering the evolution of complex industrial economies would be reduced. Such asymmetries are often seen merely as problems affecting sales of goods and services, but they have more fundamental significance in so far as they prevent comprehension of potentials for concerting entrepreneurial ventures in widening patterns of complementarities.

Exceptional leadership for consensus formation and solidarity building is clearly required. Under the strains of political uncertainties, Latin American elite cultures have been marked by opportunism, clientelism, factionalism, short termism, cognitive simplicity, distrust, and quests for populist approval, as well as communal attachments and loyalties. The challenging external model is a liberal market economy in which imperatives for coordination have to be discerned amidst all its manifestations of highly competitive entrepreneurial vigour: the USA has an image of entrepreneurial pluralism awaiting more orderly development (Hall and Soskice 2001). Increasing asymmetries in hemispheric structural interdependence, trade and investment related as in other North–South contexts (Finger and Nogues 2002), necessitate concerted Latin American responses.

Problems of competition policy cooperation in a hemispheric free trade area will assume larger dimensions and become more difficult to resolve. US competition policy must be expected to remain primarily domestic, under the influence of guidelines from the Department of Justice that have exhibited a liberal trend in recent years: this has been open to external challenge only from the European Union, and there has been no interest in giving the World Trade Organization a responsibility in this area. Mergers and acquisitions that establish a large foreign presence in manufacturing, resource industries, nonfinancial services and financial sectors can severely restrict opportunities for national firms, but tend to be accepted because of bargaining inequalities. The asymmetries in prospect are likely to become more adverse, making the implementation of Latin American structural policies more difficult.[8]

US competition (antitrust) policy has an external reach, directed mainly against the activities of other governments and firms restricting foreign market opportunities (Evenett, Lehmann, and Steil 2000). There is no clear restraint on the attainment of dominant positions in Third World markets by US enterprises through mergers, acquisitions, and competitive methods that may force host country firms into decline, or through entirely innovative ventures in the absence of host country competition. US corporations have incentives to respect the sensitivities of host governments and business groups, but with superior technology-based efficiencies and the advantages of global strategic management can unintentionally displace host country enterprises, especially if these are disadvantaged by government failures and capital flight.

If a Latin American administration seeks to promote entrepreneurial coordination between its national firms, for widening complementarities, there may be US objections that the collaboration sets up structural barriers to trade. Such objections may not be forthcoming if the entrepreneurial collaboration becomes open to foreign participation, in a spirit of collegial capitalism, but US policy may push for acceptance of rules against intercorporate cooperation similar to those operating in the United States, which in effect discourage alliances and make mergers and acquisitions more desirable for the avoidance of antitrust enforcement. Latin American policy planning, if it becomes open to the logic of promoting entrepreneurial coordination for increased and more balanced growth, can seek to reach understandings with US regulators and corporate associations about the potential for dynamic complementarities between nationally coordinated industrial development and the expansion of American enterprises in the Southern hemisphere. Quests for such understandings could be difficult, however, and any achievements may be short lived, because of Latin American policy changes but also because of shifts in US attitudes. Competition policy cooperation between Latin American administrations, if achieved, could facilitate more equal and more considerate interactions in this area with the USA.

In the North America Free Trade Area the USA, Canada, and Mexico have accepted briefly worded obligations to implement national competition laws and cooperate with each other in their enforcement (Lloyd and Vautier 1999). The USA has scope for discretion in the external application of its antitrust policy within NAFTA, and must be expected to have an interest in ensuring that this scope will be extended in any arrangements for hemispheric trade liberalization. It would however be possible for the European Union to assert its interests in the development of competition policy cooperation within the Southern hemisphere, on the basis of European direct investment positions in Latin America.

Liberal administrative guidance in the Southern hemisphere, while sensitive to competition policy issues, will have to draw on lessons from East Asia (Yamada and Kuchiki 1997), including recent studies of recoveries from financial crises that have indicated efficiencies in intercorporate coordination (Stiglitz and Yusuf 2001). Much energy will have to go into the formation of centres of innovation through public–private partnerships, to facilitate the diffusion of applied frontier research and to aid corporate planning. The promotion of innovative clustering has been neglected in the Southern hemisphere, in part because of low estimations of its political benefits, and the costs have been continuing increases in technological lags. The learning processes now needed could benefit from links with high technology centres in the USA and Europe.

Major expansions of infrastructure network industries will also be necessary. As many of these industries have been privatized, their further development has been awaiting entrepreneurial initiatives that have been discouraged by financial crises (Moguillansky and Bielschowsky 2001). Much policy-level and corporate planning is needed, more and more on a cross border basis, and this will have to be a special responsibility for Brazil, because of its size and central location. Progress in the regional development of transportation, communications and energy sectors will aid subregional market integration and activate further collaboration for the regionalization of infrastructures.

Financial markets will also have to be deepened, more effectively regulated, and regionally integrated, with emphasis on the promotion of funding for Southern hemispheric industrialization. Capital flight should thus diminish. Meanwhile, the large scale foreign penetration of Latin American financial sectors will have to be reduced, for more balanced interdependence, the avoidance of bias in lending priorities, and the lowering of risks associated with high volume speculative financial flows.[9]

POTENTIALS FOR NEW STATECRAFT

Negotiations for the establishment of a Free Trade Area of the Americas, if they make progress, will encourage corporate initiatives, especially in the USA, to increase hemispheric trade and investment. As structural interdependencies assume larger dimensions, with further asymmetries, US and Latin American corporate associations can be expected to interact more frequently, across wide ranges of issues, with supportive involvement by the Organization of American States, the InterAmerican Development Bank, and the Economic Commission for Latin America and the Caribbean. The consultations will tend to activate increased exchanges between Latin American and European commercial associations, especially because of Latin American interests in increasing diversity in foreign economic relations, and European interests in ensuring that there will be no discriminatory arrangements in a hemispheric free trade agreement.

US corporate associations are likely to be very enterprising in quests for strong consultative links with Latin American commercial groups, and may well be assisted by the strong presence which American business organizations have established in the European Union's consultative networks. Associations of firms in the Southern hemisphere will thus be challenged, and will have incentives to form more active links with their governments. The development of these will provide inputs into Latin American negotiating endeavours relating to hemispheric trade liberalization, but will also open up opportunities for administrative-corporate consultations on structural policy issues. The interactions could make possible technocratically aided patterns of coordinated entrepreneurship. These could have vital significance for the development of more knowledge based Latin American economies. Much scope for leadership can be seen from these projections, and indeed they indicate requirements for highly constructive new statecraft. Responsibilities for providing such statecraft are primarily domestic, but the problems of the Southern hemisphere may evoke far-sighted and generous US policy-level and corporate responses.

A knowledge based economy is, in several senses, a new economy, requiring governance through a new statecraft. The accelerated development of new economies in Latin America that clearly must now be promoted will have to be structured through multiple learning processes, gaining knowledge in imperatives for wide ranging entrepreneurial coordination in applications of advanced technologies, for relational cooperation in the generation of those technologies and in the multiplication of entrepreneurial complementarities, and for comprehensive social inclusion. Civic virtues and social capital will have to sustain the new learning statecraft.

A political philosophy for a knowledge-based economy, as a learning society cultivating civic virtues, must have the motivating force of high ideals. This may be considered unrealistic if political development and regional trade liberalization are considered to require pragmatism, without searches for ultimate purposes. Pragmatism, however, is reluctant to accept analysis, and tends to wait upon events, with expectations that somehow these will indicate how to proceed, without any grand design. Knowledge-intensive governance and higher technology-based growth clearly require grand designs – the logic of advanced systems building in which human creativity flourishes with relational coordination under liberal administrative guidance.

New thinking on the Washington Consensus (Williamson 2003, Ocampo 2002) has indicated the social justice and efficiency concerns that must guide interdependent hemispheric advances toward market integration, overcoming market failures and government failures, for new balances between the market and the public interest. The immediate requirement is a solution of the problem of speculation induced volatility in financial markets, to ensure stability and the comprehensive funding of growth in real economies. Prudent fiscal and monetary management, meanwhile, must provide the policy environment in which liberal administrative guidance can develop in Latin America. Collegial development of a hemispheric free trade area, then, drawing inspiration from the richest cultural traditions of the Northern and Southern hemispheres, can become a profoundly humanistic enterprise, with more and more functionally interdependent real economies, in which relational assets assume higher order values, giving greater meaning to philosophical traditions going back to Aristotle.[10]

From new economies there must be new statecraft, comprehensively constructed to meet requirements for systemic development, through coordinated collegial endeavours. An innovative statecraft of solidarity is needed throughout Latin America, and it must develop in relational cooperation with the very advanced knowledge-based American political economy, where a new collegial statecraft must also be energized for higher achievements. If the demands of myopic interest groups in the USA push its policy makers into the negotiation of hard, precise and unequal agreements on hemispheric trade liberalization, the domestic status of yielding Latin American governments will be undermined by opposition groups rousing economic nationalism. The clear imperative for the USA is a statecraft aiming at equitable and harmonious development of hemispheric structural interdependences, that is by facilitating complementary Latin American industrialization.

NOTES

1. See references to US quests for hard and precise trade agreements in Symposium on Legalization and World Politics, *International Organization*, **54**, 3 (summer) 2000; discussion of adversarial legalism in Robert A. Kagan and Lee Axelrad (eds) (2000), *Regulatory Encounters: Multinational Corporations and American Adversarial Legalism*, Berkeley: University of California Press.
2. See Reuven Glick, Ramon Moreno, and Mark M. Spiegel (eds) (2001), *Financial Crises in Emerging Markets*, Cambridge: Cambridge University Press.
3. There was political bias in the privatizations: see M. Victoria Murillo (2002), 'Political Bias in policy convergence: privatization choices in Latin America', *World Politics* **54**, 4 (July), 462–93.
4. See comments on trust and goodwill in Bengt-Ake Lundvall and Daniele Archibugi (2001), 'Introduction: Europe and the learning economy', in Daniele Archibugi and Bengt-Ake Lundvall (eds), *The Globalizing Learning Economy*, Oxford: Oxford University Press, pp. 1–17.
5. See references to the USA in Pier Carlo Padoan, Paul A. Brenton, and Gavin Boyd (eds) (2003), *The Structural Foundations of International Finance*, Cheltenham: Edward Elgar.
6. On government-corporate cooperation in the provision of public goods as interdependences increase see Christoph Knill and Dirk Lehmkuhl (2002), 'Private actors and the state: internationalization and changing patterns of governance', *Governance*, **15**, 1 (January) 41–63. See also Richard G. Lipsey and Ken Carlaw (1996), 'A structuralist view of innovation policy', in Peter Howitt (ed.), *The Implications of Knowledge Based Growth for Micro-Economic Policies*, Calgary: University of Calgary Press, ch. 8.
7. See references to financial instability in Padoan et al., *The Structural Foundations of International Finance*.
8. On the scale of foreign direct investment in Latin America see Linda S. Goldberg and Michael W. Klein (2001), 'International trade and factor mobility: an empirical investigation', in Guillermo A. Calvo, Rudi Dornbusch and Maurice Obstfeld (eds), *Money, Capital Mobility and Trade*, Cambridge, MA: MIT Press, ch. 8; and *Foreign Investment in Latin America and the Caribbean*, Santiago: Economic Commission for Latin America and the Caribbean, 2001, part 1.
9. See Glick et al., *Financial Crises in Emerging Markets*, and Andrei Shleifer (2000), *Inefficient Markets: an Introduction to Behavioural Finance*, New York: Oxford University Press.
10. See Robert C. Solomon (2000), 'Historicism, communitarianism, and commerce: an Aristotelian approach to business ethics', in Peter Koslowski (ed.), *Contemporary Economic Ethics and Business Ethics*, Berlin: Springer, ch. 6.

REFERENCES

Abbott, Frederick M. (2000), 'NAFTA and the legalization of world politics', *International Organization*, **54**, 3 (summer), 519–48.

Archibugi, Daniele, Jeremy Howells and Jonathan Michie (eds) (1999), *Innovation Policy in a Global Economy*, Cambridge: Cambridge University Press.

Archibugi, Daniele, and Bengt-Ake Lundvall (eds) (2001), *The Globalizing Learning Economy*, Oxford: Oxford University Press.

Arndt, Sven W., and Henryk Kierzkowski (eds) (2001), *Fragmentation: New Production Patterns in the World Economy*, Oxford: Oxford University Press.

Balassa, B. (1971), *The Structure of Protection in Developing Countries*, Baltimore, MD: Johns Hopkins University Press.

Bank of International Settlements (2002), *72nd Annual Report* Basel.

Calvo, Guillermo A., Alejandro Izquierdo and Ernesto Talvi (2002), *Sudden Stops, the Real Exchange Rate and Fiscal Sustainability: Argentina's Lessons*, Washington, DC: Inter-American Development Bank.

Carpenter, Robert E., and Bruce C. Petersen (2002), 'Capital market imperfections, high technology investment and new equity financing', *The Economic Journal*, **112** (477), F54–F72.

Desai, Mihir A., Fritz Foley and James R. Hines (2002), 'International joint ventures and the boundaries of the firm', National Bureau of Economic Research working paper 9115.

Dunning, John H. and Gavin Boyd (eds) (2003), *Alliance Capitalism and Corporate Management*, Cheltenham: Edward Elgar.

Finger, J. Michael, and Julio J. Nogues (2002), 'The unbalanced Uruguay Round outcome: the new areas in future WTO negotiations', *The World Economy*, **25** (3), (March), 321–40.

Grilli, Enzo, and J. Riedel (1995), 'The East Asian growth model: how general is it?' in R. Garnaut, E. Grilli and J. Riedel (eds), *Sustaining Export-Oriented Development*, Cambridge: Cambridge University Press.

Hall, Peter A. and David Soskice (eds) (2001), *Varieties of Capitalism: The Institutional Foundations of Comparative Advantage*, Oxford: Oxford University Press.

Kurtz, Marcus J. (2002), 'Understanding the Third World welfare state after neoliberalism: the politics of social provision in Chile and Mexico', *Comparative Politics*, **34**, 3 (April), 293–314.

Lerner, Josh (2002), 'When bureaucrats meet entrepreneurs: the design of effective public venture capital programmes', *The Economic Journal*, **112** (477), F73–F84.

Little, I., T. Scitovsky and M. Scott (1970), *Industry and Trade in Some Developing Countries: A Comparative Study*, New York: Oxford University Press.

Lloyd, P.J., and Kerrin M. Vautier (1999), *Promoting Competition in Global Markets*, Cheltenham: Edward Elgar.

Lopez, Ramon (2003), 'The policy roots of socioeconomic stagnation and environmental implosion: Latin America 1950–2000', *World Development*, **31**, 2 (February), 259–80.

Lukauskas, Arvid John, and Francisco L. Rivera-Batiz (eds) (2001), *The Political Economy of the East Asian Crisis and its Aftermath*, Cheltenham: Edward Elgar.

Moguillansky, Graciela, and Ricardo Bielschowsky (2001), *Investment and Economic Reforms in Latin America*, Santiago: Economic Commission for Latin America and the Caribbean.

Nonaka, Ikujiro, and David Teece (eds) (2000), *Managing Industrial Knowledge*, Thousand Oaks, CA: Sage.

Ocampo, Jose Antonio (2002), 'Rethinking the development agenda', *Cambridge Journal of Economics*, **26**, 3 (May), 393–407.

Prebish, R. (1950), *The Economic Development of Latin America and its Principal Problems*, New York: United Nations.

Prebish, R. (1970), *Change and Development: Latin America's Great Task*, Washington, DC: InterAmerican Development Bank.

Prebish, R. (1976), 'A critique of peripheral capitalism', *CEPAL Review*, **1**, 9–76.

Ramirez, J. Carlos, and Kurt Unger (1998), 'Mexico's national innovation system in the 1990s: overview and sectoral effects', in Robert Anderson, Theodore Colin, Chad Day, Michael Hewlett and Catherine Murray (eds), *Innovation Systems in a Global Context*, Montreal: McGill-Queen's University Press, ch. 5.

Shiller, Robert J. (2003), 'From efficient markets theory to behavioural finance', *The Journal of Economic Perspectives*, **17**, 1 (winter), 83–104.

Stiglitz, Joseph E. (2002), 'Information and the change in the paradigm in economics', *American Economic Review*, **92** (3), 460–501.

Stiglitz, Joseph E., and Shahid Yusuf (eds) (2001), *Rethinking the East Asian Miracle*, Oxford: Oxford University Press and World Bank.

United Nations Conference on Trade and Development (UNCTAD), 2002 *World Investment Report* Geneva: UNCTAD.

Weyland, Kurt (2001), 'Clarifying a contested concept: populism in the study of Latin American politics', *Comparative Politics*, **43** 1, (October) 1–22.

Williamson, John (2003), *After the Washington Consensus: Restarting Growth and Reform in Latin America*, Washington, DC: Institute for International Economics.

Williamson, Oliver E. (2000), 'The new institutional economics: taking stock, looking ahead', *Journal of Economic Literature*, **38**, 3 (September), 595–613.

Yamada, Katsuhisa, and Akifumi Kuchiki (1997), 'Lessons from Japan: industrial policy approach and the East Asian trail', in Louis Emmerij (ed.), *Economic and Social Development in the XXI Century*, Washington, DC: InterAmerican Development Bank, pp. 359–93.

3. Structural partnering potential of the US economy

Walid Hejazi

There are many economic, political and social issues that need to be addressed before any Free Trade Area of the Americas (FTAA) agreement can be implemented.[1] Further, although few would disagree with the view that there will be net economic benefits from such an agreement, the length of time before these benefits are achieved can be substantial. Often, there are significant economic adjustment costs involved which have important political and social implications. Through time, however, as local economies expand production in industries for which they have a comparative advantage and contract in others, the benefits will begin to emerge. This adjustment period must be well understood so that arrangements can be made to allow for flexibility in light of such significant adjustment costs.

The objective of this chapter is to look beyond these issues and focus on the impact such an agreement will have on US integration with Latin America (LA). Improving access to the enormous US market will provide a tremendous economic opportunity for the Latin American economies. In addition to market access, these economies will be better able to access US technology, capital, and foreign direct investment (FDI). The United States too will benefit as it gets improved access to the economies of Latin America.

At the same time, it is very important to consider the impact an FTAA would have on East Asia (EA), another developing region that has significant economic links with the United States. For many of these economies, the United States is their largest export market. Also, much of the growth in the East Asian economies has been export led. If there is an FTAA, then many of the goods that otherwise might have come from East Asia will be imported from Latin America, a result known as trade diversion. If this is the case, then such an agreement can have a significant impact on the economies of East Asia.

In addition to international trade, globalization involves multinational enterprises (MNEs), and hence FDI. There has been a surge in world FDI stocks. Since 1980, global stocks of FDI have increased ten fold, whereas trade flows have only doubled. To put this into a different context, in 1980, the share of inward and outward FDI stocks relative to GDP for the largest 20 economies were 4.7 per cent and 6.4 per cent, respectively. By 1998, these ratios tripled to 14.5 per cent and 19.0 per cent, respectively. There are, however, wide variations in these ratios by country. For example, of the countries listed in Table 3.1, Norway, Austria and Australia have experienced the most rapid growth in their outward FDI *relative to* the growth in their inward FDI. At the other extreme, Greece, the United States, and the Netherlands have experienced the lowest. Fourteen of the 20 countries listed have experienced faster growth in their outward than inward FDI. Therefore, to assess the impact of an FTAA on US relations with both Latin America and East Asia, the role of MNEs (FDI) must be taken into account.

In fact, many of the benefits of an FTAA will come in the form of increased FDI. It is well established in the International Business Economics literature that inward FDI brings with it many benefits, including employment, capital formation, and especially R&D.[2] Therefore, in assessing the impact of an FTAA on the economies of Latin America, it is critical to assess the impact of FDI. I argue below that any such an agreement must have provisions that address the role of FDI, and that such FDI can increase the benefits of increased economic integration.

The purpose of this chapter is therefore threefold. First, it addresses the theoretical and empirical links between increased outward US FDI and its exports and imports. Despite the low ranking of the United States in Table 3.1, it still has more outward FDI than inward – the relative growth in its outward to inward FDI is low in this table because it began the period with a relatively high ratio of outward FDI to inward. The growth in US outward FDI has caused many US policy makers to raise alarm bells, arguing that such outward FDI, especially FDI locating in developing countries, is tantamount to the export of domestic employment and capital formation. It is argued that American workers cannot compete with the relatively low costs of labor in the countries of Latin America such as Mexico, or in East Asia such as China.[3] This chapter argues that this is not necessarily the case. In particular, to the extent that FDI is a complement to trade, increases in US outward FDI will result in a direct increase in US exports of intermediates to US production facilities abroad. Also, the presence of FDI stocks abroad facilitates the flow of information, technical and otherwise, on a broad front. It does so intra-firm, as internalization approaches to FDI have long argued. This reduction in information and transactions costs between home and host countries reduces the costs involved in conducting business between them, thus leading to increases in US exports. This increase in US exports then results in an increase in US production, employment and capital formation. In addition, as low-value-added activities move abroad, resources in the United States move into higher-value-added industries.

Table 3.1 Openness to inward and outward FDI stocks (relative to GDP)

	inward 1980	outward 1980	inward 1999	outward 1999	inward 1999/1980 A	outward 1999/1980 B	B/A	rank
Developed countries	4.7	6.4	14.5	19.0	3.09	2.97	0.96	
Australia	8.8	1.5	31.6	22.5	3.59	15.00	4.18	3
Austria	4.0	0.7	11.2	9.2	2.80	13.14	4.69	2
Belgium and Lux	5.9	4.9	108.3	97.5	18.36	19.90	1.08	14
Canada	20.6	9.0	27.9	30.6	1.35	3.40	2.51	5
Denmark	6.3	3.1	20.9	21.5	3.32	6.94	2.09	8
Finland	1.1	1.4	14.5	26.8	13.18	19.14	1.45	9
France	3.4	3.6	17.1	24.7	5.03	6.86	1.36	11
Germany	4.0	4.7	13.7	18.9	3.43	4.02	1.17	12
Greece	11.3	2.1	17.7	0.4	1.57	0.19	0.12	20
Italy	2.0	1.6	9.4	15.8	4.70	9.88	2.10	7
Japan	0.3	1.9	1.0	5.7	3.33	3.00	0.90	17
Netherlands	11.1	24.5	50.1	65.7	4.51	2.68	0.59	18
New Zealand	10.6	2.4	62.6	13.3	5.91	5.54	0.94	16
Norway	10.4	0.9	21.1	25.3	2.03	28.11	13.86	1
Portugal	12.8	1.8	21.2	10.6	1.66	5.89	3.56	4
Spain	2.4	0.9	20.5	19.0	8.54	21.11	2.47	6
Sweden	2.3	3.0	32.7	47.4	14.22	15.80	1.11	13
Switzerland	8.4	21.1	29.9	73.9	3.56	3.50	0.98	15
United Kingdom	11.7	15.0	26.8	49.8	2.29	3.32	1.45	10
United States	3.1	8.1	11.1	13.0	3.58	1.60	0.45	19

Source: Hejazi and Pauly (2003).

To test these hypotheses, a gravity model is used to estimate the link between outward US FDI stocks and US trade on a bilateral basis to 52 countries over the period 1982 to 1998. The results indicate that outward FDI to a particular country causes both exports and imports to increase with that same country. Thus, outward FDI and trade are complementary. Furthermore, the predicted impact on exports is insignificantly different from the predicted impact on imports, thus indicating that all else constant, increased levels of outward US FDI have no net impact on the US trade balance. These results are consistent with the transactions costs theory of FDI. An analysis is also undertaken at the industry level.

The second objective of this chapter is to focus attention on US trade and FDI links with the Latin American economies. Given the possibility of hemispheric free trade, the natural question to ask is, to what extent are US trade patterns with Latin America consistent with comparative advantage? Within a gravity model framework, it is established that US trade with Latin America is much below what is predicted based on comparative advantage. The implication of course is that there is tremendous scope for the increased trade between the United States and countries within Latin America that would result from a hemispheric free trade agreement. Estimates are given on the magnitude of such gains. These gains are set against the impact of such an agreement on US trade and FDI linkages with East Asia. The gains will depend very much on the 'depth' of the agreement – that is, how far the agreement goes in reducing trade and investment barriers, and thus improving market access. Such depth will be the result of extensive negotiations that take into account many other dimensions of the discussion, including social and political considerations.

The third objective is to use the model estimated to *simulate* the impact of an FTAA on US trade patterns with both Latin America and East Asia. Explicit assumptions are made on the growth rates of GDP, FDI, and the depth of the FTAA negotiated. The impact of such an agreement on US trade patterns with both Latin America and East Asia is assessed over a 20-year horizon. Overall, the results indicate a large potential impact of hemispheric free trade. The impact of such an agreement will be felt in East Asia as well, and these effects are taken into account.

The format of this chapter is as follows. The following section reviews the literature. Then the motivation for the approach is discussed. Next, the model used to measure links between trade and FDI is examined, and the section following describes the data and provides empirical estimates of these links. The next section simulates the impact of an FTA on US trade patterns with Latin America and East Asia. The final section concludes.

LITERATURE REVIEW[4]

The empirical literature on both international trade and FDI is vast, but the literature that considers links between trade and FDI is much more limited. The well-known empirical trade literature or the determinants of FDI literature will not be reviewed here.[5] Instead the focus will be on studies which consider links between trade and FDI.

Trade theory itself is ambiguous on the question of whether trade and factor mobility are substitutes. While the standard trade theory regards trade and factor mobility as substitutes (see Mundell 1957), subsequent developments in the theory have left the issue unresolved: everything depends upon the model being used. A survey of the historical experience from 1870 to 1940 rejects substitutability and leans toward complementarity, but this does not resolve the issue for recent experience (Collins et al. 1997).

If we concentrate on FDI rather than on migration and capital flows more broadly defined, the results are still ambiguous, depending on the model, type of trade, and country experience. Much of the earlier literature on FDI assumed substitutability for manufactures: much inward FDI was said to be induced by protection, for example. On the other hand, FDI in the natural resource sector was trade increasing, both in terms of an inflow of goods financed by international investment and the eventual export of part of the resource. The change from decentralized to network-based MNEs might be expected to increase foreign trade as resource duplication across geographic markets is reduced through rationalization (Malnight 1996).

With regard to manufactures, a review of some recent work illustrates the difficulty in arriving at a clear or single answer on the issue of the links between trade and FDI. The articles in Globerman (1994) offer a good review of the issues involved. Graham (1994) is probably the best statement of the issues of direct interest to the present discussion. He suggests the evidence points to modest support for the idea that FDI abroad leads to net exports and to a positive contribution to the balance of payments. However, as Hufbauer and Adler (1968) demonstrated empirically in a classic study, the results depend heavily on how firms abroad respond in supplying the foreign market if home FDI does not occur: the results vary by regions, in addition. As Graham also notes, it is not clear if FDI abroad drives the increase in exports or whether both are responding to changes in the production process.

Pfaffermayr (1994) uses impulse response analysis and variance decompositions to examine the dynamic relationship between trade and FDI flows. Using aggregate quarterly outflows of Austrian FDI flows and exports over the period 1960 to 1991, the author finds a very slow dynamic response by each variable to exogenous shocks to the other. The analysis indicates the possibility of a positive effect of exogenously increased FDI on exports and a negative effect of exports on FDI. No significant long-run effects are established.

Rao, Ahmad, and Legault (1994) reinforce empirically the view that exports and outward Canadian FDI are complementary, while also indicating that the latter had no significant effect on capital formation in Canada. These and other types of macro effects are critical to the sensitive issue of the effects of outward FDI on home employment. Gunderson and Verma (1994) explore this in detail, as well as the question whether economic integration leads to harmonization of labor regulations. They conclude that these issues are largely unsettled, partly because of the lack of data. They note there is more agreement that outward FDI does affect the composition of overall output in ways which could favour higher-skill workers and damage the interests of those with lower skills. However, Blomström and Kokko (1994) express concern that the reverse may be happening with outward FDI from Sweden.

The above studies consider the link between trade and FDI flows or stocks. Brainard (1997) points out several problems with such studies. She argues that considering the link between exports and FDI is a conceptual mismatch, as the correct comparison is between exports and foreign production. There are studies however, such as those below, which are not subject to this criticism.

Lipsey and Weiss (1981) use data for 1970 on exports to a cross-section of 44 countries from the United States and 13 other major countries. The exports are at the industry level. They use a gravity model with country size, distance, and membership in a trade bloc, and add to it some variables describing direct investment by the United States and other countries. The question being asked is whether direct investment has any impact on exports beyond the country characteristics. For the 14 industries studied, the level of US affiliate production is found to be positively related to US exports to that country in the same industry, and negatively related to exports of rival producers. The presence of foreign countries' firms was negatively related to US exports and positively related to foreign countries' exports. This is interpreted as indicating that US manufacturing affiliate activity tends to promote US exports and that foreign manufacturing affiliates tend to promote foreign country exports. As a result, there is no evidence that, on balance, a country's production in overseas markets substitutes for its own domestic production and employment. Also, Lipsey and Weiss find distance is insignificant in explaining exports when affiliate sales are included as a dependent variable.

Lipsey and Weiss (1984) use unpublished firm level data from the 1970 Bureau of Economic Analysis's 1970 survey and are able to improve on their 1981 study by disaggregating further by industry, location of investment and destination of exports. By comparing US owned production and trade across countries within industries, the authors avoid biases that may arise from the presence of industry comparative advantage that promotes both trade and direct investment. Exports in 1970 to each of five areas of the world by individual firms are related to characteristics of the parent firms and to the output of their overseas affiliates and the size of the market within each area. This is done within a gravity model framework. The results indicate that parent exports to an area (whether exports to non-affiliates are included or not) are almost always positively related to manufacturing affiliate activity in that area. That is, higher levels of affiliate output were associated with higher exports by the parent. In general, at the industry level, increased foreign production increased parent exports of intermediate goods, while in final products there is either no effect or a positive one.

Swedenborg (1979) uses firm level data on Swedish multinationals to show that multinational sales and exports are complements at the level of the firm. Blomström et al. (1988) use industry level data on US and Swedish multinationals and find that exports and foreign production are complementary.

Another important limitation of studies that consider links between trade and FDI is that no formal consideration is given to their interactions. As we know, when MNEs make decisions on how to service foreign markets, both exports and foreign production are considered. That is, the decision is a simultaneous one.[6] This is extremely important for the current topic because as the Latin American economies increase their openness to US exports and FDI, the choice of how to service the Latin American economies by US MNEs will influence the economic impacts of such an agreement.

Hejazi and Safarian (2004) and Hejazi and Safarian (2001a) explain Canadian trade and FDI patterns simultaneously, employing the standard gravity model to explain the former and an augmented gravity model to explain the latter. The augmentation takes into account elements of the Heckscher–Ohlin theory, new growth theories, public policy, and institutions. The evidence for Canada and 29 of its trading partners from 1970 to 1998 measures the roles that each of these theories have in explaining Canada's FDI. The result of most interest to the current discussion is the following. The North American Free Trade Agreement (NAFTA) has reduced the attractiveness of Canada as a destination for foreign MNEs. Many non-North American firms now locate in the United States or Mexico, and have access to the entire North American market. This effect is very strong. Such a result is very important for the current study and will influence the simulations undertaken below. Specifically, what happens to US FDI in Latin America if there is an FTAA? As barriers to trade go down, US MNEs may rely less on FDI and more on trade. On the other hand, US MNEs may expand production facilities in the Latin American economies in order to increase their market shares. In other words, the impact of an FTAA on the strategies of US MNEs, and hence on US FDI patterns, in Latin America is ambiguous.

Moving to an industry level, Hejazi and Safarian (2001b) measure the impact of US outward FDI in natural resources, manufacturing and services on US trade patterns. Using trade and FDI stock data on a bilateral basis between the United States and 51 other countries over the period 1982 to 1994, the paper establishes within a gravity model framework that trade and FDI are complementary. US outward FDI is found to have a larger predicted impact on US exports than does inward FDI. On the other hand, inward FDI is found to have a larger predicted impact on US imports than does US outward FDI. These results are directly linked to patterns of intra-firm trade within the multinational enterprise, a result consistent with the transactions cost theory of multinationals. The sectoral analysis indicates that US outward FDI in manufacturing has a large predicted impact on both exports and imports, whereas US outward FDI in services has a large predicted impact on US exports but little or no predicted impact on imports. Hejazi and Safarian (1999b) undertake a sectoral analysis for Canada. They document substantial heterogeneity, but use a finer level of industry disaggregation.

This literature survey indicates that there is evidence demonstrating that outward FDI and exports are complementary. These results are consistent with the transactions costs theory of the MNE which is discussed below. Furthermore, the results underscore the importance of accounting for MNEs in explaining changes in trade. In other words, if we are to assess the impact of an FTAA on trade linkages between the United States and Latin America, careful attention must be given to the strategies employed by MNEs, and hence changes in FDI patterns must be taken into account.

MOTIVATION FOR THE APPROACH UTILIZED

In order to analyse the causal link between trade and FDI, it is not sufficient simply to look at the correlations between trade and FDI. We need to consider a formal model of international trade, which is determined by some function of comparative advantage. The three major models of international trade each appeal to a different source of comparative advantage. The monopolistic competition model appeals to increasing returns to scale and product differentiation as the source of comparative advantage. The Heckscher–Ohlin model appeals to relative factor endowments, while the gravity model appeals to transactions costs (broadly defined).

It has been shown by Deardorff (1995) that the gravity model can in fact be derived from alternative trade models. That is, the gravity equation is a testable implication of both the Heckscher–Ohlin and monopolistic competition models of international trade. Using the gravity model as a test for one of these models against the other is misleading because the gravity equation is consistent with both trade models.[7] This is good motivation for the use of the gravity model in the context of the current chapter because the objective is to model links between US outward FDI and trade, and not to decide which model is most appropriate to explain US trade. The use of the gravity model is also supported by its wide use in both the trade and FDI literatures (Feenstra et al. 2001, Grosse and Trevino 1996, Hejazi and Safarian 2004).

The approach adopted here to measure the relation between trade and FDI links transactions costs with the gravity model. The gravity model has transactions costs as its source of comparative advantage. The presence of FDI stocks abroad facilitates the flow of information, technical and otherwise, on a broad front. It does so intra-firm, as internalization approaches to FDI have long argued. MNEs, moreover, are deeply involved in spreading alliance forms of business organization.[8] In addition, spillovers of knowledge through FDI often rival national production of knowledge locally (Hejazi and Safarian 1999a, Hejazi 2001). This reduction in information and transactions costs between home and host countries reduces the costs involved in conducting business between them, thus leading to increases in international trade. Also, a large part of international trade is intra-firm[9] and such trade may respond differently to price and exchange rate changes than would arm's-length trade (Zeile 1997). As a result, one would expect the presence of MNEs to be an important determinant of trade patterns. For a thorough discussion of internalization and the MNE, see Rugman (1980, 1988).

MODELLING THE LINKS BETWEEN TRADE AND FDI: THE GRAVITY MODEL FOR EXPORTS

The Gravity Model

The gravity model has been used to explain bilateral trade flows among large groups of countries and over long periods of time (Feenstra et al. 2001, Frankel et al. 1995, Hejazi and Trefler 1996). The gravity model is used here to explain trade flows between the United States and 52 other countries over the period 1982 to 1998, the period for which bilateral FDI and trade data exist (see Table 3.2 for a list of countries and regional groupings). The analysis will be extended to take into account FDI as an additional determinant of international trade. Such an analysis will indicate whether, after controlling for comparative advantage (the gravity model), international trade and FDI are substitutes or complements.

Table 3.2 Countries used in study and regional classifications

	Country	Latin America	East Asia	Europe
1	Argentina	X		
2	Australia			
3	Austria			X
4	Bahamas	X		
5	Belgium–Luxembourg			X
6	Brazil	X		
7	Canada			
8	Chile	X		
9	China		X	
10	Colombia	X		
11	Costa Rica	X		
12	Denmark			X
13	Dominican Republic	X		
14	Ecuador	X		
15	Egypt			
16	Finland			X

Table 3.2 continued

	Country	Latin America	East Asia	Europe
17	France			X
18	Germany			X
19	Greece			X
20	Guatemala	X		
21	Honduras	X		
22	Hong Kong		X	
23	India			
24	Indonesia		X	
25	Ireland			X
26	Israel			
27	Italy			X
28	Jamaica	X		
29	Japan			
30	Korea		X	
31	Malaysia		X	
32	Mexico	X		
33	Netherlands			X
34	New Zealand			
35	Nigeria			
36	Norway			X
37	Panama	X		
38	Peru	X		
39	Philippines		X	
40	Portugal			X
41	Saudi Arabia			
42	Singapore		X	
43	South Africa			
44	Spain			X
45	Sweden			X
46	Switzerland			X
47	Trinidad and Tobago	X		
48	Thailand		X	
49	Turkey			
50	United Arab Emirates			
51	United Kingdom			X
52	Venezuela	X		

Let t index years, i index the exporting country, j index the importing country, and let X_{ijt} denote bilateral exports from country i to country j in year t. Let T_{ijt} denote transactions costs broadly defined. Also, let D_{ij} denote regional dummy variables. The gravity model can therefore be written as follows:

$$\log(X_{ijt}) = \alpha + \log(T_{ijt})\,\beta + D_{ij}\,\delta + \in_{ijt} \qquad (1)$$

The transactions cost and dummy variables included (letting GDP denote gross domestic product) are listed in Box 3.1 below.

BOX 3.1. THE GRAVITY MODEL

	Variable Description	Expected sign in trade regression
$GDPPC_{it} \times GDPP_{jt}$	product of per capita GDPs in countries *i* and *j*	+
$GDP_{it} \times GDP_{jt}$	product of GDPs in countries i and j	+
$distance_{ij}$	a measure of distance between countries *i* and *j*	–
$language_{ij}$	a dummy variable equal to unity if countries *i* and *j* share the same language.	+
exchange rate	value of the US dollar in terms of foreign currency (on a real PPP basis)	– for exports + for imports
	Dummy variables	
Adjacency	Equal to 1 for Canada and Mexico, 0 otherwise	+
Europe	Equal to 1 for countries in Europe, 0 otherwise	?
East Asia	Equal to 1 for countries in the East Asia, 0 otherwise	?
Latin America	Equal to 1 for countries in the Latin America. 0 otherwise	?
Japan	equal to 1 for Japan, 0 otherwise	?

The idea is that countries of similar size and per capita GDP have similar needs both in terms of intermediate inputs (Ethier 1982) and consumption patterns. Also, two countries' trade should be positively related to the two countries' incomes.[10] In addition, countries that are close geographically and countries with a similar language will have small transactions costs of doing business and correspondingly large levels of bilateral trade. The exchange rate is expected to have an opposite impact in the export and import regressions: increases in the US dollar are expected to increase US imports but reduce exports.

In addition, we include dummy variables for the following regional groupings: Europe, East Asia, Latin America and Japan. We also include an adjacency dummy to take into account the special geographic relationship the United States has with Canada and Mexico. It is important to point out that these dummy variables are capturing residuals in the model. If the standard gravity model variables captured all of the determinants of international trade, these regional and adjacency dummy variables would be statistically insignificant. Adding the dummy variables captures persistent unexplained trade between the United States and the regional grouping that is not explained by the standard gravity model variables.

Since we are concerned with US exports to other countries, $i = U$, denoting the United States:

$$\log(X_{Ujt}) = \alpha + \log(T_{Ujt})\,\beta + D_{Uj}\,\delta + \in_{ijt} \qquad (2)$$

The reader familiar with the literature will recognize that in this section we are trying to follow as closely as possible the work of Frankel et al. (1995) and Hejazi and Trefler (1996). This allows for simple comparisons with previous work.

EXTENDING THE MODEL TO INCLUDE FDI

After estimating the gravity model, outward FDI is included as an additional determinant of trade:

$$\log(X_{Ujt}) = \alpha + \log(T_{Ujt})\,\beta + D_{Uj}\,\delta + \log(FDI_{Ujt})\,\lambda + \in_{ijt} \qquad (3)$$

Intuitively, FDI fits nicely into the gravity model. According to the gravity model, the source of the comparative advantage is transactions costs, broadly defined. The presence of FDI would indicate that the links or networks in the foreign country have already been established, and hence the costs associated with exporting should be lower. As a result, exports should be higher. According to this hypothesis, therefore, trade and FDI are complementary. In the next section of the chapter, this hypothesis is tested.

The theory indicates that there is an interaction between FDI and trade. That is, FDI patterns are highly dependent upon patterns of trade, and vice versa. It is typically the case that MNEs first export to a country. This is followed by movement of production facilities abroad so as to avoid transportation costs and import protection, thus guaranteeing access to the local market, and generally enabling MNEs to compete more effectively with local firms.[11] As discussed in Grosse and Trevino (1996), 'the analysis supports the notion that FDI is used to preserve markets that were previously established by exports'. It is also the case that FDI promotes trade. Eaton and Tamura (1994) indicate that US FDI follows exports, whereas Japanese FDI has a beachhead effect in promoting subsequent Japanese exports. The argument that US FDI abroad serves as a beachhead for US exports has been advanced also in Encarnation (1993) and Graham (1993). Reasons for this include: FDI abroad markets home products and home-made inputs; and MNE retailers are more likely to sell home products. All of this is consistent with much US trade being infra-firm (Hejazi and Safarian 2001b).

SECTORAL FDI AND TRADE

In order to measure the impact of FDI on trade (or any other economic variables), the underlying motivation for that FDI must be taken into account. For example, US outward FDI is motivated partly by lower factor costs but mainly by market access and access to technological skills. That might follow, for example, from the fact that US outward FDI is located in both developed and developing countries but especially in the former. Furthermore, the sectoral distribution of FDI could exhibit quite different links to trade.

FDI undertaken in services, which for the most part are non-tradeables, is likely to have a positive impact on the US economy. Since services are non-tradeables, FDI does not displace exports; in the absence of the FDI, the foreign market would not be served. Such FDI may generate exports of intermediate inputs to the foreign market, thus stimulating US production and investment. There would be no impact, however, of this outward FDI on imports into the United States from the host country. Second, if the primary motivation for FDI is gaining market access (whether in tradeables or non-tradeables) then outward FDI can stimulate US activity as it stimulates intermediate production. In short, FDI motivated by these factors is likely to have either no effect or a positive effect on exports and hence on US production and investment. Here too there should be no impact of this outward FDI on imports into the United States from the host country.

Third, FDI may be stimulated by factor endowment differences and hence factor price differences. In response to these differences in factor prices, firms may transfer production facilities from the United States to countries that have lower factor costs such as wages. Finally, FDI may be stimulated by the desire to minimize costs based on the tradeoff between proximity and concentration (Brainard 1997). In both of these cases, the impact on exports, domestic production and investment as a result of outward FDI is ambiguous. Although these scenarios do stimulate outward FDI at the expense of domestic investment, there is an offsetting effect: exports of intermediates result in an increased demand for domestic production, and therefore stimulate domestic capital formation. There would also be an impact on imports back to the United States from the host country.

Factor price differences are more likely to exist between the United States and developing countries. On the other hand, US FDI in developed countries is less likely to be motivated by factor price differences, but rather by market access and technology acquisition considerations.

Therefore, the analysis in this chapter focuses on the distribution of US FDI across as many countries as possible, both developed and developing, and across several regions. The data cover US FDI within North America, Europe, Japan, and in two major developing regions, namely Latin America and East Asia. The analysis tests whether increased US FDI to these trading partners can be linked to increased levels of exports and imports with these countries and regions. The countries used in this study together with the regional groupings are noted in Table 3.2.

We also extend equation (3) to include sectoral FDI. That is, we test the impact of outward and inward FDI in each of natural resources, manufacturing, and services, on patterns of US exports and imports. Consistent with Hejazi and Safarian (2001b, 1999b), we find much heterogeneity in the link between trade and FDI at the industry level.

ESTIMATION AND INTERPRETATION OF THE RESULTS

Data Description

Bilateral US outward FDI stocks were obtained from the US Bureau of Economic Analysis. US merchandise exports and imports, on a bilateral basis, to each of these 52 countries, were obtained from The International Monetary Fund's *Direction of Trade Statistics*. In addition, purchasing power parity based exchange rates, GDPs, and population data were obtained from the Penn world tables. Finally, distance and language dummies were those used in Hejazi and Trefler (1996). Details on these data are provided in the Appendix 3.1. The sample size of our empirical tests is therefore 884 (52 countries times 17 years per country). All data have been converted to real values except for the FDI stock data. Since the stock data are reported at historical costs, it is not a straightforward task to convert to real values. See Appendix 3.2 for a detailed discussion of this issue.

Before moving to the estimation, it may be helpful to review briefly certain aspects of the actual distribution of the US trade and FDI data. These statistics are based on the 52 countries in the sample listed in Table 3.2, unless otherwise indicated.

BOX 3.2 SUMMARY OF US TRADE AND FDI DATA

Panel A. US Trade in Goods (see Table 3.3)

1. The US trade deficit in goods has increased dramatically from \$19.1 billion in 1982 to \$193.3 billion in 1998.
2. In 1982 and 1998, respectively, 58.8% and 62.7% of this trade deficit was with developed countries. Therefore, the surge in the US trade deficit cannot be attributed solely to increasing imports from developing countries.

Panel B. US Outward FDI stock (see Table 3.4. Panel A)

1. Stocks of US FDI abroad increased from \$203 billion in 1982 to over \$900 billion in 1998.
2. In 1982 and 1998, respectively, 74.86 per cent and 76.03 per cent of this FDI was located in developed countries. Therefore, US FDI abroad is not increasingly destined for developing countries.
3. In 1998, 10.86 per cent of US outward FDI was located in Canada, 2.95 per cent in Mexico, 4.58 per cent in Japan, 56.13 per cent in Europe, 14.50 per cent in Latin America, and 7.93 per cent in East Asia.

Panel C. US FDI stock position relative to world FDI (see Table 3.4. Panel B)[12]

1. Total world inward stocks of FDI increased from \$495 billion in 1980 to over \$4.0 trillion in 1998. World growth in FDI stocks has therefore grown by a factor of ten over the sample, and at a rate far greater than that for US FDI abroad.
2. Although three-quarters of US outward FDI was located in developed countries in 1998, only about 67% of world FDI stocks are located in developed countries.
3. Whereas Canada and Japan together received only 5.08% of world FDI in 1998, they received around 15% of US FDI Europe received between 39% and 44% of world FDI over the sample period, but received between 45% and 56% of US FDI.
4. It is also worth pointing out that, whereas in 1980, the US was the home for 42% of world FDI stocks, this share had fallen to less than 25% in 1998. In contrast, although the US was host to 17% of world FDI in 1980, this share has increased to over 20% in 1998.

Note: Although Panels A and B refer to the sample of countries listed in Table 3.2, Panel C refers to world FDI.

Table 3.3 Panel A. US exports and imports (billions of US dollars) (all goods traded)

	Exports			Imports			Balance		
	1982	1990	1998	1982	1990	1998	1982	1990	1998
Total (sample)	205.5	386.1	674.9	224.6	467.6	868.1	–19.1	–81.5	–193.3
Developed countries	133.7	268.7	402.3	144.9	317.7	523.5	–11.2	–49.0	–121.2
Developing countries	71.9	117.4	272.6	79.7	149.8	344.7	–7.9	–32.5	–72.1
Canada	38.7	85.2	147.8	50.6	100.8	189.9	–11.9	–15.6	–42.1
Mexico	10.6	29.2	94.0	12.0	20.4	104.5	–1.3	8.8	–10.5
Japan	23.4	51.4	62.3	39.7	94.3	123.2	–16.3	–42.9	–60.9
Europe	64.0	118.6	170.3	50.7	112.8	194.5	13.3	5.8	–24.2
East Asia	22.4	49.3	88.6	27.0	75.9	177.6	–4.6	–26.6	–89.0
Latin America	31.9	53.9	157.0	34.1	50.0	149.3	–2.3	3.8	7.7

Table 3.3 Panel B. US exports and imports (percentage distribution)

	1982	1990	1998	1982	1990	1998	1982	1990	1998
Total (sample)	100	100	100	100	100	100	100	100	100
Developed countries	65.0	69.6	59.6	64.5	68.0	60.3	58.8	60.2	62.7
Developing countries	35.0	30.4	40.4	35.5	32.0	39.7	41.2	39.8	37.3
Canada	18.8	22.1	21.9	22.5	21.6	21.9	62.5	19.2	21.8
Mexico	5.2	7.6	13.9	5.3	4.4	12.0	6.9	–10.8	5.4
Japan	11.4	13.3	9.2	17.7	20.2	14.2	85.2	52.7	31.5
Europe	31.1	30.7	25.2	22.6	24.1	22.4	–69.7	–7.1	12.5
East Asia	10.9	12.8	13.1	12.0	16.2	20.5	24.1	32.7	46.1
Latin America	15.5	13.9	23.3	15.2	10.7	17.2	11.9	–4.7	–4.0

Note 1. Only includes countries in our sample as listed in Appendix 3.1.

Table 3.4 Panel A. Distribution of US outward FDI

	Millions of US dollars			Percentage distribution		
	1982	1990	1998	1982	1990	1998
All countries	203 062	399 685	904 437	100	100	100
Developed countries	152 010	324 362	687 669	74.86	81.15	76.03
Developing countries	51 052	75 323	216 768	25.14	18.85	23.97
Canada	43 511	69 508	98 200	21.43	17.39	10.86
Mexico	5 019	10 313	26 657	2.47	2.58	2.95
Japan	6 407	22 599	41 423	3.16	5.65	4.58
Latin America	33 772	48 933	131 137	16.63	12.24	14.50
East Asia (less Japan)	10 924	20 897	71 686	5.38	5.23	7.93
Europe	91 780	213 243	507 705	45.20	53.35	56.13

Table 3.4 Panel B. Total inward FDI stocks

	Millions of US dollars			Percentage distribution		
	1980	1990	1998	1980	1990	1998
All countries	495 200	1 761 198	4 015 258	100	100	100
Developed countries	373 960	1 380 827	2 690 129	75.52	78.40	67.00
Developing countries	121 240	377 380	1 240 976	24.48	21.43	30.91
USA	83 046	394 911	811 756	16.77	22.42	20.22
Canada	54 149	112 872	143 234	10.93	6.41	3.57
Mexico	2 090	22 424	60 783	0.42	1.27	1.51
Japan	3 270	9 850	26 065	0.66	0.56	0.65
Latin America	36 317	98 193	347 462	7.33	5.58	8.65
East Asia (less Japan)	54 229	166 017	609 861	10.95	9.43	15.19
Europe	200 753	770 090	1 545 151	40.54	43.73	38.48

Notes:

1. Data in Panel A from the US Bureau of Economic Analysis.
2. Panel A includes only those countries in our sample as listed in Appendix 3.1. This sample of countries accounts for 98.0 per cent, 93.4 per cent, and 90.1 per cent of all US outward FDI in 1982, 1990, and 1994, respectively. These countries also account for 77.4 per cent, 73.0 per cent, and 73.4 per cent of all world inward FDI stocks in 1980, 1990, and 1995.
3. Data in Panel B from the *World Investment Report* (1999).

Table 3.5 Panel A. Total inward stocks of FDI in individual Latin American economies

	Millions of US dollars			Percent distribution		
	1980	1990	1998	1980	1990	1998
1. Argentina	5 344	9 085	47 114	14.71	9.25	13.56
2. Bahamas	298	336	938	0.82	0.34	0.27
3. Brazil	17 480	37 143	132 734	48.13	37.83	38.20
4. Chile	886	10 067	30 038	2.44	10.25	8.64
5. Colombia	1 464	4 904	18 125	4.03	4.99	5.22
6. Costa Rica	672	1 447	4 201	1.85	1.47	1.21
7. Dominican Republic	239	572	2 924	0.66	0.58	0.84
8. Ecuador	719	1 626	5 452	1.98	1.66	1.57
9. Guatemala	701	1 734	3 043	1.93	1.77	0.88
10. Honduras	92	383	937	0.25	0.39	0.27
11. Jamaica	501	727	2 261	1.38	0.74	0.65
12. Mexico	2 090	22 424	60 783	5.75	22.84	17.49
13. Panama	2 353	2 090	6 064	6.48	2.13	1.75
14. Peru	898	1 302	7 998	2.47	1.33	2.30
15. Trinidad and Tobago	976	2 093	5 721	2.69	2.13	1.65
16. Venezuela	1 604	2 260	19 129	4.42	2.30	5.51
Total	36 317	98 193	347 462	100	100	100

Table 3.5 Panel B. Total inward stocks of FDI in individual East Asian economies

	Millions of US dollars			Percent distribution		
	1980	1990	1998	1980	1990	1998
1. China	6 252	24 763	265 603	11.53	14.92	43.55
2. Hong Kong	22 929	46 826	109 334	42.28	28.21	17.93
3. Indonesia	10 274	38 883	68 458	18.95	23.42	11.23
4. Korea	1 140	5 186	19 043	2.10	3.12	3.12
5. Malaysia	5 169	10 318	45 241	9.53	6.22	7.42
6. Philippines	1 281	3 268	9 305	2.36	1.97	1.53
7. Singapore	6 203	28 564	72 416	11.44	17.21	11.87
8. Thailand	981	8209	20 461	1.81	4.94	3.36
Total	54 229	166 017	609 861	100	100	100

Source: *World Investment Report* (1999).

Table 3.5 provides total FDI into the individual countries within Latin America and East Asia. Although Brazil remains the largest recipient of world FDI among the Latin American economies, the share going to Mexico has increased dramatically over the period. Chile also has received an increased share. Within East Asia, the share going to Hong Kong has fallen dramatically whereas that going to China has increased.

Table 3.6 provides a description of US FDI locating in the individual countries within Latin America and East Asia. In contrast to the global share, the US share of FDI in Brazil has not fallen. But similar to world FDI shares, the share of US FDI to both Chile and Mexico has also increased. In terms of the countries within East Asia, the US share going to Hong Kong has not fallen significantly, but the share going to China has increased. What is interesting, however, is that the US share of its FDI in the region locating in China is far below world FDI locating in China.

Table 3.7 breaks US outward FDI down by three industry classifications: natural resources, manufacturing and services. Of all US outward FDI in 1998, less than 10 per cent was in natural resources, 31.35 per cent was in manufacturing, and 60 per cent was in services. The services share has almost doubled since 1982.[13] The importance of both natural resources and manufacturing has fallen, with the former falling more rapidly. The table then gives the share of all outward FDI in each sector locating in each region. For example, in 1998, 68.68 per cent of all US outward FDI in natural resources was located in other developed countries, with the remaining 31.32 per cent locating in developing countries; 73.69 per cent of US outward FDI in manufacturing located in developed countries with the remaining 26.31 per cent locating in developing countries; and 78.57 per cent of US outward FDI in services located in developed countries, with the remaining 21.43 per cent locating in developing countries.

There is an important observation to be made in terms of the difference between Latin America and East Asia. In 1998, more than double the US share of outward FDI in both manufacturing and services was located in Latin America than was located in East Asia. In contrast, the share of US outward FDI in natural resources in East Asia was almost double the share in Latin America.

Table 3.8 presents the data a little differently. It breaks US FDI into each region down into the share in each industry. For example, in 1998, of all US FDI locating in Latin America, 56.7 per cent was in services, 36.48 per cent in manufacturing, and only 5.32 per cent in natural resources. For East Asia, 48.73 per cent was in services, 33.54 per cent in manufacturing, and 17.73 per cent in natural resources. Therefore, although the share in manufacturing is about the same, US FDI in Latin America is more focused on services, whereas that in East Asia is more focused on natural resources.

Table 3.6 Panel A. US FDI in individual Latin American economies

	Millions of US dollars			Percentage distribution		
	1980	1990	1998	1980	1990	1998
1. Argentina	2864	2531	12327	8.48	5.17	9.40
2. Bahamas	3121	4577	1000	9.24	9.35	0.76
3. Brazil	9290	14384	37195	27.51	29.40	28.36
4. Chile	160	1896	9029	0.47	3.87	6.89
5. Colombia	1769	1677	3749	5.24	3.43	2.86
6. Costa Rica	142	251	2074	0.42	0.51	1.58
7. Dominican Republic	188	529	645	0.56	1.08	0.49
8. Ecuador	388	321	904	1.15	0.66	0.69
9. Guatemala	233	107	498	0.69	0.22	0.38
10. Honduras	247	262	111	0.73	0.54	0.08
11. Jamaica	386	625	1960	1.14	1.28	1.49
12. Mexico	5019	10313	26657	14.86	21.08	20.33
13. Panama	4413	9289	25924	13.07	18.98	19.77
14. Peru	1990	599	2148	5.89	1.22	1.64
15. Trinidad and Tobago	931	485	1004	2.76	0.99	0.77
16. Venezuela	2631	1087	5912	7.79	2.22	4.51
Total	33772	48933	131137	100	100	100

Table 3.6 Panel B. US FDI in individual East Asian economies

	1980	1990	1998	1980	1990	1998
1. China	49	354	6350	0.45	1.69	8.86
2. Hong Kong	2854	6055	17548	26.13	28.98	24.48
3. Indonesia	2295	3207	8104	21.01	15.35	11.30
4. Korea	690	2695	7365	6.32	12.90	10.27
5. Malaysia	1221	1466	5629	11.18	7.02	7.85
6. Philippines	1315	1355	3931	12.04	6.48	5.48
7. Singapore	1720	3975	17550	15.75	19.02	24.48
8. Thailand	780	1790	5209	7.14	8.57	7.27
Total	10924	20897	71686	100	100	100

Source: US Bureau of Economic Analysis.

Table 3.7 Geographic distribution of US outward FDI, by region

	US dollars				Shares			
	All	Nat. Res.	Manu.	Serv.	All	Nat. Res.	Manu.	Serv.
All Countries								
1982	203 062	48 456	82 377	72 154	100	23.86	40.57	35.53
1990	399 685	49 650	167 889	182 090	100	12.42	42.01	45.56
1998	904 437	76 252	283 579	542 637	100	8.43	31.35	60.00
Developed Countries								
1982	152 010	34 765	63 107	54 138	74.86	71.75	76.61	75.03
1990	324 362	38 579	135 445	150 338	81.15	77.70	80.68	82.56
1998	687 669	52 374	208 958	426 337	76.03	68.68	73.69	78.57
Developing Countries								
1982	51 052	13 690	19 270	18 017	25.14	28.25	23.39	24.97
1990	75 323	11 071	32 444	31 752	18.85	22.30	19.32	17.44
1998	216 768	23 879	74 621	116 299	23.97	31.32	26.31	21.43
Canada								
1982	43 511	10 421	18 825	14 265	21.43	21.51	22.85	19.77
1990	69 508	10 494	33 274	25 740	17.39	21.14	19.82	14.14
1998	98 200	12 282	40 504	45 414	10.86	16.11	14.28	8.37
Mexico								
1982	5 019	83	3 921	1 015	2.47	0.17	4.76	1.41
1990	10 313	79	7 784	2 450	2.58	0.16	4.64	1.35
1998	26 657	116	15661	10 880	2.95	0.15	5.52	2.01
Japan								
1982	6 407	1 650	3 058	1 699	3.16	3.41	3.71	2.35
1990	22 599	3 988	11 182	7 429	5.65	8.03	6.66	4.08
1998	41 423	4 396	11 428	25 599	4.58	5.77	4.03	4.72
Latin America								
1982	33 772	6 299	15 615	11 783	16.63	13.00	18.96	16.33
1990	48 933	3 545	23 494	21 838	12.24	7.14	13.99	11.99
1998	131 137	6 972	47 841	74 355	14.50	9.14	16.87	13.70

Table 3.7 continued

	All Countries							
	US dollars				Shares			
	All	Nat. Res.	Manu.	Serv.	All	Nat. Res.	Manu.	Serv.
	East Asia (less Japan)							
1982	10924	4468	2032	4424	5.38	9.22	2.47	6.13
1990	20897	5004	7614	8279	5.23	10.08	4.54	4.55
1998	71686	12712	24041	34933	7.93	16.67	8.48	6.44
	Europe							
1982	91780	21028	37632	33120	45.20	43.40	45.68	45.90
1990	213243	20924	84743	107576	53.35	42.14	50.48	59.08
1998	507705	31442	146615	329648	56.13	41.23	51.70	60.75

Source: US Bureau of Economic Analysis.

Table 3.8 Sectoral distribution of FDI by region

	All Countries							
	Millions of US dollars				Shares			
	All	Nat. Res.	Manu	Serv.	All	Nat. Res.	Manu	Serv.
1982	203062	48456	82377	72154	100	23.86	40.57	35.53
1990	399685	49650	167889	182090	100	12.42	42.01	45.56
1998	904437	76252	283579	542637	100	8.43	31.35	60.00
	Developed Countries							
1982	152010	34765	63107	54138	100	22.87	41.52	35.61
1990	324362	38579	135445	150338	100	11.89	41.76	46.35
1998	687669	52374	208958	426337	100	7.62	30.39	62.00
	Developing Countries							
1982	51052	13690	19270	18017	100	26.82	37.75	35.29
1990	75323	11071	32444	31752	100	14.70	43.07	42.15
1998	216768	23879	74621	116299	100	11.02	34.42	53.65
	Canada							
1982	43511	10421	18825	14265	100	23.95	43.26	32.78
1990	69508	10494	33274	25740	100	15.10	47.87	37.03
1998	98200	12282	40504	45414	100	12.51	41.25	46.25

Table 3.8 continued

	All countries							
	Millions of US dollars				Shares			
	All	Nat. Res.	Manu	Serv.	All	Nat. Res.	Manu	Serv.
				Mexico				
1982	5019	83	3921	1015	100	1.66	78.12	20.22
1990	10313	79	7784	2450	100	0.77	75.48	23.76
1998	26657	116	15661	10880	100	0.43	58.75	40.82
				Japan				
1982	6407	1650	3058	1699	100	25.75	47.73	26.52
1990	22599	3988	11182	7429	100	17.65	49.48	32.87
1998	41423	4396	11428	25599	100	10.61	27.59	61.80
				Latin America				
1982	33772	6299	15615	11783	100	18.65	46.24	34.89
1990	48933	3545	23494	21838	100	7.24	48.01	44.63
1998	131137	6972	47841	74355	100	5.32	36.48	56.70
				East Asia (less Japan)				
1982	10924	4468	2032	4424	100	40.90	18.60	40.50
1990	20897	5004	7614	8279	100	23.94	36.44	39.62
1998	71686	12712	24041	34933	100	17.73	33.54	48.73
				Europe				
1982	91780	21028	37632	33120	100	22.91	41.00	36.09
1990	213243	20924	84743	107576	100	9.81	39.74	50.45
1998	507705	31442	146615	329648	100	6.19	28.88	64.93

Source: US Bureau of Economic Analysis.

Table 3.9 describes the role of MNEs in facilitating exports and imports with the United States. For 1992, 33.4 per cent of all exports from the United States were mediated by MNEs – of which 22.5 per cent involved US MNEs and the remaining 10.9 per cent foreign MNEs. On the import side, 41.5 per cent of US imports were mediated by MNEs, of which 15.6 per cent involved US MNEs with the remaining 25.9 per cent involving foreign MNEs. The relative importance of foreign to US MNEs in facilitating trade is therefore about twice as great for imports into the United States as for exports. There are

Table 3.9 Panel A. Role of MNEs in US exports and imports by industry, 1992 (percentages)

	US exports which are intra-firm			US imports which are intra-firm		
	% of all exports	Between US parents and their majority owned foreign affiliates	Between US affiliates and their foreign owned parents	% of all imports	Between US parents and their majority owned foreign affiliates	Between US affiliates and their foreign owned parents
All countries	33.4	22.5	10.9	41.5	15.6	25.9
Canada	41.4	37.4	4.0	46.7	37.1	9.6
Mexico	26.3	24.9	1.5	34.7	30.5	4.2
Europe	35.5	26.8	8.7	46.3	11.5	34.8
Japan	70.1	15.9	54.2	71.3	2.0	69.2
Latin America	20.8	18.6	2.2	29.1	20.3	8.8
Asia	38.5	14.7	23.8	42.6	7.7	34.9

Table 3.9 Panel B. Role of MNEs in US exports and imports by industry, averages for 1982 to 1994 (percentages)

	Intra–firm trade between US parents and their majority owned foreign affiliates				Intra–firm trade between US affiliates and their foreign owned parents			
	All industries	Manufacturing	Wholesale trade	Petroleum and other industries	All industries	Manufacturing	Wholesale trade	Petroleum and other industries
Exports	100.0	66.7	29.3	4.0	100.0	20.6	73.8	5.6
Imports	100.0	75.4	8.3	16.3	100.0	20.3	73.8	5.8

Source: Zeile (1997).

dramatic variations in these ratios across countries and regions. Specifically, the importance of foreign MNEs in mediating exports to Latin America is only 2.2 per cent, but 23.8 per cent for Asia. On the import side, only 8.8 per cent of imports from Latin America are mediated by foreign MNEs, but 34.9 per cent of imports from Asia are mediated by foreign MNEs. These data therefore point to significant differences in the strategies utilized by MNEs in their trade relations with Latin America in comparison to their relations with Asia. Although it is beyond the scope of the current analysis to explain these dramatic differences in the behaviour of MNEs, this should be highlighted, and one should consider the impact an FTAA would have on these linkages.

Finally, I would like to summarize precisely the increasing openness of the US economy to the world, as well as its changing integration with the regions of Latin America and East Asia. Figure 3.1 establishes that the United States is becoming much more open to both international trade and FDI. Over the past 40 years, it is inward FDI relative to GDP that has grown most rapidly. Figure 3.2 considers the distribution of US exports and imports. The top two panels indicate that developing countries have been increasing in relative importance as a destination for US exports as well as a source for US imports. The bottom two panels indicate that both Latin America and East Asia have experienced a steady increase in their shares of US trade, both exports and imports, over the past 20 years, although the East Asian share of US imports has levelled off and their share of exports actually fell over the latter half of the 1990s. This is no doubt a transitory trend and is likely to reflect the East Asian financial crisis. Also, although Latin America's share of US exports is higher than that

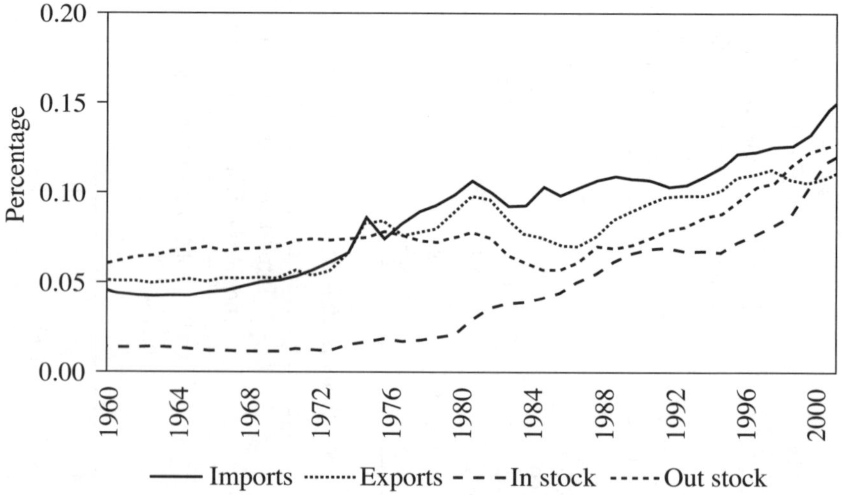

Figure 3.1 US openness to trade and FDI (relative to GDP)

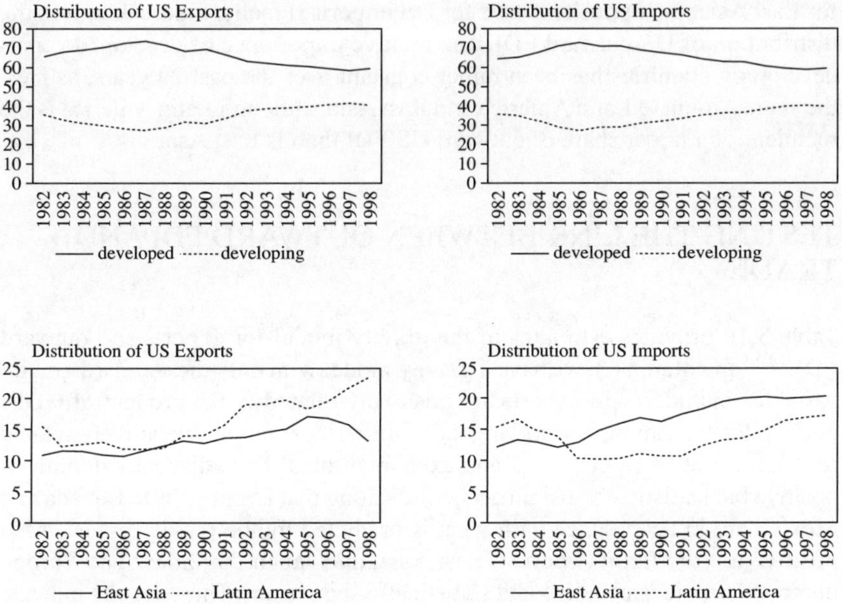

Figure 3.2 Distribution of US trade

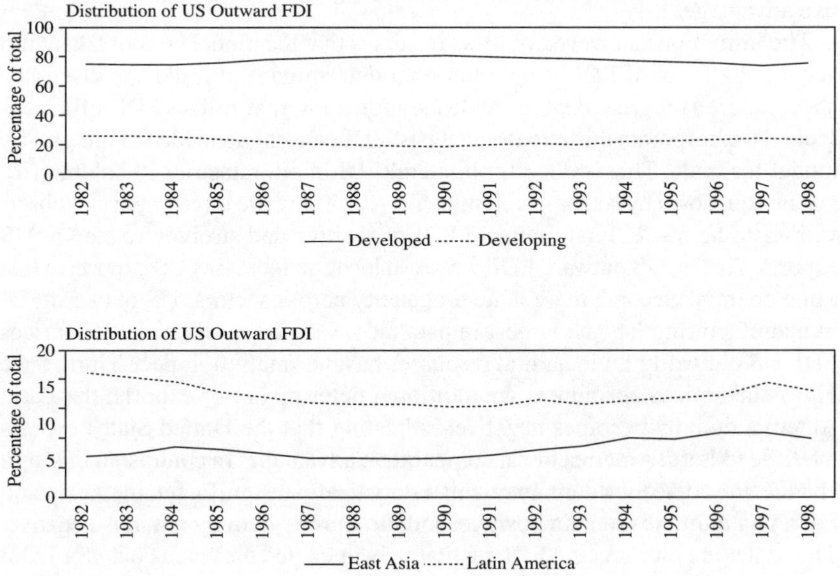

Figure 3.3 Distribution of US outward FDI

for East Asia, the opposite is true for US imports. Finally, Figure 3.3 gives the distribution of US outward FDI. The relative importance of developed versus developing countries has been rather constant over the past 20 years, as have the shares going to Latin America and East Asia, although Latin America is the recipient of a larger share of outward US FDI than is East Asia.

TESTING THE LINK BETWEEN OUTWARD FDI AND TRADE

Table 3.10 provides estimates of the gravity model for exports and outward FDI.[14,15] In column (i), we have a gravity model with only the standard gravity variables included. US exports are positively related to the product of GDPs and GDPs per capita, and to language similarities, but are negatively related to distance between countries and exchange rates. The adjacency dummy is positive but statistically insignificant, indicating that US exports to Canada and Mexico are in accordance with what is predicted by the gravity model. Also positive are the Latin America, East Asia, and Japan dummies. The Europe dummy variable is negative and statistically significant. These results indicate that US exports to adjacent countries are in accordance with the gravity model's predictions, but that the United States exports more to Latin America, East Asia and Japan, but less to Europe than is predicted by the gravity model (comparative advantage).

The limitations, however, of these results is that the model has not taken into account patterns of FDI as an additional determinant of trade. As discussed above, there is a great deal of evidence indicating that in fact FDI influences trade. To incorporate this into the analysis, FDI patterns are added to our gravity model for trade. This is done for bilateral FDI in all industries in column (ii), and broken down by sector in columns (iii)–(v). There are three important observations to be made. First, outward FDI is positive and strongly related to US exports. That is, US outward FDI to a given location increases US exports to that same country. Second, there is heterogeneity across sectors. US outward FDI in manufacturing has the largest impact on US exports, followed by Services FDI. US outward FDI in natural resources has the smallest impact. Third, once FDI is taken into account as an additional determinant of exports, the Latin America dummy becomes negative, indicating that the United States exports too little to Latin America given comparative advantage. In contrast to this sign change, the adjacency dummy remains statistically insignificant, the Japan and East Asia dummies remain positive, and the Europe dummy remains negative. That is, taking into account FDI qualitatively impacted the results only for Latin America, and hence including FDI is an important extension for the analysis.

Table 3.10 Gravity model regressions for US exports and sectoral outward FDI, 1982–1998

Independent Variables	Dependent Variable: Bilateral Exports				
	(i) no FDI	(ii) Total FDI	(iii) Natural Resources FDI	(iv) Manufacturing FDI	(v) Services FDI
Product of GDPS	0.663	0.457	0.646	0.418	0.533
	(46.96)	(30.42)	(41.40)	(25.00)	(35.39)
Product of per capita GDPS	0.754	0.414	0.736	0.412	0.442
	(27.43)	(12.81)	(25.80)	(13.91)	(12.75)
Distance	–0.840	–0.932	–0.844	–0.649	–0.939
	(–12.51)	(–19.19)	(–12.79)	(–10.31)	(–19.12)
Language	0.392	0.013	0.353	0.094	0.143
	(8.42)	(0.31)	(7.36)	(2.32)	(3.13)
Exchange rates	–0.056	–0.048	–0.056	–0.050	–0.049
	(–8.79)	(–9.80)	(–8.75)	(–9.47)	(–9.19)
Adjacency	0.226	0.103	0.226	0.197	0.009
	(1.54)	(0.81)	(1.54)	(1.47)	(0.07)
Latin America	0.291	–0.250	–0.264	–0.064	–0.142
	(3.74)	(–3.58)	(–3.41)	(–0.87)	(–2.05)
Japan	0.724	0.566	0.691	0.691	0.650
	(10.93)	(10.49	(10.52)	(12.15)	(10.89)
Europe	–0.518	–0.751	–0.525	–0.605	–0.686
	(–7.93)	(–14.53)	(–8.04)	(–11.69)	(–12.18)
East Asia	0.994	0.716	0.970	0.711	0.803
	(17.38)	(12.63)	(16.37)	(13.37)	(13.52)
Outward FDI		0.299	0.027	0.264	0.196
		(20.08)	(2.41)	(20.27)	(15.21)
Adjusted R^2	0.860	0.904	0.861	0.903	0.891

Notes: Column (i) estimates the gravity model with no FDI. Column (ii) adds total US outward FDI. Column (iii) adds outward FDI in petroleum. Column (iv) adds outward FDI in manufacturing. Column (v) adds outward FDI in services.

The next hypothesis tested is whether outward FDI has any significant impact on imports. It is often assumed that outward FDI, especially that motivated by factor price differences, results in increased imports back to the home country. To test this hypothesis, we estimate the gravity model for imports:

$$\log(M_{Ujt}) = \alpha + \log(T_{Ujt})\,\beta + D_{Uj}\,\delta + \in_{ijt} \qquad (4)$$

where M_{Ujt} are imports into the United States from country *j* in year *t*. We then test whether adding patterns of outward FDI provide any additional information to explain these patterns of imports:

$$\log(M_{Ujt}) = \alpha + \log(T_{Ujt})\,\beta + D_{Uj}\,\delta + \log(FDI_{Ujt})\,\lambda + \varepsilon_{ijt} \qquad (5)$$

These results are presented in Table 3.11.

Table 3.11 Gravity model regressions for US imports and sectoral outward FDI, 1982–1998

Independent Variables	Dependent Variable: Bilateral Imports				
	(i) no FDI	(ii) Total FDI	(iii) Natural Resources FDI	(iv) Manufacturing FDI	(v) Services FDI
Product of GDPS	0.676	0.465	0.649	0.395	0.563
	(32.41)	(16.05)	(27.01)	(12.74)	(22.15)
Product of per capita GDPS	0.662	0.312	0.632	0.271	0.390
	(9.94)	(3.98)	(8.75)	(3.64)	(4.93)
Distance	–1.068	–1.163	–1.076	–0.850	–1.155
	(–17.15)	(–17.84)	(–17.49)	(–13.53)	(–17.88)
Language	0.319	0.071	0.253	–0.022	0.101
	(5.14)	(1.21)	(4.19)	(–0.34)	(1.56)
Exchange rates	–0.019	–0.011	–0.018	–0.012	–0.013
	(–1.92)	(–1.33)	(–1.80)	(–1.65)	(–1.44)
Adjacency	0.442	0.104	0.444	0.409	0.253
	(2.90)	(0.71)	(2.88)	(2.92)	(1.74)
Latin America	0.014	–0.541	–0.029	–0.390	–0.362
	(0.12)	(–3.86)	(–0.23)	(–3.31)	(–2.69)
Japan	1.564	1.401	1.509	1.526	1.500
	(14.53)	(13.60)	(13.92)	(15.52)	(13.98)
Europe	–0.404	–0.643	–0.416	–0.503	–0.550
	(–4.10)	(–6.82)	(–4.13)	(–5.91)	(–5.78)
East Asia	1.622	1.337	1.58	1.299	1.455
	(14.51)	(11.49)	(13.19)	(12.36)	(12.77)
Outward FDI		0.307	0.044	0.301	0.017
		(11.40)	(2.65)	(12.25)	(8.70)
Adjusted R^2	0.782	0.815	0.783	0.822	0.799

Notes: Column (i) estimates the gravity model with no FDI. Column (ii) adds total US outward FDI. Column (iii) adds outward FDI in petroleum. Column (iv) adds outward FDI in manufacturing. Column (v) adds outward FDI in services.

Column (i) of Table 3.11 estimates the standard gravity model for imports. US imports are positively related to the product of GDPs and GDPs per capita and language similarities, and are negatively related to distance between countries and the exchange rate, but the exchange rate is statistically insignificant. The adjacency dummy is positive and statistically significant indicating the United States imports more from Canada and Mexico than is predicted by the gravity model. Also positive are the East Asia and Japan dummies, whereas the Latin America dummy is statistically insignificant. The Europe dummy variable is negative and statistically significant. These results indicate that the United States imports more from its adjacent trading partners, Japan and East Asia, than is predicted by the gravity model, but imports less from Europe. However, US imports from Latin America conform to the predictions of the gravity model.

In column (ii), US outward FDI is included as an additional determinant of US imports. Language now becomes statistically insignificant. Recall this was also the case in the export regressions. In other words, FDI eliminates the statistical significance of one of the transactions costs noted earlier. The coefficient estimate on the FDI variable is positive and strongly significant. This indicates that increased levels of US outward FDI to a particular country increase US imports from that same country. That is, there is a complementary relationship between outward FDI and imports. Once FDI is added, however, the coefficient on the adjacency dummy becomes statistically insignificant, indicating the important role played by multinationals in facilitating US imports from Canada and Mexico: there are no unexplained imports into the United States from its adjacent trading partners when patterns of FDI are added. The addition of FDI has now made the Latin America dummy negative. That is, once the amount of US FDI located in Latin America is taken into account, the United States imports too little from Latin America. The Europe dummy remains negative, and the Japan and East Asia dummies remain positive. These results are remarkably similar to those on the export side.

Looking at Tables 3.10 and 3.11 together reveals important implications of US FDI on the US trade balance, at the aggregate and sectoral levels. The results indicate that increased outward FDI impacts both exports and imports (columns (ii) in Tables 3.10 and 3.11), but the impact on exports is marginally smaller than that on imports, indicating a slight negative net impact on the US trade balance, although the effect on trade balance is insignificantly different from zero. We next take into account the sectoral distribution of FDI on both exports and imports (columns (iii) to (v) in Tables 3.10 and 3.11). The hypothesis is that increased US outward FDI in services will be likely to have a strong impact on US exports as US firms provide many of the intermediates needed in the delivery of such services, but little or no impact on imports back into the United States. This hypothesis is confirmed, as the results indicate a strong positive impact on US exports but a very small impact on US imports. On the other hand, the expectation is that US outward FDI into manufacturing will have a strong predicted impact on US exports of intermediates, as well as an impact on the imports back into the United States, especially of final products. These results too are confirmed, and the results indicate that the impact on exports is smaller than that on imports. US outward FDI in natural resources results in twice the impact on exports as it does on imports. This is consistent with US MNEs investing abroad to exploit natural resources, which are exported back to the United States. In short, therefore, outward FDI in services stimulates the US trade balance, whereas outward FDI in both natural resources and manufacturing stimulates a trade deficit. Over this sample period, the net impact of these two offsetting effects results in an increase in US outward FDI having no net impact on the trade balance.

DISCUSSING THE RESULTS

In both sets of regressions, the Europe dummy is negative and the Japan dummy positive. The results indicate therefore that the United States trades more with Japan than is consistent with comparative advantage, but less with Europe. These signs are as expected. Given Japan's stringent restrictions on FDI (Figure 3.4), the United States' integration with Japan relies more heavily on trade than otherwise would be the case. On the other hand, given the free trade area within Europe and trade restrictions on goods entering Europe, countries are forced to rely more heavily on FDI to avoid the barriers. Also, Europe's restrictions on FDI are less stringent than those for Japan. As a result of these FDI restrictions, the United States has far more FDI in Europe and hence less trade, and at the same time less FDI in Japan and hence more trade. The effects of these policies towards FDI are also reflected in the data reported in Table 3.4. The top panel indicates that in 1998, Japan received less than 5 per cent of all US outward FDI, whereas Europe received over 50 per cent. In the bottom panel, similar patterns hold for the distribution of global FDI.

The focus, here, however, will be on US trade and FDI relations with Latin America and East Asia. The results in Tables 3.10 and 3.11 indicate that the United States trades less with Latin America, but more with East Asia than is consistent with comparative advantage. Specifically, the United States exports only 78 per cent of what it should to Latin America given comparative advantage, and imports only 58 per cent of what it should be expected to import.[16] On the other hand, the United States exports to East Asia twice what is predicted by comparative advantage, and imports 3.8 times as much as predicted. These results should indicate the tremendous potential benefits to an FTAA – if as a result of such an agreement, US trade with Latin America reached its compara-

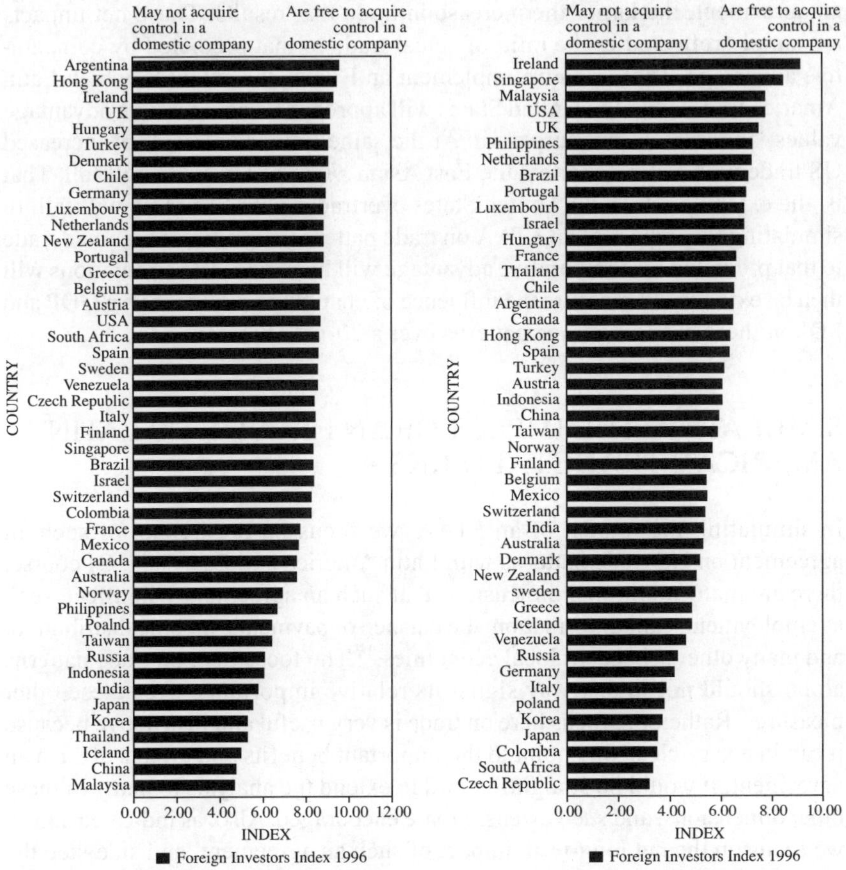

Source: *World Competitiveness Report*, 1998.

Figure 3.4 Government policies on FDI

tive advantage level, US imports from Latin America would double and US exports to Latin America would rise by 25 per cent.

These results will be used in the next section to simulate the impact of an FTAA on US trade patterns with Latin America and East Asia. Some very important assumptions must be made, however. As mentioned above, much is involved in negotiating any free trade agreement – what I focus on here is the net impact on the 'depth' of such an agreement. That is, to what extent does the agreement improve market access for US goods into the Latin American economies, and at the same time, to what extent is market access into the US improved for the Latin American economies. The larger the 'depth' of such an agreement, the larger the increase in trade that results. These net impacts are simply reflected in the ratio of actual trade to that predicted by comparative advantage. That is, as we implement an FTAA, the extent to which Latin America trades with the United States will approach its comparative advantage values, and may in fact surpass it. At the same time, as a result of increased US trade with Latin America, the East Asian *share* of US trade will fall. That is, the extent to which the United States overtrades with East Asia will fall. In simulating the impact of an FTAA on trade patterns, the ratio of assumed trade to that predicted by comparative advantage will be varied. The simulations will then be extended to measure the influence of changing growth rates in GDP and FDI on these changing trade patterns over a 20-year horizon.

SIMULATING THE IMPACT OF AN FTAA ON US LATIN AMERICAN TRADE PATTERNS

In simulating the impact of an FTAA, we focus on the impact of such an agreement on US trade patterns with Latin America and East Asia. Of course, there are many additional dimensions that such an agreement will affect, such as employment, capital formation, the balance of payments, income distribution, and many other aspects of local economies.[17] The focus here on trade patterns alone should not in any way signal its relative importance over these other measures. Rather, the focus here on trade is very useful and instructive because it can in a very clear way point to the important benefits and effects of such an agreement. It would be straightforward to extend the analysis to many of these other dimensions, and such extensions are encouraged. Also, as indicated above, we focus on the net long-term impact of such an agreement, and side-step the short-run adjustment costs. Again, this is not to say such adjustments are not important – to the contrary, they are extremely important. But the focus here is on potential long-term effects and benefits of such an agreement.

The simulations here will be of two kinds. The first looks at the impact an FTAA could have on US export and import shares with Latin America and East Asia, with the results depending on the 'depth' of such an agreement, and the extent of trade diversion that occurs. The second simulation will take us forward 20 years, and after having made assumptions on GDP and FDI growth rates in the world, the United States, Latin America, and East Asia, the impact of such an agreement can be assessed, again as a function of the depth of such an agreement.

The results of the first set of simulations are presented in Figure 3.5. We start with the trade ratios actually seen in the data for 1998, and these are reported in Table 3.3. The estimation results reported in Tables 3.10 and 3.11 indicate that US exports to Latin America were only 78 per cent of what comparative advantage predicts, and we allow this to move toward its comparative advantage level and beyond, to 1.28 times the level predicted by comparative advantage. Similarly, we allow US imports to increase from their current level of only 58 per cent of their comparative advantage values up to slightly more than is predicted by comparative advantage (108 per cent).

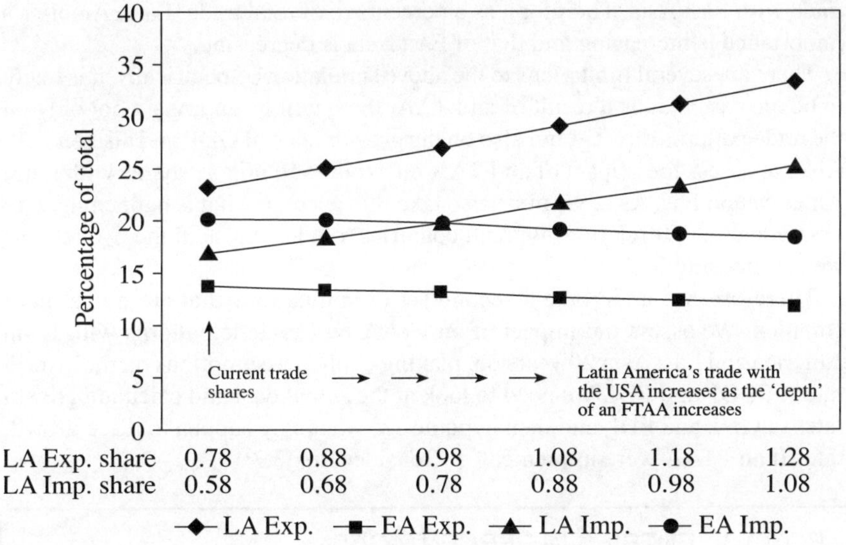

Note: There are entries here for each of US export and import shares for both Latin America and East Asia (EA). The first entries (to the far left) reflect current (1998) trade patterns, as reported in Table 3.3 of the chapter. On the horizontal axis, we have Latin America's exports and imports relative to comparative advantage: the first number of 0.78 indicates that the USA exports 78 per cent of what it should based on comparative advantage – the second number, 0.58, indicates that the USA imports 58 per cent of what it should. As we move to the right, we are moving Latin America's trade ratio higher. The last set of numbers on the horizontal axis indicates that we have let US exports to Latin America reach 1.28 times their comparative advantage values, and imports 1.08 times their comparative advantage values.

Figure 3.5 Simulating the impact of an FTAA on US export and import shares with Latin America and East Asia

It is important to note several important factors. First, an FTAA should at least move trade patterns between the United States and Latin America to the comparative advantage value, and likely beyond. Of course, how far we move will depend on the depth of the agreement negotiated. Second, throughout Figure 3.5, we are holding US exports to East Asia at twice their comparative advantage value and imports at 3.8 times, amounts predicted from the data and reported in Tables 3.10 and 3.11 above. If we were to allow for trade diversion, the results in the diagram would just become more extreme: the East Asian trade ratios would fall and those for Latin America would increase. Of course, the extent of trade diversion will depend on the industry overlap of trade.[18] Third, it is also important to note that even though the East Asian trade biases are being held constant, their ratios are falling as we move to the right because as we allow US trade with Latin America to increase, we are holding constant trade with East Asia. Therefore, as a percentage of total trade, Latin America's importance is increasing and that of East Asia is decreasing.

There are several limitations to the above simulations. Specifically, it is likely to be the case that as a result of an FTAA, there will be an impact not only on the trade patterns directly, but also on the growth rates of GDP and also on FDI. Also, to assess the impact of an FTAA on export and import shares with Latin America and East Asia, we must also take into account what is happening with US trade and FDI relations with all countries, not just those in the two regions we are focusing on.

Therefore, we undertake a second set of simulations that are much more complex. We assess the impact of an FTAA on US trade patterns with Latin America and East Asia 20 years on, making explicit assumptions on the growth rates of GDP and FDI. We need to look at the actual data and calculate growth rates in GDP and FDI, and then hypothesize what may happen to these growth rates if an FTAA were implemented. Consider Box 3.3:

BOX 3.3 ENTRIES IN PERCENTAGES

	Scenario 1 Actual Growth Rates		Scenario 2 LA GDP growth up EA GDP growth down		Scenario 3 As in Scenario 2, and LA FDI growth down	
	GDP	FDI	GDP	FDI	GDP	FDI
US/World	3.6	9.8	3.6	9.8	3.6	9.8
EA	6.7	12.5	4.0	12.5	4.0	12.5
LA	2.6	8.9	4.0	8.9	4.0	4.0

Over the 1982–1998 period, compound growth rates in GDP were 3.6 per cent in the United States, 6.7 per cent in East Asia, but only 2.6 per cent in Latin America. That is, East Asia grew at roughly twice the rate of the United States and almost two and a half times that of Latin America. US outward FDI to the world grew at an annual compound rate of 9.8 per cent. US outward FDI to Latin America grew at 8.9 per cent, and at a significantly higher 12.5 per cent to East Asia.

Our next simulation (Scenario 1) will then be as follows. Suppose that the actual growth rates in GDP and FDI were to continue for the next 20 years. We also assume that the GDP of all other countries in the sample (that is, the rest of the world) grows at the rate of US GDP growth. The results are presented in Figure 3.6. If there were no FTAA, and growth in GDPs and FDI continued as they have been over the 1982 to 1998 period for the next 20 years, then East Asia would emerge as a more important trading partner than Latin America both in terms of exports and imports. This result is driven by the fact that East Asian GDP and FDI have grown and hence are assumed to continue to grow at significantly higher rates than those for Latin America. As a result, only with an FTAA can Latin America retain its current position as a more important destination for US exports. For Latin America to change its current position relative to East Asia vis-à-vis US imports, a very deep trade agreement would be needed. As can be seen in Figure 3.6, an FTAA that was not too deep would be sufficient to make Latin America a more important destination for US exports. On the other hand, a very deep trade agreement would not be sufficient to make Latin America more important in terms of US imports – that is, the lines do not cross in the right panel of Figure 3.6.

Our next simulation, Scenario 2, leaves the growth rates in FDI unchanged, but increases the assumed growth rate for Latin American GDP but reduces it for

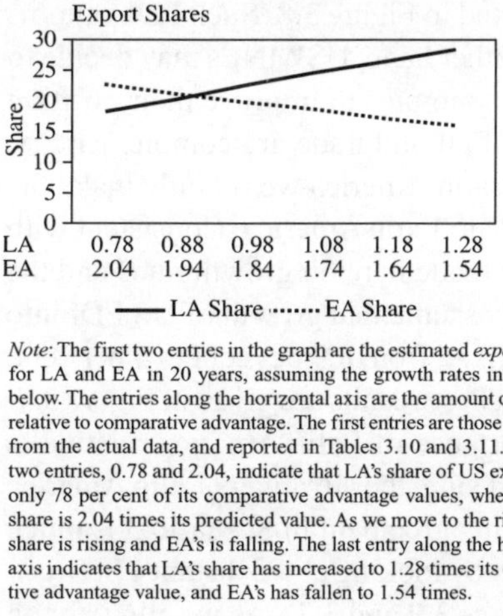

Note: The first two entries in the graph are the estimated *export* shares for LA and EA in 20 years, assuming the growth rates in the table below. The entries along the horizontal axis are the amount of exports relative to comparative advantage. The first entries are those predicted from the actual data, and reported in Tables 3.10 and 3.11. The first two entries, 0.78 and 2.04, indicate that LA's share of US exports are only 78 per cent of its comparative advantage values, whereas EA's share is 2.04 times its predicted value. As we move to the right, LA's share is rising and EA's is falling. The last entry along the horizontal axis indicates that LA's share has increased to 1.28 times its comparative advantage value, and EA's has fallen to 1.54 times.

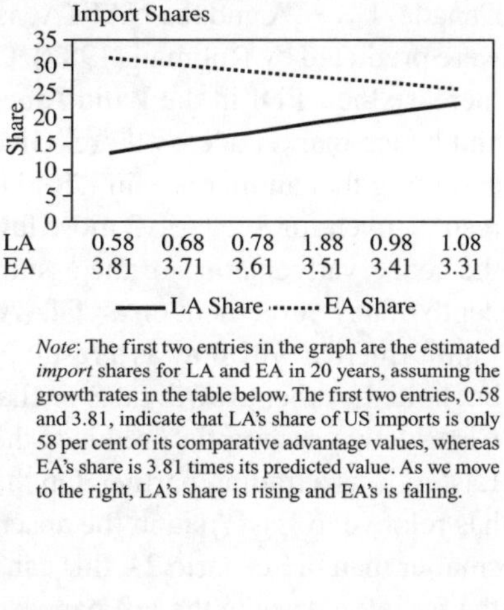

Note: The first two entries in the graph are the estimated *import* shares for LA and EA in 20 years, assuming the growth rates in the table below. The first two entries, 0.58 and 3.81, indicate that LA's share of US imports is only 58 per cent of its comparative advantage values, whereas EA's share is 3.81 times its predicted value. As we move to the right, LA's share is rising and EA's is falling.

Growth Rates (%)	GDP	FDI
USA/world	3.6	9.8
EA	6.7	12.5
LA	2.6	8.9

Figure 3.6 Scenario 1: 20 years out

East Asia. This assumption is consistent with the view that much of the growth in East Asia has been export led. If as a result of an FTAA and significant trade diversion, East Asia exports slowed, then it is likely that the GDP growth rate in East Asia would also slow. At the same time, the improved access given to the Latin American economies would stimulate their growth rates. Therefore, we assume that East Asian GDP growth falls from 6.7 per cent to 4 per cent, and Latin American GDP growth increases from 2.6 per cent to 4 per cent. The growth in US GDP is unchanged at 3.6 per cent as is the growth in the rest of the world GDP. If this were to occur, then even in the absence of an FTAA, Latin America would emerge as a more important destination for US exports than East Asia, although East Asia would maintain its import position relative to Latin America. However, as we allow for an FTAA, then the relative importance of Latin America improves, increasing its lead on East Asia as a destination for US exports, and also surpassing East Asia as a source for US imports.

Our final simulation, Scenario 3, makes the same assumptions on GDP growth rates as in Scenario 2, but changes the assumption on the growth rates for FDI. There is ambiguity as to what the impact of an FTAA would be on US FDI into Latin America. On the one hand, as trade barriers fall, US MNEs may pull back, deciding to service the Latin American economies to a greater extent through trade. This is consistent with US FDI into Canada after the Canada–US FTA and the NAFTA, as reflected in Figure 3.8. Such FDI patterns were predicted by Rugman (1987). On the other hand, US MNEs may decide to increase their FDI in the Latin American economies to improve their position and hence market access there. Given that FDI and trade are complementary, assuming that an increase in US FDI into Latin America would only make the results given for Scenario 2 more favourable to Latin America. Consistent with the conservative nature of the assumptions made here on growth rates and the depth of any agreement on an FTAA, I will assume that growth of US FDI into Latin America will slow as a result of an FTAA, from 8.9 per cent to 4 per cent, but hold the other growth rates unchanged. These results are given in Figure 3.9. Clearly, this assumption reduces the importance of Latin America relative to East Asia as a trading partner. On the export side, the advantage Latin America has relative to East Asia in the absence of an agreement in Scenario 3 is much smaller than in Scenario 2 – this can be seen by looking at the distance between the far left entries in the left panels of Figures 3.9 and 3.7). As we allow for an FTAA that is more and more deep, we move to the right in Figure 3.9 and the relative importance of Latin America over East Asia increases. On the import side, it is clear that in order for Latin America to overtake East Asia as a more important source for US imports, a deeper agreement will be needed – the lines in the import panels cross further to the right in Figure 3.9 than they do in Figure 3.7.

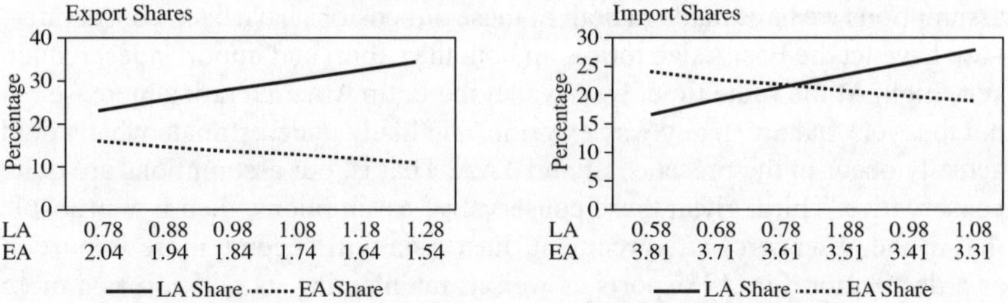

See notes to Table 3.6 See notes to Table 3.6

Growth Rates (%)

	GDP	FDI
USA/world	3.6	9.8
EA	4.0	12.5
LA	4.0	8.9

Figure 3.7 Scenario 2: 20 years out

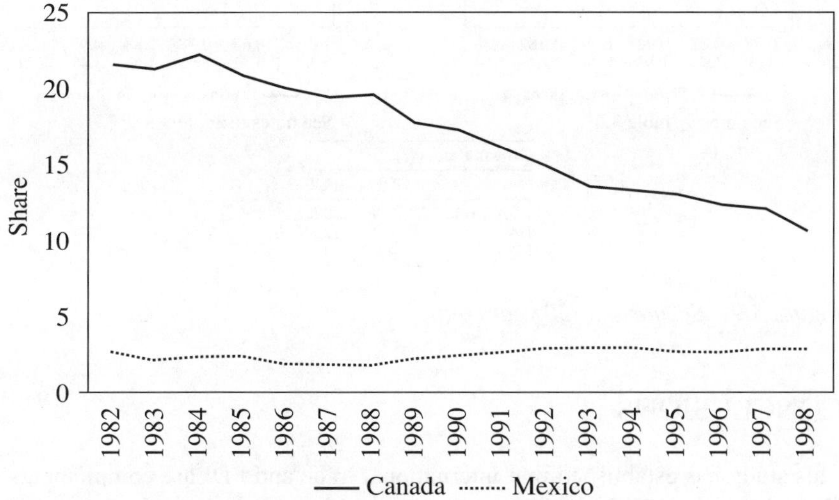

Figure 3.8 US outward FDI shares

The results of these simulations can be summarized as follows. First, in the absence of an FTAA, East Asia will emerge as a more important trading partner than Latin America both in terms of imports and exports. Second, the introduction of an FTAA will increase the ratio of US trade with Latin America relative to the amount predicted by comparative advantage. To the extent that there is trade diversion, such an agreement will reduce the East Asian trade ratios. The assumptions we have made in both of these dimensions have been conservative – we have let the East Asian ratios, on both the export and import sides, remain very high. At the same time, we have let the Latin America ratios increase but not to levels that are in any way extreme, and likely underestimate what would actually occur in the presence of an FTAA. That is, our assumptions are quite conservative. Third, given these conservative assumptions, then it is probable that in the absence of an agreement, East Asia will become more important as a destination for US exports as well as maintaining its position as a more important source of US imports. On the other hand, an FTAA that is not too deep will be likely to result in Latin America emerging as a more important destination and source for US exports and imports.

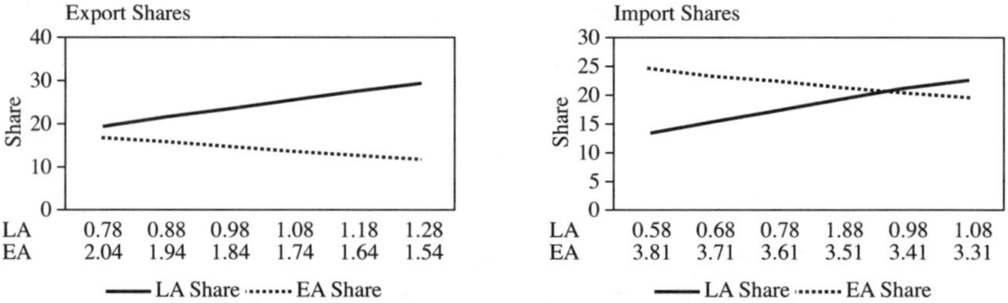

See notes to Table 3.6 See notes to Table 3.6

Growth Rates (%)		
	GDP	FDI
USA/world	3.6	9.8
EA	4.0	12.5
LA	4.0	4.0

Figure 3.9 Scenario 3: 20 years out

CONCLUSIONS

This study has established that international trade and FDI are complements. Over the period 1982 to 1998 and covering 52 countries, we show within a gravity model framework that US outward FDI stimulates domestic exports and imports. The impact of outward FDI on exports is statistically the same as that on imports, and in this sense outward FDI can be said to be neutral with respect to the trade balance, other things equal. This chapter therefore measures one important aspect of the impact that outward FDI has had on a home economy. It is important to add that the effects of FDI involve more than the effects on the trade balance, for either home or host countries. Total trade has risen, for example, and a number of non-trade variables would need to be considered for a full welfare analysis.

The analysis in this chapter has also considered the predicted impact of sectoral FDI on trade. The results indicate that US outward FDI in natural resources has a negative impact on the trade balance, as does US outward FDI in manufacturing. In contrast, US outward FDI in services stimulates large increases in exports, but only a small increase in imports. That is, US outward FDI in services stimulates the US trade surplus.

Closer examination of the estimation results indicates that US exports and imports with Latin America are much less than is predicted by comparative advantage. On the other hand, US trade with East Asia is much higher than is predicted by comparative advantage. Therefore, there are tremendous potential benefits that would stem from a free trade agreement between the United States and Latin America. Trade diversion effects, however, would result in the excessive amounts of trade with East Asia to fall – that is, East Asian growth rates will be likely to fall as a result.

The importance of R&D and technology must also be highlighted once again. Coupled with increased trade integration is increased FDI integration. Both trade and FDI have been shown to be very important channels of R&D diffusion, both among developed countries as well as between developed and developing countries. Furthermore, FDI is an important source of capital formation for local economies. Therefore, the increased trade integration that would result from an FTAA will result in tremendous productivity gains for the countries in Latin America.

APPENDIX 3.1

Data Sources and Data

Trade and FDI data

US stocks of FDI on a bilateral basis with each of 52 countries were obtained from the US Bureau of Economic Analysis. These data are reported at historical costs.

US exports and imports on a bilateral basis with each of 52 countries were obtained from the International Monetary Fund's *Direction of Trade Statistics*. These data are in current US dollars. To convert these trade data into real terms, export and import deflators were obtained from Citibase.

Aggregate inward FDI stocks into each of our sample countries (reported in Table 3.4, Panel B) were obtained from UNCTAD's *World Investment Report*, 1999. These data are reported using differing definitions. See the *World Investment Report* for details. These data were not used in our regression analysis.

Intra-firm trade data

Intra-firm exports between US parents and their majority-owned foreign affiliates as well as between foreign parents and their affiliates in the United States were obtained from William J. Zeile, 'Intra Firm Trade in Goods', *U.S. Survey of Current Business*, February 1997.

Gravity data

GDP data and GDP per capita were obtained from the Penn World Tables. These data have been constructed very carefully to allow for international comparisons (see Summers and Heston 1991), and are reported in constant 1987 US dollars.

Exchange rates were also obtained from the Penn World Tables, and are on a real PPP basis.

Distance variables were kindly provided by Werner Antweiler, and were used in Hejazi and Trefler (1996).

Dummy variables

The language dummy captures whether countries speak the same language. If the official langauge of a country is English, the dummy takes on a value of one, and zero otherwise.

The regional dummies take on a value of one if the country is in the respective region, and zero otherwise.

The countries that comprise Europe, East Asia and Latin America are listed in Table 3.2 of the chapter.

The Japan dummy takes on a value of one for Japan, and zero otherwise.

The adjacency dummy takes on a value of one for Mexico and Canada, and zero otherwise.

APPENDIX 3.2

Issues in Converting FDI Stock Data to Real Values

With the exception of the FDI stocks and foreign sales figures, the data used in this study are in real 1987 constant US dollars. The GDP and GDP per capita data for the 51 countries plus the US are available from the Penn World Tables on that basis. These data have been constructed very carefully to allow for international comparisons (see Summers and Heston 1991). US exports and imports are also converted to a constant US dollar basis.

Unlike exports and imports, it is a non-trivial task to convert the FDI stock figures from their present historical cost values to real values. The difficulty in undertaking such a transformation arises because FDI is a stock. Consider the following equation:

$$FDI_t = FD_{t-i} + \begin{matrix}\text{retained}\\ \text{earnings}\end{matrix} + \begin{matrix}\text{net}\\ \text{flows of}\\ FDI\end{matrix} + \begin{matrix}\text{price}\\ \text{appreciation /}\\ \text{depreciation}\\ \text{on } FDI_{t-1}\end{matrix}$$

The level of FDI at any point in time is defined as the level of FDI in the previous period, plus retained earnings, plus net new flows of FDI, plus price appreciation (or less depreciation). The retained earnings and the flows are in current dollars, and are simply added to the stock of FDI from the previous year, which is not in current dollars. The retained earnings and flows form the balance of payments definition of FDI. In addition, however, there is another component which involves revaluation of the FDI stocks. It is this last component which is needed to convert FDI from their historical costs to their market values.

The US Department of Commerce (1995) has published US stock figures on the basis of historical cost, replacement cost, and market values, but the country and sectoral data are available only on a historical (book value) basis. There are a variety of private and semi-official estimates of the different valuations for the US and UK stocks of FDI (Bellak and Cantwell 1996). A straightforward way to adjust stock values is through changes in security prices, as utilized in Gray and Rugman (1994) but this is subject to a number of criticisms as noted in Bellak and Cantwell (1996). We have decided to use the unadjusted data.

NOTES

1. For several country studies that consider many of these issues, see the symposium on Latin America published in the *World Economy*, July 2002. For example, there are studies that consider links between trade reform and poverty in Mexico, trade and standards in Central America, an assessment of Chile's trade and regional integration, as well as the transformation of the Brazilian economy over the 1990s and the implementation of inflation targets.
2. See, for example, Balasubramanyam et al. (1996), Barrell and Pain (1999), Blomström and Kokko (1994), Borensztein et al. (1998), Feinberg et al. (1998), Hejazi (2001), Hejazi and Safarian (1999a), Hejazi and Pauly (2002, 2003), McFetridge (1991a, b) Safarian (1985), van Pottelsberghe and Lichtenberg (2001). Many of these effects have been discussed extensively in Rugman (1990).
3. Similar concerns have been raised in Japan in terms of a hollowing out of its manufacturing sector. See Bayoumi and Lipworth (1997). The academic debate in the United States has focused on the effects of 'globalization', driven especially by trade and FDI, on domestic income inequality. See the summer 1995 and fall 1998 *Journal of Economic Perspectives,* and the summer 1997 and spring 1998 *NBER Reporter.*
4. A review of the theoretical literature is contained in UNCTAD (1996) 123–5.

5. For reviews of the empirical trade literature, see Grossman and Rogoff (1995). For reviews of the determinants of FDI, see Caves (1996), Dunning (1993), Jun and Singh (1996), Grosse and Trevino (1996), and Hejazi and Safarian (2001b).
6. For a detailed discussion of alternative modes of entry, see Bora (2002).
7. There has been work using the gravity equation to differentiate among alternative theories of trade, including Feenstra et al. (2001).
8. For references to internalization and to alliances, see *Journal of International Business Studies* (1994), **25** (4), 806–8.
9. Rugman (2000) estimates the top 500 MNEs account for 90 per cent of the world's stock of FDI and over one half of world trade.
10. Entering GDPs in product form is empirically well established in bilateral trade regressions. It can be justified by the modern theory of trade under imperfect competition. Furthermore, GDP per capita has a positive effect on trade – as countries become more developed, they tend to specialize and trade more (Frankel et al. 1995).
11. See, for example, the considerable literature on the product life cycle, inspired by Vernon (1966).
12. There is an obvious problem in comparing aggregate stocks of inward FDI across countries because each country has a different method of calculating and recording the FDI data. Furthermore, we cannot state the percentage of FDI located in a particular host economy that originates from the United States. To do so would require 'host' country data on inward FDI from the United States in addition to the aggregate inward FDI data reported in Panel B of Table 3.4. Since these data are measured differently, they should not be compared.
13. See Hejazi and von der Ruhr (2002) for a detailed description of US FDI at the industry level. Special attention is given to the role of business services in explaining changing FDI patterns.
14. All *t*-statistics reported in this chapter use estimated standard errors which are heteroscedastic and autocorrelation consistent. We have not reported the constant. Also, note that we cannot estimate a fixed effects model because such effects would be collinear with the distance measures.
15. Following Hejazi and Safarian (2004), an equation is estimated for trade and one for FDI. The results are qualitatively the same as those reported in Tables 3.10 and 3.11.
16. Since the regressions in Tables 3.10 and 3.11 are in logs, then to interpret the regression parameters on any of the dummies, we must take the exponential. Therefore, in Table 3.10, the estimated coefficient on the Latin America dummy is –0.250. By taking the exponential, we get –0.7788. That is, the United States exports to Latin America only 77.88 per cent of what is predicted by comparative advantage.
17. For a detailed discussion of the impact the NAFTA has had on Mexico's trade as well as in other dimensions, see Anyul et al. (2001).
18. Alexandroff et al. (1996) report an export similarity index for Chinese and Mexican exports to North America for 1991 of slightly over 31 per cent. This indicates that the extent of trade diversion will be significant.

REFERENCES

Alexandroff, Alan, Walid Hejazi and Leonard Waverman (1996), 'China's strategic trade patterns and the impact of NAFTA', in Leonard Waverman (ed.), *Sino-North American Trade: Challenges and Opportunities*, Toronto: University of Toronto Press.

Anyul, Martin Puchet, and Lionello Punzo (eds) (2001), *Mexico Beyond NAFTA: Perspectives for the European Debate*, London: Routledge.

Balasubramanyam, V.N., M. Salisu and D. Sapsford (1996), 'Foreign direct investment and growth in EP and IS countries', *Economic Journal*, **106**, 92–105.

Barrell, Ray, and Nigel Pain (1999), 'Domestic institutions, agglomerations and foreign direct investment in Europe', *European Economic Review*, **43**, 925–34.

Bayoumi, Tamim, and Gabrielle Lipworth (1997), 'Japanese foreign direct investment and regional trade', International Monetary Fund working paper 97/103.

Bellak, Christian, and John Cantwell (1996), 'Foreign direct investment – how much is it worth? Comment on S.J. Gray and A.M. Rugman', *Transnational Corporations*, **5**, 1, 85–97.

Blomström, Magnus, and Ari O. Kokko (1994), 'Home country effects of foreign direct investment: Sweden', in S. Globerman, (ed.), *Canadian Based Multinationals*, Industry Canada Research Series, Calgary: University of Calgary Press.

Blomström, Magnus, Robert E. Lipsey and Ksenia Kulchycky (1988), 'US and Swedish Direct Investment and Exports', in R.E. Baldwin (ed.), *Trade Policy Issues and Empirical Analysis* Chicago: University of Chicago Press pp. 259–97.

Bora, Bijit (2002), *Foreign Direct Investment Research Issues*, London: Routledge.

Borensztein, E., J. De Gregorio and J.-W. Lee (1998), 'How does foreign direct investment affect economic growth', *Journal of International Economics*, **45**, 115–35.

Brainard, S. Lael (1997), 'An empirical assessment of the proximity-concentration trade-off between multinational sales and trade', *American Economic Review*, **87**, 4 (September), 520–45.

Caves, Richard (1996), *Multinational Enterprise and Economic Analysis*, Cambridge: Cambridge University Press.

Collins, William J., Kevin H. O'Rourke and Jeffrey G. Williamson (1997), 'Were Trade and Factor Mobility Substitutes in History', National Bureau for Economic Research working paper 6059.

Deardorff, Alan V. (1995), 'Determinants of Bilateral Trade: Does Gravity Work in a Neoclassical World', National Bureau for Economic Research working paper 5377.

Dunning, John (1993), *Multinational Enterprises and the Global Economy*, Wokingham: Addison-Wesley Publishing Co.

Eaton, Jonathan, and Akiko Tamura (1994), 'Bilateralism and regionalism in Japanese and US trade and direct foreign investment patterns', *Journal of the Japanese and International Economics*, **8**, 478–510.

Encarnation, D.J. (1993), 'Beyond trade: foreign investment in the US–Japan and EC-Japan rivalries', Harvard Business School manuscript.

Ethier, Wilfred (1982), 'National and international returns to scale in the modem theory of international trade', *American Economic Review*, **72**, 389–405.

Feenstra, Robert C., James R. Markusen and Andrew K. Rose (2001), 'Using the gravity equation to differentiate among alternative theories of trade', *Canadian Journal of Economics*, **34** (2), 430–47.

Frankel, J.A., Shang-Jin Wei and Ernesto Stein (1995), 'APEC and regional trading arrangements in the Pacific', in Wendy Dobson and Frank Flatters (eds), *Pacific Trade and Investment: Options for the 1990s*, Kingston, Ontario: John Deutsch Institute.

Globerman, S. (ed.) (1994), *Canadian Based Multinationals,* Industry Canada Research Series, Calgary: University of Calgary Press.

Graham, Edward (1993), *US Outward Direct Investment and US Exports: Substitutes or Complements – With Implications for US – Japan Policy*, Washington: DC, Institute for International Economics.

Graham, Edward M. (1994), 'Canadian direct investment abroad and the Canadian economy: some theoretical and empirical implications', in S. Globerman (ed.), *Canadian Based Multinationals*, Industry Canada Research Series, Calgary: University of Calgary Press.

Gray, S.J. and A. Rugman (1994), 'Does the United States have a deficit with Japan in foreign direct investment?', *Transnational Corporations*, **3** (2), 127–37.

Grosse, Robert, and Len Trevino (1996), 'Foreign direct investment in the United States: an analysis by country of origin', *Journal of International Business Studies*, first quarter.

Grossman, Gene, and Kenneth Rogoff (eds) (1995), *Handbook of International Economics*, vol. 3, Amsterdam: North Holland.

Gunderson, Morley, and Savita Verma (1994), 'Labor market implications of outward foreign direct investment', in S. Globerman, (ed.), *Canadian Based Multinationals*, Industry Canada Research Series, Calgary: University of Calgary Press.

Hejazi, Walid (2001), 'Access to foreign R&D does not undermine domestic R&D efforts', *Policy Options*, October, 43–8.

Hejazi, Walid, and Peter Pauly (2003). 'Motivations for FDI and domestic capital formation', *Journal of International Business Studies* **34**(3), 282–9.

Hejazi, Walid, and Peter Pauly (2002b), 'Foreign direct investment and domestic capital formation', Industry Canada working paper series, 36.

Hejazi, Walid, and A.E. Safarian (1999a), 'Trade, foreign direct investment, and R&D spillovers', *Journal of International Business Studies*, **30**(3), 491–511.

Hejazi, Walid, and A.E. Safarian (1999b), 'Modelling links between Canadian trade and foreign direct investment', published in the Industry Canada Research Publications series entitled *Perspectives on North American Free Trade*, April.

Hejazi, Walid, and A.E. Safarian (2001a), *Canada and Foreign Direct Investment: A Study of Determinants*, Toronto: University of Toronto Centre for Public Management.

Hejazi, Walid, and A.E. Safarian. (2001b), 'The complementarity between US FDI stock and trade', *Atlantic Economic Journal*, **29**, 4.

Hejazi, Walid, and A.E. Safarian (2004), 'Explaining Canada's changing FDI patterns', University of Toronto working paper.

Hejazi, Walid, and Daniel Trefler (1996), 'Explaining Canada's trade with the Asia-Pacific', in *The Asia Pacific Region and the Global Economy: A Canadian Perspective*, Richard Harris (ed.), Industry Canada Research Series, Calgary: University of Calgary Press.

Hejazi, Walid, and Marc von der Ruhr (2002), 'US firms in world finance', in Gavin Boyd (ed.), *American Macromanagement*, Cheltenham: Edward Elgar.

Hufbauer, G.C., and M. Adler (1968), 'US manufacturing investment and the balance of payments', in *Tax Policy Research Study Number 1*, Washington, DC: US Treasury Department.

Journal of Economic Perspectives, entire issues, summer 1995 and autumn 1998.

Journal of International Business Studies (1994), **25**(4), 806–8.

Jun, Kwang W., and Harinder Singh (1996), 'The determinants of foreign direct investment in developing countries', *Transnational Corporations*, **5**, 2, 67–105.

Lipsey, Robert E., and Merle Yahr Weiss (1981), 'Foreign production and exports in manufacturing industries', *The Review of Economic Statistics* (November), 488–94.

Lipsey, Robert E., and Merle Yahr Weiss (1984), 'Foreign production and exports of individual firms', *Review of Economics and Statistics*, 304–8.

Malnight, Thomas W. (1996), 'The transition from decentralized to network-based MNC structures: an evolutionary perspective', *Journal of International Business Studies*, **27** (1), 43–65.

McFetridge, D.G. (1991a), 'Introduction', in *Foreign Investment, Technology, and Economic Growth*, Investment Canada Research Series, Calgary: The University of Calgary Press.

McFetridge, D.G. (ed.) (1991b), *Foreign Investment, Technology, and Economic Growth*, Investment Canada Research Series, Calgary: The University of Calgary Press.

Mundell, Robert A. (1957), 'International trade and factor mobility', *American Economic Review*, **47**, 321–35.
NBER Reporter, summer 1997 and spring 1998.
Pfaffermayr, M. (1994), 'Foreign direct investment and exports: a time series approach', *Applied Economics*, **26**, 337–51.
Rao, Someshwar, Ashfaq Ahmad and Marc Legault (1994), 'Canadian-based multinationals: an analysis of activities and performance', in S. Globerman (ed.), *Canadian Based Multinationals*, Industry Canada Research Series, Calgary: University of Calgary Press.
Rugman, A.M. (1980), 'Internalization as a general theory of foreign direct investment: a reappraisal of the literature', *Weltwirtschaftliches Archives*, **116** (2), 367–79.
Rugman, A.M. (1987), *Outward Bound: Canadian Direct Investment in the United States*, Toronto: C.D. Howe Institute.
Rugman, A.M. (1988), 'The multinational enterprise', in Ingo Walter and Tracy Murray, (eds), *Handbook of International Management*, New York: Wiley.
Rugman, A.M. (1990), *Multinationals and Canada–United States Free Trade*, Columbia, SC: University of South Carolina Press.
Rugman, A.M. (2000), *The End of Globalization*, New York: Random House.
Safarian, A.E. (1985), *Foreign Direct Investment: A Survey of Canadian Research*, Montreal: The Institute for Research on Public Policy.
Summers, Robert, and Alan Heston (1991), 'The Penn world tables (mark 5): an expanded set of international comparisons, 1950–1988', *Quarterly Journal of Economics*, **106**, 327–68.
Swedenborg, B. (1979), *The Multinational Operations of Swedish Firms: An Analysis of Determinants and Effects*, Stockholm: The Industrial Institute for Economic and Social Research.
United Nations Conference on Trade and Development (UNCTAD) (1996), *World Investment Report 1998: Investment, Trade and International Policy Arrangements*, New York and Geneva: United Nations.
United Nations Conference on Trade and Development (UNCTAD) (1999), *World Investment Report 1998: FDI and the Challenge of Development*, New York and Geneva: United Nations.
United Nations Conference on Trade and Development (UNCTAD) (2001), *World Investment Report: 2001 Promoting Linkages*, New York and Geneva: United Nations.
US Department of Commerce (1995), 'Foreign direct investment in the United States: detail for historical-cost position and related capital and income flows', *Survey of Current Business* (August), 53–78.
van Pottelsberghe De La Potterie, Bruno, and Frank Lichtenberg (2001), 'Does foreign direct investment transfer technology across borders?', *Review of Economics and Statistics*, **83**(3), 490–97.
Vernon, Raymond (1966), 'International investment and international trade in the product cycle', *Quarterly Journal of Economics*, **2**, 190–207.
World Economy, July 2002, entire issue.
Zeile, William J. (1997), 'US intra firm trade in goods', *US Survey of Current Business* (February), 23–38.

4. Economic integration in North America: implications for the Americas

Alan M. Rugman

SUMMARY

In this chapter I build on the ten years of experience of economic integration that companies have enjoyed under the North American Free Trade Agreement (NAFTA). This started on 1 January 1994, but was negotiated and largely in its final shape for all of 1993. The role of foreign direct investment (FDI) undertaken by multinational enterprises (MNEs) has been of critical importance in NAFTA. I examine the economic integration of Canada and the United States and draw implications for all of the Americas. The increasing degree of intra-regional trade and FDI in North America, both before and during NAFTA, is likely to be repeated across the Americas in the future.

INTRODUCTION

The Free Trade Area of the Americas (FTAA) is going to build on the basic principles of NAFTA. There are two of these: first is the negotiated reduction of tariffs on mainly manufactured products (with agriculture and most of traded services exempted); second is the principle of national treatment, again for manufacturing but also for resource investment (and with most of the service sectors exempted). The nature of NAFTA, and its implications for corporate strategy, have been discussed in Rugman (1994). Logically, the FTAA, being based on NAFTA, will have similar implications for business strategy. Rather than revisit this topic in this chapter, I assess the nature of economic integration under NAFTA over the last ten years. With this focus upon the actual outcome of NAFTA on business strategy, I am then in a better position to predict the economic and business outcomes of the FTAA.

More specifically, in this chapter I review data both at aggregate and also at firm level on the extent of intra-regional trade and foreign direct investment (FDI) in NAFTA. I then examine more micro firm-level data. I conclude with an assessment of the appropriate corporate strategies for the FTAA. There I argue that all firms will need to become successful in the dominant US market.

NORTH AMERICAN INTRA-REGIONAL TRADE AND FDI

In this section of the chapter I examine recent empirical data on the nature and extent of Canada–US economic integration, especially under NAFTA. The statistical evidence is that the increase in regional integration in the NAFTA region has been achieved mainly through trade. Intra-regional trade in NAFTA is now at 55.7 per cent, up from 33.6 per cent in 1980 and 49.2 per cent in 1996. At the same time, intra-regional FDI in NAFTA has declined, particularly US FDI in Canada. In contrast, very recently, the share of Canadian FDI in the United States has increased slightly, after decreasing every year since the Canada–US Free Trade Agreement (FTA) started in 1989. Trade in the automotive sector and related industries, such as in specialty chemicals and steel products, heavily influences this pattern of manufacturing regionalization by intra-regional trade. In contrast, services are now being integrated in NAFTA more by FDI than by trade, as many barriers to trade in services remain.

To examine these trends in the bilateral relationship, and to relate them to broader trade and FDI issues, data on NAFTA-based service trade and FDI are related to changes in the manufacturing sector. The data for NAFTA indicate a pattern of increased intra-regional trade in manufacturing but decreased intra-regional FDI over the last 20 years. Similar trends exist in the European Union (EU); however, there is increasing inter-regional FDI between the EU and NAFTA. The latter is part of the 'triad' effect of large MNEs operating mainly within their home-market triads of NAFTA, the EU and Asia (Rugman 2000) but also seeking to access each other's triad market. The data indicate that MNEs are strongly home triad market-based, but there is some evidence of increased EU–NAFTA inter-regional FDI in the last few years.

Previous work on Canada–US trade and FDI appeared in Rugman (1990). One of the main findings of that study was that Canadian FDI in the United States was growing, over the 1975–1987 period, at twice the pace of US FDI in Canada. In 1975, the ratio of Canadian FDI in the United States to US FDI in Canada (in stocks) was 18.7 per cent. Already by 1980 it was 33.7 per cent, by 1984 it was 48.0 per cent and by 1987 at the start of the FTA it was 57.6 per cent (Rugman 1990, p. 12).

The theoretical explanation behind this dramatic trend was that Canadian MNEs needed to access the US market through FDI. As the US market was at least ten times greater than Canada's, investing in a US business became a huge commitment for Canadian firms who needed to compete with larger US rival firms. However, access to the US market through FDI allowed Canadian MNEs to develop continental capabilities, following the example of Northern Telecom, Alcan, Bombardier and Seagram. An earlier explanation of this phenomenon of the growth of Canadian multinationals and Canadian outward FDI appears in Rugman (1987).

At the time of the FTA this information about the growth and maturity of Canadian multinationals was a counterpoint to the popular Canadian concern about US ownership of the Canadian economy. A related finding, in Rugman (1990), was that US foreign control of Canadian industry actually decreased from 28.8 per cent in 1970 to 21.9 per cent in 1985. In manufacturing, US control fell from 46 per cent in 1970 to 39.8 per cent in 1985 and, in petroleum from 77.0 per cent in 1970 to 39.6 per cent in 1985. These two events, the decline of US foreign control of Canadian industry, coupled with the dramatic increase in Canadian FDI in the United States, reduced and alleviated Canadian concerns about US economic domination. These two trends indicated that Canadian business was capable of capturing an increased relative share of the North American business system.

Canada's dependence on the US market is well known. In 2000, 87 per cent of Canada's exports went to the United States (up from 76 per cent in 1991). In 1999, 52.2 per cent of Canada's outward FDI stock went to the United States. In a complementary manner, US economic involvement with Canada is also strong and is its largest bilateral relationship. In 2000, 22.6 per cent of all US exports went to Canada (Rugman and Hodgetts 2003, p. 513). Back in 1991, US exports to Canada were 20.2 per cent and in 1981, they were 16.9 per cent of all US exports.

In contrast to the increase in intra-regional trade between Canada and the United States, the intra-regional FDI has been falling relative to FDI with non-NAFTA countries. In 1982, the share of the outward US stock of FDI in Canada was 20.9 per cent. By 1989 it was 16.7 per cent and by 2000 it was 10.2 per cent of all US outward FDI. This decrease in the proportion of US FDI in Canada is a puzzle which merits more attention than has been paid to it, although a similar result appears in Safarian and Hejazi (2001) and in Hejazi and Safarian (2002). In this chapter the reasons for the relative decline in US FDI in Canada are explored and implications for business and public policy are considered.

The Canada–US bilateral relationship, which experienced ever deeper degrees of economic interdependence over the 1950–1988 period, was finally recognized in the Canada–US Free Trade Agreement in 1989. This provided a set of trade and investment rules to govern and further facilitate this economic relationship. Subsequently, the trade and investment provisions of the FTA were used as the basis for NAFTA which began in 1994. The FDI aspects of NAFTA have been examined (Rugman 1994). The main finding of that study was that the Canada–US economic relationship would not be much affected by NAFTA but that Mexico would experience the greatest burden of adjustment and also make the largest gains from NAFTA. This prediction has been borne out in practice by subsequent events which have led to a large increase in intra-regional trade, but not in FDI, in NAFTA.

Safarian and Hejazi (2001) have also found that inward FDI into Canada has been falling in the 1990s, while outward FDI from Canada has been increasing. In a more recent study, Hejazi and Safarian (2002), using a gravity model for trade and an augmented gravity model for FDI, found that NAFTA has led to less FDI between Canada and the United States, but to more intra-regional trade. They argue that US MNEs are now better able to serve the Canadian market by trade rather than FDI. These studies are entirely consistent with the data and analysis in this chapter.

RECENT CANADA–US TRADE AND FOREIGN DIRECT INVESTMENT

The increase in regional integration under the FTA and NAFTA has been achieved mainly through trade. With the elimination of tariffs and most other barriers to trade in goods and traded services, the US and Canadian economies have a situation of virtual free trade. However, there remain barriers to trade in most of the service sectors; indeed as services are largely produced and consumed locally there is little in the FTA and NAFTA to facilitate increased trade in services. Furthermore, over half of the service sectors were excluded from the national treatment provisions of the FTA and NAFTA, which mainly applied to business services. Sectors exempted include: cultural services; health; education; social services; transportation; and financial services (Rugman 1994). Several implications arise from the institutional fabric of the FTA and NAFTA:

1. Free trade for goods and traded services has resulted in an increase in intra-regional trade, as shown in Figure 4.1; intra-regional trade is now at 55.7 per cent (up from 33.6 per cent in 1980 and 49.19 per cent in 1996). One key reason for the increasing degree of intra-regional trade in NAFTA is due to the increasing dependence of both Canada and Mexico on the US market. In 2000, 87 per cent of Canada's exports went to the United States and 88.7 per cent of Mexico's to its main NAFTA partner.
2. As can be seen in Figure 4.2, the situation with regard to FDI is more complex. There has been a decrease in intra-regional FDI as a percentage of total FDI for 1999 for NAFTA at 18.2 per cent (down from 21.1 per cent in 1997 and 30.3 per cent in 1986). The main reason is that there has been a decrease in the percentage of US FDI to Canada, as described below.

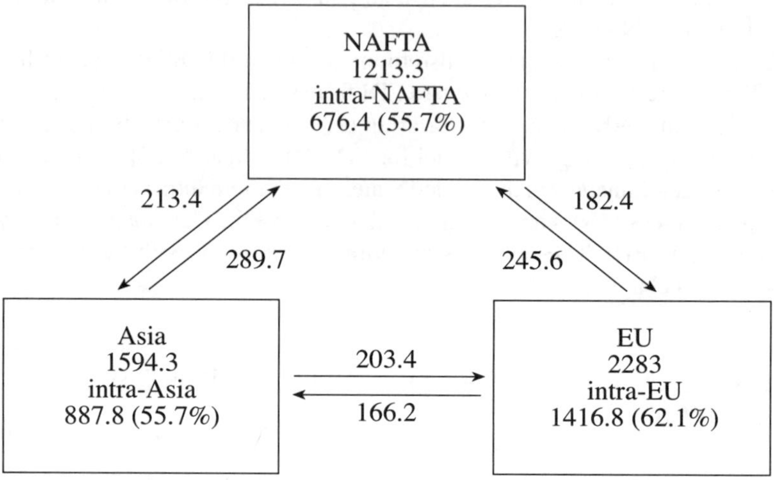

Notes: Asia and intra-Asia is the addition of Japan and Developing Asia in the IMF, *Direction of Trade Statistics Yearbook*. It does not include New Zealand and Australia.

Source: Adapted from International Monetary Fund, *Direction of Trade Statistics Yearbook 2001* (Washington DC: IMF, 2001).

Figure 4.1 Exports in the broad triad, 2000 (US$ billion)

The key trade and FDI stock data available for the years 1980, 1986, 1997, 1999 and 2000 are summarized in Table 4.1.

Table 4.1 confirms the two main points made above. First, intra-regional trade has been increasing at a steady pace within each of the markets of the triad, but it is increasing at the fastest rate in NAFTA in recent years. Going back to 1980, both NAFTA and Asia have shown similar rates of increase in intra-regional trade, but Asia's integration largely occurred before 1997, whereas NAFTA's has accelerated since then.

Second, in terms of FDI, there is a slowing down of intra-regional FDI stocks in all three parts of the triad between 1997 and 1999. This reflects greater inter-regional FDI, especially in both directions between the EU and NAFTA in recent years. However, over the 1980–1999 period, there has been an increase in intra-regional FDI in two parts of the triad – the exception is NAFTA.

The NAFTA decrease in intra-regional FDI is almost entirely due to changes in the US–Canadian economic relationship. In 1986 there were still major barriers to intercontinental business, but the Canada–US Free Trade Agreement of 1989 and NAFTA in 1994 served to open up both markets to trade, thereby

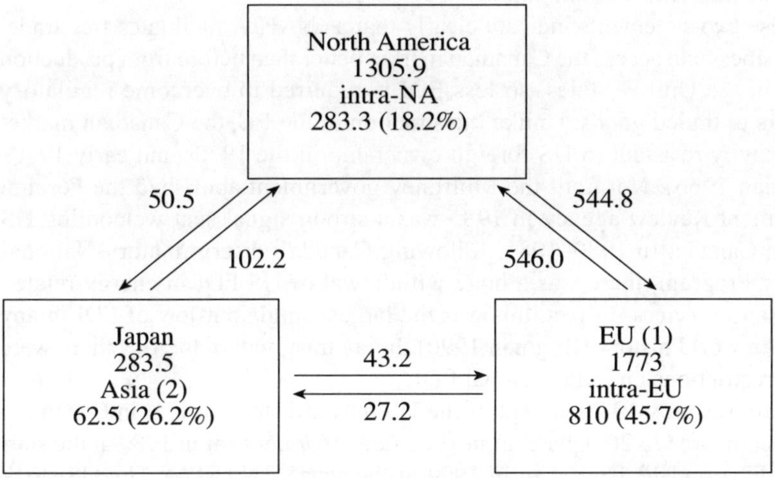

Notes:

1. Data for the European Union only include Austria, Finland, France, Germany, Italy, Netherlands, Sweden, United Kingdom, Portugal, Greece and Denmark, but include FDI to all other EU countries. Data for other EU countries are not available. For Italy, data for FDI to Asia (excluding Japan and Korea) are for 1994, the latest year available. Data for Denmark, France, Netherlands, Austria, Germany and Finland are for 1998.
2. Data for Asia do not include Australia and New Zealand. Data for Japan are for 1998.

Source: OECD, *International Direct Investment Statistics Yearbook*, 2001.

Figure 4.2 Total outward FDI in the broad triad, 1999 (US$ billion)

Table 4.1 Intra-regional trade and FDI in the triad, 1980–2000

	Intra-regional exports (%)			Intra-regional outward FDI (%)		
Year	EU	NAFTA	Asia	EU	NAFTA	Asia
2000	62.1	55.7	55.7	na	na	na
1999	–	–	–	45.7	18.2	26.2
1997	60.6	49.1	53.1	49.3	21.1	28.4
1986	–	–	–	35.8	30.3	20.5
1980	52.1	33.6	35.3	na	na	na

Source: IMF, *Direction of Trade Statistics Yearbook*, 1983–2001 and OECD, *International Direct Investment Statistics Yearbook*, 2001.

reducing the need for FDI to overcome trade barriers. This bilateral relationship is discussed in more detail below.

These two statements indicate clearly that as NAFTA facilitates free trade, US business can access the Canadian market better than before from production bases in the United States, so less FDI is required to overcome regulatory barriers to traded goods. Unlike the situation in the EU, the Canadian market was heavily resistant to US foreign ownership in the 1970s and early 1980s (Safarian 1966). Not until the Mulroney government abolished the Foreign Investment Review agency in 1985 was a strong signal sent welcoming US FDI in Canada. In 1980–1981, following Canada's discriminatory National Energy Program, there was a huge withdrawal of US FDI in energy related goods and services. In fact, this was the largest single outflow of FDI in any sector in world history (Rugman 1990). In contrast, within the EU, there were fewer restrictions on intra-regional FDI.

There was only 10.2 per cent of the US outward stock of FDI in Canada in 2000, compared to 20.9 per cent in 1982 (and 16.7 per cent in 1989 at the start of the FTA and 12.1 per cent in 1994 at the start of NAFTA). The US stock of FDI in Mexico was 2.8 per cent in 2000, about the same as in 1994, at the start of NAFTA. Canada has very little FDI in Mexico and Mexico little in the rest of NAFTA.

In addition, the United States has increased its FDI position in the EU and Asia, at the expense of Canada, as barriers to trade remain relatively stronger in these other parts of the triad. By 2000, the US stock of FDI in Europe was 52.1 per cent of its total (up from 44.5 per cent in 1982); in Asia it was 16.0 per cent (up from 13.6 per cent in 1982).

In terms of worldwide FDI stocks, by 1999, the US stock of FDI in the EU was up to 45.2 per cent (from 38.0 per cent in 1986); in Asia it was at 12.9 per cent (up from 10.3 per cent in 1986). In contrast, the US stock of FDI in the rest of NAFTA (Canada and Mexico) was 12.9 per cent in 1999 compared to 21.3 per cent in 1986.

For Canada, its stock of FDI in NAFTA (almost entirely in the United States) in 1999 was 53.3 per cent compared to 68.7 per cent in 1986, 58.3 per cent in 1991 and 53.1 per cent in 1996. In 1999, Canada's stock of FDI in the EU was 18.8 per cent; in Asia it was 5.8 per cent. A large amount, 22.1 per cent, was in tax havens, listed under 'other'.

We also need to review Canada's FDI stock in the United States alone, not across NAFTA. In 1999, the Canadian stock in the United States was 52.2 per cent (as compared to 53.3 per cent in NAFTA, including Mexico with the United States). Other than a small increase in 1998, the 2000 figure reverses a steady decrease in the share of Canadian FDI in the United States, which fell from 68.3 per cent in 1986 to 63.0 per cent in 1989 (with the FTA) and to 53.3 per cent in 1994 (with NAFTA). Rather than this relative decrease being offset by a marked increase in FDI to the other two triad regions of the EU and Asia, most of the Canadian FDI no longer going to the United States instead appears to be going into tax havens (listed as 'other'), which accounted for 22.1 per cent of Canada's FDI in 1999.

Table 4.2 relates Canada's FDI stock in the United States to the US stock in Canada. The former has continued to grow at 13.5 per cent per year, double the US rate of 6.5 per cent per year. As a result, the ratio of Canadian FDI in the United States to US FDI in Canada has continued to increase. In 1982 it was 27 per cent; in 1989 it was 47 per cent with the FTA. In 1994 it was 56 per cent and by 2000 it was 80 per cent. These data are from a US source, which actually understates the ratio, compared to Statistics Canada data used in Rugman (1990), where these ratios are much higher. The reason, as discussed in Rugman (1987, 1990), is that the Canadian-based data evaluate the Canadian stock of FDI in the United States as about 50 per cent greater than the US evaluation, due to different methodological approaches.

Overall, these data reveal a decrease in the intra-regional FDI of NAFTA, although the decrease mainly occurred before the FTA and NAFTA started. This may have been in anticipation of the FTA (Rugman 1990). Between 1986 and 1996, the US stock in NAFTA (mainly in Canada) declined from 21.3 per cent to 13.7 per cent, but then only to 12.9 per cent by 1999. Similarly, the Canadian stock in the United States fell from 68.7 per cent in 1986 to 53.1 per cent in 1996, but has actually increased slightly to 53.3 per cent in 1999. The largest change involves an increase in Canada's FDI in 'other' from 12.8 per cent in 1986 to 22.1 per cent in 1999. In short, both the United States and Canada are now less dependent upon each other in terms of FDI compared to the situation in 1986.

To keep this decrease in NAFTA intra-regional FDI in perspective, however, let us consider the situation in Europe, as was shown in Figure 4.2 and Table 4.1. In 1986, the intra-regional stock of EC FDI was 35.8 per cent; in 1997 it was 49.3 per cent but in 1999 it fell to 45.7 per cent. This recent decrease in EU intra-regional FDI stock over the last five years of data availability is actually greater in absolute values than the decrease in NAFTA intra-regional stock of FDI over the same period. The principal reason for this switch is an increase in the EU stock in NAFTA from 22.8 per cent in 1996 to 30.8 per cent in 1999. In other words, European MNEs are increasingly seeking access to the NAFTA market through FDI at a time when intra-regional trade in the EU is still increasing. The European situation is therefore exactly similar to that of NAFTA: increasing intra-regional trade but FDI becoming more inter-regional.

Returning to the importance of increased intra-regional trade in NAFTA, the United States has become more open, especially in terms of imports, which in 2000 represented almost 15 per cent of GDP. Exports accounted for nearly 11 per cent of GDP in 2000. These ratios have increased since NAFTA and have more than doubled over the last 30 years, see Table 4.2.

Table 4.2 Bilateral stocks of US FDI: Canada and the United States, 1982–2000 (millions of US$)

Year	Canada's FDI Position in the USA (1)	US FDI Position in Canada (2)	Net Position [(1)–(2)]	(1)/(2)
1982	11 708	43 511	–31 803	0.27
1983	11 434	44 779	–33 345	0.26
1984	15 286	47 498	–32 212	0.32
1985	17 131	47 934	–30 803	0.36
1986	20 318	52 006	–31 688	0.39
1987	24 684	59 145	–34 461	0.42
1988	26 566	63 900	–37 334	0.42
1989	30 370	63 948	–33578	0.47
1990	29 544	69 508	–39 964	0.43
1991	36 834	70 711	–33 877	0.52
1992	37 843	68 690	–30 847	0.55
1993	40 487	69 922	–29 435	0.58
1994	42 133	74 987	–32 854	0.56
1995	45 618	83 498	–37 880	0.55
1996	54 799	91 301	–36 502	0.60
1997	64 022	99 859	–35 837	0.64
1998	72 696	98 200	–25 504	0.74
1999	76 526	111 051	–34 525	0.69
2000	100 822	126 421	–25 599	0.80
Average % (1982–2000)	13.5	6.5	(1.3)	6.6

Note: Data are on a historical-cost basis.

Sources: Adapted from BEA, *Survey of Current Business*, June, 2002; June 1999 and July 1996.

Indeed, the US economy is now more open than the Japanese economy. The US openness coefficient is 13.1 per cent of GDP as compared to 10 per cent of GDP for Japan. The EU continues to be the most open trade bloc, according to these data, with a 35.6 per cent openness coefficient. However, the vast of majority of EU trade is intra-regional and this significantly biases upward this ratio.

SECTORAL CHANGES IN MANUFACTURING AND SERVICE SECTORS

Another way of interpreting the data on increased intra-regional trade yet decreased intra-regional FDI within NAFTA is to take into account the differences in sectoral performance. For example, it is well known that about one-third of all US–Canadian trade is in automobiles and auto-parts, transportation equipment and affiliated industries. This integration of the largest manufacturing sector has occurred over the last 40 years. When specialty chemicals, plastics, steel and related manufacturing sectors linked to the automobile sector are brought into consideration, it is apparent that probably half of all US–Canadian trade is automobile related. The dominance of this manufacturing sector in the bilateral trade statistics is extraordinary and shows the special nature of the bilateral relationship.

In contrast, in services, market access on both sides of the border is much more diversified. No one service sector dominates FDI or trade data. Therefore, the service sector will be subject to different explanations than the manufacturing sector, since the latter is dominated by automobiles whereas services are much more diversified. Theory shows that access by Canadian business to the US service sector has to be by FDI as services are produced and consumed locally. In contrast, market access for manufacturers in NAFTA is now largely achieved through trade. Consistent with this, Hejazi and Pauly (2003) shows that the share of Canadian FDI in the United States has grown by 19.2 per cent over the 1983–1995 period, whereas the share of US FDI in Canada in services has only grown by 4.5 per cent over the same period.

The United States has halved its ratio of services to goods imports over the 1971–2000 period. However, since just after NAFTA started there has only been a slight decrease from 18.8 per cent in 1996 to 17.8 per cent in 2000. In contrast, the ratio of US services to goods exported has remained high at 37.86 per cent in 2000, slightly down from 39.21 per cent in 1996. Coupled with earlier information about the increase in intra-regional trade in NAFTA and the decrease in intra-regional FDI in NAFTA, this reduced ratio of imported services suggests a switch in the United States from trade in services towards FDI in services. This is apparent only when we look at service imports to the United States. The ratio of service imports to total imports decreased from 25.15 per cent in 1971 to 15.81 per cent in 1996 and then to 15.14 per cent in 2000. So, the United States must have increased its share of manufactures in total imports. As about one-quarter of all US imports come from Canada we can infer that there must be a large increase in intra-regional manufacturing trade in NAFTA over the last three years. In contrast, access to the US market for services is now more likely to be by FDI.

In terms of services, NAFTA is a different cultural animal than the EU. Within the EU there is a policy to promote harmonization and homogenization across its internal market. There is a social charter, a single currency and, every six months, new waves of directives stemming from the commissioners in Brussels. These institutional developments are necessary due to the historical political and cultural divisions between and within the fifteen member states of the EU. In contrast, in NAFTA, there is a huge degree of existing similarity between wealthy US and Canadian consumers and the existence of variation in the service sector stems more from regulatory sovereignty than from cultural differences.

In other words, due to size asymmetries, Canadians have already taken on board the dominant cultural and social characteristics of the United States. Today, much attention is paid in the Canadian media to what are really trivial differences between middle class Canadians and Americans. In Europe, the more balanced sizes of the six large and nine smaller economies has led to a smaller signaling effect from a dominant partner.

Furthermore the close geographic proximity of Canada to the United States has resulted in Canadian business achieving a high degree of market access to its neighboring economy. The large size of the United States acts as a magnet to business. This has resulted in both greater exports and growth of FDI stocks by Canada in the United States over the last 20 to 30 years. In contrast, as the Canadian economy is only one-tenth the size of the US economy, there has been less incentive for US business to locate in Canada (in a relative sense). In particular, US FDI in Canada in the service sector is hindered because many sectors are exempted from national treatment. So this reduces potential US interest in Canadian sectors, such as banking, health care, culture (including newspapers, book publishing and other media), transportation, etc. Consequently, Canada does not attract US services FDI today in the same proportion as it did US FDI in manufacturing 20 to 30 years ago.

One key aspect of the size asymmetries has been that Canadian business has only to learn how to deal with one set of US institutions (and Americans with one set of Canadian institutions), whereas within the EU the complex array of regulations and institutional peculiarities of each of the fifteen member states has taken a longer time to resolve into a common set of institutions.

FIRM-LEVEL DATA ON INTRA-REGIONAL BUSINESS

A final checkpoint on this aggregate data comes from looking into firm-level data. The largest 500 MNEs in the world account for well over 90 per cent of the world's stock of FDI and over half of the world's trade (Rugman 2000). In a recent analysis of the intra-regional sales of the largest 100 of these MNEs it was found that 67 of the 78 cases for which data were available had a majority of the sales in their home triad (Rugman and Brain 2003). For these 67 MNEs the average ratio of home triad foreign to total (F/T) sales was 79.3 per cent. For all 78 MNEs the average of home triad intra-regional sales was 71.6 per cent.

Of the largest 100 MNEs, only three were 'global' in the sense of having at least 20 per cent of their sales in each of the three parts of the triad. (These are IBM, Sony and Nestlé.) Another four are bi-regional, with 20 per cent of the sales in two parts of the triad and under 50 per cent in the home triad (they are BP, Toyota, Nissan and Unilever). A final set of four MNEs are host-triad oriented, namely Daimler-Chrysler, ING, Royal Ahold and Honda. Overall, this is confirmation of the importance of doing business in the home triad and it supports a focus on NAFTA for Canadian-based firms.

In a related study, all 49 retail MNEs in the world's largest 500 were examined, including Wal-Mart which is currently the largest MNE. Only one of these 49 MNEs is 'global' in the above sense. This is LVMH, the luxury goods retailer (Rugman and Girod 2003).

In a later study, Rugman and Verbeke (2004) found that across the world's 500 largest companies, a startling 72 per cent of all sales are within their home region. Indeed, across the 500, for the 380 firms for which geographic sales data are available, it is only possible to classify nine firms as truly 'global'. In contrast 320 of the 380 firms are home region bound, and these 320 firms have an average of 80 per cent of their sales in their home region. Thus we need to examine the regional strategies of these 380 firms. Of the 380 firms in the top 500 for which geographic sales data are available, an additional 58 firms have zero foreign sales, that is, 100 per cent of their sales are in their home region. These firms include: Kroger; Allstate; Bank One Corporation; US Bancorp; Circuit City; Safeway; Cathay Life; Kyushu Electric, and so on. Of the 380 firms with data, 320 are home-region based. Today, MNEs largely operate within their home region of the triad, or, at best, are bi-regional (competing only across two of the triads of the EU, NAFTA and Asia). Few MNEs are 'global' and thus few MNEs are really good case studies of globalization. Instead, today, most of the largest 500 MNEs are interested in the deepening of regional trade and investment agreements in Europe, the Americas and Asia.

At the micro level the evidence of regionalism is even stronger. Of the largest 500 corporations in the world, 320 of the 380 for which geographic sales data are available have, on average, 80 per cent of their sales in their home region of the triad. For example, the world's largest company, Wal-Mart, has 94 per cent of its sales in NAFTA. Of the other top 50 companies ranked by size, General Motors has 81 per cent in NAFTA; Mitsubishi has 87 per cent in Asia; Mitsui has 79 per cent in Asia; TotalFinaElf has 56 per cent in Europe; Allianz has 78 per cent in Europe; VW has 68 per cent in Europe; Deutsche Bank has 63 per cent in Europe; Credit Suisse has 61 per cent in Europe.

Of the 380 companies for which data are available, only nine are 'global' in the sense of having at least 20 per cent of their sales in each region of the triad. These are mainly MNEs in electronics such as IBM, Sony, Philips, Nokia, Intel, Canon and Flextronics. The others are Coca-Cola and LVMH. There are also a score of 'bi-regional' MNEs with at least 20 per cent of sales in two of these regions of the triad. These include: Toyota; Nissan; Daimler-Chrysler; Honda; AstraZeneca; GlaxoSmithKline; Ericsson; Diageo; Michelin; and so on. Overall, there are incredibly few truly global firms and most MNEs operate mainly in the home region of the triad.

The importance of economic-based regionalization and the triad, and the lack of globalization, is now being reflected in political alignments. Following the definitive change in US political attitudes towards national security after the September 11, 2001 terrorist attacks, a new world political system is emerging. This is based on the triad reality of regionalization.

The United States already has economic security on a regional basis. This was affirmed by the NAFTA agreement of 1994 (Rugman 1994). Now Canada and Mexico supply energy and other natural resources to the United States in exchange for enhanced business access to the world's single largest and richest market. The NAFTA does not provide the depth of economic integration of the EU, and it has none of the EU's political and currency integration. Yet it ties together its three constituent economies in a gigantic and highly successful free trade area to the mutual economic benefit of all three partners.

So successful is NAFTA that it is in the process of being expanded to the FTAA in 2005. This will lock in all 34 countries of the Americas into an extension of NAFTA. The US economy will serve as the regional regime for growth and renewed prosperity for Latin America and the Caribbean, just as NAFTA has done for Mexico.

CANADIAN MULTINATIONALS ARE REGIONAL, NOT GLOBAL

In this section I examine some of Canada's largest multinational firms, especially as they do business in the United States. These serve as models of corporate strategy for other MNEs from the countries in the FTAA, all of which need to access the leading and dominant US market. Each year *Fortune* magazine ranks the world's largest multinationals in their annual Fortune 500 list. Canada is at number four with 16 Canadian-owned multinationals making the world's top 500. Of these multinationals, the vast majority, 14, are home-triad based, with over 50 per cent of their sales in North America. At best, two Canadian multinationals are bi-regional. These are Bombardier and Alcan. Bombardier has over 90 per cent of its sales in North America and Europe. Even then, with over 50 per cent of its sales in North America, it is better classified as a home-based MNE. This leaves Alcan with 41.1 per cent of sales in North America and 39.6 per cent in Europe as Canada's only true bi-regional MNE. None of the Fortune 500 Canadian MNEs have a strong revenue base in all three parts of the triad, let alone in other regions of the world.

The foreign-owned firms in Canada are also regional. Unfortunately, we cannot obtain data on the intra-regional sales of these subsidiaries of US multinationals. All we know is that Ford Canada has 68 per cent of its sales outside Canada; Pratt and Whitney Canada has 85 per cent outside Canada and Cargill has 70 per cent outside Canada. Most of these sales are to the United States. At the very least the foreign-owned firms have a majority of their sales in North America.

The average intra-regional sales (F/T) for Canada's top 16 multinationals is 74.1 per cent. The comparable number for the largest 169 US multinationals is 77.3 per cent. So, Canada's dominant large firms are just as focused on their home NAFTA region, as are US ones. There is a further important implication of this similarity between Canadian and US multinationals. Both sets of firms now inhabit a common North American economic space. The 16 Canadian multinationals and the 169 US multinationals in the top 500 of the *Fortune* best average 75 per cent of all their sales in North America. As both sets of multinationals depend for their success on the North American market, Canadian multinationals need to focus on bilateral issues, such as access to the US market, on the deepening of NAFTA, and on border security measures, rather than on the World Trade Organization (WTO) and other multilateral agendas.

Yet, under the Chretien government, especially in its lack of support for US policy in Iraq, there has been an unworthy flourishing of anti-American sentiment and actions. This can only penalize Canadian business. While Canadian multinationals are just as locked into the North American market as are US multinationals, there is still a border. This can be a barrier to economic success in terms of political uncertainty. Canadians need to work to achieve better relations with the United States, to deepen NAFTA and to curtail anti-American sentiment. The US multinationals could become allies in this work, since they are just as dependent on the North American region of the triad, as are the Canadian multinationals.

The new political reality in the United States is that September 11, 2001 has changed both multilateral and bilateral government policy. The priority for the United States is its national security. As Iraq has illustrated, the United States places its unilateral security ahead of the traditional multilateral activities of the United Nations. Canadian business needs to be responsive to this new reality.

One way to do this is for Canada to link security issues to the economic integration of NAFTA. Canada needs more border measures like the 'Smart Border' declaration and action plan of September 2002. As part of this agreement between the Prime Minister and President Bush, multinational firms like General Motors, Ford and others have assumed responsibility for trans-border shipments. They certify the truck drivers and seal the contents of their containers, thereby gaining faster access through border crossings. Logically, this privatization of national security could be extended to the majority of US–Canadian trade, as 90 per cent of it is conducted by as few as 50 firms.

The policy logic of this new reality is that Canada can become a true partner and thus an 'insider' with the United States. Canadian business already operates on a regional basis; the politics needs to be adjusted to catch up with this. One bargaining chip for Canada is over energy. The United States will be seeking even greater energy security in the future. Canada needs to seize the initiative by making plans to develop the Alberta Tar Sands and by arranging long-term contracts with US firms for energy supply. Regional politics need to follow from regional economics.

These data on regional economic integration tell us that corporate policy as well as government policies need to ensure Canada's access to the vital US market. Simply, without the United States as an open, accessible and free market for Canadian goods and services Canada's economic goose is cooked! At the same time Canada should try to spread its bets by increasing its involvement in the two other regions of the triad economies, Europe and the Asian economies. But this will be a long and slow process. China, especially, has the potential to be a major market for key Canadian MNEs such as Bombardier and Nortel. But this observation has also been made by multinationals in the United States, Europe and Japan and competition for the potentially huge Chinese market is enormous. But the reality of today's global economy is that Canada is firmly attached to the US economic engine and will be for decades to come. It is hard to foresee any other likely scenario. The Canadian experience in NAFTA is likely to be repeated by Mexico and all other members of the FTAA. Corporate strategy across the FTAA needs to follow the Canadian example of close economic integration with the United States, a form of continentalism.

CONCLUSIONS

The major trend over the last 20 years has been an increase in intra-regional trade within each triad bloc. This is especially noticeable in NAFTA. The US economy is now more open (at 11 per cent exports to GDP and 15 per cent imports to GDP). This is similar to Japan, where exports account for 10.8 per cent of GDP, but it is behind the EU average of 35 per cent of GDP.

Due to increased intra-regional trade in NAFTA, US FDI stocks in NAFTA as a percentage of worldwide FDI have decreased over the last 20 years. In contrast, intra-regional FDI stocks have continued to increase within the EU and Asian triad blocs. The unusual situation in NAFTA is dominated by the US–Canadian manufacturing relationship. In turn, this reflects the overwhelming importance of the automobile sector in North America. This sector accounts for one-third of US–Canadian trade. In this sector free trade has existed for over 40 years, and it has replaced the need for FDI.

In contrast, across the service sectors affected by NAFTA, FDI is still important. Indeed, it remains the only viable mode of entry in sectors, such as financial services, transportation, cultural industries, health, education and social services, which are still regulated.

Furthermore, national treatment for FDI is still denied in these service sectors. This reduces the incentive for US FDI in the service sector in Canada but (due to size asymmetries) does not discourage Canadian FDI in the United States. For example, privatization and de-regulation in the US financial service sectors now present opportunities for Canadian banks to expand into the United States. They will need to do this through FDI rather than trade owing to the need to deliver services locally and given the residual risks in this quasi-regulated sector.

At firm level, data on foreign sales by MNEs reveal that very few of the world's largest MNEs are 'global' in the sense of operating in all three triad markets. The vast majority of large MNEs mainly operate in their home-triad market. These firm-level data support the large degree of intra-regional trade in NAFTA.

The implications of this for corporate strategy are very basic; the MNEs are the drivers of regional integration. As NAFTA expands to the FTAA, the MNEs will increase their intra-regional trade and FDI. The US-based MNEs will access the other markets of the FTAA, while MNEs from all other countries in the FTAA will need to become players in the dominant US market. After the start of the FTAA in 2005 it will take some ten years or more for MNEs to grow their intra-regional trade and FDI. This will be at the expense of 'global' trade and FDI.

REFERENCES

Hejazi, Walid, and Peter Pauly (2003), 'Motivations for FDI and domestic capital formation', *Journal of International Business Studies* **34**(3), 282–9.

Hejazi, Walid, and A.E. Safarian (2002), 'Explaining Canada's changing FDI patterns', mimeo, Rotman School of Management, University of Toronto, June.

Rugman, Alan M. (1987), *Outward Bound: Canada's Direct Investment in the United States*, Toronto: C.D. Howe Institute.

Rugman, Alan M. (1990), *Multinationals and Canada–United States Free Trade*, Columbia, SC: University of South Carolina Press.

Rugman, Alan M. (1994), *Foreign Investment and NAFTA*, Columbia, SC: University of South Carolina Press.
Rugman, Alan M. (2000), *The End of Globalization*, London: Random House and New York: Amacom-McGraw Hill.
Rugman, Alan M., and Cecilia Brain (2003), 'Multinational enterprises are global, not regional', *Multinational Business Review*, **11** (1).
Rugman, Alan M., and Stephane Girod (2003), 'Retail multinationals and globalization: the evidence is regional', *European Management Journal*, **21**, 1 (January), 24–37.
Rugman, Alan M., and Richard Hodgetts (2003), *International Business*, 3rd edn, London: Pearson Financial Times/Prentice-Hall.
Rugman, Alan M., and Alain Verbeke (2003), 'Regional and global strategies of multinationals', *Journal of International Business Studies*, **35**(1), 1–15.
Safarian, A.E. (1996), *Foreign Ownership of Canadian Industry*, Toronto: McGraw-Hill of Canada.
Safarian, A.E., and Walid Hejazi (2001), *Canada and Foreign Direct Investment: A Study of Determinants*, Toronto: Rotman School Centre for Public Management, University of Toronto.

5. What institutional design for North America?

Gordon Mace and Louis Bélanger[1]

The North American Free Trade Agreement (NAFTA) is now ten years old. It was born in the context of an acute political debate, particularly in the United States, concerning its potential benefits. After ten years of implementing the accord, there are still opposing views concerning its effects. Apparently, NAFTA had a positive impact on the economies of the three member countries at the macroeconomic level but farmers in Mexico are severely hit and the Mexican government is now thinking of asking for changes in the agreement.[2] Although it is still difficult to assess all the economic, political and social consequences of the agreement, which took effect in January 1994, there is no doubt that it has greatly altered the geo-economic environment of North America.

Since the early 1990s, much academic literature has been produced on various aspects of NAFTA. The bulk of this literature has dealt with the general economic impact of the agreement and its specific costs and benefits for the three member countries as well as for their economic sectors.[3] Another part of the literature has a more general focus, reflecting on the wider contours of North American regionalism.[4] This includes important analyses of the political aspects of NAFTA, the role of political parties,[5] national legislatures and more particularly the US Congress,[6] and the negotiation process that led to the signing of the agreement.[7] Authors have also examined various other aspects and dimensions of North American integration such as the convergence of values among the three political communities,[8] the larger problematique of governance,[9] the environment[10] and, as a natural result of the September 11, 2001 tragedy, the security dimension through the North American perimeter.[11]

Only recently, however, a debate on institutions has started, on the basis of proposals by scholars as well as by policy-makers and political observers. On the political front, the Permanent Committee on Foreign Affairs and International Trade of the House of Commons of Canada has produced a substantial report which recommends, among other things, that the Canadian government study the opportunity for a North American customs union, and proposes a new trilateral intergovernmental framework based on the summitry model, so as to develop a 'strategic North American dimension' in Canadian foreign policy.[12] But the main initiative has come from the President of Mexico, Vicente Fox, who has called for the creation of a North American Economic Community with trilateral cooperation in immigration, labor, economic development and monetary policy.[13] What Fox had in mind is an evolution of regionalism in North America along a European-type integration model.[14] These proposals, however, have received little attention from the Canadian[15] and US governments.

Nevertheless, this has not prevented the larger intellectual community from reflecting upon the 'deficient institutionally' of NAFTA[16] and proposing an institutional setting for North American regionalism. Wendy Dobson, for example, in the first report of a series produced by the C.D. Howe Institute on the challenges of regional integration for Canada, calls for a 'strategic bargain' which would put NAFTA on the road to a customs union and eventually a common market.[17] However, the boldest proposal, without a doubt, was made by Robert Pastor in a book proposing the gradual establishment of a North American Community. The Community would develop policies on immigration, regional development, trade in goods, and the movement of persons, and education, while exploring the feasibility of various methods of macroeconomic coordination such as the creation of a common currency.[18] As for institutions, Pastor makes four proposals: a North American Commission which would be much leaner than its European counterpart but nevertheless independent from the three governments; a North American Parliamentary Group which would essentially merge the US–Mexican Inter-Parliamentary Conference and its Canada–US counterpart; a Permanent North American Court on Trade and Investment which would be an upgrade of the existing dispute-settlement mechanism; and, finally, meetings of Cabinet ministers on the basis of existing binational commissions.[19]

These blueprints for North American regionalism, and particularly the proposals on institutions, would seem modest in the context of the European integration. From a theoretical point of view and possibly from a business perspective, they appear to be simply a logical extension of a free trade agreement. However, this chapter will argue that, while these blueprints may be possible some years down the road, they are not probable in the current context of North American regionalism.

This chapter describes the institutional design of North American regionalism. What is the nature and extent of the NAFTA?[20] What type of legalization model does it use? It is important to understand the nature and scope of the 1994 agreement if we are to discuss the underlying reasoning of the actors both now and then. In the second section, we discuss the strategic calculus made by each government when negotiating NAFTA in the first part of the 1990s. Then, we analyse the current positioning of the three member governments in the regional context, referring to events outside the region, especially the fall-out of the intervention in Iraq. In the conclusion, we will draw on the analyses made in sections two and three to demonstrate why a change in the institutional design of the NAFTA will be difficult to bring about in the near future.

THE INSTITUTIONAL DESIGN OF THE NAFTA

Robert Pastor maintains that the preamble to the NAFTA Treaty was written like a business contract.[21] In fact, the whole agreement gives the impression of a business deal, done in the US fashion: most eventualities are covered, the duties of the contracting parties are stated clearly, the timetable is precise, and the dispute-settlement mechanisms are identified. The signatories liberalize trade among themselves. But what does 'trade liberalization' mean?

Until the 1970s, trade liberalization essentially implied a reduction of tariff and non-tariff barriers, evident in the agenda of the Kennedy Round GATT negotiations. But by comparing the agendas of the multilateral trade negotiations from the Kennedy Round to the Doha Round, Stephen Woolcock has very aptly demonstrated how the international trading environment has changed.[22] Today, the trading environment also involves subsidies and duties, public procurement, investment, services, labor standards, and so on, policies which regulate trade but also have a very significant impact on the overall functioning of national economies. In NAFTA, as pointed out by Cameron and Tomlin, the agreement also has the effect of restructuring basic property rules and state–society relations.[23] This is all the more true for Canada and Mexico given the asymmetry in power between the three member countries. Thus, the fundamental significance of the NAFTA is that it is a deal by which Washington offered relatively guaranteed access to the US market in return for which the Canadian and Mexican governments agreed to harmonize many of their economic policies, to create a fairly uniform economic environment in all of North America. Given the weight of the US economy in the region, it is reasonable to expect that the NAFTA economic environment will align itself with US macroeconomic policies. Thus, economic nationalism, for example, of the type adopted by the Canadian and Mexican governments in the 1970s, will not be possible in the NAFTA environment.

That said, what does the NAFTA signify in terms of its institutional design and why did the member governments choose that design? We will try to provide an answer in the next section but let us concentrate for the moment on the NAFTA's institutional design itself.

In their excellent article, Koremenos, Lipson and Snidal[24] propose five criteria enabling us to identify as precisely as possible the nature and scope of an institutional design and to compare it to others. These key dimensions are: membership, scope, centralization, control and flexibility. *Membership* determines who belongs to an institution. Is the membership exclusive and restrictive or inclusive? Does it involve only states or other type of actors such as NGOs? Membership impacts directly on the dynamics of an institution. *Scope* has to do with the issues or areas of activity of the institution. Is it limited to trade or does it involve larger economic questions? Does it deal with economic issues only or other areas such as culture, immigration, democracy, and so on? *Centralization* refers to the level of duties and responsibilities given to an international authority. Do participating governments devolve many or only a few functions to a superordinate body? This dimension closely resembles delegation, which is the third dimension of the concept of legalization as identified by Abbott and co-authors.[25] *Control* differs from centralization in that it is used from the perspective of the participating units and focuses attention on the weight that each actor has in monitoring the whole process. Where asymmetry is strong, the weaker actors should normally have less control over the institution. Finally, *flexibility* of the institutional design refers to the open or closed character of the institution. Does a trade agreement, for example, contain many or few escape clauses? Does it permit renegotiation or not?[26]

Some of these dimensions closely resemble the 'parameters' identified by Robert Pastor in his attempt at typology-building.[27] They are therefore included in our criteria, which are listed in Table 5.1 and to which was added Pastor's criterion of origin. Origin refers here to the basic reasons for which the institutional arrangement was adopted in the first place. Table 5.1 also compares the NAFTA design to that of the European Union (EU).

Table 5.1 Comparing institutional designs, selected criteria

	European Union	NAFTA
1. Origin	Security/ Strategic positioning	Secure market/ Strategic positioning
2. Membership	Extended	Restricted
3. Scope	Diversified	Trade/Economy
4. Centralization	Medium/High	Low
5. Control	Symmetry	Asymmetry
6. Flexibility	High	Low

A quick look at the table indicates that the institutional design of the NAFTA is fundamentally different from that of the EU. First of all, regarding *origin,* it is evident that strategic positioning inside the world system was an important consideration for all the actors who participated initially in each regional project. The European countries wanted to increase their bargaining power with both the United States and the USSR while the three NAFTA governments wanted to improve their position by creating a trading bloc able to compete with Asia and 'Fortress Europe'. There is nothing very original here in the sense that all regional projects are endeavors aimed at improving strategic positioning in the world system. The difference in the NAFTA–EU comparison lies in other considerations. In the case of the European Union, security was a major factor, as illustrated by the establishment in 1951 of the European Coal and Steel Community. In the case of NAFTA, on the other hand, economic goals constituted a principal consideration: securing access to the US market for the Canadian and Mexican governments, and, in the case of the United States, creating an economic framework for North America. This being said, it is obvious that the United States had a strategic interest in 'locking' Mexico in a liberalizing process that was political as well as economical.

Membership differs in both institutional settings. While it is restricted for the moment to the three North American governments in the case of NAFTA,[28] membership is extended to other governments in the case of the EU. With the enlargement of 2004, the EU will comprise 25 participating governments and will be much more open than NAFTA to participation by non-state actors such as political parties and NGOs.

The *scopes* of the two arrangements also vary substantially. NAFTA is essentially a normative framework for economic policies while the European Union covers a much larger spectrum of human activity including social policies, democratic behavior and civil liberties. As noted by Pastor, the philosophy behind the whole EU experiment is also fundamentally different as it implies 'a commitment to the values of internal solidarity and mutual support'.[29]

Centralization, or delegation of responsibilities by national governments to community institutions, is significant in the EU with the important role played by the Commission and its various bodies. In contrast, the institutional framework of NAFTA is extremely limited. Qualified observers such as Grinspun and Kreklewich, for example, have noted that the NAFTA already suffers from an 'institutional deficit' which limits its capacity to deal with the developments arising from the implementation of the initial agreement.[30] Pastor, for his part, remarks that the regional institutions cannot settle trade conflicts as soon as they arise and are therefore unable to prevent crises, a situation that can only weaken the North American partnership.[31] These limited institutions can neither help the three governments to 'forge North American policies or define a common agenda'. Finally, Sidney Weintraub considers the Free Trade Commission and other NAFTA structures as 'quite primitive',[32] while Isidro Morales believes that the density and the complexity of the integration process launched in 1994 will necessitate the establishment of new 'transnational' institutions.[33]

Control, for its part, is more widely distributed in the EU as it has many more member countries than NAFTA and there is a lower degree of asymmetry between the larger and smaller countries of the Union, compared with the United States and its two NAFTA partners. In North America, the US economy generates almost 90 per cent of the region's gross product which illustrates the profound asymmetry within the NAFTA.

Finally, compared with NAFTA, the EU has a much higher degree of *flexibility*[34] – in the dual sense of special treatment for less-developed member countries, and the use of negotiations to decide on various steps of integration in each area. In the case of NAFTA, however, negotiations occurred before the agreement was signed but they were no longer possible once the agreement was ratified and in the process of being implemented. At more than 700 pages, the sheer length of the NAFTA agreement – longer than the original GATT Agreement and the Treaty of Rome establishing the European Common Market, and much longer than the 12-page Treaty of Ascuncion which created MERCOSUR[35] – is a testimony to the extremely high level of precision and obligation that the member governments accepted in signing the agreement. As Abbott writes:

> NAFTA is among the most highly detailed international trade agreements ever negotiated between governments. It comprises twenty-two chapters setting out specific obligations on trade in goods, services, financial services, investment, intellectual property rights, technical barriers to trade, sanitary and phytosanitary measures, safeguards measures, and dispute settlement. It incorporates a panoply of annexes that elaborate the extent (and limits) of obligations by reference, among other things, to the internal legislation of its parties. NAFTA is broader in scope of coverage than that of the WTO agreement, and it is comparable in level of detail to the WTO agreement. NAFTA was drafted at a level of detail substantially higher than the EC treaty.[36]

Consequently, the institutional design of NAFTA as it now exists can be characterized by a particular type of legalization: a high level of obligation, a high level of precision and a low level of delegation.[37] The high level of obligation results from the binding rules contained in the agreement. The high level of precision means that the rules contained in the agreement are very detailed, leaving as little as possible to interpretation or further negotiation. The low level of delegation refers to the limited authority delegated to minimal community institutions.[38]

This illustrates the basic philosophy and innovative aspect of this regional project. In opposition to the supranational approach of the EU, whereby progress occurs mainly as a result of the work done by the community institutions, the approach in the NAFTA is one where policy convergence is sought through the application of a normative framework represented by the initial treaty.[39] In other words, precision has been preferred over delegation. This approach would explain the relative efficiency of the agreement despite the absence of strong community institutions: they can be avoided because it is the institutional framework itself which acts as a blueprint for member governments and, in so doing, steers the process forward.

CHOOSING THE DESIGN

The institutional design of NAFTA can therefore be summarized as legalization combined with a policy convergence approach which results in limited institutionality. Like all institutional designs, the NAFTA structure is fundamentally the result of particularized objectives and policy preferences expressed by the member governments when initially negotiating the agreement. These objectives and preferences are naturally constrained by the general context of the period in which each government found itself during the negotiation. In the case of NAFTA, the period extended from 1988, when President-elect Salinas first approached the US administration, to the final days of the negotiation in 1993. What was the initial calculus of each government at that time and how does this explain the choice of the institutional design?

Without going into all the intricacies of the pre-NAFTA negotiation period, which is well covered in the literature,[40] let us briefly examine the main elements of each government's strategic calculus when entering the negotiations that would lead to NAFTA. The end of the 1980s and the start of the 1990s was a difficult period for multilateral trade negotiations and this, combined with the economic difficulties of the time, gave rise to a fear of emerging trading blocs. For the Canadian and Mexican governments, the 1980s was also a time to take stock of the exact location of their respective economies in the world system – and the picture was not good. Both economies had become more and more dependent on the United States, despite policies aimed at diversification throughout the 1970s, a situation which, of course, had an impact on the standing and influence of both countries in the international system.

Given this perception of emerging rival trading blocs,[41] the fear of a looming 'Fortress Europe' for countries such as Mexico and Canada,[42] and the aggressive trade policy of the Reagan administration,[43] it is not surprising that the foremost consideration for policy-makers in Mexico and Ottawa at the time was secured access to the US market. This explains the Canadian government's decision to seek a free trade agreement with the United States as early as 1985.[44] With this in place by 1988, Canada did not really need a NAFTA, but when the idea of another FTA between Mexico and the US materialized in 1990, the Canadian government demanded to be part of the negotiation. As stated by Abbott, the move by Canada was essentially motivated by 'defensive economic purposes'.[45] The Canadian government was mostly preoccupied with protecting the gains of free trade with the US from the threat that an eventual deal between Mexico and Washington would result in the United States coming back to Canada to seek more concessions. Canada also wanted to prevent a hub-and-spoke structure in which there would be two trade deals in North America with the United States at the center of the arrangement. So the Canadian strategy in the NAFTA negotiations was fundamentally a defensive move with the same basic goal of securing access to the US market for Canadian goods.

The Mexican government of Carlos Salinas had the same goal because, like Canada, Mexico was in the same type of dependency relationship with the US economy. It is interesting to observe the similarities in the evolution of the economic relationship of these two countries with the United States over the past 40 years, and how during this period, fluctuations in their respective macroeconomic policies have followed the same pattern. But there was another consideration which was important for the administration of the new Mexican President, Carlos Salinas. Before becoming president, Carlos Salinas had served as planning minister under former President Miguel de la Madrid after his election in 1982. His work in this portfolio had convinced Carlos Salinas that the impact of the Mexican debt crisis could not be dealt with by continuing to apply the traditional economic policies pursued by the preceding Mexican governments. A fundamental change had to be made to the model of economic development in Mexico if the country wanted eventually to join the club of industrialized nations. But at the start of his mandate, the new President was aware that many groups and organizations in the country were opposed to a radical change in Mexico's economic policies. Membership in the NAFTA was therefore seen as a strategic move to 'lock in' the new economic policies that the Salinas administration had decided to implement.[46] Consequently, Mexico had much more at stake in the NAFTA negotiations than the other two participants and this greatly influenced that government's preferences in relation to the outcome of the negotiation.

In the case of the United States, it was clear to the Bush administration that a window of opportunity existed in North American and inter-American affairs and that the occasion had to be seized.[47] Like the previous agreement with Canada, here was a situation where the other party was asking for a deal. In responding, Washington would not be seen as imposing an economic blueprint but it would certainly try to use the upcoming negotiations to do so. One of the objectives pursued by the US government since the mid-1980s, and particularly in the framework of the Canada–US negotiations, was to use bilateral trade negotiations to influence multilateral negotiations directly by having the same items discussed in both forums. Influence could also be wielded indirectly by showing Japan, the EU and other commercial partners of the United States that Washington was prepared to privilege bilateral and multilateral trade agreements over multilateral ones to advance the US conception of free trade.

Other strategic objectives were the improvement of conditions of access to the Mexican market for US investment and commercial firms and of economic conditions in Mexico so as to relieve the pressure that resulted in immigration to the United States[48] and to stabilize the socio-political environment in Mexico. The objective result of all this was the imposition of a more uniform economic framework on all of North America by having the governments of Canada and Mexico harmonize their macroeconomic policies as much as possible with those of Washington.

It should first be pointed out, as was done so aptly by Abbott,[49] that neither Canada, Mexico nor the United States 'entered into NAFTA negotiations with the objective of creating a political or social union on the North American continent'. There was no intention on the part of any of the three governments to create an institutional structure or a strong regional bureaucracy to regulate business activity or activities in other areas. Why was that? In the case of the United States, it is a well-known observation in international relations that the most powerful states strive to manage their foreign policy outside institutional constraints as much as possible unless they feel that strong institutions will provide them with benefits resulting from the functioning of such institutions in a given area. This is particularly true when the institutional design is framed in such a way, in terms of obligation and precision, that cooperation is extensively regulated by that design – which was exactly the case of the NAFTA. As we stated earlier, NAFTA represents a completely innovative trajectory of regionalism. It is a case where regionalism proceeds, not on the basis of a supranational approach as is the case in the EU, but on the basis of compliance with a normative framework. The NAFTA framework is so complete that, in a way, it precludes the necessity of strong regional institutions to monitor progress and move the process forward. Therein lies the beauty of this situation from the perspective of the US government: bring the other governments to accept an economic blueprint and consequently harmonize their macroeconomic policies with that of the United States without the necessity of making a substantial investment in institutions for governance.

In the case of the two smaller countries, it is clear that they entered into the negotiations in order to reduce the uncertainty concerning access to the US market. This uncertainty resulted from what they perceived as the growing influence of protectionist forces in the United States.[50] But neither the Canadian nor Mexican governments saw the necessity of creating strong regional institutions as a logical extension of this objective. On the contrary, policy-makers of both countries wanted to prevent the establishment of an extended institutional structure of the EU type for fear that Washington would use the considerable power differential between the three countries to impose its point of view and dominate the community institutions. This preoccupation was ingrained in the particular history of the relationship of both countries with the United States. The Canada–US war episode of 1812 and the US–Mexican war of 1848, with the subsequent loss by Mexico of almost half of its territory, have nurtured an enduring theme of maintenance of independence from the United States in the political landscape of both countries.[51] A more immediate preoccupation was the domestic opposition in both countries, and in the United States for that matter, which was already portraying the NAFTA as an abandonment of national sovereignty.[52] In that context of recurring traditional political values and more immediate trade politics, the creation of strong regional institutions was certainly seen as problematic.

The institutional design of NAFTA as adopted in the period 1992–4 was therefore a result of the national preferences of the three governments. The original NAFTA deal was essentially an offer of a secured access to the US market in return for a certain harmonization of macroeconomic policies. This represented the fundamental policy preferences of the three participating governments and it was felt that the legalization model then adopted would enable each government to reach its objectives. The question that now remains concerns the current situation. What has changed in the NAFTA project or in the larger international environment that would modify the initial preferences of the participating governments and bring them to substantially alter the institutional design of NAFTA? We will try to frame the answer to that question in the next part of the chapter.

CHANGING THE DESIGN?

Proposals for a change in the institutional design of NAFTA are generally accompanied by a call for a deepening of the regional project which is perceived as being unable to manage the existing or upcoming regional agenda.[53] Both elements are linked, as the deepening of a regional project should normally affect its institutional design. This is why we must have a clear understanding of what is implied by the term 'deepening'.

The deepening of a regional project can only happen in two ways: either by making changes in the existing dimension of the process and/or by adding more dimensions to the process. Unlike the EU, the fact that NAFTA deals exclusively with economic matters currently makes it a unidimensional regional project. Because NAFTA is nominally a free trade agreement, deepening it could mean, in the first instance, a move toward a customs union, a common market or an economic union. These are the traditional stages in a process of economic integration as identified in the literature and as illustrated by the experience of the European Union since 1957. In this scenario, the transformation of a free trade area into a customs union would not normally necessitate a change of the institutional design in the sense of more delegation because what would be added to the initial agreement is the harmonization of tariffs on imports coming from third parties. This can be managed in the same way as the free trade area is already dealt with in NAFTA.

Upgrading a free trade area to a common market and to an economic union, however, is something very different. The large scale harmonization of economic policies implied here, including the introduction of a common currency, cannot be determined once and for all by a constitutive treaty as is the case for the current free trade agreement. The number of items involved, their importance for each domestic community and the uncertainty resulting from a constantly evolving situation, along with the introduction of new, sometimes unforeseen, problems, all necessitate constant bargaining which can only be done in the framework of well-structured regional institutions.

The other scenario for deepening implies adding new dimensions to the process. This would mean an extension of the initial regional project to cover other areas such as immigration/migration, the environment, health policies, security, and so on. Again, and even more than in the other scenario, strong community institutions would be necessary here as a forum for discussion, negotiation and monitoring.

With the exception of the customs union, both scenarios consequently imply a complex agenda which is impossible to manage only through a normative framework such as the one regulating NAFTA. From a functional point of view, many arguments point toward modification of the institutional trajectory of NAFTA to build stronger regional institutions. Observers have underlined the inadequacies of NAFTA in dealing with some problems of non-compliance and with what Pastor has called the 'illegitimate side of integration', namely drugs, smuggling, undocumented workers, and so on.[54] From a purely North American perspective, one can also see the benefits of strong regional institutions in terms of reducing uncertainty, facilitating the bargaining process and dealing with enforcement problems. But what are the prospects for a change in the institutional design of NAFTA in the short to medium term?

To put it bluntly, they do not appear to be very favorable in the present context. It is true that the new Mexican government of President Vicente Fox tabled a proposal in February 2001 for an expanded North American community on the model of the European Union.[55] This would establish a common market within 25 years and the adoption of a single currency and the free movement of goods, services, capital and labor. In March 2002, the Guanajuato Proposal materialized into the Partnership for Prosperity Initiative and on this occasion Jorge Castaneda, the Mexican Foreign Affairs Minister, made a call 'to build the institutions of a real North American Community'.[56]

These announcements can be considered as somewhat of a surprise given the Mexican tradition of independence *vis-à-vis* the United States. But they are not out of line with the objectives of the new Fox administration, which would like to change the ways in which Mexicans envisage relations with the rest of the world, including the United States. What is revealing, however, is the complete silence with which this proposal was received by both governments in Canada and in the United States.[57] There was no official reaction whatsoever. Why?

In the case of Canada, a debate is going on among specialists and observers of the North American scene. It has been launched, among other things, by a C.D. Howe report by economist Wendy Dobson in April 2002, one month after the announcement of the Partnership for Prosperity Initiative. The report called for a Canadian policy of 'Big Ideas' and strategic bargaining including a proposal for a customs union and for a common market.[58] The Dobson report launched a debate about the pros and cons of deeper integration.

Opponents of deeper integration argue essentially that NAFTA has not delivered in terms of helping to raise Canadian living standards and has not protected Canada against retaliatory trade measures adopted by the US administration as, for example, in the case of lumber exports. Furthermore, they maintain that NAFTA arrangements endanger Canadian sovereignty as NAFTA has already become 'an external, if virtually secret, constitution for Canada'.[59] Others fear that NAFTA could threaten the Canadian health care system if the government decided to extend the system and bring in private health care services.[60] Even the editorial team of the leading Canadian newspaper, *The Globe and Mail,* expressed concern over the far-reaching implications of the Dobson proposals and considered that the government should 'tread carefully'.[61] On the other hand, some observers stated that there was nothing wrong with NAFTA[62] and that, indeed, the building of an area of security in North America will benefit commercial relations in the region.[63]

What is most interesting for our purpose, however, is that most of the discussion on proposals ignored the trilateral relationship, instead concentrating almost exclusively on the bilateral one. Even Dobson herself, in a comment made a year after the publication of her report, called for a 'strategic framework' linking security and defense with economic goals. Among the four elements of the framework (security initiative, Canadian contribution to North American defense, secure natural-resources area and a North American economic efficiency initiative), only the last one really deals with the trilateral relationship, while the whole strategic package would be negotiated inside a 'framework agreement between the US President and the Canadian Prime Minister'.[64] Others, such as Anne Golden of the Conference Board, disagree with the Big Idea concept and prefer a step-by-step approach. But most of these steps exclude Mexico as an interlocutor.[65] Finally, the reaction of the Canadian government has been extremely reserved and when expressed, mostly by way of speeches by ministers Rock and Manley, it favored the strengthening of the *bilateral* relationship through a step-by-step approach[66] in spite of calls for a deepening of the cooperation between the three North American countries on the part of the House of Commons Committee on Foreign Affairs.[67] As for the new Canadian Prime Minister, Paul Martin never mentions the trilateral relationship in public statements on the future of Canadian foreign policy.[68]

This said, the preceding paragraphs reveal that the Canadian political and economic elite is divided concerning the future of Canada's place in North America. Majority opinion, however, still appears satisfied with the existing institutional design of NAFTA as far as the management of the trilateral relationship is concerned. It is felt that the future problems that Canada will face in North America will be dealt with more thoroughly in the framework of the bilateral Canada–US relationship. Why is this still the dominant point of view in Canada?

The first reason is that the foremost strategic consideration for Canadian policy-makers is still to get secured access to the US market. Canadian living standards are seen to depend on that access. Another reason is the perception that problems are not the same, or do not, in Canada–US relations, present themselves in the same way as Mexico-US relations. For example, the Mexican suggestion that post-September 11 border issues could be dealt with trilaterally was seen as disastrous from the Canadian perspective, given the massive migration problems along the US–Mexican border, which are completely different from what exists along the Canada–US border.[69] However, this may be partly related to a Canadian identity problem since Canadian policy-makers still perceive Canada as a first world country and Mexico as a member of the Third World. It would seem that the consequences of being a North American country have not been grasped completely in Canada as the North American perspective in Canadian foreign policy still includes only Canada and the United States. Finally, there is also the fear factor: fear that an extended institutional structure covering North America will be easily dominated by Washington, given the asymmetry between the three countries, creating multiple threats to Canadian sovereignty – a threat perceived as less important if problems are addressed in a piecemeal procedure.

As for the United States, one could believe that Washington would have a positive view of a change in the institutional design of the NAFTA given US interests in the security of North America, its future energy needs and the preoccupation with the environment. As stated previously, it is difficult to envision regular cooperation in these and other areas without more developed regional institutions. The US reaction to Mexico's proposals, however, was even more restrained than that of Canada. No official comment came from Washington and the other declarations that were made expressed US preferences for intergovernmental channels when dealing with regional problems. A former US ambassador to Ottawa, Gordon Giffin, stated for example that: 'The relationship doesn't need a new "idea", rather a renewed mutual commitment.'[70]

The recent pattern of US cooperation with its neighbors is also illustrative of the way Washington envisions its future relations with Ottawa and Mexico. Let's take, for example, security, which has been without a doubt the most important area of concern for the US government since September 11.[71]

Given the centrality of this theme throughout the US governmental structure since autumn 2001, one would expect that the optimal solution to the security problems of the US national territory would be a security perimeter covering all of North America and managed on a coordinated trilateral basis. But this was not the road taken by Washington, which chose instead to sign two bilateral agreements whose contents do not vary substantially from each other. Taking the Canada–US Smart Border Accord as an illustration, we have a 30-point plan calling for cooperation in several areas from data sharing to asylum practices and integration of enforcement and intelligence capacities.[72] As Kitchen notes, it is 'more than incremental co-operation (but) less than mega-issue cooperation on the scale of NAFTA'.[73]

Three reasons can explain Washington's refusal to envisage changes to the institutional design of NAFTA and to support the creation of significant community institutions for the management of North American affairs. The first is the traditional reluctance of large countries, and the United States in particular, to be constrained by any supranational body. As noted by Robert Pastor, Washington has a 'constant temptation to act unilaterally' and the reasons for that are the weight of a Congress whose incentive system is aimed essentially at meeting local needs plus the psychological factor associated with the feeling of 'exceptionalism'.[74] The second reason, as stated by Wilson-Forsberg,[75] is that the United States has largely secured its own interests within the existing framework of NAFTA. As we have already said, the normative or policy convergence approach of the NAFTA treaty is doing the work without it being necessary to create, for the satisfaction of US interests, strong regional institutions. And finally, there is the post-Iraq situation where both of Washington's NAFTA partners have broken with the United States over the war.[76] Given the mood of the present US administration, the refusals to support the US intervention in Iraq have, from Washington's point of view, broken a relationship of trust and have had an impact on the evolution of the North American regional project.

CONCLUDING REMARKS

Koremenos, Lipson and Snidal[77] identify four independent variables that can influence governmental choices concerning institutional designs. *Distribution problems* arise when more than one type of cooperative agreement is possible and when the relative gains expected by each parties vary from one design to another. *Enforcement problems* refer to the incentives of actors to cheat on a given agreement. An enforcement problem occurs when an actor believes that unilateral noncooperation brings more benefits than long-term cooperation. The third variable is the *number of actors*. The term 'number' refers here to the actual number of participants in an institutional design as well as to membership and the distribution, symmetrical or asymmetrical, of actors' capabilities. Finally, *uncertainty* refers to the accuracy of information that actors possess concerning the behavior of others, the state of the world, and so on.

How do these variables come into play in Mexico's preference for change in the institutional design of the NAFTA, and the Canadian and US preferences for keeping the current design? In the case of Mexico, the two variables at work appear to be distribution problems and asymmetry. Asymmetry renders the possibility of strong central institutions very slim. On the one hand, asymmetry works against a change to the institutional design that involves creating strong regional institutions because the chances are that these institutions would be dominated by the United States due to the differential in capabilities. On the other hand, central institutions that would mediate the power asymmetry would not be acceptable for the United States because of the limits it would impose on its capacity to use its leverage. But it seems that this factor is outweighted by the distribution variable. The Vicente Fox Administration is unsatisfied with the actual functioning of NAFTA, particularly its perceived impact on Mexican agriculture,[78] and hopes that a change to the institutional design of NAFTA would benefit Mexico, particularly if the changes are in the direction of the EU model. Mexico has in mind the EU Structural and Cohesion Funds which, if the idea was transferred to North America, would involve regular flows of monies to Mexico as part of regional adjustment policies.

However, in Canada the distribution factor plays an opposite role. While Canadian policy-makers do not necessarily fear that Canada would be asked to contribute more to Mexican development, they do fear that a change to the institutional design will bring Mexico closer to the United States, with possible detrimental effects for Canada. However, the more important variable in the Canadian case, again, would seem to be asymmetry. The initial objective of secured access to the US market being relatively assured, the Canadian government believes that national sovereignty could be threatened by establishing regional institutions that could be dominated by the United States. Finally, the uncertainty variable comes into play here, particularly with regard to the future behavior of the Mexican government. Ottawa appears uncertain as to the real motives of Mexican authorities and how these will impact on the functioning of a new institutional design.

Finally, as for the United States, it should be recalled that NAFTA's main purpose was to provide a blueprint for the harmonization of macroeconomic policies in North America and to act as an instrument for pressure on the multilateral trading negotiations. These objectives being more or less satisfied, Washington has been unresponsive to proposals for changes in the agreement. One reason for this is that Washington believes it would bear the costs of a change to the institutional design, particularly if that meant structured assistance to Mexico. But maybe the most important consideration, which could be called the psychological factor, lies outside the framework designed by Koremenos, Lipson and Snidal and involves two components. First, there is the element of exceptionalism in the US psyche, which was mentioned by Pastor and is at the origin of the unilateralism of US foreign policy. Second, there is a conjectural element associated with the intervention in Iraq and the Bush administration's sense of betrayal as a result of Canada and Mexico's lack of support for US action. In the present context, the combination of both elements works against more structured cooperation on the part of Washington.

On this basis, it is difficult to foresee any changes to the institutional design of NAFTA in the immediate future, at least as regards regional institutions. The institutional design of the regional project in North America can only be modified with Washington's assent, and the chances of that happening during the present US administration are very slim indeed.

NOTES

1. The authors wish to express their gratitude to the Social Sciences and Humanities Research Council of Canada and to the Fonds québécois de recherche sur la société et la culture for financial support of their NAFTA project.
2. See for example 'Floundering in a tariff-free landscape', *The Economist*, 30 November 2002, 31 and Jordan, Pav, 'Mexican farm rescue plan may seek NAFTA Checks', *The Globe and Mail*, 28 April 2003, p. B7.
3. Among the many titles are: Belous, Richard S., and Jonathan Lemco (eds) (1995), *NAFTA as a Model of Development: The Benefits and Costs of Merging High- and Low-Wage Areas*, Albany, State University of New York Press; Blank, Stephen and Jerry Haar (1998), *Making NAFTA Work: US Firms and the New North American Business Environment*, Miami: North–South Center Press, Bonser, Charles F. (ed.) (1991), *Toward a North American Common Market: Problems and Prospects for a New Economic Community*, Boulder, CO: Westview; Bulmer-Thomas, Victor, Nikki Craske and Monica Serrano (eds) (1994), *Mexico and the NAFTA: Who Will Benefit?*, New York: St Martin's Press; Cremeans, John E. (ed.) (1998), *Handbook of North American Industry: NAFTA and the Economics of its Member Nations*, Lanham, MD: Bernan Press; Globerman, Steven, and Michael Walker (1993), *Assessing NAFTA: A Trinational Analysis*, Vancouver: Fraser Institute; Hufbauer, Gary C., and Jeffrey J. Schott (1992), *North American Free Trade: Issues and Recommendations*, Washington, DC: Institute for International Economics; Hufbauer, Gary C., and Jeffrey J. Schott (1993), *NAFTA: An Assessment*, Washington, DC: Institute for International Economics; Reynolds, Clark W., Leonard Waverman and Gerardo Bueno, (eds) (1991), *The Dynamics of North American Trade and Investment: Canada, Mexico and the United States*, Stanford, CA: Stanford University Press; Weintraub, Sidney (1997), *NAFTA at Three: A Progress Report*, Washington, DC: Center for Strategic and International Studies.
4. Barry, Donald, Mark O. Dickerson and James D. Gaisford (eds) (1995), *Toward a North American Community? Canada, the United States and Mexico* Boulder, CO: Westview Press; Blank, Stephen (1993), *The Emerging Architecture of North America*, (Coral, Gables, FL: North–South Center; Doran, Charles F., and Alvin P. Drischler (eds) (1996), *A New North America* Westport, CT: Praeger; Grayson, George (1995), *The North American Free Trade Agreement: Regional Community and the New World Order*, Lanham, MD: University Press of America; Hakim, Peter, and Robert E. Litan (eds) (2002), *The Future of North American Integration, Beyond NAFTA*, Washington, DC: Brookings Institution Press; Hoebing, Joyce, Sidney Weintraub and M. Delal Baer (eds) (1996), *NAFTA and Sovereignty: Tradeoffs for*

Canada, Mexico and the United States, Washington, DC: Center for Strategic and International Studies; and Poitras, Guy (2001), *Inventing North America, Canada, Mexico and the United States*, Boulder, CO: Lynne Rienner Publishers.

5. See for example Doran, Charles F., and Gregory P. Marchildon (eds) (1994), *The NAFTA Puzzle, Political Parties and Trade in North America*, Boulder, CO: Westview Press.
6. Pastor, Robert A., and Rafael Fernandez de Castro (eds) (1998), *The Controversial Pivot, The US Congress and North America*, Washington, DC: Brookings Institution Press.
7. Bertraub, Hermann von (1997), *Negotiating NAFTA: A Mexican Envoy's Account*, Washington papers no. 173, Westport, CT: Praeger-CSIS; Cameron, Maxwell A., and Brian W. Tomlin (2000), *The Making of NAFTA, How the Deal was Done*, Ithaca, NY: Cornell University Press; and Mayer, Frederick W. (1998), *Interpreting NAFTA: The Science and Art of Political Analysis*, New York: Columbia University Press.
8. Inglehart, Ronald, Neil Nevitte and Miguel Basanez (1996), *The North American Trajectory: Cultural, Economic and Political Ties among the United States, Canada and Mexico*, New York: Aldine de Gruyter.
9. Morales, Isidro (1999), 'NAFTA: The governance of economic openness', *Annals*, **565** (September), 35–65.
10. Hufbauer, Gary C., Daniel C. Esty, Diana Orejas, Luis Rubio and Jeffrey Schott (2000), *NAFTA and the Environment: Seven Years Later*, Washington, DC: Institute for International Economics; and Kirton, John (1997), 'NAFTA's trade-environment institutions: regional impact, hemispheric potential', paper presented at the joint meeting of the Mexican Association of International Relations and the International Studies Association, Manzanillo, Mexico, 11–14 December.
11. Andreas, Peter, and Tom Bierstecker (eds) (forthcoming), *Re-Bordering North America? Integration and Exclusion After 9/11*, New York: Routledge; and Klepak, Hal (2002), 'Hemispheric security after the towers went down', Canadian Foundation for the Americas (FOCAL), policy paper FPP-02–4, Ottawa.
12. Chambre des Communes, Canada, *Partenaires en Amérique du Nord, Cultiver les relations du Canada avec les États-Unis et le Mexique,* Rapport du Comité permanent des affaires étrangères et du commerce international, Ottawa, December 2002. For the list of 39 recommendations see pp. 307–18.
13. Pastor, Robert A. (2001), *Toward a North American Community. Lessons from the Old World for the New*, Washington, DC: Institute for International Economics, pp. 2–3.
14. Wilson-Forsberg, Stacey (2002), 'Canada and Mexico: searching for common ground on the North American continent', FOCAL Policy Paper 02–3, Ottawa, FOCAL; and Maria Teresa Garcia-Segovia de Madero (2002), 'Remarks by the Mexican Ambassador to Canada', *NAMI News*, Santa Fe, NM, The North American Institute, 3, pp. 5–8.
15. See Government of Canada, response to the Parliamentary Committee Report 'Partners in North America: advancing Canada's relations with the United States and Mexico', Ottawa, 7 May 2003. According to Canadian journalist Peter Newman, however, both the Prime Minister and the Deputy Prime Minister made separate declarations at the end of October 2002 stating that the time had come to renegotiate the trade deal. For his part, Canada's International Trade Minister, Pierre Pettigrew, apparently announced that 'he has actively been discussing the redrafting of the NAFTA agreement with US Trade Representative Bob Zoellick'. See *Maclean's*, 2 December 2002, p. 46. No official statement was made however.
16. Grinspun, Ricardo, and Robert Kreklewich (1999), 'Institutions, power relations, and unequal integration in the Americas: NAFTA as deficient institutionally', in Kristen Appendini and Sven Bislev (eds), *Economic Integration in NAFTA and the EU*, New York: St Martin's Press, 1999, pp. 17–33.
17. Dobson, Wendy (2002), *Shaping the Future of the North American Economic Space: A Framework for Action*, commentary no. 162, Toronto: C.D. Howe Institute, p. 1. 'Paradoxically, a window of opportunity is now open because of the United States' 'current openness to its friends and neighbors' (p. 1). What difference a year can make.
18. Pastor, *Toward a North American Community*, chs 5 and 6.
19. Ibid., pp. 99–103.

20. Given all the material that has been produced on the NAFTA for the past ten years or so, one would think that the informed public understands clearly what is involved in this trade agreement. However, even seasoned observers such as Peter Newman misinterpret the NAFTA by seeing it as a customs union! See for example Newman, Peter C. (2002), 'Beware of freer trade', *Maclean's*, 2 December, p. 46.
21. Pastor, *Toward a North American Community*, p. 96.
22. Stephen Woolcock (1999), 'The multilateral trading system in the new millennium', in Brian Hocking and Steven McGuire (eds), *Trade Politics, International, Domestic and Regional Perspectives*, London: Routledge, pp. 26–39.
23. Cameron and Tomlin, *The Making of NAFTA*, p. 232.
24. Koremenos, Barbara, Charles Lipson and Duncan Snidal (2001), 'The rational design of international institutions', *International Organization*, **55**, 4 (autumn), 761–99.
25. Abbott, Kenneth W., Robert O. Keohane, Andrew Moravcsik, Anne-Marie Slaughter and Duncan Snidal (2000), 'The concept of legalization', *International Organization*, **54**, 3 (summer), 401–19 and particularly 415–18.
26. Koremenos et al., 'The rational design of international institutions', pp. 770–73.
27. Pastor, *Toward a North American Community*, p. 28, table 2.2.
28. Article 2204 of the NAFTA foresees the eventual accession of 'any country or group of countries' but no serious attempt at enlarging it has been pursued.
29. Ibid., p. 29.
30. Grinspun and Kreklewich, 'Institutions, Power Relations, and Unequal Integration in the Americas'.
31. Pastor, *Toward a North American Community*, pp. 83–4.
32. Weintraub, *NAFTA at Three*, p. 69.
33. 'NAFTA', pp. 35–65.
34. As is also the case in the MERCOSUR, See for example Bernier, Ivan, and Martin Roy (1999), 'NAFTA and MERCOSUR: two competing models?', in Gordon Mace, Louis Bélanger and contributors, *The Americas in Transition: The Contours of Regionalism*, Boulder, CO: Lynne Rienner Publishers, pp. 69–91.
35. Bernier and Roy, 'NAFTA and MERCOSUR', pp. 72–3.
36. Abbott, Frederick M. (2000), 'NAFTA and the legalization of world politics: a case study', *International Organization*, **54** (3), 524.
37. See Abbott et al., 'The concept of legalization', pp. 404–8.
38. Abbot offers a different interpretation by characterizing the NAFTA as hard legalization. The difference lies in the interpretation of the delegation dimension of the agreement, which he sees as moderate and which we consider as low. The difference of interpretation is due essentially to the fact that Abbot focuses basically on the dispute-settlement mechanisms of Chapters 19 and 20 while we attribute more importance to the overall institutional structure of the NAFTA. See Abbott, 'NAFTA and the legalization of world politics', pp. 519–47 and particularly pp. 535–40.
39. The 700-page document. On the policy convergence approach, see the excellent contribution of McDougall, John N. (2000), 'National differences and the NAFTA', *International Joumal*, **55**, 2 (spring), 281–91.
40. See, among others, Cameron and Tomlin, *The Making of NAFTA*, and Mayer, *Interpreting NAFTA*.
41. Belous, Richard S., and Richard S. Hartley (eds) (1990), *The Growth of Regional Trading Blocs in the Global Economy*, Washington, DC: National Planning Association, and Brand, Diana (1992), 'Regional bloc formation and world trade', *Intereconomics*, (November/December), 274–81.
42. Pentland, Charles (1991), 'Europe 1992 and the Canadian response', in Fen O. Hampson and C.J. Maule, (eds), *Canada Among Nations 1990–1991: After the Cold War*, Ottawa, ON: Carleton University Press, pp. 125–44.
43. See for example Nollen, Stanley D., and Dennis P. Quinn (1994), 'Free trade, fair trade, strategic trade and protectionism in the US Congress, 1987–88', *International Organization*, **48**, 491–525; Cline, William R. (1982), *Reciprocity: A New Approach to World Trade Policy?* Washington, DC: Institute for International Economics; and Bhagwati, Jagdish N., and Hugh

T. Patrick (eds) (1990), *Aggressive Unilateralism: America's 301 Trade Policy and the World Trading System*, Ann Arbor: The University of Michigan Press.

44. Hart, Michael, Bill Dymond and Colin Robertson (1994), *Decision at Midnight, Inside the Canada–US Free Trade Negotiations*, Vancouver: UBC Press, ch. 1.
45. Abbott, 'NAFTA and the legalization of world politics', p. 522.
46. Cameron and Tomlin, *The Making of NAFTA*, pp. 51–2.
47. For many in the Bush and Clinton administrations, the period from 1988 to 1994 was also seen as a 'turning point', a moment of 'convergence of values' between the United States and Latin America which was an important factor in the attitude of US policy-makers at the time. See Mace, Gordon, 'The origin, nature and scope of the hemispheric project', in Mace et al., *The Americas in Transition*, pp. 30–1.
48. Abbott, 'NAFTA and the legalization of world politics', p. 522.
49. Ibid., p. 523.
50. Winham, Gilbert R. and Elisabeth DeBoer-Ashworth (2000), 'Asymmetry in negotiating the Canada–US Free Trade Agreement, 1985–1987', in William I. Zartman and Jeffrey Z. Rubin (eds), *Power and Negotiation*, Ann Arbor: The University of Michigan Press, p. 39 and Cameron, Maxwell A. (1997), 'North American Free Trade Negotiations: liberalization games between asymmetric players', *European Journal of International Relations,* **3**, 1 (March), pp. 105–39.
51. Abbott, 'NAFTA and the legalization of world politics', p. 522. On Mexico see also Cockroft, James D. (1988), *Mexico's Hope, An Encounter with Politics and History*, New York: Monthly Review Press, ch. 2.
52. See for example Cooper, Andrew F., 'NAFTA and the politics of regional trade', in Hocking and McGuire, *Trade Politics*, pp. 229–45 and particularly pp. 232–3.
53. For example, see Pastor, *Toward a North American Community*, pp. 16–18. 'The main argument for deepening NAFTA, however, is the simplest: *Problems can no longer be contained in any of the three countries, and the new opportunities benefit all three*' (ibid. 18, emphasis in original).
54. Ibid., pp. 83–7.
55. Government of Mexico (2001), 'Toward a partnership for prosperity: the Guanajuato Proposal', joint communiqué. 16 February.
56. Casteneda, Jorge (2002), 'It takes three to tango', *The Globe and Mail*, 4 March, p. A13.
57. 'While Mexico may be quick to establish institutions as a solution to problems, the United States, and to an extent Canada, are equally quick to dismiss them', Wilson-Forsberg, Stacey (2002), 'Canada and Mexico: searching for common ground on the North American continent', FOCAL Policy Paper, Ottawa (February), 6.
58. Dobson, *Shaping the Future*, 'Canada's goal should be to achieve customs-union-and-common-market-like integration without full scale harmonization and the resulting erosion of political independence', p. 25.
59. Clarkson, Stephen (2002), 'Time to break free (trade)', *The Globe and Mail*, 27 September, p. A13. See also Clarkson, Stephen (2002), 'What's in it for us?', *The Globe and Mail*, 6 May, p. A15 and Dobbin, Murray (2002), 'Prescription for decline', *The Globe and Mail*, 25 October, p. A15.
60. Laghi, Brian (2002), 'Health system vulnerable to NAFTA, report says', *The Globe and Mail*, 22 October, p. A7.
61. 'Big bargain: trading economy for security', *The Globe and Mail*, 22 April 2002, p. A12.
62. Hart, Michael, and Bill Dymond (2002), 'When it comes to trade, who's fooling whom?', *The Globe and Mail*, 9 October, p. A15.
63. McKenna, Barrie (2002), 'Security zone will aid trade, Mulroney says', *The Globe and Mail*, 10 December, p. A16.
64. Dobson, Wendy (2003), 'The next big idea, trade can brush in a new border', *The Globe and Mail*, 21 January, p. A15.
65. Golden, Anne (2003), 'Building a new partnership', *The Globe and Mail*, March, p. A11.
66. Fagan, Drew (2002), 'Sweet continental harmony', *The Globe and Mail*, 29 October, p. A19.
67. Chambre des communes du Canada, *Parlenaires en Amérique du Nord*, ch. 4.

68. Martin, Paul (2003), 'Un effort constant', *La Presse*, 2 May, p. A9.
69. Fagan, Drew (2002), 'Continental integration complicated, to Mexico's dismay', *The Globe and Mail*, 4 March, p. B8. There is also an attitude of mistrust in some circles based on the perception that Mexico is using the North American community card only to obtain a privileged relationship with the United States, to the eventual detriment of Canada.
70. Cited in Golden, 'Building a new partnership'. Giffin was commenting on the Dobson proposal.
71. Bush, George W. (2002), 'The national security strategy of the United States of America', September, accessed at http://www.whitehouse.gov/nsc/nss.pdf.
72. The text of the declaration can be found at www.whitehouse.gov/news/releases/2002/01/
73. Kitchen, Veronica M. (2003), 'Re-thinking the Canada–United States security community', paper presented at the Annual Conference of the International Studies Association, Portland, OR, 1 March. On the Mexican problematique, see Hussain, Imtiaz (2003), 'Back to the security future? 9/11 and the fate of regional economic integration', paper presented at the Annual Conference of the International Studies Association, Portland, OR, February.
74. Pastor, *Toward a North American Community*, p. 149
75. Wilson-Forsberg, Stacey (2002), 'North American integration: back to the basics', FOCAL Policy Paper, Ottawa (August), p. 4.
76. Reding, Andrew (2003), 'Why Washington is isolated in its own back yard', *The Globe and Mail*, 25 March, p. A17.
77. Koremenos at al., 'The rational design of international institutions', pp. 773–9.
78. Jordan, 'Mexican farm rescue plan'.

6. The future of MERCOSUR

Heinz G. Preusse

INTRODUCTION

MERCOSUR, like most other projects of regional integration, comprises both political and economic objectives. The most important political objectives have been the de-escalation of long-standing rivalries and distrust between Argentina and Brazil and the formation of a politically more influential entity of Latin American countries in the globalizing world (and in America). While the former aspect had been prevalent during the pre-foundation period of the 1980s and progress in this field is evident, the attainment of the latter objective is still pending. In fact, to enhance the political impact of Latin America on the international arena by means of regional integration will only have a serious chance if MERCOSUR and its potential enlargements develop into a politically stable and economically prosperous region. Thus, it is not surprising that the economic conditions for successful regional integration have become a centerpiece in the discussion of MERCOSUR issues from the implementation period up to now.

At the time of writing this chapter the economic prospects of MERCOSUR are gloomy. When the turbulences of the Asian (1997) and the Brazilian crises (1999) seemed to calm down, the breakdown of the Argentine currency board almost destroyed any hope for a rapid recovery of the region. Instead, Uruguay, Paraguay, and even Brazil are on the brink of disaster. On the face of it, the misery of MERCOSUR appears to be the result of these external events. However, a closer look reveals some important deficiencies of the integration scheme itself, which have contributed to the severity of the present crisis.

I will argue here that these deficiencies are structural by their very nature. If this proposition holds, these deficiencies will not only pose constraints on the cyclical recovery of the region but may in fact threaten the long-run viability of the whole MERCOSUR project. Put differently, I shall judge the future of MERCOSUR on the basis of an analysis of these structural (conceptual) weaknesses. The following presentation will explore four fundamental questions:

1. What kind of regional integration agreement did the architects of MERCOSUR intend to establish?

2. What has been done to make this concept work?
3. Which are the main structural weaknesses of MERCOSUR?
4. What can be done to overcome them?

Finally, some conclusions will be drawn.

WHAT KIND OF REGIONAL INTEGRATION AGREEMENT DID THE ARCHITECTS OF MERCOSUR INTEND TO ESTABLISH?

The foundation of MERCOSUR has not been independent from the major structural reforms in Latin America of the 1980s. These reforms should transform the economies from the inward-looking and highly interventionist development strategies (import substitution) of the post-war period into open market-oriented economies.[1] MERCOSUR was originally designed as a conditioned opening up strategy, which can be interpreted as an integral part of the overall concept. This is to say, MERCOSUR has been founded under the principles of 'open regionalism' (Bergsten 1997, Reynolds 1997) and should eventually lead to a common market with a low degree of external protection. Further to trade liberalization, the initial concept of MERCOSUR stands for an open capital account and, in particular, a modern FDI regime that recognizes the principal virtues of multinational enterprises (MNEs) for developing countries.[2]

The idea to develop a common market indicates that its proponents have also been sympathetic to the concept of 'deeper integration' (Lawrence 1996) and intend to broaden the scope of intra-regional cooperation beyond purely economic issues.[3] Unfortunately, the concept of deeper integration is inherently ambiguous because it comprises quite different options for the extension of regional integration beyond the free trade area (FTA) and the customs union (CU) status. This makes it difficult to identify the exact meaning of deeper integration in the case of MERCOSUR without going into a detailed analysis. And even such an analysis would soon face the problem that there is no definite answer yet to the question how the 'common market' MERCOSUR should finally be organized, once non-committal political declarations are omitted.

In order to answer the lead question of this chapter it is advisable to restrict the analysis to some basic principles which have been recorded in the treaty of Asuncion. These are (see Kaltenthaler and Mora 2002, pp. 75–6):

1. trade liberalization between member states,
2. the formation of a common external tariff (CET), which implies a customs union,

3. the coordination of macroeconomic policies,
4. the adoption of sectoral agreements.

Principles 1 to 3 define openness between member states and outsiders and emphasize the importance of stable and reliable macroeconomic conditions (a relatively stable real exchange rate, in particular) for the integration of local markets.

The fourth point is more difficult to interpret. The explicit inclusion of sector policies suggests that the founders of MERCOSUR were aware of the difficulties which arise for distinct parts of local economies from opening-up, and they claimed specific treatment for these sectors from the beginning. While the definition of specific sensitive areas which should receive special treatment is a common practice in trade negotiations, it is the concrete handling of these sectors that matters. Building on the spirit of open regionalism one would expect special treatment *first* to be limited to a small number of exceptions, and *second* to be subject to strict phase-in mechanisms which definitely confirm that special treatment remains a transitory phenomenon.

In fact, experience warns against too much emphasis on sectoral policies. These measures not only intensify the discriminatory character of regional integration but tend to be self-perpetuating, once the beneficiaries get accustomed to protection. As a result, a proliferation of protection rather than the stimulation of flourishing open (regional) markets takes place. Skepticism concerning sectoral (industrial) policies is especially appropriate in view of the Latin American experience under import substitution regimes. Consequently, the definition and management of sectoral policies in MERCOSUR should be scrutinized carefully.

Another important aspect of deeper economic integration is the institutional framework under which the agreement will have to develop. This framework is both important for the functioning of the agreement at any time and for the development of more profound structures of coordination as integration proceeds. Generally, one would expect a shallow institutional structure to be appropriate for a simple FTA, and a more complex structure to be required as integration deepens. Likewise, an initial negotiation and implementation period which is dominated by a continuous political decision-making process and adaptive reforms should give way to a rules-based system as the integration process proceeds.

Last but not least, the concept of 'deeper integration' maintains that the adaptation of the nation states and their economies to the conditions of the integrated market stimulates the creation of new and efficient institutions which are appropriate to overcome traditional bottlenecks of development. It is clear that the effect of integration on the modernization of institutions (and on the reform process of the participating countries in general) may have an important positive impact on the growth performance of the region.[4]

WHAT HAS BEEN DONE TO MAKE THIS CONCEPT WORK?

It has been extensively documented that MERCOSUR started a most successful process of creating an FTA between 1991 and 1994. During this period tariffs and non-tariff barriers have been rapidly dismantled both externally and internally. In 1995 the customs union came into being and, despite being incomplete, this event appeared to demonstrate the firm commitment of the member countries to the integration project. Also the successful implementation of the '*plano real*' that has quickly converted Brazil into an economy with relatively healthy macro-economic conditions,[5] and the growing credibility of the Argentine 'Currency Board' have stimulated the creditworthiness of the integration process and attracted new investors. Last but not least, a number of regional infrastructure and educational projects helped to create the kind of community spirit that was appropriate to build sympathy for the project in the population.

Despite some hesitance on behalf of the ongoing political progress of region building after 1995 intra-regional trade still grew rapidly in 1996–1997 and so did FDI inflows. Consequently, in studies concentrating on this period, MERCOSUR receives excellent grades and has been celebrated as a prototype of the growth-promoting concept of open regionalism (Devlin and Estevadeordal 2001, Estevadeordal et al. 2000).

Meanwhile, the situation has changed dramatically both in terms of integration policies and economic performance. The member countries, in order to re-build walls against inter- and intra-regional competition resorted more and more to old-fashioned protectionist measures. Argentina and Brazil in particular, the leading protagonists of regional integration, began to raise tariffs, re-activated non-tariff barriers (NTBs), and withdrew concessions unilaterally and without prior consultation, on which they had already agreed.

It does not come as a surprise under these conditions that the hotly debated and repeatedly delayed automotive program, too, became a mirror image of the general situation. Rather than designing a future-oriented program to integrate the automotive sector into the concept of open regionalism the agreement of June 2000 forced the industry into a stiff corset of managed trade and will raise external protection by a pre-fixed phase-in mechanism. This program is in clear contradiction to the phase-out procedures of the early integration period.

Critics also point out that under the pressure of the economic downturn the weak institutional framework of MERCOSUR has been unable to prevent a growing politicization of the integration policies. Increasing politicization, in turn, downgraded the significance of any systematic process of region building based on the principles of open regionalism and opened the door to rivalry protectionism among the partner countries. When new macroeconomic turbulences hit the region (the US and world recession in 2001 and the breakdown of the Argentine currency board in 2002), the adverse developments in the field of microeconomic regulations and the deficiencies in institution building became disclosed and the future of MERCOSUR began to be openly discussed.

To sum up, after an impressive record before the implementation of the customs union in 1995, the MERCOSUR performance slowed down in the second half of the decade. In 2002 it is apparent that MERCOSUR has lost most of the credibility that it had gained during the successful start-up period. Both external and internal tariffs are higher today than in 1995. NTBs have reconquered the regional markets and restrictive sector agreements are strangling much of intra-regional trade. As a result, intra-regional re-allocation of resources has become risky, locational decisions made on the strength of the political commitment to open regionalism proved to be wrong, and investment slowed down. Macroeconomic policy coordination had never worked, and this has provoked extreme swings in real exchange rates which have added to uncertainty (Preusse 2001). Last but not least, the institutional framework of MERCOSUR is not appropriate to managing the region efficiently. Consequently a high degree of politicization substitutes for a reliable rules-based system. The problems arising from this state of affairs are felt the more painfully, the less favorable the external conditions are. But they will not become extinct automatically when the external environment improves. Thus, the need for structural reforms will stay on the agenda.

WHICH ARE THE MAIN STRUCTURAL WEAKNESS OF MERCOSUR?

Given the present state of affairs it is unlikely that MERCOSUR will survive without a comprehensive removal of its most severe weaknesses. According to the analysis in the previous chapters, three major obstacles to a better performance of the region can be identified:

1. institutional weakness,
2. missing macroeconomic coordination,
3. the retreat of national trade policies to unilateralism and increased protectionism.

In what follows the first and the second obstacles will be discussed only briefly. Emphasis, instead, will be put on the third topic.

INSTITUTIONS

Until today MERCOSUR is operated on a highly informal institutional basis. The highest decision-making body is the Common Market Council (CMC) which consists of the ministers of foreign affairs and the economy. This council is complemented by the Common Market Group (CMG) which consists of another selection of high ranked officials. Coordination and administration is done in the tiny MERCOSUR secretariat located in Montevideo.

In both institutions political representatives are prevalent. In essence, this means that MERCOSUR is managed politically rather than by commonly agreed and binding principles (rules-based system). This impression is underlined by the fact that these groups are themselves constrained by the presidents (from Brazil and Argentina in particular) who used to decide on vital questions of the MERCOSUR project on a strictly personal level. One can conclude from this situation that the present institutional provisions of MERCOSUR are weak and still heavily biased by intimate and personalized political decision-making procedures. This political configuration may have been adequate (and even helpful) during the inauguration period, but as integration proceeds and the day-to-day management of increasing interdependence becomes a central task, it will become less and less supportive.

In fact, from a political point of view, institutional weakness may become a major restriction upon the ongoing integration process because it hinders participatory decision-making procedures among the partner countries. In particular, for a common market with close political and economic relations to function smoothly, it is indispensable to establish a transparent system of checks and balances that allows for democratic voting procedures and the adequate articulation of minority groups. Vasconcelos has emphasized the importance of these kinds of provisions 'to help balance power across the participating states and protect them from excessively strong leadership by any member'.[6] In the case of MERCOSUR a rules-based power-balancing mechanism appears to be particularly important in order to manage the two-tiered asymmetry between Argentina and Brazil vis-à-vis Paraguay and Uruguay, and Brazil *vis-à-vis* all of her partners. Though the institutional deficits of MERCOSUR have been recognized even in Brazil,[7] it will be most difficult to come to a solution of the problem as long as the sovereignty of the nation state remains an overriding principle of foreign (economic) policy in the region.

What should be emphasized in this context is that the relative importance of institution building is not independent from the type of regional agreement that is envisaged. As a matter of rule, the 'optimal institutional content' of preferential regional agreements varies with the profundity of integration. In turn, the maximum attainable level of regional institutions and cooperation varies with the readiness of each single member country to share sovereignty. Thus, the readiness to share sovereignty determines the scope for institution building and this should determine the optimal degree of (deeper) regional integration. Following this argument, one would expect a low level of readiness to share sovereignty to correspond with a lower level of integration. In the most restricted case this would make it advisable to limit economic integration to a simple FTA. A high degree of willingness to share sovereignty, in turn, is conducive to the development of more sophisticated forms of cooperation and supranational region building and may eventually lead to the successful formation of a deeper integration area.

Applying these principles to MERCOSUR, and taking into consideration that under increased economic pressure all four countries quickly fell back to unilateralism suggests that an integration level beyond a FTA is likely to run into serious problems of credibility and reliability under the present conditions. Only from a more visionary perspective might one be willing to speculate that integration building is itself a dynamic process that helps to create more profound regional sentiments over time. In this case, the viability of the customs union may at least be within the range of the realistic options. However, even deeper forms of integration which call for binding supranational institutions and more demanding forms of sovereignty sharing are unlikely to become a reality in the foreseeable future. Following this argument, closing the gap between aspiration and political reality (and at the same time pushing for a more open minded stance in sovereignty-sharing commitments) would be one important approach to revitalizing MERCOSUR.

MACROECONOMIC COORDINATION

The problem of missing macroeconomic coordination has been discussed extensively in the literature. Without going into details of this discussion it is important to note that the different concepts of macroeconomic management, for example the Argentine currency board and the Brazilian system of managed floating, turned out to be a major factor of uncertainty for the determination of reliable competitive positions within the region.[8] After the Brazilian crisis of January 1999, the incompatibility of both concepts could not be overlooked any more and eventually turned out to be one of the driving forces of the Argentine crash of 2001/2[9], which by now has itself become a major threat for MERCOSUR.

It is worth noting that after the release of the currency board in Argentina the fundamentally oppositing positions on macroeconomic coordination of Argentina and the rest of the MERCOSUR countries do not seem to exist any more. Not withstanding the severe new problems that the Argentine crash has brought, this means that macroeconomic coordination, based on similar ideas of stabilization, public and exchange rate policies, may come to be realized more easily, once the present shock situation has been brought under control.[10] Thus, if the region succeeds in stabilizing the crisis there may be a better chance now of eliminating this second obstacle to integration of the 1990s by agreeing on a regional macroeconomic framework that allows for the management of stable real exchange rates.

INTEGRATION AND TRADE

Provided that, first, some minimum standards of macroeconomic coordination can be established, and, second, that an institutional framework can be installed which allows for the substitution of a more rules-based system for political muddling-through strategies and personal (presidential) decision-making procedures, the reorganization of trade (and investment) policies remains the crucial reform project of MERCOSUR. Taking into consideration the sobering experience with import-substitution policies in less developed countries (LDCs), and in Latin America in particular, and the existential threat that the formation of closed trading blocs would pose for the world economy, the revitalization of MERCOSUR is conditional on the reversal of the existing trade policy trends. More precisely, if regionalism in the Southern Cone should again become a promising future option at all, this will definitely be in the form of 'open regionalism'. So far, the trade policy agenda of MERCOSUR is fairly clear. It will simply have to return to its original objectives.

What seems to be not so clear, however, is the exact opening-up strategy that MERCOSUR should follow. During the first decade of region building this strategy had been based on the creation of so-called 'intra-industry trade' IIT). *IIT within the region* should become the lead strategy for the development of trade and international competitiveness. This notion has been derived from the observation of trade and specialization structures in advanced industrialized countries, Europe in particular, which shows specialization *within* narrowly defined industries to be particularly marked (SITC three to five-digit levels).[11] This kind of trade specialization does not follow differentials of factor endowments as in the case of the traditional trade model, but rests on the exploitation of economies of scale (ECS) in differentiated product markets.[12]

For the MERCOSUR countries, and Brazil in particular, the charm of IIT is based on two interrelated aspects. First, specialization and trade within industries seems to open up a large potential for national producers to react to trade liberalization without the need to restructure between industries. Thus, the existing structures of (industrial) production can by and large be saved. Second, the kind of adjustment procedures which have to be undertaken in IIT are also believed to be less costly for both capital and labor because the need to acquire new production knowledge in different industries will be minimized. Last but not least, the costs of regional factor movements are relatively low when adjustment takes place within the same industry (or firm). In turn, specialization based on inter-industry trade (INT) relations, that is essentially North–South trade, is thought to be a second-best opening-up strategy. The point is that, in this latter case, structural adjustment takes place predominantly between industries and according to comparative advantage. And this is perceived to be economically more costly and politically less attractive.

In fact, Brazil (MERCOSUR), by opening up after decades of import-substituting industrialization, entered world market competition with relatively highly diversified structures of industrial production, which pay virtually no tribute to comparative advantage (see for example Yeats 1989). Thus, trading freely with countries having different factor endowments will surely enforce major structural adjustments. Industries with a comparative advantage on the world market can be expected to expand, while those with a comparative disadvantage are likely to shrink.

Some proponents of MERCOSUR, by pointing to the allegedly soft structural adjustment procedures in IIT, have concluded that MERCOSUR should enforce these structures in order to save as many industries as possible from restructuring and to keep adjustment costs low. Only after an extended learning period should the more sophisticated intra-industrial specialization structures of MERCOSUR be exposed to world market competition.

In order to check the validity of this argument it is necessary to analyse the relative importance of inter- and intra-industry trade for LDCs more seriously. INT which can be interpreted as Heckscher–Ohlin (HO) trade in the case of manufactured exports, derives static benefits (gains from trade) from the exchange of goods and services at different relative prices and from specialization according to comparative advantage. Dynamically, the gains from INT are seen to be the result of the exposure of national producers to stiffer international competition and the drive of export demand on the global market. These effects may induce investment and help to exploit ECS more forcefully. Last but not least INT, enlarges the capacity to import high quality/low price inputs and technology (Conolly 1999, Conolly and Gunther 1999). Differentials of factor endowments are the motor for these kinds of gains from trade, and they are obviously the more pronounced the larger the differences in factor endowments and the less competition that existed on the local market before trade opened up. Put differently, INT offers little or no gains from trade if factor endowments are equal between the trading partners. This is the case, for example, in North–North trade where IIT prevails. The (static) gains from North–North trade, then, derive basically from the exploitation of ECS in differentiated markets.

From a dynamic perspective, things are less transparent. If IIT has no effect on competition relative to INT, the effect of ECS on productivity and the improved choice of consumers (and producers) among highly differentiated products are the only significant benefits to be expected from IIT. However, it has been argued that competition between firms which compete on similar products within narrow market segments might be more challenging than under the typical conditions of INT. One reason is that entry barriers may in fact be low in these markets. Another one is that IIT trade and specialization among industrialized countries prevail in high tech sectors where stiff innovational competition is present. If competition is stronger in industries where IIT prevails, relative to the competitive situation in INT, an additional welfare-increasing effect of IIT has to be taken into consideration.[13]

The crucial question for the MERCOSUR trade strategy is, whether a country (a region) does really have the option to decide between INT and IIT as its dominant trade strategy. For industrialized countries the situation is clear. They employ both strategies at a time. Because North–South trade is limited by market size in the LDCs, North–North trade evolves as a complement and adds to the gains from INT.

For LDCs the situation is different. They have a competitive advantage in North–South trade. And if they are ready to exploit their comparative advantages, the world markets are large and eager to absorb these goods. But LDCs are not well equipped for IIT because product differentiation is low in low-income countries. Accordingly, the scope for specialization within industries is limited and so is the potential for intra-industry specialization and trade. In a dynamic interpretation this means that the enforcement of IIT within a regional market consisting of low-income countries may produce an initial boost in IIT (when artificial barriers to trade are eliminated), but the scope for further expansion will be limited.

Sustained trade expansion will be even more challenged if IIT comes at the expense of INT, because technological upgrading is fostered most efficiently in North–South trade (and by expanding high quality imports from the North). The IIT strategy, therefore, runs into quite a number of difficulties. First, by scaling down North–South trade relations, it diminishes the inflow of technologies from the North. Additional exports from out of the sectors which are engaged in IIT cannot substitute for this loss because they are not competitive internationally (that is, outside the region). Second, by scaling down technology-bearing imports from (advanced economies) abroad, the upgrading process within the industries which are inter-linked by IIT on the regional level will also slow down. Third, many industries for which IIT specialization is important are depending on larger markets than a common LDC region can offer. The exploitation of ECS will, therefore, remain limited compared to the possibilities that the world market offers (and which competitors take advantage of), and productivity levels remain low.[14]

The idea, therefore, to privilege IIT within the region in order to avoid a costly restructuring process between industries is flawed.[15] By avoiding inter-industry restructuring and pushing intra-industry trade (and specialization), inefficient sectors of the national industry are being nurtured at the expense of efficient industries, and the important benefits from North–South trade are neglected. As the technology transfer from the North slows down, technological upgrading, too, will diminish and convergence of competitiveness towards the world market level will not take place. In the end, this IIT strategy is likely to run into similar problems as the import-substitution strategy which it had been intended to overcome.

Three objections might be raised against this diagnosis. First, in the case of MERCOSUR it could be argued that the region covers a relatively large geographical area and income per capita is already at the average emerging market level. Thus, markets may be sufficiently large to provide the scope for the simultaneous exploitation of product differentiation and economies of scale, that is necessary for IIT to evolve. Second, measured IIT coefficients indicate that IIT already plays a certain role in MERCOSUR. Third, imports from outside the region grew particularly rapidly for most of the 1990s so that technology transfer should not have been limited by the expansion of IIT.

On closer inspection these arguments cannot bear the facts. First, it is correct to argue that, because of the relatively high level of income per capita in Argentina (before the crash) and the sheer size of Brazil in terms of geography and population, MERCOSUR is in a favorable situation compared to a CU formed by typical small LDCs. Nevertheless, this observation is not sufficient to dampen down the concern that IIT will be limited because of its market size. In fact, Brazil (MERCOSUR) is still not large enough in terms of purchasing power to develop a sophisticated system of intra-industrial specialization. A simple comparison of the absolute size of GDP of MERCOSUR with that of some advanced industrialized countries (regions) may clarify this point. In the year 2000, the combined GDP of MERCOSUR was US$908 billion. Brazil accounted for US$596 billion, Argentina for US$285 billion, Uruguay for US$20 billion and Paraguay for US$7 billion respectively. This combined product of MERCOSUR is smaller than that of Italy alone (US$1.068 billion), that of Brazil is smaller than that of Canada (US$690 billion), and that of Argentina is smaller than that of the Netherlands. Germany alone has a GDP that is more than twice that of MERCOSUR. But no one in Germany, Canada or Italy would propose a national IIT specialization. On the contrary, Europe has become unified exactly because modern industrial markets require a much larger size than a single country, even a large one, can provide. The same holds true for Canada which entered NAFTA and kept markets open to non-NAFTA countries.

Second, IIT coefficients are available on the three-digit SITC level from the MERCOSUR Report 2000–2001 (see Table 6.1). They show that IIT is relatively high on average in SITC one-digit groups 5 (chemicals and similar products) and 7 (machines and transport equipment). But they are low in groups 6 (manufactures by type of material) and 8 (various manufactured articles). To get a better understanding of the meaning of these coefficients, two things can be done. One is to compare these indicators with those of the highly developed countries in Europe. Drawing on data from Nunnenkamp et al. (1994), IIT coefficients in Europe in 1991 were between 78.5 per cent in clothing and 96.4 per cent in road vehicles. These figures suggest that IIT in MERCOSUR is still in an infant stage.

Next, it is indicative to check how the coefficients have changed over time. In Europe, IIT coefficients have risen continuously since the 1960s because growing income and increased integration of the European Market offered a large potential for specialization. Comparing the development of the MERCOSUR coefficients for 1990 and 2000 with the European experience is sobering. There are only small increases in chemicals (from 0.64 in 1990 to 0.71 in 2000) and machines (from 0.62 to 0.66), but a reduction in manufactures by type of material (from 0.38 to 0.35) and various manufactured articles (from 0.40 to 0.33). That is, by and large, the share of IIT has been stagnating over the 1990s. Combining these findings of relatively low and stagnant IIT coefficients supports the view that the growth potential for IIT at the present stage of economic development of MERCOSUR is not impressive. This conclusion is strengthened by two other observations. One is that IIT in the most important categories (5 and 7) mainly consists of trade in intermediate goods which, in the case of automobiles at least, has been enforced by strict trade-balancing regulations rather than efficiency-based firm decisions. The other is, that trade in intermediate products is most often based on vertical product differentiation which is particularly prone to include 'false' IIT (Blanes and Martin 2000). Altogether, it can be concluded from these observations that IIT has not developed the dynamic trade forces expected by the proponents of this strategy.

Third, imports from non-member (industrialized) countries have indeed grown rapidly during the 1990s. This fact has occasionally been taken as evidence that MERCOSUR is indeed an 'open' region that has no problems to finance technology-bearing imports from abroad. There are also some reservations to be made against this argument. One point is that, leaving capital flows aside, imports must be financed out of export receipts. When exports and imports are balanced politically or by means of IIT within MERCOSUR, these trade activities do not release any net receipts from intra-regional trade which can be used to finance extra-regional imports. Thus, when extra-regional exports are stagnating because IT is discriminated against, extra-regional imports will be depressed, too.

Table 6.1 MERCOSUR: Trends in intra-industrial trade (Grubel and Lloyd Index), 1990–2000

SITC	Description	1990	1991	1992	1993	1994	1995	1996	1997	1998	1999	2000	Trade in 2000 (%)
5	Chemical and similar products	0.64	0.65	0.61	0.46	0.50	0.57	0.62	0.59	0.66	0.74	0.71	18.3
6	Manufactures, by type of material	0.38	0.28	0.17	0.22	0.27	0.42	0.46	0.44	0.40	0.38	0.35	20.1
7	Machines and transport equipment	0.62	0.57	0.41	0.58	0.65	0.73	0.66	0.69	0.65	0.69	0.66	54.1
8	Various manufactured articles	0.40	0.64	0.36	0.29	0.33	0.60	0.62	0.63	0.53	0.38	0.33	7.5
	Total SITC 5–8												100.0

Source: Taccone J. and U. Nogueira, eds. 2001. *MERCOSUR Report 2000–2001* (Buenos Aires: INTAL), p. 35.

The second point is that capital imports may be used to compensate for the gap in foreign currency as long as foreign investors are willing to engage in the region. This has been the case in MERCOSUR as long as the integration project was believed to be a successful venture internationally. In fact, FDI inflows into MERCOSUR have increased dramatically from an average of US$ 2.23 billion (in constant 2000 prices) during the 1980s to US$ 6.29 billion from 1991–1995 and US$35.38 billion from 1996–2000.[16] There are doubts, however, whether the latter figure is a reliable indicator for the present (and future) attractiveness of the region for FDI. A year-on-year breakdown of the figures reveals that, after the peak year 1999, FDI inflows have decreased from US$53.0 to US$26.0 billion in 2001 and are expected to decrease even further in 2002 (see Table 6.2). While this decrease is of course heavily influenced by the Argentine crisis,[17] the peak level may have been biased by some extraordinarily large transactions such as the YPF–Repsol deal and other mergers and acquisitions.[18]

Table 6.2 FDI inflows into MERCOSUR, 1990–2002 (US$ billion)

	1990–95	1996	1997	1998	1999	2000	2001	2002
Argentina	3.5	7.0	9.2	6.8	24.1	11.2	3.2	2.7
Brazil	2.0	10.8	19.0	28.9	28.6	32.8	22.5	–
Paraguay	0.10	0.14	0.23	0.34	0.10	0.10	0.15	–
Uruguay	0.10	0.14	0.13	0.16	0.24	0.29	0.32	–
MERCOSUR	5.7	18.1	28.6	36.2	53.0	44.4	26.0	–

Source: UNCTAD. 2002. *World Investment Report*. (New York and Geneva: UNCTAD).

It is too early to judge seriously the relative importance of cyclical and one-shot phenomena *vis-à-vis* a possible change of the trend. However, some of the available information warns against too much optimism. First, a huge share of capital inflows during the 1990s has been directed towards the acquisition of privatization ventures. This development is temporary by nature. That is, it only can attract a limited amount of capital inflows over a limited time period (and this period may have come to an end already in Argentina).[19] Once the privatization activities come to an end, new capital inflows can only be attracted if the economic prospects of the region are (and are expected to remain) sufficiently favorable. This conclusion leads to the second point: capital inflows, net of privatization, will depend on the growth potential of the local (regional) market (size and rate of growth of the regional economy) and the conditions under which the global markets can be served. This brings in the IIT strategy once again. This strategy adversely affects growth prospects, so that future FDI inflows may diminish. According to a recent Miga report (conducted before the crash in Argentina) this fear may be justified: only Brazil is likely to attract foreign investors in both manufacturing and services in the future.[20]

Another proof of this argument is the automotive industry, which is a centerpiece of MERCOSUR's industrial development strategy. The objective of industrial policies in this sector was to transform the highly inefficient inheritance of the import-substitution era into a competitive industry.[21]

Under the emerging MERCOSUR regime and supported by the 'popular car policy',[22] Brazil pushed the production of motor vehicles[23] from 914.5 thousand units in 1990 to 2067 thousand units in 1997. And in Argentina production even rose from 99.6 thousand units to 445.9 thousand units over the same period.

What appears to be a tremendous success at first glance becomes less impressive once it is analysed more seriously. First, the recovery of the 1990s was nurtured by the strong catch-up of demand after the depression of the so-called 'lost decade' (automobile production had dropped by about 50 per cent between 1980 and 1990), and it became heated up even more by the Brazilian 'popular car policy', which steered local demand into a higher quantity of lower priced cars. Second, stiff external protection (with tariffs as high as 70 per cent and flanked by NTBs) prohibited any significant increase of imports. Likewise, new competitors from Asia remained largely excluded from the regional market,[24] so that local producers were enabled to expand production for the regional market without any significant competition from abroad. Another effect of this situation was that exports aimed at the international markets remained low,[25] because the increase of productivity lagged behind international developments.

In order to make the consequences of this strategy more transparent a brief look at the Mexican experience may be helpful. In the early 1990s Mexico found itself captured in a similar situation to MERCOSUR. After the long-lasting import-substitution era the inefficient automobile sector, producing mainly for the local market (about two-thirds of total output), had to be transformed substantially. When Mexico decided to join NAFTA it had to accept that protection would be definitely phased out within a limited time period. That is, it would have to face import competition from the world market, the USA and Canada in particular, but it also gained the chance to take advantage of these large markets of its own. In order to meet this challenge, Mexican car manufacturers (basically the same MNEs that produce in MERCOSUR) had to undergo tremendous restructuring procedures to upgrade their plants and to integrate Mexico into the US–Canada production system.

In 1997 Mexican vehicles production had risen to 1,338 thousand units. This is a lower rate of growth than in MERCOSUR, but the value per unit of output has grown in Mexico, while it has dropped in MERCOSUR. What is more important, however, is the fact that the upgrading procedures have raised the productivity of labor of Mexican plants close to international standards and substantially ahead of MERCOSUR.[26] Mexican producers, today, are ready to export to the most advanced markets in the USA, Canada, and Europe and they do so ever more forcefully. In 1997, nearly three-quarters of Mexican production (884 thousand units) were exported (about 90 per cent to the US market).

These are crude figures, but they are indicative of the different long-term perspectives of both markets, and the quality of the underlying political strategies. While the Mexican automobile industry has caught up with world markets and will be able to grow at the rate of world demand and even above that rate in the future, MERCOSUR producers are still restricted to their low income, low scale, and highly volatile emerging market. Within this market, the same MNEs which are operating efficiently in Mexico and elsewhere are producing at lower standards and higher prices because the incentive system of MERCOSUR teaches them to do so.[27]

Following the above analysis of the relative importance of inter- and intra-industry trade for emerging markets, one would conclude that the prospects for sustained high rates of capital inflows are not encouraging. While the incentives for foreign investors, to step into newly privatized markets are diminishing, the conditions for regional growth are becoming less favorable because of the inherent obstacles to IIT expansion and the relative discrimination of extra-regional exports under this strategy. As a result, the capacity to import technology will most probably diminish, and MERCOSUR growth performance will suffer.

WHAT COULD BE A VIABLE TRADE STRATEGY FOR MERCOSUR?

The basic message of this chapter will be that the priority of trade policy must be shifted from intra-industry to inter-industry trade. Such a shift of strategy would call for lower protection against outsiders in order to diminish (and at best eliminate) the relative discrimination against exports to non-member countries.[28] At the same time the trend towards increased protection within MERCOSUR must be reversed. Such policies would also help to redirect MERCOSUR towards the concept of 'open regionalism'.

One crucial point is that, once the relative discrimination of North–South trade has been ended, trade expansion will quasi-automatically turn to inter-industry trade, because for LDCs, exploiting comparative advantage on the global market is still the most promising way to use trade as a 'handmaiden' of growth (Kravis 1970, Riedel 1984). The growth-promoting effect of North–South trade would help to develop the local (regional) market, and, as growth proceeds, this would also broaden the scope for intra-industry trade. Thus, instead of pushing intra-industry trade by external protection and stiff internal regulations (automobiles), INT will be pushed by trade liberalization both at home and abroad, and IIT will follow later on and according to the development of the regional market.

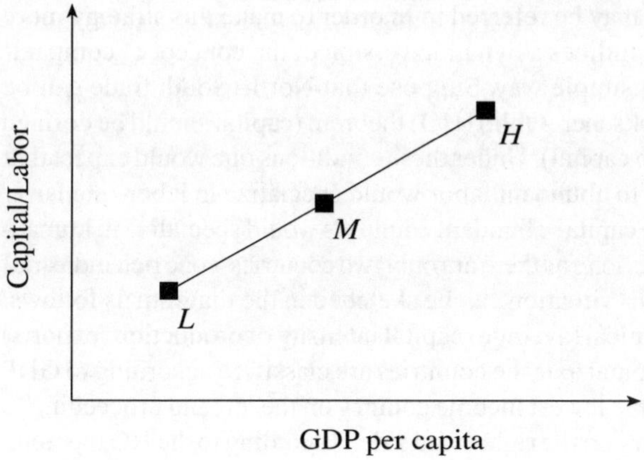

Figure 6.1a Continuum of comparative advantages

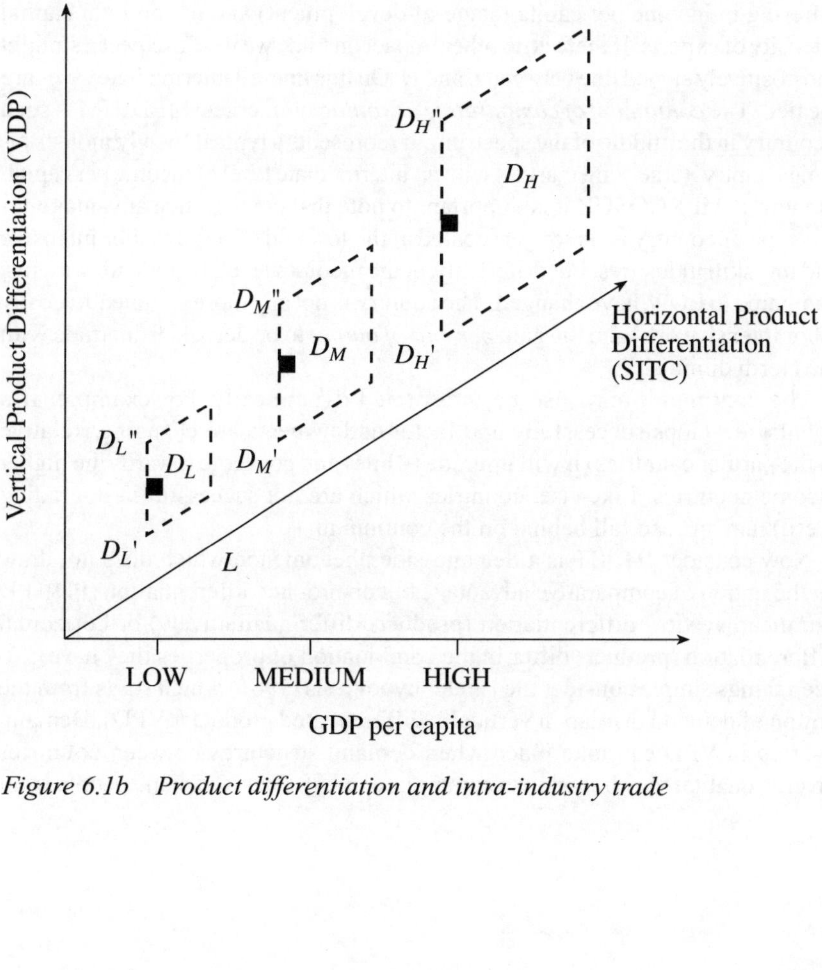

Figure 6.1b Product differentiation and intra-industry trade

Figures 6.1a and 6.1b may be referred to in order to make this strategy more transparent. Figure 6.1a outlines a dynamic version of the concept of comparative advantage in a very simple way. Suppose that North–South trade can be approximated by the Heckscher–Ohlin (HO) theorem (capital should be defined broadly to include human capital). Under these conditions one would expect that low income countries with abundant labor would specialize in labor-intensive/low-skill products, while capital-abundant countries would specialize in human-capital intensive goods. As long as there are only two countries – one rich industrial nation and one LDC – this situation can be sketched in the diagram as follows: on the vertical axis the typical (average) capital intensity of production (exports) is depicted. On the horizontal axis the countries are classified according to GDP per capita, starting with the lowest income country on the left and proceeding to the highest income country on the right-hand side. According to the HO theorem, low (high) income countries are labor (capital) abundant. Thus, with only two countries we will find the low income country (LOW) positioned at point *L* and the high income country (HIGH) at point *H*. Now consider a multi-goods, multi-country world[29] (but remain within the capital-labor framework) with countries differing in income per capita (stage of development) and the optimal capital intensity of exports. If there is no other impact on trade we would expect a straight and positively sloped line between *L* and *H*. On this line, all intermediate cases are located. The *continuum of comparative advantages* emerges. MEDIUM is such a country in the middle of the spectrum. It represents a typical 'newly industrializing country' (emerging market) with an intermediate level of income per capita. In view of MERCOSUR it is important to note that comparative advantage for this type of country is no longer located at the low end of purely labor intensive and low skill industries. Put differently, at the medium level, factor endowments, compared to LOW, have changed. The country is not any more an 'unequivocally labor intensive one' and the gain *per unit of output* to be derived from trade with the North diminishes.[30]

The continuum may also be interpreted dynamically. For example, if a country develops successfully and factor endowments are changing (relative to the partner countries) it will upgrade (Chile) and converge towards the higher income countries. Likewise, countries which are not successful in upgrading (Peru) may instead fall behind on the continuum.

Now consider IIT. IIT is a demand-side phenomenon which does not draw on the notion of comparative advantage but on product differentiation (PD). PD can mean vertical differentiation (products differ qualitatively) or horizontal differentiation (products differ in the combination of properties they have). To keep things simple consider the Linder hypothesis (1961) which starts from the notion of demand overlap in vertically differentiated products (VPD). Demand overlap in VPD can take place when demand structures between countries diverge qualitatively but retain a common segment. That is, if some people from country A prefer products which are exclusively produced in B and vice versa, intra-industry trade emerges.

Consider LOW in Figure 6.1b. On average LOW people demand the low quality product D_L. Assuming that income is distributed unequally and people are demanding distinct qualities in relation to income, a demand structure emerges in LOW which extends from D_L' to D_L". Now turn to HIGH, which has a higher average quality level of demand than LOW, and it will also have a higher spread of qualities. The reason is an increased diversification of demand at a higher average level of income per capita. Let VPD spread from D_H' to D_H" in the high income country. In this high–low income country scenario no demand overlap exists. That is, even the highest quality demand in LOW will not cause significant demand from poor people in HIGH. Accordingly, no IIT can develop.

Now introduce intermediate country MEDIUM as in the HO case (newly industrializing country/emerging market). This country is assumed to be situated right in the middle between LOW and HIGH and it will have a spread of demand that overlaps with both HIGH and LOW. Within the overlapping segments, two-way trade (IIT) can develop (note that comparative advantage is not involved in this argument). What is important from a dynamic point of view is the notion that VPD increases with increasing income levels and so does the scope for IIT.

Now consider horizontal product differentiation (HPD). HPD means that products do not differ in quality but may have different combinations of properties (two equal cars, for example, differ in their engines, one having a gas engine and the other a similarly powered diesel engine).[31] HPD, too, will broaden as income per capita rises and so will the margin for IIT. In order to include HPD in Figure 6.1b let us suppose that HPD can be approximated by the degree of differentiation of any given SITC category (the more positions enter the higher is the degree of horizontal product differentiation). HPD can be depicted on a third axis. This axis will exhibit few entrants in LOW because HPD is only poorly developed in low income markets. But it will rise as per capita income rises, Thus in MEDIUM, HPD has already grown and in HIGH, diversification is highly sophisticated.

Both models are very basic and mechanistic presentations. Nevertheless, by comparing both figures (6.1a and 6.1b) we can recognize some fundamental aspects of the INT–IIT puzzle. While the scope for gaining from INT with the North diminishes as per capita income (and implicitly factor endowments) converge towards the highest income countries, the scope for IIT expands. For low income countries, maximizing the gains from trade is closely linked to the exploitation of comparative advantage. Pushing IIT at the expense of INT would definitely be an inferior strategy. Such a country would have to do without the (full) exploitation of comparative advantage but the conditions for the expansion of IIT are not appropriate to substitute for this loss. Things are more complicated in MEDIUM which shows already a (slightly) advanced level of product differentiation and where there exists some scope for IIT. Nevertheless, it would not be advisable to push IIT *at the expense* of INT. The basic reason is that technology transfer via imports from the North still remains the most important effect of trade on local (regional) growth. Cutting INT for the sake of IIT, therefore, diminishes the prospects for convergence directly and, by slowing down the process of product differentiation, also indirectly.

Switching back to an INT strategy is not an easy task in the case of MERCOSUR because it will inevitably cause challenging restructuring procedures to take place. Basically, MERCOSUR cannot evade this challenge, because the structures of production, after decades of import substitution and futile adjustment evasion strategies, are still not appropriate to face global competition. Turning more courageously to the global market under these conditions must be accompanied by prudent political activities which should not be restricted to trade policy. Rather, what has been uncovered by the turbulences of recent years is the fact that, while opening up the trade account may well be a necessary condition for growth and development, it is by no means a sufficient one. Prudent economic policies for growth and development will also have to be implemented. They should take care of adequate macro- and micro-economic devices which foster incentives to invest, provide the basic infrastructure (material and immaterial – education!) and facilitate market access for those who were left behind by the traditional approach (informal sector, unemployment and so on). Further, if structural adjustment is to be enhanced, efficient adjustment assistance for those who may lose their jobs in declining industries is a necessary complementary policy. It may also be growth promoting, inasmuch as it helps to weaken opposition to change.

Last but not least, the political economy of transformation points to the fact that general welfare-enhancing policies may fail because of strong vested interests. In Latin America, because of its long history of non-democratic governments and monopolistic structures of production, nurtured by and closely inter-linked with politics, these interests appear to be particularly influential. What is missing after decades of economic reforms are equally profound political reforms which are appropriate to strengthen the democratic control mechanisms and to encourage the forces of change at the expense of vested interests. Without going into detail on this point, recent developments in Argentina are alarming in this respect. Apparently, the political system of this country has abused the economic stability borrowed from the currency board for years and was unable to respond to the economic challenges of the late 1990s even in the face of economic and political suicide.[32] Argentina is an especially drastic but by no means singular case. The political occurrences in the run-up to the Brazilian crises of 1999, for example, do exhibit similar political (mis-)perceptions of the economic constraints that the economy faces in a globalized world (though it has to be admitted that Brazil at least reacted quickly and prudently, once the crises had erupted).

Thus, deficits in the political management of the young democracies may pose another threat to the future of Latin America in general and MERCOSUR in particular.

CONCLUSIONS

There are two major threats to the future of MERCOSUR. One is the present economic and political crisis. Without a speedy recovery from this crisis the chances of MERCOSUR surviving are not encouraging. Assuming that such a recovery does take place, the future of the agreement still remains in doubt as long as a return to the principles of open regionalism and a reliable integration strategy do not succeed.

In this chapter, three structural deficits of the present concept of MERCOSUR have been discussed: the institutional weakness, the lack of macroeconomic coordination, and the intra-industry trade strategy. The first two of these deficits have been mentioned only briefly. In principle, they can be corrected

- by adjusting the relatively demanding concept of a 'Common Market' to the political realities (taking into account the readiness to share sovereignty), and by replacing the highly personal decision-making procedures by a more rules-based system, and
- by avoiding macroeconomic concepts at the national level which threaten to produce distorted real exchange rates within the region.

The third structural weakness, the IIT strategy, is fundamental, and its removal is difficult but imperative. IIT is a phenomenon that can be observed most clearly in trade between high income countries. The reasons are twofold. On the demand side, the scope for IIT depends on the extent of product differentiation, which, in turn, depends on the size of the market. On the supply side, IIT most often prospers in the competitive environment of innovational competition. In order to succeed in these markets technological knowledge and organizational and management experience is urgently needed. Both prerequisites for success are scarce in LDCs.

Low income countries which are trying to push IIT (South–South trade) at the expense of INT are most likely to fail under these conditions. They hinder the expansion of the more growth-enhancing trade relations with industrialized countries (thereby diminishing technology transfer) without being able to provide the essential preconditions for beneficial IIT to evolve.

Considering MERCOSUR in the light of these arguments makes it clear that its IIT strategy is flawed. First, in order to gain ground internationally in IIT, firms from MERCOSUR would have to compete directly on the world market, and in an environment of fierce innovational competition. In this field they would surely be in a disadvantaged position. The response of MERCOSUR to this challenge has been to maintain a relatively high level of external protection for strategic industries (the automobile industry in particular).

External protection implies discrimination and leads back to a new form of import substitution policy. But, following the traumatic experience of the so-called 'lost decade', the import-substitution strategy had been overthrown exactly because of its dramatic failure: by establishing and maintaining inefficient structures of production, the large benefits that could have been derived from trade with economically advanced countries remained unexploited. This failure eventually resulted in depression. In the 'new' IIT variant, import substitution is likely to hinder the development of the regional market, thereby decreasing the scope for market-driven intra-industry specialization. Enforcing regional IIT by means of administrative protection and managed trade is no solution to this problem. Rather, *it is* the problem.

Second, defending the IIT strategy because of its low adjustment costs (relative to INT) is a popular but not a convincing argument. It is correct to state that some complicated forms of adjustment under INT (regional migration, complete depreciation of specific knowledge) are less frequent under IIT, but this is not sufficient to qualify IIT as less costly. Just as IIT and intra-industry specialization are likely to prosper in strongly contested markets and under the conditions of innovational competition, changes in demand and supply structures are taking place frequently and rapidly in this environment. As a result, a higher speed of change is reigning in these markets and structural adjustment, though remaining within industries, may still bear heavy costs.

According to these arguments MERCOSUR must inevitably restructure its productive capacities following comparative advantage. Presently, one cannot recognize that this approach is considered seriously. Thus the third structural weakness still remains to be solved. If this weakness is taken seriously it is clear that the future of MERCOSUR must remain in doubt, even if the present economic turbulences can be overcome.

NOTES

1. For a comprehensive analysis of these reforms see Edwards (1995).
2. Theoretically, a profound switch from the political power (Hymer 1976) to the transaction cost theory of the multinational enterprise (Caves 1996) can be diagnosed.

3. In fact, the European Union has quite often been cited as a model for the formation of MERCOSUR as a common market. For a discussion of the similarities and differences of both approaches see Vasconcelos (2001, p. 139).
4. This argument has been discussed intensively in Europe when the Single European Market had been proposed. See for example Cecchini (1988).
5. See Averbug (2002, p. 925).
6. Vasconcelos (2001, p. 141).
7. F. H. Cardoso (1998), cited in Vasconcelos (2001, p. 141).
8. See Preusse (1998, pp. 12–23).
9. After the devaluation of the *real* the Brazilian government changed to inflation targeting and imposed a more ambitious anti-inflation policy. Nevertheless, the initial target rate of inflation of 6 per cent was still much higher than that of Argentina. Thus, while the peso still appreciated against the US dollar, the Brazilian *real* depreciated even further. See Averbug (2002, p. 934).
10. For a profound discussion of these topics see Tavlas and Ulan (2002).
11. The empirical and theoretical studies on intra-industry trade (IIT) are numerous. They began with the early work of Linder (1961), Hesse (1974) and Grubel and Lloyd (1975). Later on, theoretical models by Lancaster (1980), Helpman (1981) and Krugman (1981) among others have given the 'new' trade phenomenon a theoretical basis. For more recent publications see Greenaway and Hines (1991) and Blanes and Martin (2000).
12. Note, however, that a considerable share of (conventionally) measured intra-industry trade is due to measurement errors (between 25 and 35 per cent). The main problem is that of 'categorical aggregation' (Greenaway and Milner 1986, Grimwade 1996). To the extent of the error margin IIT should better be attributed to traditional trade mechanisms.
13. Note that, under these conditions, the question of the severity of adjustment pressure in both trade regimes has also to be reconsidered. Inasmuch as competitive pressure is rising under IIT, so does the speed of structural change. If this pressure also spurs innovational competition in high tech markets, specific skills (human capital) may become the scarce factor. Thus structural adjustment in the IIT environment will be both speeding up relative to the conditions under INT and drawing heavily on human capital (that is, the scarce factor in LDCs). It is unlikely that structural adjustment in LDCs under these IIT conditions is less demanding than under INT.
14. According to recent empirical research on the causes of economic growth, policies which are appropriate to enhancing productivity are the most important growth-promoting factor. See Prescott (2002, p. 10); Bergoeing et al. (2002, p. 19).
15. Discriminating against extra-regional imports has further serious consequences which cannot be treated in depth here. First, in the case of MERCOSUR, extra-regional trade will be predominantly INT. Thus, discrimination will most likely push trade structures in contradiction to comparative advantage (Yeats 1998). Second, the Vinerian claim of trade diversion gains the more ground, the higher is protection against outsiders. Third, systematic price changes may occur at the expense of non-member countries. Chang and Winters have calculated that MERCOSUR trade policies had in fact significantly negative effects on the prices of extra-regional exports. In particular, based on 1991 exports to Brazil, the total loss of export revenue of five major exporters (Chile, Germany, Japan, South Korea and the USA) amounted to nearly US$ 9.5 billion. The USA (US$ 5.4 billion) and Germany (US$ 2 billion) were most severely affected. Thus, trade diversion, if practiced strategically and extensively, may give rise to new trade disputes. See Chang and Winters (1999, p. 31 and table 7).
16. Chudnovsky and López (2002).
17. UNCTAD (2002), World Investment Report, Transnational Corporations and Export Competitiveness, pp. 62.
18. UNCTAD (2002, p. 65).
19. Ibid., p. 66.
20. MIGA 2002, cited from UNCTAD (2002, p. 65).
21. According to Mortimore, in the heyday of import substitution 'the main success of ... the policy led promotion of the auto industry in Latin America was to create a functional automobile

industry ... supplying the domestic market ... in a totally unacceptable way as measured by international standards of efficiency and productivity' (Mortimore 1998, p. 11).

22. Under this program, taxes on vehicles with motors of less than 1000 ccm were reduced from 34.5 per cent in 1990 to 17 per cent in 1993 (and again increased to 23 per cent in 1995). This measure pushed small car production from 201 000 units in 1990 to 882 000 units in 1997 (64 per cent of all passenger car sales). For more details see Mortimore (1998, p. 21).
23. Including passenger cars, commercial vehicles and other.
24. According to Mortimore these policies have been effectively lobbied for by some European volume producers, FIAT in particular. It remains unexplained, however, why these lobbying activities have been met by success in the case of MERCOSUR, but not in Mexico.
25. In 1997 about 42 per cent of the value of Brazilian auto exports were due to trade with Argentina, and 86 per cent of Argentine exports went to Brazil (Mortimore 1998, p. 20).
26. A crude estimation based on the data presented by Mortimore suggests that the average productivity of labor in Mexico is about 50 per cent higher than in MERCOSUR.
27. During the last few years, some isolated new plants have been established in MERCOSUR which meet international standards. Most of these plants, however, do work as export platforms operating under special regimes (the Daimler-Chrysler E-class production in Brazil is a case in point).
28. For the definition and elaboration of a concept for a non-discriminatory trade regime (sometimes called 'export orientation') see for example Perkins et al. (2001, ch. 18).
29. Theoretically these ideas have been outlined in the so-called 'chain-theorem of comparative advantages' (see Deardorff 1982).
30. Note, however, that new opportunities arise for trade with poorer countries. Moreover, because the level and the structure of demand increase as income per capita rises, so does the scope for INT, and the total gains from trade will still rise. The demand-side aspects of trade will be discussed below.
31. For a theoretical exposition see Lancaster (1980).
32. See Pastor and Wise (2001).

REFERENCES

Averbug, A. (2002), 'The Brazilian economy in 1994–1999: from the Real Plan to inflation targets', *The World Economy*, **25** (July), 925–44.

Bergoeing, R. et al. (2002), 'Policy driven productivity in Chile and Mexico in the 1980s', *American Economic Review*, **92**, 2 (May) 16–21.

Bergsten, F.G. (1997), 'Open regionalism', Institute for International Economics, Working Paper 97–3.

Blanes, J.V. and C. Martin (2000), 'The nature and causes of intra-lndustry trade: back to the comparative advantage explanation? The case of Spain', *Weltwirtschaftliches Archiv*, **136** (3), 423–41.

Caves, R.N. (1996), *Multinational Enterprises and Economic Analysis*, 2nd edn, Cambridge: Cambridge University Press.

Cecchini, P. (1988), *The European Challenge*, Aldershot: Wildewood House.

Chang, W., and A.L. Winters (1999), 'How regional blocks affect excluded countries: the price effects of MERCOSUR', The World Bank, globalization working papers no. 2157, August.

Chudnovsky, D., and A. López, (coord.) (2002), *Integratión regional e inversión extranjera directa: El caso del MERCOSUR*, Banco Interamericano de Desarrollo, BID-INTAL.

Conolly, M. (1999), 'North–South technological diffusion: a new case for dynamic gains from trade', Duke University Economics Department working paper 99–08, September.

Conolly, M., and J. Gunther (1999), 'MERCOSUR: implications for growth in member countries', Federal Reserve Bank of New York, *Current Issues in Economics and Finance*, **5**, 7 (May), 1–6.

Deardorff, A.V. (1982), 'The general validity of the Heckscher–Ohlin-Theorem', *American Economic Review*, **72** (September), 683–94.

Devlin, R., and A. Estevadeordal (2001), 'What's new in the new regionalism in the Americas?', INTAL ITD-STA working paper 6.

Edwards, S. (1995), *Crisis and Reform in Latin America. From Despair to Hope*, Washington, DC: The World Bank.

Estevadeordal, A., J. Goto and R. Saez (2000), 'The new regionalism in the Americas: the case of MERCOSUR', INTAL ITD working paper 5.

Greenaway, D., and R. C. Mines (1991), 'Intra-Industry specialization, trade expansion and adjustment in the European economic space', *Journal of Common Market Studies*, **29**, 6 (December), 602–22.

Greenaway, D., and C. Milner (1986), *The Economics of Intra-Industry Trade*, Oxford: Oxford University Press.

Grimwade, N. (1996), *International Trade Policy*, 2nd edn, New York: Routledge.

Grubel, H.G., and P.J. Lloyd (1975), *Intra-Industry Trade*, London: John Wiley.

Helpman, E. (1981), 'International trade in the presence of product differentiation, economies of scale and monopolistic competition: a Chamberlin-Heckscher-Ohlin approach', *Journal of International Economics*, **11**, 305–40.

Hesse, H. (1974), 'Hypotheses for the explanation of trade between industrial countries, 1953–70', in H. Giersch (ed.), *The International Division of Labor: Problems and Perspectives*, International Symposium, Tübingen, 39–49.

Hymer, S.H. (1976), 'The international operations of national firms: a study of direct foreign investment', Ph.D. dissertation, Massachusetts Institute of Technology.

Kaltenthaler, K., and F.O. Mora (2002), 'Explaining Latin American economic integration: the case of MERCOSUR', *Review of International Political Economy*, **9**, 1 (March), 72–97.

Kravis, J.B. (1970), 'Trade as a handmaiden of growth', *Economic Journal*, **80**, 850–72.

Krugman, P.R. (1981), 'Intra-industry specialization and the gains from trade', *Journal of Political Economy*, **89** (5), 959–73.

Lancaster, K. (1980), 'Intra-industry trade under perfect monopolistic competition', *Journal of International Economics*, **10**, 151–76.

Lawrence, R.Z. (1996), *Regionalism, Multilateralism and Deeper Integration*, Washington, DC: Brookings Institution.

Linder, S.B. (1961), *An Essay on Trade and Transformation*, Uppsala: Almquist & Wiksell.

Mortimore, M. (1998), 'Corporate strategies and regional integration schemes in developing countries: the case of NAFTA and MERCOSUR automobile industries', *Science, Technology & Development*, **16**, 2 (August), 1–31.

Nunnenkamp, P., E. Gundlach and J.P. Agarwal (1994), *Globalization of Production and Markets*, Kieler Studien 262, Tübingen: Mohr.

Pastor, M., and C. Wise (2001), 'From posterchild to basket case', *Foreign Affairs*, **11/12**, 60–72.

Perkins, D.H. et al. (2001), *Economics of Development*, 5th edn, New York and London: W.W. Norton.

Prescott, E.C. (2002), 'Prosperity and Depression', Richard T. Ely Lecture reported in *American Economic Review*, **92**, 2 (May), 1–15.

Preusse, H.G. (1998), 'MERCOSUR and the formation of a common market, some lessons from the European experience', Cuaderno de Negocios Internacionales e Integración, 20, Universidad Catolica, Montevideo, Uruguay, 12–23.

Preusse, H.G. (2001), 'MERCOSUR – another failed move towards regional integration?', *The World Economy*, **24**, 7 (July), 911–31.

Reynolds, C. (1997), 'Open regionalism, lessons from Latin America for East Asia', Kellog Institute working paper 241, August.

Riedel, J. (1984), 'Trade as an engine of growth in developing countries, revisited', *Economic Journal*, **94** (March), 56–73.

Taccone, J., and U. Nogueira (eds) (2001), *MERCOSUR Report 2000–2001*, Buenos Aires: INTAL.

Tavlas, G.S. and M.K. Ulan (special eds) (2002), 'Exchange-rate regimes and capital flows', *The Annals of the American Academy of Political and Social Science*, **579** (January).

UNCTAD (2002), *World Investment Report*, New York and Geneva: UNCTAD.

Vasconcelos, A. (2001), 'European Union and MERCOSUR', in M. Telò (ed.), *European Union and New Regionalism*, Aldershot: Ashgate, ch. 7.

Yeats, A. (1989), 'Developing countries' exports of manufactures: past and future implications of shifting patterns of comparative advantage', *The Developing Economics*, **27** (2), 109–45.

Yeats, A. (1998), 'Does MERCOSUR's trade performance raise concerns about the effects of regional trade arrangements?', *The World Bank Economic Review*, **12** (1), 1–28.

7. The European experience of economic integration

Paul Brenton and Miriam Manchin

It is now more than 50 years since countries in Europe embarked upon the road of fundamental economic integration. The European experience has subsequently been characterized by the deepening and widening of the policy mix applied at the European level, together with successive enlargements. At the end of the first quarter of 2002 12 EU countries removed their national currencies and fully adopted a common currency, the euro. Every day over 300 million Europeans now have a physical representation of the extent of European economic integration in their pockets and purses. Judged in terms of its longevity and the increasing depth of cross-country relationships, the European integration project has been a success and one which, together with increasing exploration of regional in conjunction with multilateral trade liberalization, has stimulated countries throughout the world to confront the possibilities for regional integration within their locality. Despite the overall success of the project, however, there are aspects of the integration exercise in Europe that, with the benefit of hindsight, have not been economically beneficial. These too should provide some important pointers to new integration schemes.

It is in this context that this chapter provides a brief overview of the historical origins of the European integration process, the initial impacts of this process and some of the lessons that might be drawn from the European experience. Clearly, closer economic relations in Europe arose from a precise set of historical circumstances that will never be repeated, nevertheless, it is clear that certain preconditions were necessary for this process to be successful and these are of equal relevance to contemporary considerations regarding the prospects for closer regional economic ties in Asia, the Americas and Africa. Fundamental amongst these is *a willingness to open up* on the part of all partners and to effectively liberalize. This entails a commitment to confront the inevitable adjustment costs that will arise in the attainment of the net economic benefits that many economists are confident will arise from *suitably designed* integration schemes. European integration suggests that a key element in such a design is internal liberalization, together with external openness. Further, the European model is one where substantial social safety nets have been in place to mitigate the adjustment costs that have arisen from market liberalization. It is also worth noting from the outset that the European experience of integration is one of progressively increasing economic ties, whilst at the same time maintaining an essential degree of national diversity, economic, political and social.

THE BACKGROUND TO EUROPEAN INTEGRATION

European integration rose from the ashes of the second devastating war to hit the continent within 25 years. However, it is important to note that the big step towards integration taken in the Treaty of Rome in 1957, which founded the European Economic Community, followed a relatively long period of integration initiatives and learning by doing in Europe. The background to European integration was a period immediately after the war in which the need for reconstruction was dominant and the economies of Europe were characterized by widespread restrictions on international commerce and severe international imbalances.

European integration commenced after the failure of the multilateral approach initially favoured by the United States to address the post-war problems facing Europe (Pelkmans 1997). In the immediate post-war period European trade was tariff and quota ridden, there were enormous supply bottlenecks, unconvertible currencies and a crucial lack of foreign exchange. This was the environment facing those seeking fundamental and rapid reconstruction where Europe required substantial inflows of funds for investment.

Initially the United States proposed a multilateral response in the form of the establishment of three global institutions: the IMF (International Monetary Fund), World Bank and the ITO (International Trade Organization). However, this approach failed. The ITO, suffering from lack of political support, was not ratified by the US Congress and was substituted by a much weaker organization, the GATT (General Agreement on Tariffs and Trade), which initially was only concerned with reducing tariffs, whilst the IMF and the World Bank were not suitable vehicles for dealing with the massive European needs for funds for reconstruction.

A further fundamental factor influencing the US approach to Europe was the emergence of the 'cold war'. The divide in Europe that emerged during the latter part of the 1940s undermined the multilateral approach. As a result US policy evolved and in 1948, under the Marshall Plan, direct aid was provided to European countries on the condition of increasing intra-European integration. The framework for this was provided by the Organisation for European Economic Co-operation (OEEC, which later with non-European members became the OECD). Economic cooperation between Western European countries was seen as the best way of preventing renewed conflict, of stimulating economic growth and hence of resisting the spread of Soviet communism.

Today the multilateral system is much stronger with the WTO (World Trade Organization) presiding over the rules-based system of world trade. Thus, regionalism must now be a complementary, rather than an alternative, mechanism for achieving economic integration and stimulating trade and growth. However, security issues, of a vastly different nature, are still paramount and regional economic integration may still play a role in combating these issues. Indeed, a key feature of earlier and recent European external trade policy has been the use of economic integration to achieve foreign policy and security objectives, primarily on the borders of Europe. However, as we shall discuss in more detail below, the fulfilment of these objectives has been undermined by the design of the EU's trade agreements with neighbouring and developing countries. Thus, whilst integration in Europe has not compromised the European commitment to the multilateral trade system and (non-agricultural) external trade barriers have been substantially reduced, the economic benefits of bilateral agreements with other countries have been severely constrained by the rules that the EU imposes within these agreements.

The decade following the shift towards a regional approach in US policy saw a number of successful integration initiatives, such as the creation of a customs union between Belgium, Luxembourg and the Netherlands (Benelux) in 1948, and the creation of the European Coal and Steel Community (ECSC) in 1950. The ECSC was essentially an attempt to solve what at the time was seen as 'the German problem' and to integrate the two sectors of the economy of particular strategic importance in this period, in the sense of being essential for military purposes. Integration of these sectors was also seen as a necessary response to the threats under the cold war and, crucially, provided the basis for Franco-German reconciliation and subsequent cooperation.

However, there were also a number of setbacks and failures during this period. For example, France and Italy negotiated a bilateral customs union, which was never implemented. There followed seven years of various proposals after the ECSC was created until six countries (the Benelux countries, France, Germany and Italy) signed the Treaty of Rome to lay the main foundation for European integration. This process over ten years in Europe highlights the difficulty of achieving regional integration, particularly amongst modern economies with a high degree of regulation, and the important role of the learning process in Europe.

THE LESSONS FROM 'LEARNING BY DOING IN EUROPE'

Following Pelkmans (1997) we can identify three key lessons from the European experience in the late 1940s and 1950s concerning regional economic integration which are of relevance to countries in other regions contemplating such a development.

1. Partial forms of integration are less likely to be accepted or successful. In the immediate post-war period the OEEC was given the task of dismantling quantitative restrictions in Europe, whilst the GATT had the reduction of tariffs as its focus. In many ways this approach failed, but particularly since it prevented low tariff countries from effectively participating in negotiations on quota reductions. This argues against excluding particular trade policies from integration schemes. Similar arguments are equally pertinent with regard to sectors. Picking and choosing which sectors to include and which to exclude is unlikely to provide the basis for a sound integration agreement.
2. Free trade agreements can be viewed as a deepening of multilateral liberalization and are not suitable for a deepening of regional integration itself. Free trade agreements liberalize certain border trade policies on internal trade (tariffs and quotas), whilst others (contingent protection (anti-dumping and safeguards), rules of origin) are maintained. Free trade agreements impinge very little on the policy autonomy of members. More advanced, or deep, forms of integration require attention to a range of non-border policies that affect trade and investment flows and segment markets along national lines. The effective removal of the barriers to trade caused by regulatory policies, such as those relating to health and safety, often requires a degree of common regulation and harmonization of policies. This is not to say that free trade agreements are necessarily economically inferior to deeper forms of integration but that if the aim is to achieve free movement of goods and services then simple free trade agreements will not be suitable.
3. The environment in which integration is built is important. European integration was facilitated by a period of strong economic growth and also, of particular relevance to current contemplation of regional integration, a strong *willingness to open up* and to liberalize backed by intense mutual economic dialogue and communication, and genuine efforts towards mutual understanding.

THE FOUNDATION OF EUROPEAN INTEGRATION: THE TREATY OF ROME

The Treaty of Rome, which created the European Economic Community in 1957, was, at the time, a very bold initiative, which aimed to create something much more than a free trade area. The founders of European integration sought from the start to create a common market based upon four freedoms: the freedom of movement of goods, services, capital and people. In the initial stage of integration between 1959 and 1968 the EEC was able to achieve the comprehensive removal of border trade barriers and the adoption of a common trade policy consistent with a customs union.

The Treaty of Rome committed members to remove 'tariffs and all charges having equivalent effect'. It is, however, only recently with the creation of the Single Market in 1992 that the EU countries have provided a framework by which the objectives with regard to freedom of movement can be fully achieved. Indeed there is still much to be done to provide for the freedom of movement of services, and in certain cases product integration is far from complete. Nevertheless, the founders of European integration in the 1950s recognized that the implementation of national regulatory policies could interfere with freedom of movement.

From the outset European integration was characterized by supranationality: the transfer of certain powers from the national to the European level. This sharing of sovereignty is not a feature of less ambitious integration schemes, such as a free trade area. The Treaty of Rome created the European institutions: the Commission, the Council and the Court of Justice. Thus in certain areas, for example, trade policy for goods and competition policy, competence was transferred from the national to the European level. In these areas European law superseded national law and compliance with the provisions of the Treaty was subject to judicial review.

It is important to note that from the outset integration in Europe has been based upon the idea of 'an open market economy with free competition' (Art. 3a) and that the Treaty contains a commitment that increasing integration between European countries should not be accompanied by the raising of external barriers to third countries. Article 110 of the Treaty of Rome commits the Community to 'the harmonious development of world trade, the progressive abolition of restrictions on international trade and the lowering of customs barriers'. As we shall argue in more detail below, an important feature of the initial phase of integration in Europe is that the internal removal of tariffs and quantitative restrictions was, with the exception of agricultural products, accompanied by external liberalization.

Nevertheless, this period witnessed increasing intervention within national economies, in terms of increasing regulation of labor markets and the greater use of industrial policy to support particular industries and firms ('national champions'), at the same time as trade barriers against products from European partners were removed and barriers against third countries were reduced. In some ways this increasing national intervention was a response to the increasing integration that was taking place. The 1950s and 1960s also saw the creation of extensive welfare states in European countries such that the social consequences of adjustment to integration and economic change were substantially cushioned.

Finally, in this section, we briefly address the issue concerning the role of politics versus economics in driving European integration. It is clear that the initial stimulus to European integration was political. The vision of the founders of European integration, as encapsulated in the Treaty of Rome, was of 'an ever closer union among the peoples of Europe'. Hence, *from the start integration was seen as a process rather than a single step.* Nevertheless, given this vision, subsequent developments in Europe have been driven by market integration. It is only very recently that very limited steps have been taken towards, for example, a common foreign and security policy or towards a European policy for justice and home affairs. Even so the key developments in the evolution of European integration remain economic. Recently, this has been apparent in the creation of the Single Market and then the Single Currency.

EUROPEAN INTEGRATION: INITIAL ACHIEVEMENTS

Tariffs and quotas on intra-EEC trade flows were fully removed 18 months ahead of schedule. This highlights, on the one hand, the genuine commitment towards liberalization throughout Europe during the 1950s and 1960s, and on the other, that initial integration was not accompanied by politically unsustainable adjustment costs. This will be discussed in a little more detail below. This period of initial integration was reflected in a strong increase in the absolute and relative importance of intra-EEC trade flows. Trade between the six member countries increased from around 34 per cent of their total trade in 1958 to over 50 per cent at the start of the 1970s.

As mentioned above, this strong growth in internal trade took place at the same time as external tariff barriers against imports of goods from third countries were being reduced under a series of negotiating rounds of the GATT. This helped to ensure that European integration did not cause conflicts with other countries in the world and that on balance the initial stage of integration was trade creating rather than trade diverting and therefore led to improved economic efficiency within Europe. Here the experience of European integration has clear lessons for contemporary discussions concerning regional integration. Such schemes are more likely to generate economic benefits to the members if they take place at the same time as external trade barriers are reduced. So countries evaluating various regional trade policy options should be putting their full weight behind the current round of trade negotiations under the WTO, which were launched by the Ministerial Declaration in Doha in November 2001.

Another important feature of the European experience of the 1950s and 1960s is that whilst trade liberalization led to increasing specialization, the source of the economic benefits that accrued from this specialization tended to occur within industries rather than between industries. This is reflected in the very strong growth of intra-industry trade between European countries during this period. Indeed it was the European experience which led to the development of both empirical and theoretical research to understand the phenomenon of intra-industry trade.

The importance of the growth of intra-industry trade relates to the issue of structural adjustment following trade liberalization. Traditional trade theories, based upon the notion of specialization according to broad industrial sectors (textiles, steel, motor vehicles and so on) led to the expectation that European integration would require the adjustment of resources between sectors. In practice, however, the growth of intra-industry trade entailed that much of the adjustment to trade liberalization took place in the form of the reallocation of resources within industries and to greater specialization of more narrowly defined activities. Recent integration between the EU and the Central and Eastern European countries (CEECS) has also been accompanied by the rising importance of intra-industry trade. In the early 1990s many commentators expected that integration would stimulate the CEECS to specialize in 'sensitive' labor-intensive industries such as textiles and clothing and furniture. However, there has been an enormous increase in two-way trade in engineering products as these countries have become integrated into European-wide product networks. Again, this appears to have reduced the adjustment implications of integration and confounded those who predicted substantial economic dislocations.

The rapid integration between European countries in the 1950s and 1960s does not appear to have caused any substantial problems of adjustment that called into question the broad support for trade liberalization. This reflects three factors: that trade expansion occurred mainly through intra-industry trade; the period was one of relatively strong economic growth and low unemployment; European countries created comprehensive social safety nets to protect those who bore the costs of adjustment to the new liberal trading environment in Europe. The latter suggests that policies to protect social welfare and trade liberalization may not necessarily be incompatible, as some suggest in the current debate over globalization.

The EEC countries experienced relatively rapid growth in the 1960s and early 1970s, in the region of 5 per cent per annum and in this regard the European countries outperformed the United States during this period. Growth rates slowed substantially during the latter part of the 1970s and during the early 1980s before picking up again in the late 1980s. This shows that the initial period of European integration took place during a period of relatively high growth. Average rates of unemployment in Europe in the 1960s and early 1970s were very low by contemporary standards. Again European performance exceeded that of the United States during this period, but again there was a substantial deterioration in unemployment in the 1970s and 1980s, with no recovery in the late 1980s.

A relevant issue is to what extent the strong growth performance of the 1960s and early 1970s was a determinant of the successful integration process in Europe and how important integration was in stimulating growth in European countries in this period. Traditional trade theory stresses the static efficiency gains that may accrue from economic integration.[1] There is little scope within the confines of this theory for a link from trade to growth. More recently, however, trade economists have begun to consider how international trade and foreign direct investment flows may affect economic growth. Economic integration by providing a larger international market allows for technological spillovers from one country to another and a larger international market raises the potential returns to innovators and hence the rate of innovation. Increased trade flows due to economic integration can also increase investment since the traded sector tends to be more capital intensive than the non-traded goods sector, cheaper intermediate goods can reduce the price of investment goods and integration can reduce the price of imported capital equipment. Foreign direct investment provides a direct means for the transfer of technologies and can be important in augmenting the domestic capital stock.

Thus, whilst it is undeniable that the initial stage of European integration took place under particularly favourable global economic conditions of strong growth and low unemployment, integration itself may have contributed to the growth process in Europe during the 1950s and 1960s. Integration may have played both an economic role in terms of stimulating investment and growth but also in terms of providing for greater stability and predictability in Europe and hence an environment more conducive to long-run investment decisions. Increasingly it has been recognized that regional trade agreements can play a role in providing a more certain policy environment and in allowing countries to effectively 'lock-in' planned reform programmes that they would otherwise have difficulty in implementing.

Regional integration may provide a strong mechanism, and one that is stronger than the WTO, for locking in domestic economic and institutional reforms. An international treaty on trade and investment, as well as other internal policies, may provide a strong anchor for domestic reforms, ensuring that the reversal of policy reform becomes more difficult. A number of 'deep integration' issues covered by a free trade agreement are not covered by the WTO, or are covered in a weak or partial way. Investment issues and the right of establishment are barely touched upon by the WTO. WTO rules relating to the service sector are rather weak relative to those pertaining to trade in goods. We return to the issues of services below.

Credibility will be enhanced more if the enforcement mechanisms in the free trade agreement are stronger than those under the WTO. If a free trade agreement helps to provide a credible signal that domestic reforms cannot easily be overturned then it may contribute to providing a more favourable climate for investment by both domestic and foreign firms. A positive response from investors will then further enhance the process of economic reform and contribute to economic progress.

The key issue is the extent to which countries who sign a free trade agreement are penalized if they renege on key commitments under the agreement. If the costs of deviating from an agreed liberalization package are made sufficiently large then the temptations of governments to provide protection for particular sectors or groups will be easier to resist. This in turn will instil a degree of credibility into the reform process. However, a free trade agreement can be at best a complement to domestic reform. A free trade agreement will have little or no impact if the domestic reform process itself is not coherent and credible. A bilateral agreement can make a direct contribution in this regard by providing clear mechanisms by which penalties will be imposed when commitments are reneged upon. Further, if the agreement is seen as part of a process towards further integration then it will create a constituency which will perceive future gains and will resist attempts from other groups to resist and roll back reforms.

Thus, for example, certain traditionally high inflation EU countries have recently been able to move to a low inflation trajectory by using membership of the monetary union as a credible commitment by which to conquer domestic inflationary expectations. During the 1990s countries in Central and Eastern Europe have been able to implement widespread economic reforms and liberalization anchored initially on trade agreements with the EU and then on accession to the EU. The economic impact of this has been reflected in rapidly rising trade and investment links between the two regions. However, certain of the CEECs have been less bold in reform and less effective in implementing reform policies and have not experienced the substantial foreign investment inflows or rapid economic growth that is a feature of other CEECs. Yet all of the CEECs have free trade agreements with the EU. This suggests that a free trade agreement is not a panacea for investment and growth. It is clear that domestic policies and their implementation are by far the most important determinant of domestic economic outcomes. A free trade agreement can act to enhance domestic liberalization and provide credibility to reform programs.

Another of the achievements of European integration in the 1950s and 1960s was the emergence of Europe, in the form of the six members of the EEC, as an important actor in global negotiations. This was most apparent in the GATT. In the Kennedy Round, for example, although individual members, the six negotiated together as the EEC. This had an important impact upon the perception of 'Europe' as an identity and challenged the dominant position of the United States, which substantially modified its expectations of the round and negotiating positions.

LESSONS FROM INITIAL INTEGRATION IN EUROPE

The Importance of 'Behind the Border' Barriers to Trade

Integration in Europe was able to proceed due to a genuine and deep-seated commitment throughout the members to liberalize. This was apparent throughout the 1950s and 1960s and enabled the successful dismantling of internal border trade barriers (tariffs and quotas). This in turn may well have contributed to the strong growth performance of the EEC countries during this period. In the 1970s and 1980s, however, it became apparent that a range of non-border barriers remained and were even replacing tariffs and quotas as significant impediments to trade. During this later period the process of integration slowed down and even went into reverse, if measured by the share of intra-member trade in total trade.

This highlights that protectionist elements will look to alternative policies once tariffs and quotas are removed and that the removal of all market-segmenting barriers requires attention to a range of regulatory policies, which in practice, although this may not be their true intent, act as constraints upon trade. It was the realization that trade barriers due to differences in technical and safety regulations and due to different testing and conformity assessment procedures were proliferating in Europe which led to the creation of the Single Market in Europe, which addresses the impact of market-segmenting regulatory barriers.

The basic principle adopted in Europe to remove these regulatory barriers in the field of goods is that of mutual recognition, whereby goods manufactured and tested in accordance with a partner country's regulations are deemed to offer equivalent levels of protection to those provided by corresponding domestic rules and procedures. Thus, products produced in partner countries can be accepted without the need for further agreement with the presumption that they will not undermine basic regulatory objectives concerning health and safety and so on. This clearly requires a high degree of trust in partners. In practice, for the principle of mutual recognition to work often requires accreditation of testing and certification bodies and a mutual recognition arrangement (MRA) between bodies because member states often regulate for the same product risks in slightly different ways (or in the same way but requiring duplication of conformity assessment).

The principle of mutual recognition now plays an important role in guiding integration in Europe. CEC (1999) argues that the application of mutual recognition is 'consonant with the idea of a dynamic approach to the application of subsidiarity; by avoiding the systematic creation of detailed rules at Community level, mutual recognition ensures greater observance of local, regional and national traditions and makes it possible to maintain the diversity of products and services which come onto the markets'. In short, mutual recognition preserves the multiformity of tastes and preferences in Europe. Governments maintain substantial freedom to apply their own rules to domestically produced products but have to accept products produced to rules stipulated elsewhere. Thus, mutual recognition is a powerful tool for achieving integration, whilst maintaining a degree of national autonomy and diversity.

In certain cases, however, 'equivalence' between levels of regulatory protection embodied in national regulations in Europe cannot be assumed, and the only viable way to remove trade barriers has been for the member states to reach agreement on a common set of legally binding requirements. Subsequently, no further legal impediments can prevent market access of complying products anywhere in the EU market. EU legislation harmonizing technical specifications has involved two distinct approaches, the 'old approach' and the 'new approach'. The old approach mainly applies to products (chemicals, motor vehicles, pharmaceuticals and foodstuffs) by which the nature of the risk requires extensive product-by-product or even component-by-component legislation and is carried out by means of detailed directives. In the main achieving this type of harmonization was very slow for two reasons. First, the process of harmonization became highly technical since it sought to meet the individual requirements of each product category (including components). This resulted in extensive and drawn-out consultations. Second, the adoption of old approach directives was based on unanimity in the Council. As a result the harmonization process proceeded extremely slowly. Indeed the approach was ineffective since new national regulations proliferated at a much faster rate than the production of EC level directives on a limited set of products (Pelkmans 1987).

Increasingly it was recognized that there was a need to reduce the intervention of the public authorities prior to a product being placed on the market. Moreover, the decision-making procedure needed to be adapted in order to facilitate the adoption of technical harmonization directives by a qualified majority in the Council. This has been done by the adoption of the 'new approach' and applies to products, which have 'similar characteristics' and where there has been widespread divergence of technical regulations in EU countries. What makes this approach 'new' is that it only indicates 'essential requirements' and leaves greater freedom to manufacturers as to how to satisfy those requirements, dispensing with the 'old' type of exhaustively detailed directives.

The new approach directives provide for more flexibility than the detailed harmonization directives of the old approach, by using the support of the established European standardization bodies, CEN, CENELEC and the national standard bodies. The standardization work is achieved in a more efficient way, is easier to update and involves greater participation from industry. A further feature of the new approach is the use of market surveillance and the choice of attestation methods that are available: by self-certification against the essential requirements, by using generic standards or by using notified bodies for type approval and testing of conformity of type. The point of this is to highlight that deep integration requires a high degree of trust between partners together with the construction of common policies and harmonized regulations.

Since the GATT and now the WTO have been instrumental in substantially reducing border trade barriers across the world, it is barriers due to the application of domestic regulatory policies that are the main impediments to international trade flows in many sectors. At the same time the prevalence of regulatory interventions to achieve genuine policy objectives such as those concerning health, safety, and the environment, has increased. Thus, the degree of trade integration generated by regional agreements that tackle only border trade barriers may be limited.

Facing up to the Problems caused by Specific Sectors – Agriculture

Another important feature of European integration that should provide a lesson for others contemplating regional integration is the role and difficulties posed by the agricultural sector. The European experience shows that protectionism and subsidies towards a particular sector can quickly become entrenched and that political economy factors may render it extremely difficult to adjust and amend such policies towards economically rational outcomes. Whilst the Treaty of Rome laid down the key objectives regarding agricultural policy in Europe, it did not specify the means by which these objectives should be achieved. This suggests that where agriculture, or any sector, is singled out for special treatment it is important for both economic and political economy reasons that clear objectives together with constraints on the policies for achieving those objectives should be specified. In Europe, by the late 1980s, agriculture, a sector which contributes less than 5 per cent of GDP in the EU and which provides a similarly small proportion of total employment, was absorbing around one half of the total budget expenditures of the European Union!

The Treaty of Rome provided for the establishment of the Common Agricultural Policy (CAP) and laid down the main objectives of the CAP. These objectives were the following: increase agricultural productivity, ensure a fair standard of living for the agricultural community, stabilize markets, assure the availability of supply and ensure reasonable prices for consumers. By the end of the 1960s for most agricultural products a system of protection and support was introduced through the common market organization (CMO) which used target prices, intervention prices, threshold prices at the common frontier and export subsidies.

This highly interventionist and protectionist agricultural policy achieved the goal of self-sufficiency in several key products, such as grains, beef, dairy and sugar, but then led to massive overproduction with excessive costs for consumers due to high prices, damaging environmental consequences, and budgetary difficulties for the EC budget. Throughout the 1970s and 1980s the EU was unable to implement reforms which could have led to a more sensible approach to supporting farmers in Europe. Ultimately, the excesses of the CAP resulted in increasing tension with trade partners and eventually the GATT/WTO negotiations under the Uruguay Round of the late 1980s and early 1990s put growing pressure on the EU to change its protectionist agricultural policy.

The first substantial attempt to change the policy, undertaken in the 1980s, had sought to reduce price support and depress production. To discourage production the 'co-responsible principle' was introduced which established production quotas and maximum guaranteed quantities (above which farmers could not receive the full guaranteed price or had to pay a tax or could not sell their surpluses to the intervention authorities). Structural policies were also designed to discourage overproduction by providing compensation for the setting aside of land. Finally a strict limit was established for agricultural expenditures which aimed to constrain the increase of the CAP budget.

These amendments failed to reduce overproduction and prices remained high and the CAP continued to fail to meet its key basic objectives laid down in the Treaty of Rome, to ensure a 'fair' standard of living for farmers and reasonable prices for consumers. The vast majority of support was distributed to a small proportion of wealthy farmers whilst high border barriers continued to ensure that prices for basic agricultural products in Europe were considerably higher (sometimes by as much as a factor of three or four) than world prices. As a result it was increasingly recognized that the CAP was an extremely regressive mechanism with poor consumers, who spend proportionately more of their income on food, bearing the brunt of the costs of the policy.

The lack of impact of these changes to the policy, the coming EFTA enlargement with a need for an increase in agricultural expenditures and pressure from the Uruguay Round negotiations led to the MacSharry reform launched in 1992. The main objective of the MacSharry reform was to decouple financial support from the price mechanism. This was achieved by giving direct payments to farmers as compensation for reductions in intervention prices, additional assistance for reducing production through set-aside and by accompanying measures aiming at achieving more environmentally friendly agricultural production. The MacSharry reform replaced variable import levies and quantitative restrictions with tariffs as part of the final agreement under the Uruguay Round, although it does not appear that this led to any substantial declines in border protection. Some sectors, such as sugar and dairy, were completely excluded from these and subsequent reforms.

However, the MacSharry reform could not achieve a complete decoupling of support from production, the subsidy level remained high and the set-aside requirement had only limited effects. International criticism of the CAP continued to rise consonant with increasing awareness of the disastrous impact that the CAP had had on the agricultural sectors of many developing countries. In 1999 Agenda 2000 was launched, building on the previous MacSharry reform. Agenda 2000 emphasized the importance of direct aid instead of price support. Moreover it aimed to further integrate environmental objectives into the CAP, to lower prices further and achieve greater competitiveness of EU products on world markets, guaranteeing the safety and quality of food, and a stable income for farmers.

The aim of the recently conducted mid-term review was to examine the achievements of the objectives set in the Agenda 2000 and to propose further policy developments in order to realize the objectives set in the Agenda 2000. Thus the goals of the mid-term review of the Common Agricultural Policy remained essentially the same as those which were established in Agenda 2000: achievement of a competitive agricultural sector, food quality, preservation of environment, animal welfare, landscapes, cultural heritage and 'social balance'. These goals have to be reached within the same budgetary framework that was set in Agenda 2000. The mid-term review proposes new ways of achieving this objective. Rural support measures have a more pronounced role with an expanded scope of available instruments. The mid-term review proposes a further step to support producers rather than products by introducing a system of a single income payment per farm, integrating all existing direct payments. This new system of direct payment would also be WTO compatible. All direct payments would be conditional on cross-compliance with food quality, environmental and animal welfare criteria. The mid-term review proposes the introduction of a compulsory dynamic modulation system reducing all direct payments by 3 per cent each year to reach 20 per cent.

This brief review highlights the problems that can arise once protectionism of a specific sector becomes entrenched as well as the difficulties in effectively reforming established but bad economic policies. The CAP is, hopefully, an extreme case, nevertheless this all suggests that great care should be taken in regional trade agreements in allowing for sectoral exemptions from liberalization and in creating special policies for specific sectors. At the very least, if particular sectors are to be given special treatment then the objectives for those sectors should be clearly enunciated and the appropriate policies for achieving those objectives should be clearly defined after careful analysis of their potential impact on all affected parties, consumers as well as producers.

The Need to Pursue Genuine External Openness

Another feature of economic integration in Europe has been the evolution of a very complex set of external trade policy agreements. Whilst the EU has been very active in multilateral negotiations under the auspices of the GATT and more recently the WTO, it has, at the same time, established a broad web of preferential trade agreements.[2] This reflects, in part, the fact that a bilateral trade agreement has been the main mechanism, out of a very limited set of available policy instruments, for achieving EU foreign policy objectives. A key feature of free trade agreements is the use of rules of origin to ensure that products under preferential trade schemes do in fact originate in preferential trade partners and that trade from non-partners is not deflected through countries which face zero or low tariffs in the EU. The problem is that rules of origin can be specified in such a way as to shift protection to the external borders of free trade partners and to stimulate trade in intermediate products between the countries in the free trade agreement.

The specification of rules of origin has become particularly important in recent years as technological progress and globalization have led to the increasing fragmentation of the production process into different stages or tasks which are undertaken in different locations. A number of general approaches to origin are available. The simplest way of defining origin is probably change of tariff heading. Alternatively there can be rules relating to the amount of domestic value-added or to specific technical requirements that the product may satisfy.

In the EU's bilateral trade agreements the basic rule that it adopts is that of the change in tariff heading at the four-digit level of the CN or HS. However, in a very large number of cases this basic rule is supplanted by, often restrictive, specific requirements. For example, with the basic rule of change in tariff heading, a country which imports woven cotton fabric (HS 5208) to produce cotton shirts (610510) would satisfy the rule of origin and qualify for preferential reduction of the tariff on cotton shirts. However, in EU free trade agreements the change of tariff classification is replaced with a requirement that the product should have been manufactured from yarn. In effect this imposes the requirement that two stages of production must be undertaken in the partner or qualifying area to confer origin – not only the sewing together of the fabric but also the production of the fabric itself. Clothing products made in free trade partners of the EU but which are made up of fabrics imported from third countries, such as China, will not satisfy the EU origin rules and will not qualify for tariff reduction.

In Europe it would appear that to be able to satisfy rules of origin to achieve preferential access to the EU market requires a degree of sophistication on the part of firms in the free trade partner to be able to carefully track and show the origin and movement throughout the company of imported intermediate inputs. It also seems that a modern and efficient customs service is a necessary precondition for the proper implementation of the complex rules of origin that have been established by the EU in all of its free trade and preferential trade agreements. This suggests that other countries contemplating free trade agreements should consider carefully the possible role of rules of origin.

European (and North American) experience would suggest that complicated technical rules of origin should be avoided if trade agreements are to deliver genuine improvements in market access. A web of free trade agreements in, say, the Americas, with complex and restrictive rules of origin, may in practice have little impact on trade flows in final products, but rather may bring about a shift in the pattern of intermediate products, with the strong possibility that this will lead to a less efficient allocation of resources. Rules of origin should have a neutral impact on trade after achieving their basic objective of avoiding trade deflection. Often, however, this is not the case.[3]

The Importance of Services in the Modern Economic Environment

A further lesson from European integration is the importance, particularly in the modern context, of liberalizing trade in services. Services have come to play an ever-increasing role in national economies and in international trade. Services provide fundamental inputs to a range of economic activities. Yet the EU has found it very difficult to liberalize cross-border transactions relating to a range of service products. Again, the European experience suggests that the benefits from regional integration will tend to be larger if services are included, and accompanied by external trade liberalization of the services sector. Again, as for trade in goods, the economic benefits of preferential trade liberalization in services will be enhanced if accompanied by multilateral liberalization. This shows the importance of agreement on further liberalization under the General Agreement of Trade in Services (GATS) in the current round of trade negotiations at the WTO.

The majority of economic activity is concentrated in the service sectors and barriers to effective trade in services are typically much higher than those facing goods. It is clear then that there may be substantial gains from including services in an FTA. Given that constraints upon trade in services are often prohibitive, then preferential trade liberalization cannot cause actual trade diversion – there is no trade to divert. In addition, there will not be a loss of tariff revenue since the main barriers to trade are regulatory barriers, which do not generate revenue for the government. In this case a FTA could only cause ‘potential’ trade diversion in the sense that potential additional gains from non-preferential liberalization are foregone.

There are a number of reasons why free trade agreements provide an easier and more effective means of achieving liberalization of services than the multilateral route. Effective service liberalization may require a degree of labor mobility so that service providers can establish themselves locally. This may be easier to achieve in a bilateral free trade agreement than on a global basis. In many service sectors governments seek to achieve legitimate public policy objectives, such as protection of consumers, through regulatory intervention. Deep integration in these services sectors will therefore require a degree of harmonization and mutual recognition which may also be easier to achieve on a country by country basis than for all countries together.

The importance of services is further magnified by the fact that many services are vital inputs into production processes so that if regional integration leads to lower priced and better quality services there will be additional indirect effects on industrial sectors. Inefficient domestic production of services behind trade and investment barriers can act as a tax on production of goods. In the absence of services liberalization there may be no incentive to increase the output of a goods sector which is not receiving protection but where the services that it uses are protected, hence raising their price and so the costs to industries which rely on them.

Indeed, the liberalization of services may be necessary for industrial sectors to be able to benefit fully from the direct opportunities that are made available by the removal of trade barriers and the harmonization of regulatory regimes. For this reason it may be preferable to give services a high priority from the start of any negotiations rather than postpone liberalization until the later phases of an agreement. Including liberalization of services on the agenda from the start is also important since the removal of barriers to trade and establishment of barriers that constrain service provision is likely to take longer than the border barriers affecting goods, and indeed effective liberalization will require some degree of harmonization of national regulatory regimes.

The magnitude of barriers to trade in services and the importance of services as inputs in both manufacturing and agricultural sectors suggests that a free trade agreement which includes services is likely to generate much more substantial economic efficiency gains than an agreement which is confined to barriers to trade in goods alone. The service sector also plays a crucial role in economic growth. Just as with trade in goods, liberalization of trade in services can lead to technology transfer and technology spillovers. These can arise both through cross-border provision of services and through foreign direct investment to establish commercial presence. Such technology transfer will be the source of additional growth.

There is one key difference that distinguishes services from goods liberalization, in terms of their impact on growth. Services liberalization often implies a larger scale of activity in the domestic economy, which provides greater scope for the growth-enhancing characteristics which are present in many service sectors such as learning by doing and knowledge generation, raising product variety and product quality (Mattoo et al. 2001). This larger scale of activity arises because for many services the simultaneity of production and consumption entails that a local presence is necessary to supply the market. This requires factors of production to move to the consuming country. Further, many barriers in services sectors constrain entry to the market, not just for foreign entrants but also for new domestic providers. Hence, the liberalization of services sectors can result in more competition from both foreign and new domestic firms, which implies a larger scale of activity.

Within the services sector particular attention is often given to financial services owing to the role that they play in directing investment funds to the most productive uses and in so doing providing for growth of output and incomes. Financial systems also play other important roles which can affect efficiency and growth. These functions comprise the trading and pooling of risk, the collection and dissemination of information concerning different investment opportunities and the monitoring of managerial performance and hence the means and incentives for improved corporate control, the mobilization of savings through the provision of innovative financial instruments and the facilitation of trade in goods and services through the provision and maintenance of payment systems.

If liberalization of financial services leads to higher savings and investment and/or the more productive use of capital then a higher level of per capita income will result. Growth rates will increase during the transition period to this higher level of income but ultimately growth will return to its equilibrium rate. Permanently higher growth rates will arise if financial liberalization leads to faster innovation in the financial sector or engenders processes such as learning by doing. A number of studies have demonstrated the importance of the depth of financial markets for economic growth (King and Levine 1993, Barthelemy and Varoudakis 1995), although the role of policy and the impact of trade in financial services are not clarified. More recently, Francois and Schuknecht (1999) postulate a causal link from liberalization of trade in services to performance in financial sectors and economic growth. Trade liberalization promotes competition and higher quality financial services through entry. In an empirical exercise they find that moving from closed financial markets to a more open financial system increases the degree of competition in the provision of financial services which is associated with a higher growth rate. Mattoo et al. (2001) find that countries with open financial and telecommunications sectors have tended to grow as much as 1.5 percentage points faster than less open countries.

The empirical literature on trade liberalization in services and economic growth is still at a relatively early stage and there is no available direct evidence on the impact of bilateral and regional integration on the services and growth nexus. Nevertheless, there are strong grounds to believe that the inclusion of services in a free trade agreement will increase substantially the economic benefits of such an agreement in terms of both the efficiency gains and the impact upon economic growth. The reasoning above suggests that liberalization of services should commence early in the implementation of an agreement rather than being delayed, so that these gains are made available quickly, and growth is enhanced, and to ensure that the potential gains in industrial sectors can be fully reaped.

CONCLUSIONS

This chapter has looked briefly at the early period of European integration and sought to consider some of the key lessons, particularly in the area of product market integration, which may be of relevance to countries currently contemplating regional integration initiatives. In particular, we have stressed that European integration was based upon firm foundations in terms of a widespread and genuine commitment to liberalize, accompanied by a strong desire for mutual cooperation and understanding based upon clear and effective communication. It is also clear that the root of European integration, the Treaty of Rome, emerged from a fairly long period of learning by doing with regard to regional integration in Europe, during which a number of initiatives failed.

The initial phase of European integration took place during a particularly favourable period in terms of economic growth, unemployment and inflation. This together with the evolving importance of intra-industry trade and the construction of widespread social safety nets in Europe entailed that the adjustment costs from economic integration in Europe were rather muted and that those who did suffer adverse economic effects were supported by the social policies implemented in the individual members of the EEC. Thus, widespread support for the initial integration initiative was never compromised.

The European experience of internal trade barrier removal was accompanied by the successive reduction of external trade barriers. This helped to ensure that integration was efficiency enhancing. In the modern context, those embarking on regional initiatives should play an active and constructive role at the WTO in reducing external trade barriers.

The European experience suggests a number of key issues that may be relevant for future integration exercises elsewhere:

- Effective integration will require attention to a range of behind the border policies which can constrain trade. With the highly fragmented production networks that characterize many sectors today, successful integration will often require the provision of an environment that allows local firms or firms with foreign involvement to participate effectively in these networks. This often requires a degree of approximation and sometimes harmonization of technical regulations and standards to ensure compatibility with product requirements in major markets.
- The benefits of integration will be eroded if particular sectors are provided with special treatment in the form of exemptions from regional liberalization, high external protection, and/or substantial domestic support which is trade distorting.
- The gains from a regional free trade agreement will be undermined if the agreement is accompanied by a rise in external protection and/or

restrictive rules of origin. Restrictive rules of origin will also compromise any policy objectives that the region may have through the use of trade preferences to particular groups of countries.

- Liberalization of services is an essential ingredient in a successful integration exercise. Since the gains from liberalizing trade in goods are in part dependent upon the liberalization of services the latter should commence early in any agreement and should not be unduly delayed.

NOTES

1. A preferential trade agreement will have a positive effect upon welfare when new trade between the partners is generated. This trade creation occurs if relatively inefficient domestic output is substituted by goods produced more cheaply in the partner. However, if the preferential reduction of trade barriers increases trade between the partners at the expense of more efficient producers in the rest of the world then there will be trade diversion. Here the maintenance of the tariff against non-members entails additional costs from importing from relatively high cost producers within the free trade area and the loss of tariff revenues. If the latter detrimental effect on welfare exceeds the positive effect from trade creation then overall welfare or real income will decline.
2. For a more detailed description of EU trade policies see Brenton (2002).
3. For more discussion of rules of origin in EU trade agreements see Brenton and Manchin (2002). Flatters (2001) provides a useful discussion of the development of rules of origin in the South African Development Community (SADC).

REFERENCES

Barthelemy, J.-C. and A. Varoudakis (1995), 'Thresholds in financial development and economic growth', *Manchester School of Economic and Social Studies*, **63**, 70–84.

Brenton, P (2002), 'The changing nature and determinants of EU trade policies', in T. Brewer, P. Brenton and G. Boyd (eds), *Globalizing Europe*, Cheltenham: Edward Elgar.

Brenton, P. and M. Manchin (2002), 'Making EU trade agreements work: the role of rules of origin', Centre for European Policy Studies working document, Brussels.

European Commission (1999), 'Mutual recognition in the context of the follow-up to the action plan for the single market', communication to the European Parliament and the Council.

Flatters, F. (2001), 'The SADC trade protocol: which way ahead', *Southern African Update*, **10**, 1–4.

Francois, J. and L. Schuknecht (1999), 'Trade in financial services: procompetitive effects and growth performance', discussion paper 2144, Centre for European Policy Studies, London.

King, R. and R. Levine (1993), 'Finance, entrepreneurship and growth: theory and evidence', *Journal of Monetary Economics*, **32**, 513–42.

Mattoo, A., R. Rathindran and A. Subramanian (2001), 'Measuring services trade liberalisation and its impact on economic growth: an illustration', World Bank working paper, Washington.

Pelkmans, J. (1987), 'The new approach to technical harmonisation and standardisation', *Journal of Common Market Studies*, **25**.

Pelkmans, J. (1997), *European Integration: Methods and Economic Analysis*, Harlow: Addison Wesley Longman.

8. Hemispheric monetary cooperation

Gavin Boyd

The growth, employment, and community building effects of hemispheric trade liberalization will depend on the development of regional monetary cooperation to facilitate productive interaction between financial sectors and the real economies. For the orderly expansion of regional trade and transnational production, it will be imperative to work collectively for the elimination of exchange rate risks, and this collaboration will have to extend into the management of financial markets, with an emphasis on productive funding and the restraint of potentially destabilizing speculation. The extremely disruptive consequences of high risk and high volume speculation in the USA during the 1990s – speculation which gave impetus to numerous forms of large scale corporate fraud – have indicated the vital importance of linkages between monetary policy and administrative measures for the reform of financial markets. Policy level and corporate understanding of these linkages has been challenged by the difficulties of recovery from the recession in the USA and by the magnitude of exchange rate problems associated with its unsustainable current account deficits. For Latin American states, with pathetic records of macromanagement failures, the clear requirement for regional monetary cooperation has to be recognized with awareness that market led dollarization in their economies, activated mainly by persistent financial crises, will accelerate with hemispheric trade liberalization, despite the problems of macromanagement in the USA.

Latin American states are losing elements of monetary sovereignty as their weak currencies are being undercut by the US dollar. This kind of problem was experienced by European states before the formation of their monetary union (Mundell 2002), but Latin American administrations do not have the resolve and competence to work for the establishment of such a union in the Southern hemisphere. Their principal option is to facilitate continuing market led dollarization, while striving to form very active consultative links with US monetary authorities and building more coordinated national economies, with increased openness to each other. Dollarization entails vulnerabilities to stresses in the US economy, changes in the international role of the US dollar, and shifts in US monetary policy, as well as in the operations of US financial enterprises. These vulnerabilites could be reduced by the development of stronger investment and trade links with the European Union, but such links are likely to grow slowly, because of Europe's economic and political problems. The challenges of increasing asymmetries in structural and financial hemispheric interdependences will tend to make Latin American initiatives for intensive consultations with the USA more and more urgent.

ANALYTICAL PERSPECTIVES

Research on issues of hemispheric monetary cooperation has led to major, conclusions, for policy levels and corporate managements. Dollarization can put Latin American countries on a fast track toward monetary stability (Calvo 2001), but with vulnerabilities to adverse trends in the US economy which have become evident since the collapse of its speculative boom, which dramatized failures in regulatory discipline, market discipline, and monetary policy, as well as trade policy and fiscal policy. The dollarization to be anticipated will constitute a unilateral and uncooperative monetary union, with uncertain prospects for evolution into a system of multilateral co-determination (von Furstenberg 2002); the tradition of fully independent monetary management remains very strong in the USA, and Latin American states lack status as prospective partners in monetary cooperation.

Questions about economic advice to governments relating to the evolution of fundamentals in regional trade liberalization however necessitate consideration of monetary cooperation options in a larger context of theorizing about deepening integration. A common currency, if under sound management, reduces transaction costs and risks, thus facilitating commerce (Rose 2001) as well as production specializations that can be planned with security, subject to the orientation of financial sectors toward service of the interdependent real economies. The entire pattern can be viewed with beliefs in the efficiencies of totally competitive corporate behaviour, and in its equilibrium effects, and therefore in the restriction of governance functions to minimal regulatory requirements, allowing the formation of a liberal regional market economy. New thinking in behavioural macroeconomics, however, (Stiglitz 2002) has aided understanding of the efficiencies of cooperation, recognized in parallel thinking about intercorporate technological interdependences (Foss and Mahnke 2000) and the development of human capital in knowledge based economies (Archibugi and Lundvall 2001). Research in behavioural finance, meanwhile (Shiller 2003), has indicated how intense competition between financial enterprises for speculative gains can seriously retard growth by diverting investment from productive use, pushing asset appreciations, then abrupt declines, weakening market discipline, and subjecting the evolution of structural interdependences to the effects of manipulated volatility in foreign exchange markets.

Institutional economics[1] has been challenged by behavioural macroeconomics and behavioural finance, especially because of the increasing magnitude of corporate and intercorporate governance issues and collective management issues. As structural interdependences become larger and more complex the regional pattern of structural linkages is distinguished by the formation of transnational production systems and by associated concentration trends, which in combination weaken national macromanagement capabilities, thus setting requirements for new institutional development. This is a context in which the scope of behavioural finance has to be extended, to take account of the dangers and costs of failures in productive funding by international financial markets, the distortions in interactions between financial sectors and real economies, and the resultant problems for macroeconomic policies.

Altogether, policy learning related to issues of monetary cooperation in a hemispheric free trade area has to become open to requirements for international public goods in a vast setting in which market efficiencies and failures and government efficiencies and failures extend across borders, within and outside regional patterns of structural and policy interdependence. The management of US monetary policy to serve the common good is not a responsibility confined to the national economy, and will have to assume hemispheric dimensions as structural and financial linkages expand in a Free Trade Area of the Americas, with increasing dollarization. Complementary responsibilities will also have to be accepted by Latin American administrations. A larger and more difficult requirement, however, will be collaborative, although asymmetric, regulation of the operations of international financial enterprises providing large volumes of credit outside monetary transmission mechanisms for productive and speculative transactions affecting growth, inflation, and exchange rates. Liberalized trade in financial services, to be expected in freer hemispheric commerce, will be in effect beyond the external reach of US monetary policy, while contributing to further market led dollarization in Latin America. US banks active in securities sectors will have more extensive double roles in this context. At the same time US financial market regulators, striving to tighten discipline at home, will have to cope with external surveillance problems as the enterprises under supervision expand operations in the Southern hemisphere.

One of the major contrasts between a hemispheric free trade system and the expanding European Union is that the erosion of monetary sovereignty in the Union by securities sectors (Hartman, Maddaloni, and Manganelli 2003) may be less than that expected in Latin America, while dollarization continues in conjunction with deeper penetration by US financial enterprises: the regional dimension of US monetary authority will be weakened. Throughout the hemisphere, linkages between monetary policy and financial market regulation will demand attention.

MARKET LED CURRENCY CHANGE

Dollarization tends to increase in Latin America because of general interest in greater access to the US market, the effects of financial crises on public confidence, and expectations of larger trade and investment flows in the hemisphere. National firms expanding commerce with and production in neighbouring countries, while developing linkages with US enterprises extending regional operations, tend to make more and more use of the US currency. The overall trend is likely to become stronger as hemispheric trade develops at higher volumes, and especially as US firms build more extensive transnational production systems. European firms in Latin America will tend to contribute to the dollarization through transactions with host country and US enterprises related to the increasing scale of hemispheric commerce.

Political instability, financial crises, and indications of continuing policy level incompetence and indecision must be expected to add to corporate and household incentives to transact and hold reserves in US currency, especially while the US presence in financial sectors becomes more visible. The dollarization, moreover, will encourage expansion of that presence, and of US involvement in manufacturing, retailing, and resource based sectors. European corporate rivalry is likely to have diminishing significance for US enterprises in Latin America because of Europe's technological lags, lower growth, outflows of passive investment, and the interests of European firms in alliances with US enterprises rather than with each other.

Monetary union in Europe has not significantly challenged the prominence of the US dollar as the international currency of the Southern hemisphere, and any European initiatives for trade and investment expansion in Latin America are likely to have weak impacts unless there are extraordinary increases in European Union leadership capabilities and entrepreneurial vigour. The achievement of monetary union in Europe has somewhat remote significance for Latin America because of the record of failures in Southern hemispheric regional cooperation, and because much absorption in intraregional affairs is evident in the image projected to the outside world by the European Union. European monetary union however has demonstrated the logic of regional monetary integration for the operation of an internal market. As understanding of this logic will have increasing influence in corporate associations and policy communities that will become regionally active in a hemispheric free trade area, the dollarization trend will demand constructive responses from US monetary authorities and, it must be stressed, from US regulators of financial markets. There may well be increases in dollarization on a scale that will require immediate attention as hemispheric trade liberalization develops.

What Latin American administrations and corporate groups can hope for, and encourage, is enlightened US monetary and regulatory cooperation, in a spirit of collegial capitalism, indicating prospects for the development of a coordinated regional market economy. There is a danger that Southern hemispheric aspirations will have to cope with the influence of US interest groups pushing for aggressive negotiation of hard and precise agreements on reductions of regional trade barriers, with the advantages of superior bargaining power, and of the opportunities for the trading of political favours in the shaping of US trade policy. Problems of advanced political development in the USA, affecting the management of foreign economic relations and the entire policy mix, have become serious because of the divisive effects of growth and distributional as well as structural issues resulting from coordination failures (Hall and Soskice 2001).

Difficulties of political development in Latin America, meanwhile, may be aggravated while dollarization increases and prospective disparities in gains from hemispheric trade liberalization become more evident. Policy learning requirements set by dollarization and freer regional commerce will be more urgent and more challenging. Imbalances in the spread of benefits from liberalized commerce have to be expected because of adversarial moves that have affected the atmosphere of initial negotiations. These moves have revealed US interest in securing Latin American commitments to liberal foreign direct investment policies, excluding anti-dumping practices from the negotiations, and meeting the demands of protectionist groups which had secured concessions in the Congressional processes that had granted Trade Promotion Authority to the administration in 2002. The intended openness to foreign direct investment has been understood to entail very limited freedom for structural policies and virtually no scope for competition policy, while the intent to protect US producers of citrus fruits, sugar, textiles and steel has signalled that the terms of trade liberalization will be unequal, to the detriment of Latin American prospects for export led growth.

Adversarial trends in the dominant approach to trade liberalization[2] overshadow discussions about dollarization even though the probability of greater but imbalanced trade liberalization will tend to increase Latin American use of the US currency. The likely costs of further dollarization will then be more challenging for Latin American states. The management of US monetary policy will retain a strong domestic focus, while the role of the US dollar in foreign exchange markets will be subjected to downward pressures because of the continuation of heavy current account deficits and the attitudes of investors to the nation's overall debt levels. US financial enterprises will develop a strong presence in Latin America through mergers and acquisitions, with extensive scope for speculative operations that may be large in comparison with productive funding, which may well accord priorities to US firms. In the perspectives of US policymakers, dollarization is a result of spontaneous Latin American choices in reaction to macromanagement failures throughout the Southern hemisphere, and those failures discourage recognition of any Latin American entitlements to representation in US monetary policy processes, or in the regulation of US financial markets.

INTERDEPENDENCIES IN US MONETARY POLICY AND FINANCIAL REGULATION

Public goods issues in the USA's management of hemispheric economic relations set clear requirements to work for consultative responsiveness to Latin American problems, with concerns for fairness, reciprocity and social justice, in line with the new thinking in behavioural macroeconomics, and in recognition of the disruptive potentials of speculation in financial markets that have received attention in behavioural finance. But continuing dollarization in Latin America is tending to intensify competitive pressures, in conjunction with expansions of cross border commerce encouraged by prospective trade liberalization, and US firms gaining larger market shares in the intensified competition will influence monetary policy through financial communities interacting with the Federal Reserve. The overall efficiency effects, with the development, decline, and relocations of industries, may be viewed with expectations of progress toward competitive regional equilibrium, dominated by the most productive enterprises, while vigorous entrepreneurial cultures develop in reaction within Latin America. Seeking policy level collaboration with Latin American administrations accepting dollarization may thus not seem to be a high priority option.

Literature on US policy making suggests that relevant public goods will be neglected (Dam 2001, Aberbach and Rockman 2000), but there are clear imperatives for learning, and these have to relate to the dangers recognized in behavioural 'finance, which point to extremely urgent requirements for knowledge intensive and high principled decision making. The necessary policy learning has to be motivated by understanding that dysfunctional dynamics have very serious effects in US macromanagement, through the consequences of political trading, and through neglected structural policy issues as well as through the strong speculative propensities of the financial sector. It must be reiterated, moreover, that while the problems of regulating that sector will become more difficult as its operations extend in Latin America, there will be greater scope for undetected corporate fraud as US firms increase their presence outside the home country's regulatory reach, unless much Latin American cooperation is forthcoming in response to collegial orientations in US policy.

The imperative is to develop a functional monetary policy in a comprehensively functional policy mix, which must include reform and regulation of the securities industry, with the cultivation of a spirit of collegial capitalism that will inspire Latin American corporate and political cooperation while higher moral standards are established in the home economy. The image projected by the liberal market economy has been severely tainted by corporate fraud and by decline after grossly irrational speculation. Sustained resolution to change this image would help Latin American decision makers to see more substantial benefits from their acceptance of market led dollarization.

A fundamental challenge is to regain sufficient monetary sovereignty, for sound macromanagement, through functional change in the securities industry, with emphasis on promoting shifts to stakeholder corporate governance,[3] substantially greater use of bank financing, the taxation of trade in financial assets, and an enlightened competition policy that will discipline the market for corporate control. Sustained policy level and corporate articulation of these objectives is needed for stable growth with diversifying complementary entrepreneurial specializations, in a more advanced knowledge intensive political economy. The affirmations of principles and values could be joined by Latin American contributions to the necessary policy learning, for the development of a hemispheric policy consensus on fundamentals.

The USA's high level of monetary and financial interdependence with the European Union could well become more open to collaborative management if there is a reorientation toward collegial policies in relations with dollarizing Latin American countries, linked with quests for more cooperative Atlantic interactions. The enlargement of the European Union is strengthening its significance in world finance, and is adding to its importance for the USA while conflicting pressures are affecting the US currency's exchange rates. European goodwill could be gained by considerate treatment of Latin American interests that would indirectly benefit European economic ties with the Southern hemisphere. A US negotiating style expressing aggressive unilateralism in pursuit of trade concessions and indicating intent to discriminate against European commercial opportunities in Latin America would cause strains in Atlantic relations.

Dollarization, as it continues, will reduce transaction costs and risks in Latin America for Southern hemisphere firms, European enterprises, and US corporations, while increasing US interests in regional financial stability, economic openness, and improvements in macromanagement. The dynamics of accelerating hemispheric financial linkages, moreover, will increase the importance, for the USA, of working for understandings with Latin American administrations about the vital requirements for prudent fiscal policies throughout the region, and, thus, establishing the foundations of a hemispheric stability pact.[4] Regional consultations for this purpose could be very appropriately sponsored by the USA, through the Organization of American States,' with support from the International Monetary Fund. The consultations could also facilitate the development of consensus on regulation of the Southern hemisphere's financial sectors, and on the involvement of US regulators in this process. Greater security would then be provided for commerce and the funding of industry throughout the region.

HEMISPHERIC MONETARY AND FINANCIAL INTERDEPENDENCES

Monetary and financial interdependences in the hemisphere are evolving, through the independent operations of nonfinancial and financial enterprises, in a context of regionalized market efficiencies and failures, and government efficiencies and failures. Linkages between monetary, financial, and trade as well as structural policies are becoming more active and more complex throughout the hemisphere, while efficiencies and failures in the increasingly linked markets are assuming larger dimensions, challenging policy levels and corporations to work for the provision of more public goods, restraint on concentration trends, the harmonization of positive externalities, and the development of more functional information flows. Collaborative management of the hemispheric monetary and financial interdependences is becoming more and more necessary for the necessary enhancement of market functions, and will have to be aided by that enhancement. This must be stressed because overall growth prospects in the hemisphere depend especially on major reductions of the uncertainties which impose caution on entrepreneurial initiatives and provide opportunities for potentially destabilizing speculation.

Full clarification of the dynamics of monetary and financial interdependences in a gradually integrating hemispheric market would be a very valuable service for the region by the USA, as a contribution to general understanding of its policy orientation, and to the development of consensus with Latin American elites. There is a similarity here between requirements for transparency in corporate financial statements, which have become urgent because of the numerous corporate frauds in the USA: Latin American administrations accepting and assisting market led dollarization need to know how the USA is managing its monetary policy and regulating its financial sector, and what changes are likely in response to current and anticipated problems, relating especially to the stability of the economy and the persistent trade deficits. There are special grounds for concern about the financial sector because US regulatory tightening since the collapse of the speculative boom has not engaged effectively with the clear requirement to control the operations of hedge funds. The capacities of these funds for speculative attacks on the currencies of industrializing countries are sources of deep anxiety. The regulatory efforts moreover have encountered difficult problems in the securities sectors which have lost investor trust (Coffee 2003).

For Latin America a key dynamic associated with dollarization is the increased funding of industry by an expanding US financial presence (Peek and Rosengren 2000). Domestic funding is limited, has higher costs, entails greater uncertainties, and is affected by capital flight. Reputations established with US lenders moreover increase prospects for further financing, although that may be affected by priorities given to US firms expanding transnational production in the Southern hemisphere. Credible policy level promises of considerate treatment of Latin American interests in this increasing dependence, and its tendency to accelerate dollarization, would help to build up the USA's status as a nation committed to relational cooperation.

The considerate treatment to be hoped for by Latin American policymakers and corporate managements is acceptance of basic imperatives for progress toward more equal diversified hemispheric structural interdependences, with transformations of Southern hemisphere economies into more coordinated and higher growth systems. The integrative intent necessary for establishing high levels of trust and goodwill will have to be made evident throughout the US business culture, with emphasis on fairness and reciprocity, social justice and the formation of human capital. Diffusion of the new thinking in behavioural macroeconomics, for greater efficiency, equity, and stability and collegiality in American capitalism, will have to become stronger as the political economy becomes more knowledge intensive, with more extensive external structural linkages.

Latin American decision makers have concerns that US negotiating strategies will strive for hemispheric market openness on terms that will severely limit the scope for structural policies in the Southern hemisphere that could develop more balanced interdependences, while US enterprises would have the advantages of indirect subsidies such as those aiding export firms which only the European Union has been able to challenge. The expected insistence that Latin American enterprises be totally self-reliant, under understandings to be set out in hard and precise agreements, can be seen to reflect tacit confidence that the superior efficiencies of US corporations will ensure highly imbalanced gains from the liberalized regional commerce. Significantly phased reductions of Latin American import barriers, if negotiated, would be viewed with fears that substantial enhancements of corporate performance, in the absence of industrial aids, would be difficult to achieve within the agreed periods, and that this prospect would discourage entrepreneurship, while motivating capital flight. These consequences would be all the more likely if large increases in openness to incoming direct investment were required in advance of phased reductions of import barriers.

Altogether, the logic of a highly constructive US stance on management of hemispheric monetary and financial interdependences, while dollarization trends accelerate, should ideally be linked with a collegial and relational approach to regional market integration, to eliminate fears of aggressive unilateralism and adversarial legalism, as well as of unrestrained concentration trends and of destabilizing speculation. The asymmetries of interdependence which Mexico has experienced in NAFTA, as consequences of market integration with hard competition (Cardero 1999, Montamen-Samadian and Cruz 1999) have to be recognized in the rest of the for Southern hemisphere, with understandings that the requirements for high principled US statecraft are very demanding. Hyper-pluralism, as a problem of advanced political development in the USA, will tend to increase after hemispheric trade liberalization, unless there is enlightened administrative leadership for an integrative and knowledge intensive approach to the building of a new regional system.

Commitments to the development of such an approach will be more meaningful and more inspiring if the European Union is drawn into collaborative participation, instead of being implicitly threatened with increasing discrimination against its interests in commercial ties with the Southern hemisphere. European participation, it must be reiterated, would help to reduce inequalities in the hemispheric negotiations, assist policy learning, and induce US responsiveness to fundamental issues of collective management. Market led dollarization could be managed more effectively by Latin American administrations and firms if there were an active secondary pattern of Euro use, increasing with the growth of European trade and investment links, and offering possibilities for adaptation to dollar exchange rate fluctuations. A stronger European financial presence moreover could help to supplement the market discipline and regulatory discipline associated with the American financial presence, while contributing to independent development of Latin American financial sectors that would otherwise have very limited opportunities for growth.

The policy learning facilitated by European involvement, with the expanded accountability and monitoring that would result, would benefit Latin American and European elites, while tending to make their interactions with US decision makers more productive. There are urgent imperatives for triangular policy learning, and European clarification of these would be a vital part of the knowledge intensive interactions. The key concern for the European Union is the stability of the US currency in world financial markets, which is linked with the state of the US economy – its high debt burdens, its current account deficits, and its vulnerability to destabilizing speculation. While the role of the Euro is consolidated in world finance, as the European Union enlarges and extends its network of preferential trading arrangements, the management of Atlantic monetary interdependence will have to ensure smooth adjustments.[5] These may well tend to be increasingly difficult because of the further weakening of US monetary sovereignty and resumptions of high volume speculation by US financial enterprises. Accelerating dollarization in Latin America, with the growth of a larger US financial presence, will affect a secondary process of market led use of the Euro – in prospect as the most important trend in the international consolidation of the Euro's role as a leading currency.

For Latin American countries, especially Brazil and Argentina, use of the Euro on a significant scale while dollarization continues could moderate risks about exchange rates for the US currency, as well as about future sequences in the US business cycle, while keeping open channels for alternative financing in the evolution of hemispheric finance. Meanwhile in the triangular consultations that would tend to develop, the European involvement could well be a source of challenges for the USA, evoking possibly more knowledge intensive and more collaborative responses to monetary and financial issues emerging in liberalized regional commerce.

The principal area of manageable large scale deepening integration in the USA's interdependencies is the Atlantic, where cultural affinities facilitate understanding and the building of goodwill. Problems in East Asia compete for policy level attention, especially because dollar depreciation, due to current account deficits, is slowed by informal fixing of exchange rates in this region to the US currency, thus contributing to the persistence of large trade imbalances. The problems, for the USA, are intractable, and accordingly can be seen to increase the importance of Atlantic cooperation. That cooperation, it must be reiterated, would benefit from US endeavours to work with the European Union for the expansion of its ties with Latin America while a free trade area of the Americas is established.

PROSPECTS AND PLANNING

Regional market integration has to be planned, in the common interest, with emphasis promoting relational cooperation, for the resolution of market failures and policy failures. The planning must avoid short termism and the narrow perspectives that can be induced by pressures of political and corporate competition, and that contribute to institutional weaknesses. Enlightened and highly dedicated leadership is required. The interdependencies that increase with market integration evolve with losses of economic sovereignty to transnational firms, and accordingly international corporate collaboration becomes necessary for comprehensively constructive statecraft. Such statecraft has to engage with complex problems of coordination in the promotion of regional economic integration, and in the formation of a free trade area of the Americas the most important economic diplomacy will have to be undertaken by the USA. This will have to respond to the dollarization which is occurring in advance of hemispheric market integration, and will have to express a resourceful political will, constantly, for the building of relational assets, across borders, and across sectors, combining entrepreneurial dynamism with magnanimity.

There is a danger that the constructive imperative will receive inadequate attention while growth prospects appear to be improving in Latin America, with dollarization and advances toward regional trade liberalization, and while inflows of investment from the USA increase. These inflows will include speculative ventures that will tend to activate booms in equities and property, with much inflation, adversely affecting export growth. Requirements to guide investment into productive operations therefore may not be met, the wealth effects of the booms will tend to go in large measure into consumption, and the unwarranted optimism generated by the booms will undoubtedly push asset appreciations higher, until investor confidence collapses. The vicious sequences of the speculative boom and decline in the USA may thus be repeated in the Southern hemisphere while the USA's own recovery remains slow, in part because of the drift of investment into Latin America, in search of higher short term yields, that is while interest rates at home remain low, to aid the hoped for recovery. While completion of the dollarization remains uncertain, moreover, the speculative financial involvement in Latin America will tend to include exploitations of volatility in the area's foreign exchange markets. Altogether, then, the well recognized tasks of financial market development and reform in the Southern hemisphere will be made increasingly difficult, but in an atmosphere of unfounded confidence, in the USA as well as in Latin America.

The problems identified in behavioural finance, based especially on the destructive effects of the collapse of investor confidence in the USA, indicate the vital requirements for a US policy stance, combining hemispheric monetary cooperation with prudential regulation and guidance of the home financial sector, as the basic elements in a design for regional financial reform and development. This, it will have to be made clear, will be all the more important for broad societal discipline in support of the limited reach of the regulatory discipline that is intended to deal with corporate fraud in the home economy.

The need for a comprehensively constructive stance has an extremely important domestic dimension: the prospect of hemispheric trade liberalization is viewed with fear by US labor unions, and by members of Congress attentive to constituency interests. Well-publicized increases in investment flows to Latin America will arouse apprehensions about the effects on employment at home. There may well be growing awareness that monetary loosening to facilitate economic recovery makes it very profitable for financial enterprises to borrow at low rates for investment at much higher rates in Latin America. The imperative to eliminate corporate fraud moreover has become linked with the requirement for reform in financial markets, to ensure their service of productive functions; the potentially very large rewards of speculation tend to attract high risk operations, with misrepresentations intended to be rectified before they are detected, it being understood that opaque financial instruments can delay detection.

The challenge for the US administration is to demonstrate, through vigorous policy initiatives, a solidarity building commitment to domestic industrial development and financial market reform, with a highly constructive doctrine of hemispheric economic cooperation. The dangers of renewed destabilizing speculation in the home economy, and of deindustrialization in the course of regional trade liberalization, will have to be overcome, with extensive corporate cooperation, and the promotion of fully productive interaction between the financial sector and the real economy. In the context of this new knowledge intensive statecraft the USA will be able to offer relational cooperation to Latin American administrations facilitating dollarization.

European cooperation in the development of a new regional economy – a coordinated regional market economy – could become collegial, instead of being virtually restricted within mundane adversarial bargaining over the interests of European firms in Latin America. The Europeans have to fear a large scale destabilizing speculative boom in Latin America, and have to be sensitive to the danger of a stronger and more risky speculative propensity in the US financial sector while its global operations become more extensive, with concentration trends that add to the appetite for risk, and for market manipulation to exploit volatility.

Latin American advances in policy learning, with increases in external accountability, in wider ranging interactions with the USA and the European Union, would be conducive to fiscal prudence and cooperation as dollarization continued in the process of regional market integration. This prospect would have to be given explicit recognition in communications affirming the major elements of the new American policy stance. US sponsorship of hemispheric consultations, with European participation, could then very appropriately lead to institutional innovations, to ensure orderly development of a broad policy consensus, in which Latin American representatives would have a sense of autonomous knowledge intensive involvement.

Integrative rather than instrumental policy planning would express the new policy stance. The objective would be not to lock Latin American administrations into hard and precise agreements through aggressive unilateralism, but to open up opportunities for entrepreneurial partnering, to form dynamic and balanced structural interdependences in a region of monetary stability. Relational cooperation would be sought with unswerving purpose, avoiding experimental and disjointed approaches with shifting biases that would discourage positive responses and induce interest in continuous bargaining. Within the US policy making institutions the collaborative orientation would have to become well established.

Interactions between interest groups and policy communities throughout the hemisphere will tend to increase with trade, investment flows, and dollarization. Of the US institutions that will have to assume responsibilities for highly constructive quests for consultative partnering with the Southern hemisphere the Federal Reserve can have special significance, because of the challenges of dollarization for the role of the US currency in regional market integration. A further reason for this significance is that the Federal Reserve, standing apart from the pluralist dynamics of trade policy, may well be able to assume a very potent function in shaping and sustaining a strongly collaborative orientation in US administrative management of relations with Latin America.

The Federal Reserve could have an extremely important role in pressing for control of the myopic protectionist demands of interest groups seeking to restrict imports of Latin American primary products and low technology manufactures: Southern hemisphere countries need revenues from such exports to repay their external debts, and to finance industrialization for more balanced structural interdependence with the USA. The public interest function which the Federal Reserve could assume in this context, especially through forthright advocacy in its policy oriented research studies, would command Latin American respect, as well as the attention of US legislators with capacities for policy learning, while making more evident the vital requirement for comprehensive management of the monetary and financial linkages which are increasing with the Southern hemisphere. A major achievement would be an active role in drawing Latin American administrations into a regional stability pact, for common fiscal restraint.[6] This would provide greater security for increasing dollarization, while reducing exchange rate risks associated with the continuing use of national currencies.

The dual public interest advocacy could be supplemented by the European Central Bank, on the basis of a necessary enlargement of its surveillance functions required by monetary and financial links with Latin America, and by European involvement in IMF regional advising, as well as by the problems in Atlantic monetary interdependence that are related to stresses in the US economy. An enlightened encouragement of a European role would be a highly productive element in US policy, and would help to build trust and goodwill in Latin America, for relational cooperation.

NOTES

1. See Oliver E. Williamson (2000), 'The new institutional economics: taking stock, looking ahead' *Journal of Economic Literature*, **38**, 3 (September), 595–613.
2. See symposium on legalization, *International Organization*, **54**, 3 (summer) 2000.
3. Agency type corporate governance in the USA tends to cause short termism and underinvestment, and contributes to high volume destabilizing speculation in stocks. See Andrew P. Dickerson, Heather D. Gibson and Euclid Tsakalotos (1995), 'Short-termism and underinvestment: the influence of financial systems', *Manchester School Papers*, **63**, 4 (December), 351–67. On stakeholder corporate governance see Margaret M. Blair and Thomas A. Kochan (eds) (2000), *The New Relationship: Human Capital in the American Corporation*, Washington, DC: Brookings

Institution; James E. Post, Lee E. Preston, and Sybille Sachs (2002), *Redefining the Corporation*, Stanford, CA: Stanford University Press.

4. A stability pact could also include understandings about monetary restraint. The Federal Reserve's monetary loosening, for recovery from the recession, is in effect making funds available at low rates for high volume speculation. See comments by Martin Barnes (2003), 'Cheap Money means a Bond Bubble', *Financial Times*, 24 June. See also comments by John Plender (2003), on speculation affecting the status of the Federal Home Loan Mortgage Corporation, *Financial Times*, 16 June.
5. See symposium on European Monetary Union, *Oxford Review of Economic Policy*, **19**, 1 (spring) 2003; and *The World Economy*, **24**, 10 (November) 2001.
6. European Central Bank initiatives could provide vital support.

REFERENCES

Aberbach, Joel D. and Bert A. Rockman (2000), *In the Web of Politics: Three Decades of the Federal Executive*, Washington, DC: Brookings Institution.

Archibugi, Daniele, and Bengt-Ake Lundvall (eds) (2001), *The Globalizing Learning Economy*, Oxford: Oxford University Press.

Calvo, Guillermo A. (2001), 'Capital markets and the exchange rate', *Journal of Money Credit and Banking*, **33**, 2 (May), 312–34.

Cardero, Maria Elena (1999), 'Trade agreements between unequal partners: does NAFTA deal with these inequalities?', in Kirsten Appennini and Sven Bislev (eds), *Economic Integration in NAFTA and the EU*, New York: St Martin's Press, pp. 193–208.

Coffee, John (2003), 'Wall Street's conflicts cannot be settled', *Financial Times*, 29 April.

Dam, Kenneth W. (2001), *The Rules of the Global Game: a New Look at US International Economic Policymaking*, Chicago: University of Chicago Press.

Foss, Nicolai, and Volker Mahnke (eds) (2000), *Competence, Governance and Entrepreneurship*, Oxford: Oxford University Press.

Hall, Peter A. and David Soskice (2001), 'An introduction to varieties of capitalism', in Peter A. Hall and David Soskice (eds), *Varieties of Capitalism*, Oxford: Oxford University Press, ch. 1.

Hartmann, Philip, Angela Maddaloni and Simone Manganelli (2003), 'The Euro-area financial system: structure, integration and policy issues', *Oxford Review of Economic Policy*, **19**, 1 (spring), 180–211.

Montamen-Samadian, Sima, and Etelberto Ortiz Cruz (1999), 'Successful integration and distress: the new dual economy – the case of Mexico in NAFTA', in Kirsten Appenni and Sven Bislev (eds), *Economic Integration in NAFTA and the EU*, New York: St Martin's Press, pp. 209–26.

Mundell, Robert A. (2002), 'Exchange rate systems and currency integration: prospects for the twenty-first century', in Thomas J. Courchene (ed.), *Money, Markets and Mobility*, Montreal: McGill-Queens University Press, pp. 269–324.

Peek, Joe and Eric S. Rosengren (2000), 'Implications of the globalization of the banking sector: the Latin American experience', in Eric S. Rosengren and John S. Jordan (eds), *Building an Infrastructure for Financial Stability*, Boston: Federal Reserve Bank of Boston, June, pp. 145–70.

Shiller, Robert J. (2003), *The New Financial Order: Risk in the 21st Century*, Princeton: Princeton University Press.

Stiglitz, Joseph E. (2002), 'Information and the change in the paradigm of economics', *American Economic Review*, **92**, 3 (June), 460–501.
Rose, Andrew K. (2001), 'Currency unions and trade: the effect *is* large', *Economic Policy*, **16**, 33 (October), 433–62.
von Furstenberg, George M. von (2002), 'Unilateral and multilateral currency integration: reflections on Western hemispheric monetary union', in Thomas J. Courchene (ed.), *Money, Markets and Mobility*, Montreal: McGill-Queens University Press, pp. 253–68.

9. Western hemisphere energy development: the continuing search for security

Stephen J. Randall

A range of international and domestic challenges in the first decade of the 21st Century have reinforced the importance of Western Hemisphere energy development for the security of the United States as well as other regional nations. Such security concerns, as this chapter underlines, considerably predated the political, diplomatic and then military conflict with Iraq in early 2003, the terrorist attack on New York and Washington, DC on September 11, 2001, or the US-led coalition which employed military action to remove the Taliban from power in Afghanistan in the course of 2002. Oil shortage scares in the early 1970s and in 1979–80 at the time of the Iranian crisis and the Soviet invasion of Afghanistan had already underscored once again the fragility of the Near and Middle East, a fragility that was exacerbated by the end of the Cold War.

The larger global energy context is critical for an understanding of the environment in which US energy policies in general and in particular toward the Western Hemisphere are evolving. The UN Energy Commission for Europe in 2001 effectively captured the European situation in its brief description of the circumstances that confront the region, although the description could also be applied to much of the world's energy development. 'The winds of change', the report concluded with a sense of drama, 'are blowing across the ECE region, buffeting energy markets, industries and enterprises. Governments in central and eastern Europe as well as central Asia are busy reshaping, restructuring and, in some cases, privatizing their energy industries. In Western Europe and North America, governments are aggressively opening up and liberalizing energy markets, notably the natural gas and energy markets. At the same time, liberalization and globalization are favouring the agglomeration or concentration of capital and labor into ever larger and larger multinational energy companies, raising concerns about excessive market power.'[1]

The International Energy Agency in its 2001 analysis of the energy outlook reached cautiously more optimistic conclusions, indicating that the reserves of oil, natural gas, coal and uranium are 'more than adequate to meet projected demand growth at least until 2020'. At the same time it suggested that a massive investment in energy production and transportation infrastructure would need to occur if there is to be effective exploitation of those resources. It noted that for oil the ability and willingness of Middle East producers to exploit lower cost reserves were a source of uncertainty and that in the case of natural gas the cost of supply and the 'impact of technology' would be critical. The report concluded, rather optimistically one might suggest, that 'beyond 2020, new technologies such as hydrogen-based fuel cells, clean coal burning and carbon sequestration hold out the prospect of abundant and clean energy supplies in a world largely free of climate destabilizing carbon emissions'.[2] It is difficult to envisage such a rosy situation in such newly industrializing states as China.

HEMISPHERIC AND WORLD ENERGY SUPPLIES

There are several observations by analysts that are important to the current discussion of energy security for the United States and other major industrial consuming nations. The first is that since the price downturn in the mid-1980s, OPEC's share of world oil production has increased. As David Greene indicates, OPEC 'holds the majority of the world's oil resources, the overwhelming majority of the world's low cost reserves, and ... is drawing down its reserves at half the rate of the rest of the world'. The fact that Venezuela is a member of OPEC, and under President Hugo Chavez has been a very proactive member, is reasonable cause for concern in the Western Hemisphere. A second important observation, also by David Greene, is that the supply of oil is primarily an economic rather than a geological issue, and the supply is highly subject to monopolistic behaviour by those controlling production or to such shocks as war that disrupt supply and in some instances severely reduce production capacity for an extended period of tune. Greene contends that the US economy is no less vulnerable to oil price shocks than it was before the 1973 crisis, with oil costs as a share of GDP remaining relatively constant at about 1.4 per cent. Nor, he concludes, does the establishment of the US Strategic Petroleum Reserve (SPR) substantively alter US dependence on foreign supplies since the SPR has the capacity to replace only 3 per cent of total supply reduction, thus being useful for only extremely brief disruptions in supply.[3]

As political scientist Gawdat Bahgat has suggested, the imbalance between energy supply and demand in the United States, unless corrected, would continue to undermine economic growth; second, he correctly observed that US energy use remains dependent on the three main fossil fuels, with natural gas representing the fastest growth in demand, in part because of environmental considerations. Third, he suggests that domestic production of energy is highly unlikely to keep pace with demand, leaving the United States dependent on foreign sources of

Table 9.1 US petroleum imports by country of origin, 1980–2001

Year	Persian Gulf Nations	Selected OPEC Countries: Iraq	Nigeria	Saudi Arabia	Venezuela	Total OPEC	Selected Non-OPEC Countries: Canada	Colombia	Mexico	Norway	United Kingdom	Total Non-OPEC	Total Imports	Imports From Persian Gulf Nations as Share of Total
	Thousand Barrels per Day													Percent
1980	1519	28	857	1261	481	4300	455	4	533	144	176	2609	6909	22.0
1981	1219		620	1129	406	3323	447	1	522	119	375	2672	5996	20.3
1982	696	3	514	552	412	2146	482	5	685	102	456	2968	5113	13.6
1983	442	10	302	337	422	1862	547	10	826	66	382	3189	5051	8.8
1984	506	12	216	325	548	2049	630	8	748	114	402	3388	5437	9.3
1985	311	46	293	168	605	1830	770	23	816	32	310	3237	5067	6.1
1986	912	81	440	685	793	2837	807	87	699	60	350	3387	6224	14.7
1987	1077	83	535	751	804	3060	848	148	655	80	352	3617	6678	16.1
1988	1541	345	618	1073	794	3520	999	134	747	67	315	3882	7402	20.8
1989	1861	449	815	1224	873	4140	931	172	767	138	215	3921	8061	23.1
1990	1966	518	800	1339	1025	4296	934	182	755	102	189	3721	8018	24.5
1991	1845	0	703	1802	1035	4092	1033	163	807	82	138	3535	7627	24.2
1992	1778	0	681	1720	1170	4092	1069	126	830	127	230	3796	7888	22.5
1993	1782	0	740	1414	1300	4273	1181	171	919	142	350	4347	8620	20.7
1994	1728	0	637	1402	1334	4247	1272	161	984	202	458	4749	8996	19.2
1995	1573	0	627	1344	1480	4002	1332	219	1068	273	383	4833	8835	17.8
1996	1604	1	617	1363	1676	4211	1424	234	1244	313	308	5267	9478	16.9
1997	1755	89	698	1407	1773	4569	1563	271	1385	309	226	5593	10162	17.3
1998	2136	336	696	1491	1719	4905	1598	354	1351	236	250	5803	10708	19.9
1999	2464	725	657	1478	1493	4953	1539	468	1324	304	365	5899	10852	22.7
2000	2487	620	896	1572	2546	5203	1807	342	1373	343	366	6257	11459	21.7
2001[1]	2731	778	854	1657	1538	5447	1786	280	1423	327	306	6172	11619	23.5

Note: [1] 2001 – preliminary data.

Source: US Department of Energy. Energy Information Administration/Annual Energy Review 2001.

supply.[4] That external dependence reinforces the importance of both the Persian Gulf region and Western Hemisphere producers of energy.

Concern about the security of the global supply of energy in 2001–2002 was offset to some degree by other factors. For instance, the US Department of Energy in early 2002 indicated that decreased world oil demand as a result of slowed economic growth had combined with OPEC overproduction to increase inventories and sharply lower prices on world markets.[5] Conversely, the weaker US economy was offset in the course of 2002–2003 by the deterioration of the global situation, in particular the conflict with Iraq, where uncertainty over the consequences of war combined with the severe cold of the 2002–2003 winter in some parts of North America to produce a spike in energy prices, followed by a subsequent price decline once the United States and Britain opened the war in Iraq.

The identification of energy security as a high priority among policymakers has not been limited to Europe and North America, of course, nor to the period since September 11. Of particular significance is the increased concern over energy supplies and security that has emerged in Asia in recent years and which will become more acute as economic development progresses. As large Asian nations industrialize, they will come more directly into competition with the United States in its search for international energy supplies. The Japanese senior vice-minister for foreign affairs, Seishiro Eto, for instance, told a seminar on energy security in Asia in 2001 that the region's economic growth required an increase in its supply of energy from outside the region. He suggested that by 2020 Asia's energy demand was expected to account for 35 per cent of world energy demand, making the region the leading energy consumer in the world. China, he noted, has been a net importer of oil since 1993, and the IEA has observed that China's oil imports over the next decade are expected to increase rapidly and surpass many countries in the OECD. At the same time its imports of natural gas will increase as it seeks to address the environmental impact.[6] In the course of the 1990s China diversified its sources of crude oil supply. In 1990 China drew 39 per cent of its supply from the Middle East and 61 per cent from Asia-Pacific suppliers; by 1997 reliance on the Middle East had risen to over 47 per cent, but the Asia-Pacific had dropped to 26 per cent, with Africa now providing almost 17 per cent and other sources providing almost 10 per cent of China's requirements.[7] Japan is far more dependent on Middle East resources than the United States, with 24 per cent from Saudi Arabia, 23 per cent from the United Arab Emirates (UAE), 10 per cent from each of Iran and Kuwait, 9 per cent from Qatar.[8] Even Malaysia and Indonesia, major producers, will likely become net importers within a decade or so. Each of these countries will need to rely more heavily on Middle East exports. Given transportation distances, supply will be vulnerable to the vagaries of natural disasters as well as sabotage.

Table 9.2 Natural gas imports, exports, and net imports, 1980–2001

Year	Imports by Country of Origin									Net Import
	Algeria	Australia	Canada	Mexico	Nigeria	Qatar	Trinidad and Tobago	United Arab Emirates	Total	Percent of US Consumption
1980	86	0	797	102	0	0	0	0	985	4.7
1981	37	0	762	105	0	0	0	0	904	4.4
1982	55	0	783	95	0	0	0	0	933	4.9
1983	131	0	712	75	0	0	0	0	918	5.1
1984	36	0	755	52	0	0	0	0	843	4.4
1985	24	0	926	0	0	0	0	0	950	5.2
1986	0	0	749	0	0	0	0	0	750	4.2
1987	0	0	993	0	0	0	0	0	993	5.5
1988	17	0	1276	0	0	0	0	0	1294	6.8
1989	42	0	1339	0	0	0	0	0	1382	6.7
1990	84	0	1448	0	0	0	0	0	1532	7.5
1991	64	0	1710	0	0	0	0	0	1773	8.4
1992	43	0	2094	0	0	0	0	0	2138	9.5
1993	82	0	2267	2	0	0	0	0	2350	10.6
1994	51	0	2566	7	0	0	0	0	2624	11.6
1995	18	0	2816	7	0	0	0	0	2841	12.1
1996	35	0	2883	14	0	0	0	5	2937	12.3
1997	66	10	2899	17	0	0	0	2	2994	12.5
1998	69	12	3052	15	0	0	0	5	3152	13.5
1999	76	12	3368	55	0	20	51	3	3586	15.3
2000	47	6	3544	12	13	46	99	3	3782	15.1
2001[1]	65	2	3781	8	38	23	99	0	4029	16.1

Note: [1] 2001 – Preliminary data.

Source: US Department of Energy. Energy Information Administration/Annual Energy Review 2001.

HEMISPHERIC NEEDS

Although the price of oil has not risen to the higher levels feared, and supplies from the Middle East have not experienced serious disruption during the lead up to or the actual war against Iraq, the fragile nature of the post-Cold War world order and the uncertainty of supply have placed increased importance on the development of alternative sources of supply from Western Hemisphere countries, in particular Canada, Mexico and Venezuela. The search for energy security has been part of a larger agenda to promote free trade, privatization and liberalized investment markets in the Western Hemisphere. Market liberalization has also gone hand in hand with a focus on the promotion of democratic political institutions in Latin America, an orientation that was emphasized at the Miami, Santiago and Quebec summits of the Americas.

The focus on open markets was also, of course, an integral part of the conclusion in the late 1980s of the US–Canada free trade agreement (CUSFTA) and the trilateral North American Free Trade Agreement (NAFTA) in 1994. The conclusion of a Free Trade Area of the Americas (FTAA), which has a target date of 2005, has remained more elusive, impeded in part by growing opposition in Latin America to the entire neo-liberal agenda of privatization and open markets for investment and trade. That opposition has been reinforced by the widely held view that continued high levels of unemployment and poverty throughout the continent, the Argentine financial/economic collapse, and economic instability in Brazil are derived in part from trade and investment liberalization.

Shortly after his inauguration, President George W. Bush sought to address the perceived general energy crisis facing the United States by announcing the creation of the National Energy Policy Development Group, under the direction of Vice-President Richard Cheney. Establishment of the group reflected a general consensus that the United States did not have a coherent and integrated strategic energy policy and was badly in need of one. Access to oil reserves of course remains one of the main concerns, and the Bush administration has focused on expanding supply rather than on the conservation measures more characteristic of the Presidency of Jimmy Carter. The emphasis on expanded supply is reflected in the controversial intention to open a portion of the Alaskan Wildlife Refuge to development and efforts to normalize Iranian–US relations. Consistent with this orientiation, the NEPD Group recommended that the President direct the Secretaries of Energy and State, in cooperation with the Secretary of the Interior and the Federal Energy Regulatory Commission, to work closely with Canada, Alaska, and all other interested parties to expedite the construction of a pipeline to deliver natural gas to the lower 48 states.[9]

During the Québec Summit of the Americas in 2001 President Bush called for the establishment of a North American energy policy. There was some surprise in Canada over this appeal, since both the CUSFTA and NAFTA provide an effective free market environment for trade and investment in oil and natural gas in Canada, and there is little more that the United States can gain in terms of access to Canadian energy resources. Conversely, in the Mexican case, privatization of Pemex and the opening of the Mexican oil sector to foreign company development has long been an elusive goal that is attractive to Canadian as well as US officials and industry.

The Bush administration's call for a North American energy policy at the Quebec Summit did not reflect a new departure. The United States, with Venezuela, was already part of a process known as the Hemispheric Energy Initiative. A month prior to the Québec Summit of the Americas, Mexico hosted a Summit of the Americas Hemispheric Energy Ministerial Meeting, at which the region's energy ministers pledged to support integration and sustainable development policies, in particular transparent and consistent regulatory policies. The Heads of State Meeting at Québec the following month reconfirmed their commitment to hemispheric energy cooperation and integration.

Such developments as power brownouts in California in recent years and then the post-September 11 fear of terrorist attacks on energy facilities in North America have intensified concerns over security. Immediately following the terrorist attacks on New York and Washington, DC in September 2001 there was particular concern about the security of nuclear generating facilities in the United States and Canada, with the result that security precautions were intensified. But the concern about energy security in the North American context is much wider than the need for enhanced security at nuclear facilities. North America has in the past half century become an economic unit, and that includes interdependence in the energy sector. Alberta natural gas is an important source of energy for California, and Alberta's vast oil sands provide significant resources for future development. Hydro-electric power from northern Québec is important to the northeastern United States.

US ENERGY POLICY

US officials in recent years have become increasingly aware of the importance of energy supplies from Mexico and Canada. In mid-2002, for instance, the House of Representatives Committee on Foreign Relations held hearings on 'Oil Diplomacy: Facts and Myths Behind Foreign Oil Dependency'. Committee Chair, Henry J. Hyde, stressed that 'As Americans, we count on energy to protect our security, to fuel our cars, to provide heat, air conditioning and light for our homes, to manufacture goods, and to transport supplies. In all of these ... we pay the price for fluctuations in the global energy market.' He went on to indicate that, contrary to popular belief, 'Canada is already our largest source of imported oil, including crude oil and refined petroleum. It also supplies

93 per cent of our natural gas imports. Electricity from Canada comprises a significant portion of the US supply and is projected to grow stronger over the next few years. Our imports of energy from Mexico are at a much lower level, but Mexico's potential export capacity is enormous, especially in the area of petroleum.' Hyde concluded his remarks by proposing the creation of the North American Energy Alliance.[10]

There was a general consensus among those who provided testimony before the House Committee on International Relations. Spencer Abraham, Secretary of Energy, stressed that oil accounted for approximately 40 per cent of total US energy consumption, and projections indicated that demand would continue to grow from 19.7 million b/d in 2002 to over 26 million b/d in 2020. Over that period the forecast was that domestic production would show little increase, thus placing an even heavier demand on imports and alternative energy sources. Abraham also noted that dependence on imported oil could rise from 52 per cent in 2002 to 62 per cent in that same period. Abraham indicated that one of the highest priorities was to work closely with US neighbors in the Western Hemisphere, specifically with Mexico and Canada through the North American Energy Initiative or Working Group, which had been endorsed by President Fox and Prime Minister Chretien. That group had already begun to develop the policies needed to enhance North American energy trade and interconnections and to address the issue of energy security. Abraham reported that US officials were also working closely with the governments of Bolivia, Brazil, Colombia, Ecuador, Peru and Venezuela to accomplish similar goals.[11]

Increasingly, Canadian sources of oil and natural gas as well as hydro-electricity have been channeled to energy-hungry US markets, especially in the western US states, with the result that such rich resource bases as the Alberta Tar Sands have taken on new significance for US security. Canada has become a major supplier of oil and natural gas to US markets in recent years and, for reasons of politics as well as geographic proximity, provides a far more secure source of supply than either the Middle East or Latin America. Although Canada has had a stronger tradition of state involvement in natural resource development than has the United States, the strongly nationalistic policies of the Liberal Governments of Pierre Elliott Trudeau in the 1970s and early 1980s are unlikely to be revisited, and there is a lingering distrust of federal government policies among the governments as well as private oil and gas producers of Western Canada. The commitment to private enterprise and opposition to federal government energy and environment initiatives is especially strong in Alberta. In the course of 2002, as the Canadian government debated ratification of the Kyoto environmental accord, there was strong opposition to ratification among Western Canadian producers and in particular the Alberta provincial government, which has been concerned that Kyoto would injure the oil and gas industry by significantly increasing costs of production and reducing Canadian competitiveness in the US market.[12]

The Alberta Oil Sands, which contain bitumen, constitute a major source of supply for future generations, although the costs of extraction remain high relative to the much lower costs of Middle East operations. According to the Energy and Utilities Board of Alberta, the Tar Sands contain an estimated 174.8 billion barrels of oil. Through 2001 only 2 per cent of the initial established crude bitumen reserve has been produced. Alberta's reserves of conventional crude oil in 2001, on the other hand, were estimated at only 1.7 billion barrels, with the ultimate potential recoverable reserves of crude estimated at 19.7 billion. Consequently, future supply clearly will shift in the long term from conventional to bitumen, and natural gas exports to the United States will become increasingly significant. Given the substantial difference between Saudi Arabian and Alberta conventional crude oil reserves, Alberta would never constitute a reasonable alternative to Middle East supplies.[13] Nonetheless, the *Oil & Gas Journal* suggests that the potential development of the Tar Sands reduces OPEC's share of total world oil reserves from 79.4 per cent to 67.5 per cent. Taken together Canada and Mexico constitute a logical regional energy source for the United States. Canada's relatively low population density results in lower domestic demand than in the United States. In the first nine months of 2001 Mexico and Canada each provided 14 per cent of US crude oil imports, compared with 18 per cent from Saudi Arabia and 20 per cent from the rest of South America. The data for late 2002 indicate that Mexico and Canada together provide approximately 45 million b/d, which is 30 per cent of US daily oil imports.

Southern Hemisphere Energy

The growing importance of Canadian energy supplies for the United States has been compounded by several trends in the oil rich countries of Latin America. One major consideration has been the political and economic instability of the region in spite of the optimism that accompanied the shift toward democratic, or at least largely democratic, governments throughout the region in the course of the 1980s and 1990s as well as the liberalization of foreign investment regulations in the natural resource sector of most Latin American countries. The most pronounced political problems have occurred in Venezuela in 2002–2003 in a direct confrontation between the state oil company PDVSA and the populist government of Hugo Chavez. Venezuela's neighbor, Colombia, has experienced intensified military conflict involving guerrilla, right-wing paramilitary groups and narcotics insurgencies, all of which have made energy development in the country a high risk. In the course of 2002 Argentina experienced financial crisis and economic collapse, and in Brazil 2002 elections brought to power a labor government which increased economic uncertainty. A second factor in the Latin American context has been the expansion of domestic energy demand with increased industrialization, urbanization and modernization throughout the area. A third factor which is seen as limiting the energy expansion of a number of Latin American countries, in particular Mexico and Brazil, has been the continuing adherence to statist policies, which in turn have limited the foreign capital investment essential to industrial expansion.

It is difficult to make meaningful differentiation between politics and economic policies in Latin America since reforms in the latter area depend entirely on the capacity of Latin America to achieve meaningful political reforms as well.[14] A 1998 report of the Carnegie Economic Reform Network observed that although there had been an encouraging degree of political support for market-oriented economic reforms, one could not discount a slowdown or reversal of such support, in particular because of the impact, perceived and real, of such reforms on people's jobs in a 'volatile, competitive and globalized economy'. The same report indicated that banking systems remain vulnerable to economic shocks, and the economic meltdown in Argentina during 2001–2002 is an indication of how quickly an economy can shift from apparent progress to crisis.[15]

In a recent overview of Latin American trends in the coming half century, Caltech researchers presented two very divergent scenarios for Latin America in the coming decade. The first was what they called a Fortress World Scenario in which economic disparity increased and along with it intensified political violence and conflict over scarce resources, with the wealthier segments of Latin American society even more isolated than in the past. That scenario also witnessed continued high levels of outmigration by professionals and others seeking better opportunities, continued power and activity by narcotics cartels, destabilization of governments by the combined forces of populist politicians and organized crime, the flight of foreign investment capital and tourists to other more stable regions of the world.[16]

The Caltech group indicated that given current levels of economic disparity, where today approximately 100 million people, equal to 20 per cent of the region's population, face day to day challenges of survival and where the poorest 20 per cent of the population receive a smaller share of the region's income than in any other region of the world, some level of violent political conflict is to be expected.

The Caltech group also presented a second scenario, however, this one entitled the 'Transformed World', in which the shift to open, market driven economies and global markets was supplemented by progressive reforms designed to alleviate poverty, improve the quality of and access to education, land reforms that improved access for currently landless groups of farmers to currently under-utilized agricultural land, the passage and enforcement of anti-corruption laws and public accountability. This scenario depends on a shift not only in current practice but also in political culture, and it is noted that neither the political will nor that value shift is sufficiently developed at present for there to be much optimism that the scenario will be realized in the near future. Interestingly, this highly optimistic scenario is close to the view that the first Clinton administration projected, in its policy of 'enlargement and engagement'.

That optimistic view, with some cautions, is also consistent with the report produced at the end of 2000 by the US National Intelligence Council, an arm of the US intelligence community. That report reflects not just official views but those of non-governmental and largely academic experts brought together to provide their perspectives. The report projects a highly positive perspective:

> By 2015, many Latin American countries will enjoy greater prosperity as a result of expanding hemispheric and global economic links, the information revolution, and lowered birthrates. Progress in building democratic institutions will reinforce reform and promote prosperity by enhancing investor confidence. Brazil and Mexico will be increasingly confident and capable actors that will seek a greater voice in hemispheric affairs. But the region will remain vulnerable to financial crises [the report was written before the Argentine meltdown] because of its dependence on external finance and the continuing role of single commodities in most economies. The weakest countries in the region, especially in the Andean region, will fall further behind. Reversals of democracy in some countries will be spurred by the failure to deal effectively with popular demands, crime, corruption, drug trafficking and insurgencies.
>
> Latin America – especially Venezuela, Mexico and Brazil – will become an increasingly important oil producer by 2015 and an important component of the emerging Atlantic Basin energy system. Its proven oil reserves are second only to those located in the Middle East.[17]

Critics of the view of free trade as the route to political freedom, economic growth and stability have noted that elected civilian governments in Latin America are fragile, in many instances threatened by military or other non-democratic forms of intervention. In a report on US policy in Latin America prepared for the Inter-hemispheric Resource Center, it is suggested that 'the neoliberal economic model is simply not capable of addressing fundamental problems like the lack of employment opportunities and the inequitable distribution of income and resources. Moreover,' the report concludes, 'it fails to take into account the very real danger of sharp reversals in the positive regional trends of democratization, demilitarization, and greater respect for human rights.'[18]

Clearly that report is more negative than the 2000 CIA study, but in fairness to the latter, it contained a significant range of cautions about the next decade and a half. It suggested, for instance, that by 2015 the improved demographics that would ease unemployment and poverty in some countries would not be shared to the same extent by Bolivia, Ecuador, Honduras, Nicaragua, Guatemala and Paraguay. It also concluded that although in countries such as Chile, Mexico, Argentina and Brazil democratic institutions appear to be moving toward consolidation, other governments will continue to experience considerable impotence in their capacity to redress poverty, control crime and civil strife. The group predicted that criminal activity could 'overwhelm' some Caribbean countries.[19]

Latin American energy consumption for domestic and industrial use over the next 50 years is predicted to increase by 250 per cent, and industrial growth in that period is anticipated to be more than 600 per cent. Such high levels of industrial activity will inevitably produce a higher level of toxic emissions which in turn will require cleaner technology, more effective environmental policies and more effective enforcement of those policies.[20] There is a better balance among oil production, consumption and surplus in Latin American countries than in other oil producing regions of the world, and as consumption increases there is likely to be a decline in the region's export capacity. In 2000, Latin America produced ten million barrels of crude oil per day and consumed approximately six million. North America, Europe and Asia have significantly higher consumption than production. The United States in 2000 produced ten million barrels a day but consumed twice that amount. Middle Eastern consumption, by contrast, is very low relative to production, thus leaving a high percentage for export.[21]

There have been significant developments in the energy sectors of the major Latin American countries in the past decade, and those trends will continue to have repercussions well into the 21st century. Although a detailed analysis of energy developments in all countries of the region is not feasible in this relatively short chapter, there are developments in several countries that require emphasis. Latin America in general is a vital source of oil, with Mexico and Venezuela accounting for more than 90 per cent of proven reserves in the early 1990s and approximately 70 per cent of production in the region. It is estimated that Latin America could continue to produce crude oil for more than 40 years at 1992 levels of production.[22] Venezuela and Mexico have led production in the region since the 1920s, although both have been plagued with problems historically and currently. The region is less significant as a source of natural gas. In 2000 Latin America had only 5 per cent of proved natural gas reserves, in contrast to 35 per cent in the Middle East and 38 per cent in the former Soviet Union, although geographic proximity to North American markets, combined with the greater costs associated with natural gas transport, increase the importance of such Latin American natural gas producers as Mexico.[23]

Latin American oil producers are, with the exception of Venezuela, to some extent disadvantaged in attracting foreign investment by the higher costs of production than apply in the Middle East. Iraq (at least when it is stabilized and the infrastructure renewed in the aftermath of war), Kuwait and Saudi Arabia have production costs ranging from $1.50 to $2 a barrel, in contrast to production costs in the United States in excess of $3. Given the volume of its reserves and relative ease of access, PDVSA's production costs in Venezuela are similar to those of Kuwait and Saudi Arabia. Pemex's production costs are the second lowest among Latin American producers at slightly more than $2 a barrel, with Petroecuador, Petrobras, Argentine and Colombian production ranging between Pemex and US costs.[24]

In the course of the 1990s most of the Latin American producers moved toward a significant liberalization of private investment in their oil industries. In most instances this involved providing opportunities for joint ventures between state-owned companies and the private sector. The exceptions were Argentina, Bolivia, and Peru, which privatized their oil industries entirely, and Mexico, where liberalization made virtually no inroads into the monopoly exercised by Pemex. One result of this opening in the 1990s was that in the second half of the decade, foreign direct investment in oil exploration and development in Latin America increased more rapidly than in any other oil producing region of the world. Again, Mexico was the exception. Brazil's and Venezuela's state oil companies continued to dominate the industry but opened their upstream activities to foreign direct investment. With the exception of Mexico and Venezuela, all Latin American countries have permitted private companies and state enterprise to construct and operate pipelines for the transport of oil and oil products. There has also been deregulation of price controls in the sector. Argentina, Brazil, Chile, and Peru leave prices to be determined by market conditions. Bolivia, Ecuador and Mexico, on the other hand, set prices.[2S]

Investment liberalization also combined with relatively low oil prices from the mid-1980s to provide an incentive for corporate mergers and acquisitions in the oil sector. Repsol of Spain, for instance, in 1999 acquired 98 per cent control of YPF in Argentina (Yacimientos Petroliferos Fiscales), and minority shareholders acquired 18 per cent of Petrobras in Brazil in 2001.[26]

Venezuela is especially important. It produces on average in excess of three million barrels of oil per day and has proven reserves above 72 billion barrels and 143 trillion cubic feet of natural gas. [7] For the past 20 years, Venezuela has welcomed foreign participation in the petroleum sector, but the stability of the industry and of the Venezuelan economy has been undermined by political instability during the presidency of the populist regime of former lieutenant-colonel Hugo Chavez and the specific confrontation between the presidency and PDVSA. There was a brief period after his inauguration when it appeared that President Chavez would continue the previous administration's policies of market liberalization and positive relations with the United States. His appointment as first President of PDVSA of Roberto Mandini seemed to point in that direction, but he was soon dismissed to be followed by a series of executives who often found themselves in conflict with the Presidency. The appointment as Energy Minister of Ali Rodriguez Araque, a long-time Congressional critic of liberalization, sent a different signal from that of Mandini's appointment, and increasingly Chavez came into conflict with the company and other advocates of previously established policy directions. Under Chavez, Venezuela cut oil production to accommodate OPEC's desire for an increase in Saudi production. Between the first Riyadh agreement in 1998 and 2000, Venezuela cut production by 650,000 b/d, all of which impacted PDVSA. Mexico on the other hand cut back on oil exports rather than production to adhere to the OPEC mandate. Only Chevron among the foreign operators in field operation contracts was asked to cut production, but that was also shortly reversed. Analysts were concerned that PDVSA would not be able to return to its pre-1998 production levels, since budget and production cutbacks over a two-year period made some 74 field drilling crews redundant.

The perspective of foreign investors became increasingly negative. Those who hoped the Chavez government would liberalize further the policy of 'apertura' and renegotiate unfavorable contracts were soon disappointed. Particularly troubling was the fact that the newly adopted Venezuelan constitution banned the privatization of PDVSA, making Venezuela even more restrictive than Mexico in terms of private investment in the upstream sector. Confronted with little hope of investing in the upstream sector of the industry as well as with unfavorable royalties on oil and gas production, private investors began to withdraw. To cite a few examples: BP Amoco sold its Pedernales field reactivation contract to France's Parenco; Chevron stopped its plans for a joint venture on the Paraguana Peninsula.[28] Political conflict has seriously compromised the reliability of Venezuelan oil production and exports. The Venezuelan situation in the period since Chavez came to power in 1999 has been particularly disturbing to US security interests. President Chavez was the first elected head of state to visit *Iraq* since the Gulf War. On that same tour of oil producing countries he also visited Iran. With Iraq holding the world's second largest oil reserves, Iran the world's largest oil producing nation, and Venezuela the major producer in Latin America, those three nations hold a significant degree of potential control over the world's energy resources, with the result that their political and economic stability and effective working relationship with the major industrial nations has to be a critical security objective of the United States.

For *Mexico*, the main challenge is to overcome the bureaucratic lethargy in the oil sector that is identified with Pemex and to attract the massive levels of foreign capital investment in the industry that are critical if the industry is to realize its potential growth. Since the election of Vicente Fox to the Mexican presidency, there has been some reason for optimism that Pemex will be transformed and that the energy sector will be more open to foreign capital involvement. In 2001 the Mexican congress approved significant additional funding for the state oil company, after years in which its revenues had been diverted to general state operations. Analysts agree that domestic investment will not be sufficient to bring Mexican energy development to a new level however. That will require substantial foreign capital, and in 2002, for the first time in 50 years, the Mexican government indicated that international oil and gas companies would be invited to participate in oil and gas tenders for developing Mexico's onshore natural gas fields through multiple service contracts.[29]

In the case *of Brazil*, its integration into the global economy and industrial expansion has increased its vulnerability to changes in international oil prices and supply.[30] In the course of the last decades of the 20th century, Brazil became the largest importer of oil and oil products in Latin America, and it was also an importer of coal for industrial use. With a population now exceeding 150 million, a highly urban population, and major industrial development, Brazil has long had the highest energy consumption in Latin America. Middle East, especially Kuwait, producers have been its main source of supply (approximately *69 per cent* in 1991), although in the course of the 1990s, like the United States, it sought to reduce its dependency on the Middle East by increasing its imports from Argentina and exploiting several large offshore hydrocarbon basins that were discovered in the 1980s. Brazil is still far from reaching its target date of 2005 for self-sufficiency, but it has moved aggressively with development of new oil wells. The objective is to increase production from 1.4 mbd in 2002 to 2.2 mbd in 2005. Although Brazil imports coal as well as oil, it has the second highest coal reserves in Latin America, after Colombia, and has major potential as a producer of hydro-electricity.[31] Natural gas pipeline developments to link major Brazilian markets with sources of supply in Bolivia have been both a reflection of Brazil's growing energy needs and the increasing integration of the energy sectors in the Southern Cone. In 1997 Brazil opened its upstream sector to international competition. In January 1998 the government established the National Petroleum Agency (ANP) to facilitate investment by domestic and foreign interests other than Petrobras. The first licensing round took place in June 1999. The government also deregulated its fuel market and opened the country to fuel imports in January 2002 after decades of government-controlled prices.[32]

To some degree *Argentina* stands in marked contrast to the Brazilian situation. The fourth largest oil producer in Latin America, in contrast to Brazil, Argentina has been a net exporter of oil and has been largely self-sufficient, although it imports natural gas, coal and some refined oil products.[33] The development of natural gas pipeline linkages with Chile and Bolivia has also facilitated the integration of the Argentine economy into the Southern Cone. Its economic development appeared to be enhanced by a major commitment to privatization of state owned and operated enterprise in the course of the late 1980s and 1990s, although its financial and general economic collapse in the early years of the 21st century have severely undermined confidence in trade and investment liberalization. At the same time its declining oil reserves loomed on the horizon as a threat to its previous self-sufficiency and net exporter status.[34]

Colombia, Ecuador and Peru although still important producers of crude oil are less significant than either Venezuela or Mexico. Colombia has long been a net exporter of oil, although that situation is expected to change as domestic demand increases. In 2001 Colombia exported approximately 321,000 b/d from total production of 626,000 b/d. The government of Andres Pastrana projected that the country would remain self-sufficient in oil until at least 2008, unless new discoveries were made, but the country was in the process of drilling approximately 35 new wells annually. Colombia's main challenge currently is not the discovery of new reserves but rather resolving its decades-long internal civil conflict. The guerrilla insurgency combined with the associated narcotics industry and right-wing paramilitary groups have compromised the country's political process and economy. The ELN (National Liberation Army) has long targeted oil pipelines for destruction, resulting in significant economic loss and environmental damage. Guerrilla activities have made exploration and development extremely hazardous for a number of years, and the escalation of the conflict with US support for the government of Alvaro Uribe has increased the risks for both Ecopetrol, the state oil company, and private sector companies operating in more remote regions.[35]

Ecuador's oil production for 2001 was approximately 420,000 b/d, and like Colombia its relatively low domestic demand has facilitated a high percentage of exports, primarily to the United States and Europe. Oil exports constitute the main source of the country's revenues, and there is considerable potential for expansion of those exports with the completion of a pipeline to carry heavy crude oil from the Amazon interior to the port of Balao. Petroecuador's objective is to double exports with the completion of the line, but although construction began in 2001 the project has encountered considerable opposition locally and internationally from environmental groups concerned about damage to the sensitive ecological system in the region. Ecuador's regulatory structure is far more favorable to foreign investment than is currently the case in either Venezuela or Mexico. Foreign companies are allowed to drill and produce oil, and are presently producing as much as the state oil company, but they lack the transport capacity to take maximum advantage of the production and export potential. With considerable oil reserves, without ties to OPEC (since 1994 when Ecuador withdrew from OPEC) and without the level of civil disorder that has characterized Colombia, Ecuador is currently in a potentially very advantageous situation if it is able to resolve its transportation problems, address the environmental concerns that are impeding the completion of the pipeline, and establish a stable pricing system for its current exports from the Oriente Basin to make the oil consistently competitive on world markets.[36]

Peru is a very minor producer of oil in comparison to other Latin American producing countries. Its production in 2001 was approximately 96,000 b/d. Unlike Colombia and Ecuador, Peru has had a more negative approach to privatization and liberalization of its investment opportunities in the energy sector, although it liberalized the fuels market in 1993, and Shell was the first company to invest in the sector following liberalization. In 1996 the Peruvian government began to privatize its energy assets, transferring 60 per cent of assets belonging to the La Pampilla refinery to a consortium led by Repsol YPF. Some other assets that were privatized were given as temporary concessions to private industry. By 2000, however, privatization had lost its political appeal, largely because of a perceived link between increasing prices for refined products and privatization, with the result that Petroperu discontinued the shift toward liberalizing the industry. Peru's main hope in expanding its production capacity is the development of a large natural gas field in the eastern jungle region, Camisea, but there are high costs of development and uncertain markets for the gas, unless a connection can be made between the Camisea fields and the Brazil–Bolivia pipeline, which would give Peruvian supplies access to the huge Brazilian market.[37]

CONCLUSIONS

Several conclusions are unavoidable about the current and prospective state of energy development in the Western Hemisphere. The first is that energy security continues to be a major policy objective for the United States. In that respect there has been little if any change in the past thirty years. A logical corollary of the ongoing US quest for energy security is that a dual track policy has been pursued. The first track is reflected in a renewed focus on encouraging collaboration among Western Hemisphere energy producers, in particular North American partners. US policymakers have continued to encourage trade and investment liberalization in energy in the hemisphere. The other track has been to attempt to bring stability to the Persian Gulf and Middle East region, an objective that has to date been elusive.

Within the hemisphere the challenges have been associated less with the existence of energy resources than with the political, diplomatic, and increasingly social, economic and environmental challenges involved in energy development, especially though not exclusively where direct foreign investment is concerned. Governments as well as foreign investors have sought assurances that there is secure access to supplies, a reasonably level playing field in regulatory policies throughout the hemisphere, openness to private foreign investment, and respect for contracts. Most Latin American and Caribbean nations have moved toward considerable liberalization, as noted earlier. Mexico has been the most resistant, but is slowly transforming Pemex from the overblown bureaucracy and closed system that it has represented since its inception. Colombia has long worked on a joint venture basis in natural resource development, and its main challenges are not the availability of resources but the need to resolve the domestic war. Argentina, Bolivia, and Ecuador have also moved in the direction of investment liberalization over the past decade, and Brazil has more recently done so. Venezuela, on the other hand, is in political and economic crisis under the Chavez Presidency, and the oil industry, or more specifically PDVSA, is in disarray. Given the importance of Venezuelan production, the importance of the oil industry to its economy and to the economies of other nations, resolution of the Venezuelan situation is an important objective for the international community. The final factor is the increasing impact of environmental and social considerations on energy policies. A decade ago, those factors were of considerably less significance. In the current climate, however, there is no country in the Western Hemisphere where corporate social responsibility is not a factor and no country in which international firms are investing where the range of issues associated with corporate social responsibility is not an overriding consideration.

Unfortunately, the Bush administration's focus on increasing the supply of energy rather than addressing conservation issues domestically has served primarily to increase the level of anxiety over the security of supply. That focus has also challenged those who would place more emphasis on environmental and social considerations both in the developed nations and in the producing nations in the Western Hemisphere which are still developing economies with high levels of poverty, mal-distribution of income, and serious problems of environmental degradation.[38] It is unlikely that social and environmental factors will come to outweigh strategic and economic ones for the United States or for the developing nations in the foreseeable future, but both foreign investors and strategic planners can anticipate that they will increasingly have to respond to challenges from those forces anxious to protect the environment, indigenous peoples and natural resource wealth.

NOTES

1. UNECE (2001), 'Concern about energy security is growing', Geneva, 22 November, http://www.unece.org.
2. International Energy Agency (2001), 'World Energy Outlook: 2001 Insights', http://www.iea.org.
3. David L. Greene (1997), 'Economic scarcity: forget geology, beware monopoly', *Harvard International Review*, **19**, 3 (summer), 16–22.
4. Gawdat Bahgat (2001), 'United States energy security', *The Journal of Social. Political and Economic Studies*, **26**, 3 (fall), 515–42.
5. US Department of Energy, Energy Information Administration (2002), 'Energy situation analysis report', 3 January, http://www.eia.doe.gov/security.
6. International Energy Agency, 'China's Quest for Energy Security', cited at http://www.iea.org/public/studies. The book documents how China is creating energy relationships across the

Middle East, Southeast Asia, Russia, Central Asia and Africa and predicts that China would in the near future seek to participate in the management of overseas energy facilities.
7. 'Diversification of Chinese Oil Import sources', http://www.iea.org/public/studies/china.
8. US Department of Energy, Energy Information Administration (2002), 'Energy Situation Analysis Report', cited.
9. National Energy Policy Development Group (2001), report, 'Reliable. affordable, and environmentally sound energy for America's future', Washington, DC, see especially ch. 8, 'Strengthening global alliances: enhancing national energy security and international relationships'.
10. http://wwwa.house.gov/internationaLrelations/107/hyde0620.htm.
11. US Congress, House of Representatives, Committee on Foreign Relations hearings on 'Oil diplomacy: facts and myths behind foreign oil dependency', http://commdocs.house.gov/committees/intlrel.
12. In the autumn of 2002 the author organized a series of public presentations at the University of Calgary on government and industry reaction to the Kyoto Accord. Presenters included: Murray Smith, Alberta Minister of Energy; David Anderson, Federal Minister of the Environment; Patrick Daniel, CEO, Enbridge; Robert Page, Vice-President Sustainable Development, TransAlta; David Schindler, Ecologist, University of Alberta; CEO, Climate Change Central, Calgary. Copies of these presentations are available on request.
13. Alberta Energy and Utilities Board (2002), 'Alberta's reserves 2001 and supply/demand outlook 2002–2011', Calgary, p. 2.
14. Carnegie Endowment for International Peace (1998), 'The political challenges of advancing economic reforms in Latin America', prepared by the Carnegie Economic Reform Network, a group of former government ministers and other senior policymakers, February.
15. Ibid. Banking issues identified included: opening banking systems to foreign bank participation; need for independent superintendencies of banks; penalizing poor bank performance; clear and transparent laws to deal with insolvent banks and other firms; establishing limits on insurance for depositors and enforcing bank shareholder losses.
16. Which World, 'Scenarios for the 21st century', http://mars3.gps.caltech.edu/whichworld.
17. 'Global trends 2015: a dialogue about the future with nongovernment experts' The full report is available on the CIA website at www.odci.gov/cia/publications/globaltrends2015.
18. Coletta Youngers (1999), 'US policy in Latin America: problems, opportunities, recommendations', Interhemispheric Resource Center, *Bulletin*, no. 53 (March), www.zianet.com/ircl/bulletin/bull53.
19. 'Global trends 2015: a dialogue about the future with nongovernment experts', cited.
20. *Which World*, 'Scenarios for the 21st century', cited.
21. UN, ECLAC (2001), 'Foreign investment in Latin America and the Caribbean', report prepared for United Nations Economic Commission for Latin America and the Caribbean, p. 128.
22. Kang Wu (1995), *Energy in Latin American Production. Consumption, and Future Growth*, Westport: Praeger, pg. 2.
23. UN, ECLAC (2002), *Foreign Investment in Latin America and the Caribbean. 2001 Report*, p. 129, table IV.2.
24. Ibid., p. 133, figure IV.4.
25. Ibid., pp. 136, 138, 143.
26. Ibid. p. 142, table IV.4.
27. *Oil and Gas Investor*, Denver, **17**, 7 (July 1997), 22–235.
28. Maria Kielmas (2000), 'Venezuela: oil industry remains tied to foreign policy', *Petroleum Review*, no. 641 (June), 20–21.
29. *Petroleum Review*, London, no. 661 (February 2002). George Baker (2000), 'Mexican energy sector reforms include foreign operators' participation in E&D,' *Oil & Gas Journal*, **100**, 6 (11 February), 64–9.
30. Etel Solingen (1991), 'Managing energy vulnerability: Brazil's adjustments to oil dependency', *Comparative Strategy*, **10** (April–June), 177–99, reprinted from Raju Thomas and Bennett Ramberg (eds) (1990), *Energy and Security in the Industrializing World*, Lexington: Kentucky University Press.
31. Wu, *Energy in Latin American Production*, pp. 69–72.

32. Trade Partners UK (2002), 'Oil, Gas, refining and petrochemical market in Brazil', (September), www.tradepartners.gov.uk/oilandgas/brazil/profile.
33. Wu, *Energy in Latin America*, pp. 92–100.
34. Ibid., p. 100.
35. www.platts.com/features/LatinAmericancrude/colombia.
36. www.platts.com/features/LatinAmericancrude/ecuador.
37. www.platts.com/features/LatinAmericancrude/peru.
38. Michael Grubb and David Ulph (2002), 'Energy, the environment, and innovation', *Oxford Review of Economic Policy*, **18**, 1 (spring), 92–106.

REFERENCES

Bacher, Jorge, and Ezequiel Mirazon (1998), 'South America's southern cone becoming integrated energy center', *Oil & Gas Journal*, 23 February.

Bahgat, Gawdat (2001), 'United States energy security', *The Journal of Social. Political and Economic Studies*, **26**, 3 (Fall), 515–42.

Baker, George (2002), 'Mexican energy sector reforms include foreign operators' participation in E&D', *Oil & Gas Journal*, **100**, 6 (11 February).

Banco Interamericano de Desarrollo (1998), '*Elementos estratégicos para el sector energia en América Latina y el Caribe*', (18 September).

Barbosa, Fabio (2001), 'Mexico's new government launches major projects to boost oil production', *Oil & Gas Journal*, **99**, 19 (7 May 7), 66–9.

Dudley, Steven and Mario Murillo (1998), 'Oil in a time of war', *NACLA Report on the Americas*, **31**, 5 (March–April), 42–8.

Greene, David L. (1997), 'Economic scarcity: forget geology, beware monopoly', *Harvard International Review*, **19**, 3 (summer).

Grubb, Michael, and David Ulph (2002), 'Energy, the environment, and innovation', *Oxford Review of Economic Policy*, **18**, 1 (spring), 92–106.

Klare, Michael T. (2002), 'Global petro-politics: the foreign policy implications of the Bush Administration's energy plan', *Current History*, no. 653 (March).

Lander, Luis, and Margarita López-Maya (2002), 'Venezuela's Oil Reform and Chavismo', *NACLA Report on the Americas*, **36**, 1 (July–August), 21–3.

Martinez, Gonzalo (2001), 'Crisis energética y geopolítica del petróleo', *La Jornada Perfil* (13 July).

McLarty, Thomas F. (1999), 'Energy integration in Latin America', paper presented to the conference on The Geopolitics of Energy into the 21st Century, Center for Strategic and International Studies, Washington, DC, 8–9 December.

Mexico (2000), '*Programa sectorial de energía 2001–2006: un país con energía es un país con future*', Plan Nacional de Desarrollo, Mexico.

'Mexico energy policy: between safe play and confusion', *Petroleum Review*, no. 653 (June 2001), 12–13.

O'Brien, Dennis (1997), 'Mightier than the sword: energy markets and global security', *Harvard International Review*, **19**, 3 (summer), 8–14.

'Oil Industry remains tied to foreign policy', *Petroleum Review*, no. 641 (June 2000), 20–1.

OLADE, Energy Statistics: Oil 1999; Natural Gas 1999; Electricity 1999.

Pastor, Robert A. (2001), *Toward a North American Community: Lessons from the Old World for the New*, Washington, DC: Institute for International Economics.

'Pemex – on the brink of major change', *Petroleum Review*, no. 661 (February 2002).

Philip, George (1999), 'When oil prices were low: Petroleos de Venezuela (PdVSA) and economic policy-making in Venezuela since 1989', *Bulletin of Latin American Research*, **18**, 3 (July), 361–76.

Rodriquez Valladares, Mayra (2002), 'South America, the continent keeps plodding along', *World Oil*, **223**, 8 (August).

Salameh, Mamdouh G. (2001), 'A third oil crisis?', *Survival*, The International Institute for Strategic Studies, **43**, 3 (autumn), 129–41.

Secretaria de Energia y Mineria, República Argentina (2000), *Reservas de Petróleo y Gas*, Informe Estadfstico.

Secretaria de Energia, Republica Argentina (2001), *Reservas Comprobadas y Probables de Petroleo y Gas Natural*.

Smil, Vaclav (2000), 'The energy question, again', *Current History*, **99**, 641 (December), 408–12.

Solingen, Etel (1991), 'Managing energy vulnerability: Brazil's adjustments to oil dependency', *Comparative Strategy*, **10** (April–June), 177–99.

United Nations Economic Commission for Latin America (2002), *Foreign Investment in Latin America and the Caribbean, 2001 Report*, October.

United States Department of Energy, Energy Information Agency.

Wade, John (2000), 'Violence, crime continue to cast shadow over future oil investment in Colombia', *Oil and Gas Journal*, **98**, 3 (17 January), 32–6.

Wu, Kang (1995), *Energy in Latin America. Production, Consumption, and Future Growth*, Westport: Praeger.

10. Hemispheric alliance capitalism and structural partnering

Gavin Boyd

The formation of a free trade area of the Americas can be an arm's length process, to establish an elementary system of regional market integration, without prospects for evolving closer and more extensive cooperation, to manage the interdependencies which will increase through trade and investment flows between the member countries. As those interdependencies become larger, however, with asymmetries that must be anticipated, the logic of managing them collectively may well become persuasive for North and South American policy communities and corporate associations.

In the prospective hemispheric market integration, US transnational enterprises, advantaged by large resources and substantial involvement elsewhere in the global economy, will be especially active in the development of cross border structural links, and in related concentration trends. Intense competition between these firms is likely to express their dynamic rivalries in the home economy. This is a liberal market economy (Hall and Soskice 2001) which however, has coordination problems: the public good of spontaneous order that could be provided by substantial intercorporate cooperation has yet to be produced. There is a clear imperative to achieve a better balance between competition and cooperation, for greater efficiencies, higher stability, and increased social justice.

Alliance capitalism is a concept which could inspire more coordination in the liberal US market economy (Dunning and Boyd 2003), with shifts toward the introduction of stakeholder systems of corporate governance. Widening intercorporate cooperation for the development of entrepreneurial complementarities would promise higher and more stable growth. The promotion of a collegial management culture would be expressed in an integrative approach to the establishment of a hemispheric free trade area. A coordinated regional market economy could then be planned for, because of the leading role which the USA will have to play in the sponsorship of hemispheric market integration, and because Latin American firms could be expected to be responsive to the opportunities for productive collaboration with US enterprises.

A spirit of alliance capitalism motivates the development of relational bonds between firms, for stable but expanding entrepreneurial complementarities, with collaborative adjustment to unexpected challenges. Informal accountability, in corporate networks, can thus become a source of collective discipline, and this can have the special effect of orienting the financial sector firmly toward funding producer enterprises. The importance of such a function can be stressed in view of the extremely destabilizing consequences which can result from large scale high risk speculation by major financial enterprises.

The coordinating potential of alliance capitalism can be given effect in structural policy cooperation, and this can contribute to community formation in a free trade area. Such collaboration on a large scale, involving groups of enterprises, and supported by official infrastructure projects, could become a major feature of the development agenda in a hemispheric free trade area. Technocratic assistance from member countries in the area, focussed on advising on exploration of opportunities for entrepreneurial complementarities, would help to align intercorporate synergies with the complexities of the public interest, to ensure continuity in structural policy cooperation.

A hemispheric free trade area based on relational entrepreneurial coordination would constitute a dynamic pattern of corporate specializations, benefiting from collaborative technocratic consulting services. The formation of cross border corporate associations would tend to develop in conjunction with the expansion of clusters of coordinated ventures, and could thus aid aggregations of interests across national boundaries in the free trade area, facilitating the development of transnational policy communities. Dedicated policy level and corporate leadership would be necessary, and, if provided, could help form a regional culture of collegial capitalism.

Sharp contrasts between the capabilities of US and Latin American enterprises could discourage efforts to promote alliance capitalism, and, without such efforts, a common trend could be the contraction of alliances between strong US firms and weak Latin American companies, followed by acquisitions of the latter. Trade and investment liberalization in the hemisphere would encourage aggressive expansion by US corporations seizing opportunities to rationalize their operations on a regional basis. This prospect influences Latin American perspectives, and must be expected to motivate negotiating strategies to limit openness to foreign direct investment, while ensuring degrees of discretionary control over such investment.

To meet widely shared aspirations for equity and dynamic growth in a hemispheric free trade area, highly constructive leadership by US policymakers and corporate elites will be necessary. There is a basis for concerns that the costs of regional integration will add to the costs of globalization experienced by US workers, and that incoming foreign enterprises will force many Latin American firms into decline. Negotiation of the terms of trade and investment liberalization will have to demonstrate much US goodwill, and this will have to be expressed with sincere commitments to wide ranging collaboration for community formation. Latin American interactions with US elites, while influenced by inequalities in bargaining strengths, will have scope to contribute to shared policy learning through exploration of the dynamics of structural and policy interdependencies in free trade areas.

ASYMMETRIES IN MARKET INTEGRATION

Regional market integration, depending on the terms on which it is negotiated, provides scope for increased economies of scale and scope that can result in higher overall growth, although with imbalances due to differences in corporate competitiveness and structural competitiveness. The terms of increased economic openness may be set out in hard and precise agreements, as in the establishment of the North America Free Trade Area,[1] or in affirmations of principles for discretionary application, to build trust and goodwill. The first alternative is not conducive to community formation, and can generate much adversarial legalism, especially in the treatment of issues arising out of unequal terms of market openness, but the degrees of precision can facilitate trade and investment flows, thus reducing transaction costs. Rising volumes of these flows may then activate policy level initiatives to increase the economic openness, on more equal terms, and to cooperate in other areas of interdependence. Softer agreements for regional market integration can be initially more suitable for relational cooperation, but political will to continue such cooperation may be eroded by reactions to differences in the spread of gains from increased discretionary openness.

Policy orientations, and degrees of coordination in the expression of those orientations, become very significant for management of the interdependencies that rise in a free trade area. Mercantilist orientations result in pressures to increase advantages derived from the terms of openness, and can thus be reciprocated, while becoming sources of contests for nationalist support that make intrazonal relations adversarial. Demands by interest groups are mainly responsible for mercantilist orientations, but these can be moderated if interest groups become linked across borders and promote greater market integration, and if cross investment increases the dimensions of structural interdependence. Integrative policy orientations tend to develop only under strong and enlightened leadership during the establishment of a free trade area, and to be effective must have the support of coordinated domestic groups, but for the development of regional cooperation, that is for transnational interest aggregation and consensus formation, collaboration between these groups and those of regional partners must be encouraged.

Collaborative planning of a free trade area has to be based on shared awareness that, with increased openness between the members, on asymmetric terms because of differing policy orientations and bargaining strengths, imbalances are likely to become greater as intrazonal structural interdependencies become larger and more complex. This is the likely effect of more active corporate competition in trade, transnational production, and finance, in the course of which contrasts in structural competitiveness will tend to become sharper, unless there are initiatives to develop structural policy cooperation. While structural interdependencies increase, microeconomic and macroeconomic policy interdependencies will also increase, with related asymmetries, especially in terms of the ranges of cross border effects and of bargaining capabilities.

In the integrating regional economy, then, market efficiencies and failures, and government efficiencies and failures, will assume larger dimensions, in conjunction with changes in the overall spread *of* gains from the pattern of freer commerce. Differences in that spread of gains will challenge governments to enhance structural competitiveness, and to resort to leverage on issues of market access, but also to seek more integrative cooperation. Choices for governments and firms, however, will be complicated by structural and policy linkages with the international political economy. These linkages will continue to expand, especially because of the building of transnational production systems by multinational firms, which will increase the significance of policies implemented by outside states.[2]

Market efficiencies that extend across borders in a free trade area result principally from the increasing scale of production specializations, intrazonal and international. The dynamic and allocative aspects of these efficiencies however change as competitive pressures drive weaker firms into declines or into absorption by stronger enterprises. Concentration trends thus increase, unless there is a collective will to engage in competition policy cooperation. Meanwhile there are externalities, including degrees of deindustrialization, and sectoral disruptions, associated with corporate restructuring and production relocations. Opportunities for the development of entrepreneurial complementarities will be restricted as the concentration trends continue. Further, there may be destabilizing speculation, which has to be recognized as a form of market failure. Associated with this, moreover, there can be capital outflows to a country experiencing stock appreciations. Intrazonal financial market integration will facilitate such movements of capital from less developed to more developed countries within and outside the free trade area (Singh 2001).

Government efficiencies assume larger cross border effects in a free trade area, and, with policy failures, are influenced by the market efficiencies and failures. As the market changes result mainly from the operations of transnational enterprises, the government efficiencies and failures evolve with losses of economic sovereignty, that is while structural interdependencies in the area increase. A liberal policy orientation in effect allows considerable loss of economic sovereignty, and wide scope for independent corporate activities that shape economic structures and their linkages. The policy orientation of a coordinated market economy results in considerable collective control over the operations of national firms. Striving to develop such control, in order to enhance structural competitiveness, is a rational choice for a less developed state entering a free trade area with more industrialized members. If structural policy cooperation on equitable terms becomes possible with partners in the area, however, that will constitute a vital public good.

A liberal policy orientation that permits strong concentration trends, disruptions of economic structures, and large scale destabilizing speculation, results in multiple forms of policy failure. Meanwhile the internal political competition in a liberal political economy can drive strong fiscal expansion – a further type of policy failure.[3] By raising public debt and drawing investment away from productive use this deficiency can in effect contribute to strong outward movements of direct investment from an industrialized state, thus intensifying problems of external balance.

Altogether, the mixes of efficiencies and failures in the dynamics of market processes and government activities that demand attention in the negotiation of a regional free trade agreement necessitate consideration of systemic developmental issues as well as probabilities in the interacting effects of bargaining over market access, the strategies of national and transnational enterprises, and the macromanagement activities of governments. There are clear imperatives for concerted knowledge intensive and highly constructive policy planning, and for the development of cross border policy communities, with participation by corporate groups and associations.

CONSENSUS BUILDING

A hemispheric consensus on interdependent macromanagement is needed, and it will have to combine a revised Washington consensus with a new philosophy of liberal governance in the USA. The Washington consensus will have to be reformulated to take account of the ways in which structural and policy interdependencies tend to evolve in a free trade area, as it is a set of prescriptions for Latin American administrations acting independently, from the perspective of a liberal political economy. Principles of liberal governance in the USA will have to be adapted and expanded to engage with problems of external balance, resulting from autonomous corporate operations, and problems of stability, caused by speculative stock appreciations to unsustainable levels. As interventionist measures would conflict with the liberal tradition, a philosophy of consultative entrepreneurial coordination for productive rather than rent seeking ventures will have to be promoted, offering technocratic advising in return for the concerting of entrepreneurial endeavours in complementary patterns aligned with common interests.

In the Washington consensus economic liberalization was expected to benefit Latin American states by facilitating the expansion of technological and managerial capabilities, and the related formation of social structures providing stable support for responsible administrations (Williamson 1997). This however did not meet Latin American concerns about the vulnerabilities of structural interdependence that were to be expected after increased economic openness. The necessary revision, to guide development, with reduced vulnerabilities, will have to incorporate lessons from the achievements of alliance capitalism in East Asia. These have been achievements of relational intercorporate cooperation, with technocratic guidance and support.[4] The significance of these achievements has been obscured by the East Asian financial crises, but these revealed problems of economic openness to volatility in international financial markets rather than flaws in growth strategy.

The industrializing coordinated East Asian market economies experienced high outward oriented growth for two decades before their financial crises in the 1990s, and these were the results of vulnerability to speculative operations in financial markets – vulnerability due to premature financial liberalization, introduced without adequate supervisory and regulatory systems , and apparently without understanding of the predatory capabilities of major financial enterprises in the USA and Europe. Ambitious private investment projects relied heavily on bank lending during the growth years, and this became very risky as financial liberalization opened the way for the exploitation of volatility by opportunist foreign traders in financial assets.[5] The scope for such exploitation, moreover, happened to widen because the export earnings of these East Asian countries were adversely affected by a competitive devaluation of the Chinese currency (Huh and Kasa 1998).

The functional significance of coordinated entrepreneurship in producer enterprises would have been made more evident, with dynamic continuity, if this coordination had been extended into discipline of the financial sector, under prudent management. The key lesson for Latin America is that synergies of organized collaboration between outward oriented producer firms are vital requirements for industrial progress toward levels necessary for full openness to commerce with industrialized states, and that strong associations of producer enterprises are necessary for subordination of the financial sector to the funding of those enterprises. The logic of this conclusion has become quite strong in view of the problems of large scale high risk mismanagement and fraud in major US financial enterprises. In negotiations for a hemispheric free trade area, moreover, Latin American administrations can argue quite firmly that their financial sectors must be managed for the service of stable growth, and that vulnerabilities for all developing countries are tending to increase because of the weakening of regulatory discipline and market discipline as restraints on risky and fraudulent speculative operations by financial enterprises in advanced countries.[6] A special concern has to be that efforts to strengthen regulatory discipline in the USA can motivate shifts of questionable practices to areas outside the US economy.

The basic solution for weakened regulatory and market discipline, as a problem resulting from much sophistication in the use of financial instruments, and from related information deficiencies, has to be strong diffuse pressure for accountability from well-institutionalized peak economic associations. This, it must be made clear, is necessary in Latin America, and it is also necessary in the USA, where difficult problems of corporate governance, dramatized by cases of high risk corporate fraud, have opened up questions of macromanagement in a liberal market economy.[7]

American macromanagement has to be guided by the system building effects of functional and equitable balance between intercorporate competition and cooperation: this balance becomes increasingly important as a high order public good in a knowledge based political economy with very extensive structural interdependencies that are evolving with losses of economic sovereignty. The need for the appropriate balance has to be stressed because of imperatives for order and stability that have become evident in the effects of intensely competitive corporate expansion and of financial sector rent seeking. These effects, while indicating that the development of a liberal market economy *as a system* depends on civic virtues, have given prominence to problems of entrepreneurial coordination and political cooperation (Padoan, Brenton, and Boyd 2003).

Liberal macromanagement, based on recognition of basic individual rights to undertake entrepreneurial ventures, recognizes the efficiency effects of competition, but tends to be less open to understanding of the efficiency effects of intercorporate cooperation; these however are becoming more significant as technological advances increase production interdependencies between firms, and their interdependencies in the exploration of potential entrepreneurial complementarities – the generation of innovative knowledge through collaboration. A further problem in understanding of the efficiency effects of competition is that this tends to draw support from expectations that rivalries for market shares result in balances between the most productive enterprises, subject to impartial governmental regulatory functions. Confidence that concentration trends will thus be restrained however is challenged by the scope for tacit oligopolistic collusion, and by the domestic market advantages derived by US firms from their international operations.[8] Further, it has to be recognized that the funding priorities of major financial enterprises favour enterprises gaining prominence in concentration trends.

In addition the speculative propensities of the financial sector have to be seen as a grave problem because they push stock appreciations to unsustainable levels and then cause declines, after failures to generate productivity increases that would sustain the appreciations.[9] Recoveries, moreover, are then hindered by orientations toward further rent seeking rather than productive investment: the growth promoting objectives of monetary loosening during a recession are thus frustrated.

The promotion of extensive intercorporate cooperation, for general increases in entrepreneurial complementarities, with encouragement of relational contracting and of collegial competition, has become a primary macromanagement task in the USA, for resolution of the problems of external imbalance, internal order, and financial sector reform. The task is difficult because the generation of political will is hindered by much dysfunctional political competition, but policy level and corporate initiatives could help to build consensus, especially through emphasis on the potential efficiencies of technocratic sponsorship of entrepreneurial conferences. A vital public good to be provided through such conferences would be the generation of knowledge about the formation of systems of innovation (Andersen et al. 2000) for commercial applications of frontier research.

The development of generally stable corporate identities, through encouragement of changes from agency type to stakeholder systems of corporate governance, would support the cultivation of corporate orientations toward productive partnering.[10] Another beneficial effect would be a reduction of share trading opportunism – the large scale speculation by financial enterprises which, with tacit collusion, inflates stock prices and encourages unreal expectations that monetary loosening will aid recovery from any post-boom recession (Miller, Weller, and Zhang 2002).

The extensive relational corporate cooperation could generate very constructive contributions to the policy mix. A positive result could be strong restraint on the political competition that drives fiscal expansion. Reduction of the problems caused by such expansion, and reduction of tendencies to impose related costs of adjustment on other states, would facilitate stronger focus on the coordination of entrepreneurial energies in the US economy.

The effects on trade relations could be very significant. The management of US foreign commerce is dominated by the problem of heavy external imbalance, which is becoming more serious but which is not evoking broadly collaborative corporate responses. The clear imperative is to promote intercorporate cooperation for structural change that will provide a sound basis for necessary adjustment of the current account, without dependence on speculative capital inflows. This requirement, it must be stressed, is urgent, because of the danger that current account deficits will cause destabilizing depreciation of the dollar.[11]

For hemispheric relations the need to establish structural foundations conducive to regionally and globally balanced commerce has several dimensions. A reconstituted pattern of US production, to bring domestic output into line with internal demand, with functional balance between home output and foreign production, could facilitate the development of more symmetry in hemispheric structural interdependence. Without the clearly required changes in US corporate orientations however the pattern of linkages would probably tend to become more imbalanced, with the spread of dispersed assembly type production processes limiting technology transfers and the scope for related host country industrial development.

STRUCTURAL PARTNERING

Liberalized hemispheric commerce would enable US manufacturing enterprises to develop regional vertical specialization patterns on an extensive scale in Latin America, taking advantage of investment bidding rivalries, with the use of sites in less developed parts of the free trade area to produce for the area as a whole and especially for the more industrialized member countries. This regional rationalization and expansion would be influenced by the complexities of the arrangements for liberalized commerce, but also by the prospective attractions of emerging diversified clusters of innovative industrial activity, especially in Brazil, the main location of competitive European industrial involvement. Brazil's trade and investment links with the European Union roughly balance those with the USA (OECD 2001).

Overall economic conditions and macromanagement patterns in Latin America encourage dispersals of production stages across borders by US firms. The complexities and uncertainties to be reckoned with in estimating possibilities for economic policy cooperation between Latin American administrations, moreover, must be expected to incline US enterprises all the more firmly toward the geographic spreading of production stages.[12] The choices of these firms, in rivalries with each other and with European companies, may well remain largely uncoordinated, owing to the fragmentation of corporate associations in the home economy.[13]

The US political economy as a whole, however, would benefit in the long term from comprehensive complementary industrial growth in Latin America, aided by broadly coordinated partnering strategies that could be implemented by American enterprises with a spirit of collegial capitalism. Collaborative diversified industrial development in Latin America could be promoted, with support for the upgrading of clusters which have formed in low technology sectors (Albaladejo 2002). This is a prospect which could become a special focus for technocratic sponsorship of entrepreneurial conferences in the USA, and for the concerting of US corporate strategies in business associations expanding as a result of such conferences. The extensive high order entrepreneurial coordination that has become necessary in the USA, for more effective macromanagement, has to engage with problems of structural interdependence in all major areas of external economic relations. In the hemisphere this will require very constructive structural partnering, with integrative motivations that will help to upgrade Latin American production capabilities. Systemic development considerations, in a context of cross border market efficiencies and failures, and government efficiencies and failures, demand affirmation as a basis for the structural partnering, that is through consultative integration and harmonization of entrepreneurial endeavours.

Latin American corporate learning and policy learning would have to develop in synergistic interaction with American collegial capitalism. This must be stated with reference to interdependencies related to regional public goods, and, more broadly, with reference to issues of efficiency and social justice that are evident in the asymmetries of those interdependencies. These issues are mentioned in much of the research literature on the development agenda in Latin America, which reflects consensus on US imperatives to assist growth in that area (Emmerij 1997, Salazar-Xirinachs and Robert 2001).

The importance of high principled dedication in US initiatives for the introduction of a spirit of collegial capitalism into structural partnering with Latin America can be affirmed with new understandings of moral imperatives in the development of the American political economy. The extraordinary cases of large scale fraud-related bankruptcy in the USA during the 2001/2 recession were examples of collusive crony capitalism that could have destructive international effects. Hoped for reforms, it was clear, would have to be extended into the foreign operations of US transnational enterprises, but this would depend more on the strength of the moral commitments of US managements, as regulatory surveillance would be weaker outside the home economy. The structural partnering that can be advocated for hemispheric development would be basically a process of coordinated entrepreneurial ventures, through which there could be diffuse communications of values, to build trust and goodwill.

Elaborations of principles of hemispheric structural partnering, by US policymakers and corporate leaders, in dialogue with Latin American elites, would be vital for planning and community building. The contextual factors that should be stressed, in the logic of this partnering, would be the gravity of the US current account deficits, the influence of rent seeking incentives on the activities of major US financial enterprises, and the constraints on outward oriented growth in Latin America, both domestic and external. The main principle to be affirmed would be the imperative to increase regional market efficiencies and overcome regional market failures, in conjunction with efforts to enhance interdependent performance in macromanagement.

For all the necessary coordination, economic theory guiding policies and corporate activity would have to be revised. Concepts of individuals as unprincipled self-seekers would have to become more humanistic through recognition of the vital importance of civic virtues,[14] and through understandings of potentials for interdependent organization building and performance. In large technologically interdependent producer enterprises and major financial corporations, monitoring tasks become extraordinarily difficult if there is pervasive self-seeking. This problem has been dramatized by the numerous cases of managerial corruption that have disrupted the US economy. This liberal market economy has become knowledge based through multiplications of collaborative advances in applied technology, but also through wider understandings that these advances require much trust and goodwill. With these understandings it can be appreciated that the security and peace provided by trust and goodwill facilitates technological and entrepreneurial innovations, with the sharing of tacit and codified knowledge on a scale much greater than is possible in the guarded interactions associated with intense competition.[15]

Initiatives for hemispheric structural partnering, through the promotion of entrepreneurial complementarities, however, would have to be combined with efforts to develop competition policy cooperation. This would be a prudential requirement in a free trade area because liberalized commerce allows major firms to expand more actively through mergers and acquisitions, and to form production and marketing alliances. In the negotiation of regional trade liberalization, the USA would have interests in extending its system of antitrust enforcement, with the advantages of superior bargaining strength. This bargaining strength would be especially significant for small less developed Latin American states, as their investment bidding efforts could be hindered by assertions of their interests in facilitating the development of their national firms. Brazil, Argentina and Mexico are better placed to assert such interests, but would probably lack political will to negotiate in this policy area as a group. Brazil and Argentina, because of their substantial trade and investment links with the European Union, could be expected to seek its support for their preferences on hemispheric competition policy issues, while aligning with its tendency to press for the development of a competition policy responsibility at the World Trade Organization.

A very constructive US policy would be to press for the establishment of a hemispheric competition policy authority, with substantial Latin American judicial representation, while working to spread a spirit of collegial capitalism through policy communities and corporate associations, and particularly in the course of officially sponsored entrepreneurial conferences. The endeavour to promote the culture of a coordinated market economy would help to make the concept of a hemispheric competition policy authority more acceptable in Latin America. This concept moreover would have domestic appeal as an alternative to European Union proposals for a World Trade Organization responsibility in international competition policy. Further, Atlantic competition policy cooperation could become more extensive as the hemispheric authority became more involved in interactions between the European Commission and US antitrust authorities.[16]

BUILDING LINKAGES

The promotion of linkages between host country firms and the subsidiaries of major transnational enterprises in developing countries – a major operational concern of the United Nations Conference on Trade and Development – would be a very important process in the hemispheric structural partnering that could be inspired by a spirit of collegial capitalism.[17] Foreign corporations producing in Latin America seek host country suppliers, and dependence on them can increase, with mutual benefits that can result from their organizational development and technological advances. Transnational enterprises with international supply chains, however, can become less and less dependent on host country suppliers: satellite industrial development may thus diminish, after initial growth, unless there are vigorous official promotional endeavours. The uncertainties and disadvantages to be considered by host governments and corporate associations would be reduced if incoming US firms demonstrated firm commitments to relational cooperation, for the coordination of entrepreneurial ventures with host country partners. This integrative engagement would encourage initiatives by host country entrepreneurs who could otherwise lose confidence in their capacities to operate effectively in environments made more competitive by the foreign enterprises.

US corporate initiatives for the development of industrial linkages in a collegial spirit could have great significance for Mexico, as a country that has become very heavily dependent on the expansion of trade and investment links with the USA, while failing to develop substantial diversified structural interdependencies with Latin American neighbours.[18] The pattern of linkages emerging in Mexico can be expected to spread into those neighbours, mainly as a result of US corporate operations, and this could accelerate in a regional system of liberalized commerce. Less developed and smaller Latin American countries would tend to be drawn into the expanding pattern of linkages, in which supply chains would become more regional. The building of integrated regional production systems by US enterprises could help to activate increasing host country entrepreneurship, but it must be stressed that this would depend on the integrative spirit demonstrated by the US firms.

A collegial spirit in European capitalism, which could have effects mainly in Brazil and Argentina, would challenge and complement integrative US corporate regional involvement. The European presence is somewhat fragmented, has weaker entrepreneurial drive, and is internationally less competitive, but can be influenced by ideals of social solidarity affirmed in the European Union's policy networks and corporate associations. If structural policy cooperation begins to develop between the USA and the European Union, as could occur because of recognition of problems of adjustment in Atlantic structural interdependencies, this could extend into collaborative involvement in Latin America.[19] A challenge for the European Union is that the development of its commercial links with Latin America could be reduced by the formation of a hemispheric free trade area (Schott and Oegg 2001).

For the vital processes of financing domestically based growth and activating vigorous Latin American entrepreneurship, integrative European involvement, matching US engagement in a spirit of collegial capitalism, could give great impetus to regional development. In addition the European presence could broaden the agenda of free trade negotiations between the USA and Latin American countries, especially to focus attention on fundamental issues of market efficiency and failure, macromanagement performance, and hemispheric structural balance. This focus could result in more knowledgeable and more active Latin American concerns to press for the development of a hemispheric system of competition policy cooperation. Further, it could assist the development of Latin American understandings of structural policy imperatives, and of the importance of political will to respond to those imperatives through consultative interactions with national and foreign firms. Functional requirements for coordinated entrepreneurship, it must be stressed, have to be recognized as key elements in the regional development agenda, and to meet these requirements there clearly must be continual exploration of opportunities for entrepreneurial complementarities, with technocratic contributions based on concerns with public goods.[20]

An orderly pattern of dynamic linkages between Latin America firms, evolving in conjunction with linkages between those firms and the USA as well as European enterprises, could become self-sustaining with accumulations of technocratic expertise and the collaborative alignment of managerial orientations, supported by intensive exchanges of information. The general effect would be to build a culture of coordinated innovation. The relatively most favourable conditions for the development of coordinated linkages are in Brazil, because of the scale and diversification of its national industries and the mix of structural interdependencies with Europe and the USA. Macromanagement failures discourage optimism about Brazil (Colitt and Lapper 2002), but if initiatives for consultative coordination are taken, the influence of concerted corporate views and preferences on the broader policy process could be very beneficial.

In Brazil and most other Latin American countries the representation of corporate interests is quite fragmented, and relations between different associations are often adversarial (Fischer 1999). The major categories of firms are producers and exporters of primary products; low and medium technology manufacturers who had benefited from former import substitution policies; and new locally based transnational enterprises with medium technology capabilities that tend to be of special interest for alliance and merger and acquisition strategies implemented by US and European firms. For the development of a coordinated market economy it will be essential for national administrations to encourage integration of the various business associations into peak corporate organizations capable of interacting effectively with technocrats in the home economy as well as across borders, and with foreign transnational enterprises. In these interactions the promotion of relational linkages between foreign and home corporations, for the development of expanding complementarities, would have to be the main objective. Interest in the stability of the US and European partners would thus have to be made clear, and firm affirmations of this by groups of Latin American peak corporate associations would help to evoke reciprocal understanding in US economic organizations.

In this context the external significance of imperatives for shifts to stakeholder corporate governance by US enterprises can become more evident.[21] Such changes, it must be stressed, are needed for the economic stability in which collegial capitalist can develop, with efficiencies and social justice, and with the reorientation of the financial sector toward productive rather than rent seeking operations. At the policy level, then, resolute commitments to the sponsorship of entrepreneurial conferences have to be seen as urgent requirements for the extensive partnering to be promoted in hemispheric relations. The neglect of public goods issues, which has increasing costs in a liberal market economy as its uncoordinated structural interdependencies expand, is a challenge to formulate a new philosophy for the American political economy, and for its transnational corporations that are losing their national attachments and loyalties.

FINANCIAL MARKETS

Financial market liberalization in Latin America is a US objective in the negotiation of a hemispheric free trade area, and is a principle of the original Washington consensus, affirmed because of the importance of mobilizing savings in developing countries for domestically based growth. Such liberalization however facilitates capital flight, and inflows of portfolio investment that can be rapidly reversed, even when economic fundamentals in the host country are sound. The recent history of financial crises in Latin America and East Asia obligates caution in interactions with the USA, especially because of large differences between the resources and bargaining strengths of US financial enterprises in the area and those of local firms, as well as because of the magnitude of surveillance and regulatory problems associated with the presence of large foreign banks and securities enterprises (Singh 2001).

Inadequate regulatory arrangements entail serious vulnerabilities, but commitments to liberalize can be made under pressure while regulatory capabilities are still weak, or can be motivated by naive hopes of attracting productive investment. The most important vulnerability is exposure to speculative attack by large scale predators in world financial markets. The development and communication of a spirit of collegial capitalism in the USA would help to relieve Latin American anxieties about the risks of financial liberalization and about the problems of financial deepening under effective regulation, especially in conditions of uncertainty about prospects for growth.

Increasing hemispheric financial openness will mean that Latin American countries will be more directly affected by speculative booms and subsequent declines in the USA, unless these destabilizing problems are overcome by the coordinating effects of collegial capitalism; they will not be sufficiently moderated by improved regulatory discipline on the financial sector. Regulatory improvements depend on, and can be altered by, the dynamics of political competition for influence on policy, and the outcomes tend to lag behind the levels of sophistication reached by traders in financial assets.[22]

The preservation of stability in Malaysia and Taiwan during the East Asian financial crises of the 1990s has illustrated what could be achieved by Latin American states seeking to reduce the vulnerabilities of economic openness. The key lesson to be absorbed is that very firm prudential regulation of developing financial markets, with a readiness to resort to interventionist measures, is of vital importance, to ensure increasing and stable funding of emerging national industries, to limit capital flows to higher growth areas, and to reduce vulnerabilities to speculative attack and to recessions in the USA.[23] Endeavours to develop the necessary regulatory capabilities will depend on the political will and competence of ruling elites, and on external encouragement, which could come from advocates of collegial capitalism in the USA and Europe. The difficulties of developing regulatory discipline, although more serious in Latin American countries than in the USA, should not deter efforts to follow the achievements of Malaysia and Taiwan, or to work for the development of a culture of integrative cooperation that can promise later relaxation of the currently necessary regulatory discipline.

For Latin American states, deeper European financial involvement in their economies would help to reduce bargaining inequalities in negotiations on issues of hemispheric financial market liberalization. Resolute bargaining can be combined with vigorous efforts to promote a culture of relational collaboration, in concert with endeavours by American advocates of a new philosophy of hemispheric solidarity. In the USA, it must be reiterated, such advocates have been challenged to work with exceptional vigour because of the acute financial sector problems revealed by bankruptcies and frauds during 2002.

Premature financial liberalization has exposed Latin American countries to volatility in exchange rates and stock prices that has caused major uncertainties for national firms, while facilitating capital outflows.[24] Savings and investment rates have been low, especially compared with those in industrializing East Asian countries. Needs for controls on capital flows have been evident, but the necessary administrative capabilities and political will have been lacking. Sympathetic understanding of these problems, if evident in a US regional policy influenced by concepts of collegial capitalism, could help to build hemispheric solidarity. Optimism about this, however, may not be warranted in view of the influence of financial sector groups on US regional policy. These groups, because of focus on the exploitation of speculative opportunities in world financial markets, may well be less open to concepts of collegial capitalism than associations of producer enterprises with long term interests in regional production operations, and in stability in exchange rates and stock prices. It seems necessary to emphasize, moreover, that groups in US financial sectors, under increased domestic regulatory pressure since mid-2002, could press for increased financial market liberalization in Latin America, partly because of expected opportunities for risk taking operations outside the domestic regulatory framework.

MONETARY COOPERATION

Deepening integration in a regional free trade system increases monetary policy interdependencies. These have been developing in the hemispheric context with large asymmetries, in conjunction with structural links that have growth potentials dependent on an orderly pattern of collaborative monetary policy management. Hemispheric monetary relations are dominated by the USA, because of the extensive conditioning effects of externalities associated with its monetary management, and because it has wide scope for initiative in interactions with Latin American governments about monetary policy issues. US monetary policy however has a strong domestic orientation, especially because of the difficult task of facilitating recovery from the recession that ended the speculative boom of the 1990s. The high priority external concerns moreover are to ensure exchange rate stability in relations with the European Union and Japan, while moderating downward pressures on the dollar caused by very large trade deficits. Incentives to give attention to questions of monetary policy cooperation with Latin America are relatively weak and may not be expected to become significant until after the formation of a hemispheric free trade system.

Developmental issues in Latin America and the tasks of macromanagement in the USA are overshadowed by growth of largely uncontrolled international financial markets that are eroding monetary sovereignty in the USA and that are making monetary policies less significant in Latin America. In Europe trading in financial assets is on a much smaller scale than in the USA, and monetary sovereignty is less weakened, but US financial enterprises are vigorously expanding their European operations, and are linking the Union's securities sectors more and more with those in the USA. Very large flows of portfolio investment were moving from Europe to the USA until the US recession was worsened by the numerous large scale fraud-related bankruptcies in 2002.

US monetary policy is intended to facilitate national growth with low inflation, in a context in which political competition tends to drive fiscal expansion, thus contributing to inflationary pressures while setting borrowing requirements that limit productive investment. The pricing strategies of firms becoming prominent in concentration trends however contribute to inflation, but wage costs are kept relatively low by extensive corporate use of foreign production sites. Monetary tightening can be an ineffective restraint on speculative stock and property appreciations, because of the availability of credit from the securities sectors.[25] This credit moreover tends to flow in considerable volumes into rent seeking at home and abroad rather than the funding of productive activity. Monetary loosening to facilitate recovery from a recession does little to alter that speculative orientation, and accordingly recovery can be slow.

Exchange rate stability at levels appropriate for external balance is intended to result from the management of monetary policy, but Federal Reserve and Treasury capabilities for intervention in foreign exchange markets are small compared with the very high volumes of speculative flows moving constantly in world financial markets. This trading in financial assets draws investment because of prospective returns and low tax exposure; meanwhile US banks, whose financial operations are intended to respond to monetary policy objectives, are strongly attracted by the speculative opportunities in world financial markets. An intractable problem in this context is that the very large deficits in the current account, due to the persistence of heavy trade imbalances, are not reduced by the downward pressures on the exchange rate which they tend to cause, because of flows of speculative investment into the USA.

Latin America, after Europe, is a source of the investment flows to the USA, and these flows may well increase with the development of financial markets that can be projected after the formation of a hemispheric free trade area. This has to be stressed because of its negative implications for the funding of national firms in Latin America that will be encountering stronger foreign competition. The long history of macromanagement failures in Latin America (IMF 2002) must be expected to continue affecting investor attitudes.

The attraction of entering a zone of monetary stability through close association with the USA influences Latin American administrations, but not as strongly as the European Monetary Union draws outside governments toward its area of stability. Deepening subordinate involvement in international financial market activity centred on the USA that is expanding with diminishing responsiveness to US monetary policy, and that generates potentially destabilizing volatility, is the prospect that has to be reckoned with. The currency risks of cross border transactions within Latin America, and between Latin America and the USA, would be reduced, with very positive implications for overall growth, by the formation of a hemispheric monetary system, but the vulnerabilities of financial interdependence in such a system would tend to increase. Concentration trends in the US financial sectors would be major factors in this process.[26]

Reorientation of US financial sectors toward stable funding of productive activity, for growth in the real economy, has become a vital macromanagement imperative. This calls for regulatory changes, and the taxing of trade in financial assets, but at a deeper level changes to stakeholder systems of corporate governance are necessary, with substantially reduced trading in shares. Public education about inefficiencies in financial markets, and about the speculative attractions they can have for managements of producer enterprises, would assist the necessary functional changes. An even more important endeavour would be the promotion of a spirit of collegial capitalism, which would increase dynamic efficiencies in the economy, through stable patterns of entrepreneurial coordination. An important result would be a restoration of monetary sovereignty (Rugman and Boyd 2003).

For Latin American elites the fundamentals of monetary and financial interdependence demand comprehensive dialogue with US policymakers, despite the disadvantages of inferior status and weak capacities for consensus formation. The urgent systemic changes that have become necessary in the USA however will depend on the generation of domestic political will, to achieve general increases in productive coordination through relational blends of competition and cooperation. The opportunity is to sponsor, through policy level and corporate endeavours, conferences on the development of parallel ventures in the use of applied frontier technology, in the hope that the spirit of collaboration will spread into medium technology sectors as these absorb new innovations and become more directly linked with the higher technology industries. Increasing awareness of shared interests in the development of human capital, and in corporate stability, could be expected to develop at such conferences, that is with long term perspectives on the discernment of technology based complementarities through exchanges of tacit knowledge.

HEMISPHERIC COMMUNITY FORMATION

Economic advice to governments, firms, and corporate associations has to give much attention to issues of interdependence within and between sectors in knowledge based political economies, and between those political economies.

Efficiency and social justice considerations are challenged to converge on system building imperatives for the coordination of production functions shaping all those interdependencies. The contexts are achievements and deficiencies in macromanagement, and differing levels in the performance of markets. The productive effects and equities of relational cooperation between firms become more significant as their operational interdependencies assume larger dimensions, especially with the introduction of new technologies. The logic of such collaboration can be extended upwards in industry groups, and can be given further application at the national level if functional balances between competition and cooperation can be achieved.

The generation of collaborative synergies in an ambitious plan for hemispheric *infrastructure* development would contribute to the development of a culture of solidarity in which a spirit of collegial capitalism could have increasingly extensive effects. A design for large scale development of hemispheric infrastructure network industries, especially in energy sectors, could be put into effect with diverse partnering arrangements involving construction firms and government agencies, and could be linked with the formation of transportation systems and research centres serving new industrial clusters. Intensive involvement by Latin American technocrats and entrepreneurs in the preparation and implementation of the hemispheric infrastructure design would inspire investor confidence and contribute to the emergence of innovative public spirited Latin American elites.

The rationale for government–private sector partnering in large scale infrastructure development can be more readily acceptable in the USA and in Latin America than that for entrepreneurial conferencing, focussed on manufacturing complementarities, under policy level and corporate sponsorship.[27] Linkages increasing in the infrastructure partnering could then have learning effects, conducive to the development of relational bonds, on a scale that would facilitate general understanding of the potentials of the entrepreneurial conferencing. These potentials have great significance for dynamic and balanced interdependent growth, especially because of the cross border market efficiencies and failures that assume larger dimensions with the expansion of multinational enterprises: the degrees to which they compete and cooperate, as they extend their activities, have widening growth and employment effects. Coordination of these activities, in the public interest, through technocratically sponsored consultations, has to be seen as a vital public good. The proposed infrastructure partnering would help to set orientations for the exploration of entrepreneurial complementarities recognized in view of technological advances. At the same time the entrepreneurial conferencing would contribute to the development of the infrastructure partnering.

A grand design for hemispheric infrastructure development, supplementing the formation of a free trade area of the Americas, would greatly enhance growth prospects in Latin America, and could infuse new vitality into the US political economy, while contributing indirectly to a more functional balance between the domestic operations of US manufacturing firms and their foreign activities. In addition, a new class of technocrats and of managerial elites with expertise in structural partnering would be able to participate constructively in national policymaking. Adaptation of the intensely competitive spirit of the US political economy for the coordination of very large scale transnational production and marketing activities may seem a less feasible alternative to regulatory solutions for problems of market failure in an area of liberalized commerce, but such solutions do not help community formation, and indeed can encourage adversarial legalism.[28]

Dialogue on fundamentals has become urgent in the initial stages of negotiations on hemispheric trade liberalization, to achieve consensus that will provide the vision of a grand design, with an integrative orientation that will make the legal specifics of increased market openness more relational, with trust and goodwill. The consensus must set out, in fraternal language, a philosophy of interdependent macromanagement, for structural partnering with the efficiencies of collegial capitalism, and equities conducive to community formation. American commitment to the public good of coordinated entrepreneurship will have to be affirmed with emphasis on its importance for stronger orientation of the financial sector toward productive funding, for the development of functional balance between domestic and foreign production, for structural partnering with Latin America, and for prudent fiscal restraint. Latin American endorsement of the concept of collegial hemispheric capitalism will have to stress institutional development with domestic technocratic-corporate collaboration, extending into hemispheric collaboration, with increased economic openness between Latin American states.

The solidarity building thrust of the grand design for hemispheric infrastructure development could be made especially effective if this could be launched in the early stages of free trade negotiations. Rapid construction of major initial projects would help to generate goodwill and confidence in the endeavours to achieve continental market integration, and would give greater significance to the consensus on principles of interdependent hemispheric macromanagement.

NOTES

1. See Frederick M. Abbott (2000), 'NAFTA and the legalization of world politics: a case study', *International Organization*, **54**, 3 (summer), 519–48; and Kerry A. Chase 'Economic Interests and regional trading arrangements: the case of NAFTA', *International Organization*, **57** (winter), 137–74.
2. See UNCTAD (2001), *World Investment Report 2001: Promoting Linkages* Geneva: United Nations Conference on Trade and Development.

3. See James M. Poterba and Jurgen von Hagen (eds) (1999), *Fiscal Institutions and Fiscal Performance*, Chicago: University of Chicago Press.
4. See Ajit Singh (1997), 'Catching up with the West: a perspective on Asian economic development and lessons for Latin America', in Louis Emmerij (ed.), *Economic and Social Development into the XXI Century*, Washington, DC: Inter American Development Bank, pp. 222–65.
5. See Reuven Click, Ramon Moreno, and Mark M. Spiegel (eds) (2001), *Financial Crises in Emerging Markets*, Cambridge: Cambridge University Press; and Arvid John Lukauskas and Francisco L. Rivera-Batiz (eds) (2001), *The Political Economy of the East Asian Crisis and its Aftermath*, Cheltenham: UK, Edward Elgar, especially ch. 9, section 1.
6. Regulatory discipline in the USA, although tightened during 2002, is primarily domestic, and is made difficult by highly sophisticated financial instruments for risk spreading; use of these instruments also weakens market discipline. During a boom (which may follow a recession) investors, entrepreneurs, financial institutions and regulators, moreover, tend to become overly optimistic when estimating risks. See comments *in Bank of International Settlements Annual Report*, Basel, 11 June 2001 and 8 July 2002. Risk taking propensities have to be considered in the context of strong concentration trends in financial markets, noted in the latter report, ch. VI.
7. The fragmentation of business associations in the USA is a problem. On policies required for stability in the US financial system see observations in *Bank of International Settlements Annual Reports*, ch. VII.
8. Concentration trends in the US financial sector have not been restrained by antitrust enforcement: see review of these trends in *Bank of International Settlements Annual Report*, 8 July 2002, ch. VI. On overall concentration trends in the world economy see UNCTAD (2000), *World Investment Report*, Geneva: United Nations Conference on Trade and Development.
9. On the gravity of the stock declines see *Bank of International Settlements Annual Report*, 8 July 2002, ch. VIII.
10. On the rationale for stakeholder governance see Margaret M. Blair and Mark J. Roe (eds) (1999), *Employees and Corporate Governance*, Washington, DC: Brookings Institution. See also comments on stakeholder systems in Mary 0'Sullivan (2000), 'The innovative enterprise and corporate governance', *Cambridge Journal of Economics*, **24**, 4 (July), 393–416.
11. See *Bank of International Settlements Annual Report*, chs. VII and VIII.
12. On the logic of production dispersal see *World Investment Report 2001*.
13. See references to this and other coordination problems in Thomas L. Brewer and Gavin Boyd (eds) (2000), *Globalizing America*, Cheltenham: Edward Elgar.
14. See Walter J.Schultz (2001), *The Moral Conditions of Economic Efficiency*, Cambridge: Cambridge University Press.
15. See references to trust in Anoop Madhok (2000), 'Inter-firm collaboration: contractual and capabilities based perspectives', in Nicolai Foss and Volker Mahnke (eds), *Competence, Governance and Entrepreneurship*, Oxford: Oxford University Press.
16. On the Atlantic cooperation see Simon J. Evenett, Alexander Lehmann, and Benn Steil (eds) (2000), *Antitrust goes Global*, Washington, DC: Brookings Institution.
17. See *World Investment Report 2001*.
18. On Mexico's developmental problems see Nora Lustig (2001), 'Life is not easy: Mexico's quest for stability and growth', *Journal of Economic Perspectives*, **15**, 1 (winter), 85–106.
19. The most important involvement would be in Brazil. See OECD (2001), *Economic Survey, Brazil*, Paris: Organisation for Economic Co-operation and Development, June, and Andre Averbug (2002), 'The Brazilian economy in 1994–1999: from the real plan to inflation targets', *The World Economy*, **25**, 7 (July), 925–44. On the significance of the aerospace industry in Brazil see Andrea Goldstein (2002), 'The political economy of high-tech industries in developing countries: aerospace in Brazil, Indonesia, and South Africa', *Cambridge Journal of Economics*, **26**, 4 (July), 521–38.
20. The public goods aspects of linkages between foreign and host country firms are implicit in the *World Investment Report 2001*, but this lacks understanding of the importance of technocratic functions. For general comments on potentials for synergies in government interactions with private sector actors see Christoph Knill and Dirk Lehmkuhl (2002), 'Private actors and the

state: internationalization and changing patterns of governance', *Governance*, **15**, 1 (January), 41–63.

21. See Blair and Roe, *Employees and Corporate Governance*, and 0'Sullivan, 'The Innovative Enterprise and Corporate Governance', whose work indicates that stakeholder concepts of corporate governance have to incorporate understandings of the importance of organizational performance under insider control for continual innovation with the use of new technologies.
22. With the extensive use of derivatives, financial markets become opaque – see David Folkerts-Landau and Peter M. Garber (1997), 'Derivative markets and financial system soundness', in Charles Enoch and John H. Green (eds), *Banking Soundness* and *Monetary Policy*, Washington, DC: International Monetary Fund, ch. 13. The hedge fund industry, operating largely outside regulatory control, relies heavily on the spreading of risks through derivatives. On problems of regulatory surveillance outside the hedge fund industry see comments on the Enron case in *Bank of International Settlements Annual Report*, 2002, ch. VIII.
23. See Glick et al., *Financial Crises in Emerging Markets*, and Lusauskas and Rivera-Batiz, *The Political Economy of the East Asian Crisis and its Aftermath*.
24. Ibid.
25. See *Oxford Review of Economic Policy*, **15**, 3, 1999, symposium on Financial Instability.
26. See observations on concentration in *Bank of International Settlements Annual Report 2002*. On Latin American monetary policy options see George M. von Furstenberg (2002), 'Unilateral and multilateral currency integration: reflections on Western hemispheric monetary union', in Thomas J. Courchene (ed), *Money, Markets and Mobility*, Montreal: McGill-Queens University Press, pp. 253–68.
27. The public interest in infrastructure development is more apparent. On policies for the development of infrastructure network industries see 'Symposium on European network infrastructures', *Oxford Review of Economic Policy*, **17**, 3 (autumn) 2001.
28. On the significance of adversarial legalism see Robert A. Kagan (2001), *Adversarial Legalism: The American Way of Law*, Cambridge, MA: Harvard University Press.

REFERENCES

Albaladejo, Manuel (2002), 'The determinants of competitiveness in SME clusters', in Homi Katrak and Roger Strange (eds) *Snail Scale Enterprises in Developing and Transition Economies*, Houndmills: Palgrave, ch. 12.

Andersen, Birgitte, Jeremy Howells, Richard Hull, Ian Miles and Joanne Roberts (eds) (2000), *Knowledge and Innovation in the New Service Economy*, Cheltenham: Edward Elgar.

Colitt, Raymond, and Richard Lapper (2002), 'Brazil faces old demons', *Financial Times*, 2 August.

Dunning, John H. and Gavin Boyd (eds) (2003), *Alliance Capitalism and Corporate Management*, Cheltenham: Edward Elgar.

Emmerij, Louis (ed.) (1997), *Economic and Social Development into the XXI Century*, Washington, DC: InterAmerican Development Bank.

Fischer, Klaus Peter (1999), 'Business and integration in the Americas: competing points of view', in Gordon Mace and Louis Bélanger et al., *The Americas in Transition*, Boulder, CO: Lynne Rienner, ch. 10.

Hall, Peter A. and David Soskice (eds) (2001), *Varieties of Capitalism*, Oxford: Oxford University Press.

Huh, Chan and Kenneth Kasa (1998), 'Export competition and contagious currency crises', Federal Reserve Bank of San Francisco *Economic Letter*, 98–1, 16 January.

International Monetary Fund, (2002), *World Economic Outlook*, April, ch. 2.

Miller, Marcus, Paul Weller and Lei Zhang (2002), 'Moral hazard and the US stock market: analysing the "Greenspan Put"', *The Economic Journal*, **112**, 478 (March), C171–C186.
OECD (2001), *Economic Survey, Brazil*, Paris: Organization for Economic Co-operation and Development.
Padoan, Pier Carlo, Paul A. Brenton and Gavin Boyd (eds) (2003), *The Structural Foundations of International Finance*, Cheltenham: Edward Elgar.
Rugman, Alan M., and Gavin Boyd (eds) (2003), *Alliance Capitalism for the New American Economy*, Cheltenham: Edward Elgar.
Salazar-Xirinachs, Jose M., and Maryse Robert (eds) (2001), *Toward Free Trade in the Americas*, Washington, DC: Brookings Institution.
Schott, Jeffrey J. and Barbara Oegg (2001), 'Europe and the Americas: toward a NAFTA-South?', *The World Economy*, **24**, 6 (June), 745–60.
Singh, Ajit (2001), 'Financial liberalization and its implications for industrializing economies', in K.S. Jomo and Shyamala Nagaraj (eds), *Globalization versus Development*, Houndmills: Palgrave, ch. 7.
Williamson, John (1997), 'The Washington consensus revisited', in Louis Emmerij (ed.), *Economic and Social Development into the XXI Century*, Washington DC: InterAmerican Development Bank.

11. Developmental issues posed by the FTAA

José M. Salazar-Xirinachs[1]

Latin American and Caribbean (LAC) countries are interested in the FTAA because they see major benefits in terms of growth, development and poverty reduction. However, the connection between free trade, new trade rules and development is complex and multifaceted. Despite much discussion about the FTAA there is surprisingly limited literature analysing its developmental impacts. This chapter tries to fill the lacunae by providing a selective, although fairly comprehensive, discussion of some of the main developmental issues posed by the FTAA. This is an issues chapter. Its main objective is to raise relevant questions and review different academic and expert positions as well as existing empirical research results surrounding them. In light of the complexity of the subject matter, it would be over-ambitious to provide definite answers to these issues. Thus the spirit of this chapter is more analytical and positive than normative or prescriptive.

The developmental benefits and issues posed by the FTAA for LAC countries, are grouped in six issue areas:

1. market access in industrial goods and agriculture;
2. market access and rules in services and investment;
3. other rules related issues in areas such as intellectual property, subsidies and industrial policy;
4. treatment of differences in size and levels of development,
5. technical assistance and capacity building issues, and finally,
6. governance issues and the relationship between open markets and political institutions.

Given that in terms of trade rules in a number of areas WTO agreements provide if not the floor, at least a very important reference point for the FTAA, the chapter makes frequent reference to WTO rules and their developmental implications.

DEVELOPMENTAL BENEFITS OF ENHANCED MARKET ACCESS IN GOODS

Enhanced and more secure market access for industrial goods and agricultural products is arguably one of the major, if not the major, benefit for LAC countries in terms of growth and development. Reciprocal trade liberalization produces of course both benefits as well as costs.

Building on Existing Economic Interdependence

As a first approximation, some basic orders of magnitude suggest the potential for gains. The US market represents 78 per cent of the aggregate GDP of the Western Hemisphere. This figure alone underlines the importance for LAC countries of achieving increased and more secure access to the US market. Between 40 per cent and 50 per cent of the total exports of Central American, Caribbean and Andean countries are destined for the United States and Canada. These economies enjoy quite extensive access to those markets via the Generalized System of Preferences, the Caribbean Basin Initiative, and the Andean Trade Preferences Act. However, these are unilateral preferences; they are more uncertain than a reciprocal arrangement, they do not have a dispute resolution mechanism, and key products are excluded. Therefore, in terms of market access these countries still have an important margin of benefit to gain from the FTAA.

In the case of MERCOSUR, 20 per cent of its total exports are destined for the United States and Canada, 26 per cent to Europe, 31 per cent to the rest of LAC, and 16 per cent to the rest of the world. While the share of exports going to the US is less important for MERCOSUR than for the other LAC countries, the fact remains that more than 50 per cent of total MERCOSUR exports go to other countries in the Americas, and this makes the FTAA project potentially very significant for the economic dynamics of MERCOSUR.[2]

It is not only better access to the US and Canadian markets that makes the FTAA an attractive proposition for all countries, but also reciprocal access between the LAC group of countries themselves. For instance, from 1990 to 1999 the growth rates of exports to other LAC countries as a group were higher for all sub-regions of LAC than the growth rates of exports to other regions in the world.

Evidence from Computable General Equilibrium Models

A more direct estimate of potential gains from the FTAA is derived from various integration and trade liberalization scenarios in Latin America using multi-country Computable General Equilibrium (CGE) models. Such studies have tried to assess not only the effects of multilateral trade liberalization, but also the impact of regional initiatives, most notably an FTAA.

According to Roland-Hoist and van der Mensbrugghe (2001), for the Americas the multilateral removal of tariffs would translate into a $605 billion increase in total trade, while the removal of tariffs under an FTAA would expand the region's total trade by $125 billion. Diao, Diaz-Bonilla and Robinson (2001) estimate that the change in real GDP associated with the FTAA would be positive for all its members, and would range from less than 1 per cent for the larger economies (United States and Canada) to over 5 per cent for Argentina, Central America, and Colombia.

Empirical assessments of the effects of trade liberalization on the Americas not only underscore the key importance of market access in their liberalization strategies, but also raise questions as to the priority that countries should assign to different liberalization initiatives at the multilateral, regional or unilateral levels. In this context, several studies have sought to estimate the benefits of particular trade liberalization scenarios. One such study by Roland-Hoist and van der Mensbrugghe (2001) did not find evidence in support of the widely held view that unilateral liberalization is welfare-superior to regional arrangements. To the contrary, for each of the six countries considered by the authors,[3] and for Latin America and the Caribbean as a whole, the FTAA is more beneficial in the aggregate than unilateral trade liberalization.

Monteagudo and Watanuki (2001) also estimate gains under different trade integration scenarios and find that for hemispheric partners, the FTAA is the best option, generating the largest economic gains and export growth. The exception is MERCOSUR, for which the FTAA is the second-best option after integration with the European Union when tariff-only liberalization is considered. However, the FTAA is the best option also for MERCOSUR when both tariff and non-tariff barriers are considered. The FTAA increases Latin America's exports by 11 per cent in the entire hemispheric market, and generates the strongest export growth of light manufactures in all Latin American members except Mexico. Another interesting finding is that, in general, the FTAA boosts the region's manufactured exports through intra-industrial trade, while integration with the EU expands mainly agriculture-related exports.

The authors estimate that the elimination of tariffs under the FTAA would lead to a 6.5 per cent increase in MERCOSUR's total exports. In the case of a free trade agreement with the European Union, MERCOSUR'S total exports would increase by almost 8 per cent. Expressed in terms of income growth, the EU option would be superior for MERCOSUR, as it would result in a 3.21 per cent increase in its real GDP – 0.37 percentage points more than the FTAA option. These results are broadly consistent with those of Decreux and Guerin (2001), who found that the growth of total MERCOSUR exports under an

EU-MERCOSUR free trade area (12.7 per cent) would exceed the growth of the region's exports under the FTAA (11.3 per cent).

However, once the models are expanded to take into account welfare effects resulting from the elimination of both tariff and non-tariff barriers (NTBs), the FTAA appears as the welfare-superior option for the MERCOSUR countries. Specifically, Monteagudo and Watanuki (2001) estimate that the elimination of all tariffs and NTBs under the FTAA would result in a 6.27 per cent increase in real GDP for MERCOSUR, compared with a 6.1 per cent increase in the case of a free trade area with the European Union. Interestingly, these results are magnified significantly under a 'combined' scenario involving the completion of an FTAA and a free trade area between MERCOSUR and the European Union. Under such a scenario, MERCOSUR'S exports increase by over 30 per cent, and its real GDP by almost 12 per cent.

A general conclusion of these estimates is that RTAs, such as the FTAA or the potential agreement between MERCOSUR and the European Union, are good for the participants and have little impact on non-participants. Trade creation greatly exceeds trade diversion in most cases. And in general, the gains are found to be larger for the Latin American participants than for their large potential partners, the United States and European Union. These results are consistent with earlier studies of NAFTA, which predicted small positive gains for the United States and large gains for Mexico. It should be noted that the positive impacts of full market access from trade agreements such as the FTAA tend to be under-estimated in these CGE exercises, due to the imperfect treatment in these models of non-tariff barriers and of dynamic gains from trade.

Agriculture

Agricultural trade liberalization has always been surrounded by special sensitivities owing to some characteristics of agricultural activities and their unique role in the economies of both developed and developing countries: its importance in rural employment and standards of living; the potential impact of agricultural liberalization in rural–urban migration, particularly in developing countries where 20, 30 or even higher percentages of the population live in rural areas; food security arguments; the complex systems of domestic support/subsidy in place, particularly in developed countries; the traditionally high degree of organization and political influence of agriculture and agribusiness interests; and more recently, the different attitudes among the public and consumers over food safety and quality standards.

As Table 11.1 shows, agricultural production, employment and trade is very important for most of the Americas. Agricultural production is more than 15 per cent of GDP for Paraguay, Guatemala, Honduras and Nicaragua. In terms of employment it accounts for 46 per cent in Guatemala, 34 per cent in Paraguay,

32 per cent in Honduras, 21 per cent in Mexico and Colombia, and 16 per cent in Brazil, Chile and Dominican Republic. In addition, trade in agricultural products represents more than 19 per cent of their total trade for Paraguay, Guatemala, Honduras, Nicaragua, Argentina, Barbados and Chile, despite the fact that the trade potential is dampened by agricultural protectionism in major markets.

Table 11.1 Share of agriculture in selected countries in the WH

Countries	GDP			Employment	Intra-FTAA
	1975	1985	1999	2000	Trade
Argentina	11.9	7.7	4.6	9.8	19.6
Barbados	13.3	6.4	6.0	4.0	19.0
Brazil	8.3	7.1	8.5	16.7	12.8
Mexico	9.6	8.6	5.0	21.0	5.8
Chile	9.8	8.0	10.3	15.7	20.7
Colombia	25.2	16.5	12.8	20.4	18.5
Dominican Republic	17.5	17.8	11.3	16.7	16.8
Guatemala	28.0	25.9	23.0	46.1	28.0
Honduras	29.3	19.6	16.2	31.7	25.3
Nicaragua	23.4	30.2	31.6	20.0	27.9
Paraguay	34.7	26.9	29.2	34.4	36.0
United States	3.3	2.0	1.2	2.1	6.2
Venezuela	6.7	5.7	5.0	8.0	13.0

Source: Adapted from Berrios et al. (2002).

FTAA countries present a very diverse set of negotiating priorities, owing to the diversity of agricultural exports, net trade position (net importers versus net exporters), level of development, and agricultural export potential. However, a number of evaluations of the impacts of FTAA agricultural liberalization on LAC economies using multi-region, multi-sector CGE models conclude that their benefits can be very significant for all LAC countries. Burfisher, Robinson and Thierfelder (2002) find that despite the trade liberalization that has already occurred through MERCOSUR, NAFTA and bilateral trade pacts, the FTAA can still lead to significant expansion in the region's agricultural trade: 'If the full elimination of all tariffs (agricultural and manufacturing) is accomplished in an FTAA, annual agricultural trade within the hemisphere will increase by nearly $4 billion, or about 7 per cent. Agriculture will account for about 20 per cent of the expansion in Hemispheric trade due to an FTAA (Burfisher, Robinson and Thierfelder 2002, p. 5).

US participation in FTAA agricultural liberalization is key to enabling all countries, including the Unites States, to achieve the potential benefits of the FTAA. It is estimated that annual US agricultural exports to the hemisphere will increase by $1.3 billion (about 7 per cent) and imports by $1.1 billion (about 5 per cent) due to an FTAA.

The estimates also suggest that the concerns by some countries that they may be hurt by an FTAA because their margin of preference, particularly in the US market, will be eroded, is misplaced. Model estimates suggest that all countries are expected to increase their agricultural exports to the region under an FTAA, with the Andean region and the Central American/Caribbean region presenting the highest rates of growth of their agricultural exports (6 per cent and 4 per cent, respectively), with most exports destined for the US market, owing largely to the fact that they face relatively high US trade barriers on some of their agricultural products, particularly on processed foods. The Andean and Central American/Caribbean regions will also have relatively large increases in agricultural imports under an FTAA (13 per cent and 14 per cent, respectively), reflecting their relatively high tariffs on imports.

Monteagudo and Watanuki (2002) develop several scenarios of agricultural reform in the Americas under the FTAA by estimating the impacts of eliminating three main policy instruments: tariffs, domestic support and export subsidies. They estimate that tariff elimination would increase LACs' agricultural exports to the hemisphere by 14 per cent and that all hemisphere countries would benefit from tariff elimination. Exports to the United States account for 40 per cent of LAC countries' increased exports to hemispheric markets. Brazil and Chile are the most benefited countries (their exports expanding by 26 per cent and 28 per cent respectively). By product, as processed food sectors are more protected than primary goods, they enjoy relatively faster export growth. Latin America expands exports of dairy products, beverage/tobaccos and poultry meat by more than 25 per cent, while exports of sugar are estimated to increase by 23 per cent and of oilseeds/soybeans by 19 per cent. In contrast to these impacts of tariff elimination, the removal of domestic support has only a modest positive effect on LAC agricultural exports of 0.5 per cent.[4] The elimination of export subsidies has negligible to negative impact on LACs exports. One of the most important conclusions is that tariff reduction is the policy that would have by far the largest positive agricultural export growth impact on LAC as a result of the FTAA, even if domestic support and export subsidies issues remained to be negotiated in the Doha Round.

Jank, Fuchsloch and Kutas (2002) develop and estimate an innovative index called the Regional Export Sensitive Tariff index (REST), which allows a comparison between a country's faced tariffs from its trading partners with that country's imposed tariffs. More specifically, the REST index aggregates all tariffs faced and imposed by each country at the regional level into a single indicator, representing a ratio of the weighted value of those tariffs.[5] The analysis of agricultural trade in the Americas using the REST index shows that NAFTA, Caribbean and most Andean countries impose higher weighted MFN tariffs than they face in the Western Hemisphere (REST below 1). The biggest face-off is Mexico and Canada, where high tariffs imposed on a very small group of key products are significant to potential FTAA partners. In other words, these countries are net liberalizers within the integration process in terms of agricultural tariff protection. On the other hand, most MERCOSUR members, Chile, and most Central American countries would have net gains in terms of agricultural market access. Brazil would rank first in this process above Uruguay, Chile and Argentina, as a result of the very high tariffs faced by Brazil's sensitive products such as sugar, orange juice and tobacco, especially in the US (Jank, Fuschloch and Kutas 2002, p. 37).

In conclusion, empirical scenarios estimated by economists show that there would be major benefits for LAC countries if the FTAA negotiations achieve a significant reduction of barriers to agricultural trade in the Western Hemisphere. According to some estimates, these benefits are significant even if the distorting effects of producer subsidies remain to be negotiated in the WTO during the Doha Round.

In most LAC countries reciprocal agricultural liberalization would expand imports and exports of agricultural products. On the export side many LAC countries will find ample opportunities from increased market access given their comparative advantages in agricultural exports. On the import side, increased imports could produce serious dislocations, including potentially significant rural–urban migration, particularly in countries where agricultural employment is a high percentage of the labor force. Therefore, even in those countries where the net effect is expansionary, the agricultural sectors would experience significant transformation. This poses important issues about the role of agriculture and the peasantry in LAC countries.

Rural Development in an Open Economy

Agricultural activities and rural livelihoods have been subject to great stress in most LAC countries as a result of economic openness and modernization. As one analyst observes in the case of Mexico, over decades 'peasants have been semiproletarized, subsumed, modernized, subsidized, made migrants and poverty-ridden, excluded, and included in the sweep of national development projects' (Appendini 2003, p. 270).

As development proceeds, the long-term trend is one in which part of the rural population is increasingly engaged in non-farm activities. International experience shows that the process of economic development involves structural change toward manufacturing and tertiary activities, as the demand for food grows at a slower rate than the demand for non-food goods and services, and as economies diversify into higher productivity, knowledge and skill-intensive activities. It is in the interest of countries to promote this process since the long run trend in agricultural commodity prices is downward.

However, this process is not painless and it is one that has taken decades for many now developed countries. One of the most difficult policy challenges is how to influence and manage this transformation. Naturally, governments and civil societies want to avoid employment-reducing/poverty-increasing paths and aim instead for employment-expanding/poverty-reducing growth.

Policies on two fronts will influence the speed, costs and benefits of agricultural adjustment. On the external front, are the FTAA-negotiated transition periods by specific sector and product and the treatment given to the agricultural sensitivities of different countries. On the internal front, the agricultural transformation process that the FTAA will induce requires investments in rural development, education, communications, transportation infrastructure, export diversification, sanitary and phytosanitary and food safety capacities.[6] The FTAA Hemispheric Cooperation Program could develop hemisphere-wide cooperation in agriculture to facilitate these transformation, diversification and agricultural capacity building processes. But ultimately, each country must find the right balance and pace for rural transformation, including the challenge of increasing modernization via new investments and large-size highly integrated agribusiness, while preserving space for the small and medium-sized producers.

Safeguard Protection and Contingent Protection

Market access benefits from the FTAA would also flow from reduced trade and investment uncertainty associated with disciplining safeguard and contingent protection.

Broadly defined the term safeguard protection refers to a provision in a trade agreement permitting governments under specified circumstances to withdraw – or cease to apply – their normal obligations in order to protect (safeguard) certain overriding interests (Hoekman and Kostecki 2001, p. 303). There are several economic and political rationales for safeguard protection: they provide a safety valve to protect local producers from import surges and they play a political role in that without them governments and business will not be willing to sign agreements that reduce protection substantially. Thus, safeguard protection mechanisms are critical to the existence and operation of trade liberalizing agreements. However, the recent proliferation in the use of some of these mechanisms has raised the concern that they provide excessive opportunities to reimpose protection and negatively affect market access opportunities for all countries, particularly developing countries.

Safeguard protection provisions can be separated into two categories. First, those that allow for the *temporary suspension* of obligations, also called contingent protection provisions. In the GATT/WTO system these include antidumping (AD), countervailing duties (CVDs), balance of payments provisions, infant industry provisions, emergency protection, special safeguards and general waivers. Second, there are those that allow for *permanent exceptions* from the general obligations. In the GATT/WTO system these include General Exceptions to safeguard public morals, health and the environment (Article XX GATT and XIV GATS); National Security provisions, and provisions that allow the renegotiation or modification of schedules. One of the key developmental challenges of the FTAA is to design an appropriate safeguard protection system to limit opportunities for protectionist abuse of these measures. Particularly sensitive is the issue of antidumping, in light of the recent drastic increase in the use of this instrument.

During the 1980s, the global use of antidumping measures intensified but was limited mostly to a relatively small club of traditional developed country users. During the 1990s developing countries became major users of AD. Non-traditional users of AD involved mainly Argentina, Brazil, India, Korea, Mexico and South Africa, but the list keeps growing.[7]

A disaggregated analysis done by Tavares, Macario and Steinfatt (2001) shows the relevance of AD for the Americas:

- From 1987 to 2000 the United States and Brazil were the leading targets of AD investigations in the region, representing 63 per cent of the cases initiated against FTAA countries. A second group was involved in around 30 per cent of the investigations and includes Argentina, Canada, Mexico and Venezuela, while 12 countries received the remaining 7 per cent of investigations. Sixteen FTAA countries were not affected by AD measures during this period.
- The distribution by users of AD has a similar profile: Argentina, Brazil, Canada, Mexico and the United States were responsible for 93 per cent of total investigations initiated in the FTAA area, while ten countries accounted for the remaining 7 per cent. Nineteen FTAA countries have never used AD.
- One of the most revealing facts is that 485 of the 638 cases affecting FTAA economies, that is three of every four cases, originated in the region; there is therefore more density in the use of these measures between FTAA countries than between the rest of the world and the FTAA group.
- However, the main users of AD in the Americas direct their actions mostly against the rest of the world: of 1744 investigations initiated by FTAA

countries, 485 (38 per cent) were against other FTAA countries and 1259 against the rest of the world.

The increased use of AD in the Americas is part of a global trend. As Thomas Prusa puts it 'The AD genie is out of the bottle. A multitude of countries have only recently enacted AD statutes and these new users are now filing a larger and larger number of cases' (Prusa 1999, p. 8).

What is the developmental impact of this trend? AD actions have at least four types of negative effects: on exports and imports, distortion of competitive conditions, costs imposed on consumers due to price increases, and rent-seeking behavior by import competing firms. There is clear evidence of a decline in exports following the opening of an investigation, regardless of whether a duty is finally imposed. Prusa (1999) found that import quantities in the United States fell by 50–70 per cent on average over the first three years following the imposition of a measure, while import prices rose by more than 30 per cent during the same period. Even rejected petitions caused damage by reducing import volumes on average by 15–20 per cent. Similar results are found by Messerlin (1989) for the European Union and in numerous comparisons of import levels before and after the initiation of an AD investigation (Neufeld 2001). Some of these studies also argue that the disruption of AD is even worse than that of normal trade protection given the element of uncertainty about where and when it is going to hit.

In the Western Hemisphere, as for most of the rest of the world, the aggregate amounts of trade directly affected by AD tend to be very small. However, from 1987 to 2000 about 80 per cent of the cases initiated by, and targeted at countries in the region, were concentrated in six industries: base metals (mostly steel products), machinery and electrical equipment, chemicals, plastics, pulp and paper and textiles. This concentration and the importance of these products in the total exports of some countries such as Brazil, Mexico and the United States, means that for these countries more than 50 per cent of their exports to other countries in the Western Hemisphere are hampered by AD-induced uncertainty and instability (Tavares, Macario and Steinfatt 2001).

Developing countries are particularly hurt. Besides being frequent targets of AD measures, their enterprises are vulnerable to the extent that they are infant entrants in the international market or are typically in an economically weaker competitive situation or context. Under these circumstances developing country industries find it more difficult to face the uncertainty and unpredictability that AD rules produce than is the case with well-established exporters. And despite the fact that Article 15 of the WTO AD Agreement states that 'special regard must be given by developed country Members to the special situation of developing country Members when considering the application of antidumping measures', and directs members to 'explore ... constructive remedies before applying antidumping duties where they would affect the essential interests of developing country Members' these have remained best endeavor clauses not accompanied by concrete criteria and have therefore found no concrete expression (Neufeld 2001).

Improving the current system by designing an appropriate AD and safeguard protection system that limits protectionist abuse can have significant market access and developmental impacts for LAC countries. This is indeed one of the most difficult and complex issues in both the FTAA and WTO negotiations. In Doha, Ministers agreed to negotiations aimed at 'clarifying and improving disciplines ... while preserving the basic concepts, principles and effectiveness of these Agreements and their instruments and objectives, and taking into account the needs of developing countries and least-developed participants' (Doha Development Agenda 2001, paragraph 28).

In addition, the Doha Decision on Implementation-related Issues and Concerns expanded this Ministerial mandate by, among other aspects, directing the Council to make specific recommendations on how to operationalize Article 15 cited above by November 2002. Numerous countries have presented proposals in the WTO that reflect a great divergence of views.

Much will depend on the politics of antidumping reform in the United States. During the last weeks of the discussion of the Trade Promotion Authority Bill in 2002, the US Congress had before it a proposed amendment, the so-called Dayton–Craig Amendment, that called for a commitment on the part of US negotiators to ensure that the negotiations in the WTO did not diminish the ability of the United States to vigorously apply its trade remedy laws. The amendment in its original form was dropped in conference but is indicative of the prevailing sentiment on the issue. In its final form the US Trade Act of 2002 states that 'The principal negotiating objectives of the United States with respect to trade remedy laws are: (A) to preserve the ability of the United States to enforce rigorously its trade laws, including the antidumping, countervailing duty, and safeguard laws, and avoid agreements that lessen the effectiveness of domestic and international disciplines on unfair trade, especially antidumping and subsidies'. This language tends to reduce the room for manoeuvre by US negotiators. On the other hand, there are several potential constituencies for AD reform in the United States: the increasing number of US exporters hurt by the proliferation of foreign AD actions, as well as the downstream US import-using industries and consumers, who are harmed by the price increases and supply disruptions caused by AD protection. Their influence could change the politics of AD reform in the next few years as the US public debate and policy-makers widen their view to include the victims and costs of US AD law in addition to its beneficiaries. There is a growing recognition of the specific and systemic dangers posed by the spread of AD in other countries.[8]

DEVELOPMENTAL ISSUES RELATED TO INVESTMENT AND SERVICES

Investment

Increased investment is also one of the major benefits expected from the FTAA for LAC countries. International experience offers at least three important lessons:

- the benefits of FDI tend to exceed its costs,
- policies can make a very important difference to maximizing benefits, minimizing costs and promoting the shift from low skills/low wage to increasingly higher skills/higher wage foreign investor operations ('climbing the ladder'), and
- most of this policy responsibility lies with the host country, including areas such as macroeconomic stability, infrastructure, human capital, as well as regulatory, environmental and competition issues.

While maximizing the developmental benefits of FDI is first and foremost a domestic challenge there is also an important role for international rules and collective actions. Indeed, internationally negotiated investment rules, such as those under the Doha Development Agenda or the FTAA, pose abundant development related issues.

Following Sauve (2002), investment rule making and their developmental impacts can be discussed in terms of: (a) investment protection; (b) investment distortions; (c) investment liberalization; and (d) international cooperation to enhance investment climates and promote good governance.

Investment protection

Investment protection encompasses obligations to provide protection for foreign investment and investors and specific procedures with respect to issues such as expropriation and compensation; transfer of funds; protection and compensation in case of civil strife; fair and equitable treatment, and other standards of protection. In recent years there has been a dramatic increase in rule making for investment protection on two tracks: negotiation of bilateral investment treaties (BITs) and negotiation of bilateral and regional trade agreements, such as NAFTA, a model that has been extended quite widely to western hemisphere countries. An FTAA investment chapter will actually build on these existing agreements.

The developmental argument for the protection dimension of investment agreements is that by reducing uncertainty and providing signals that the host country is committed to abiding by international laws, they are an important additional factor in an attractive investment climate. It is important to note that investment agreements by themselves do not attract FDI. Available evidence strongly suggests that FDI flows respond to more fundamental determinants such as economic stability, quality of infrastructure and skills and other institutional factors. However, by reducing uncertainty, increasing policy credibility and positive signaling, investment agreements could make a difference at the margins of companies' decision to invest. To the extent that investment agreements include a significant market access component they may, however, have a large impact on FDI flows and associated benefits.

Some key concepts and standards of traditional investment protection and treatment law have caused difficulties of interpretation and raised public concern, particularly in respect to the ability of countries to regulate in the public interest. This is particularly the case of NAFTA chapter 11 provisions on investor–state arbitration procedures. It is beyond the scope of this chapter to enter into the complex legal aspects of this debate. Suffice it to say that despite much recent concern on this issue, the argument in favor of investor–state arbitration procedures is that, when properly designed and circumscribed, they can be a good way of taking intergovernmental and foreign policy considerations out of investment disputes.

Investment distortions

The investment distortion trade and development agenda includes the following important questions: What policy instruments can host countries put in place to maximize the flows and benefits of FDI? Which specific instruments will be disciplined away by international investment rules and is this good or bad for development policy? Table 11.2 contains examples of FDI policy instruments distinguishing between positive and negative incentives.

Positive investment incentives, including fiscal incentives, have proliferated as part of the increased international competition to attract investment both between and within countries; and yet there has been no significant effort either at the multilateral or regional levels to bring them under discipline. Properly defined rules in the context of the FTAA can help not only to maximize the benefits from FDI, but also to minimize the dangers and costs of locational incentive competition among countries, and within them, to attract the externality rich sourcing patterns of international investors (Moran 1999).[9] However, there is very limited interest, particularly in federal states (where investment incentives programs are actively used as instruments of industrial or regional development policy) in addressing the issue of distortions associated with locational competition, either at the global or regional levels. Yet, it may be in the interest of smaller economies to discipline locational competition, given their more limited fiscal capacities to engage significantly in such competition.

Table 11.2 Examples of FDI policies

Positive Incentives	Negative Incentives
• Tax holidays • Tax treaties to avoid double taxation • Exemptions on import duties on capital goods and raw materials • Other exemptions or relaxation of rules in priority sectors • Land grants • Training grants • Establishment grants	• Nationalization or expropriation • Double taxation • Domestic content requirements for intermediate inputs • Domestic employment restrictions • Export requirements • Screening • General foreign equity limits • Sectoral foreign equity limits • Landownership restrictions • Joint-venture requirements • Restrictions on remittance of profits • Limitations on transfer of shares or liquidation of the company

Source: Adapted from Hoekman and Saggi (2002).

While there has been practically no movement on positive investment incentives, negative incentives and other distorting effects of TRIMs have been subject to negotiated disciplines at regional and multilateral levels. Many developing countries have used performance requirements, including domestic content provisions, technology sharing arrangements, or export/import balancing requirements, as instruments to maximize or capture the benefits of FDI for their local economies. However, the WTO Trade Related Investment Measures (TRIMs) agreement, and a number of RTAs, request countries to phase out these instruments.

The key developmental question is how development friendly is the TRIMs agreement or RTAs that prohibit the use of these instruments? More research is needed to assess the developmental effects of various types of performance requirements. With the present state of knowledge there are two positions on this subject.

In the past, conventional wisdom has held that domestic content, joint-venture and other technology sharing requirements might harness FDI to a country's development goals. A number of empirical studies reveal that some performance requirements, particularly those related to export performance or local training requirements, can have positive developmental effects,

However, Moran (2001, 2002), based on a number of case studies, argues in favor of a 'new paradigm' that suggests that a much more effective means of capturing the benefits of FDI is to minimize distortionary interventions and allow foreign subsidiaries to be integrated as tightly as possible into the regional or global sourcing networks of their parent firms. Using evidence from the automotive, computer and electronics industries, where the globalization of the higher-skill investor operations has been most far-reaching, Moran compares the operations of foreign subsidiaries – and the backward linkages and spillovers to the host economy – under these two alternative approaches, and finds that the conventional approach is not only less successful but is in many cases actually harmful to growth and development. The best policies that host countries can implement to develop dynamic backward linkages are found to be a combination of a performance requirement-free environment, coupled with vendor development programs, including upgrading support to local suppliers and nurturing of local supplier relationships with foreign investors and operations, like those used by Singapore and Malaysia.

As suggested, the jury is still out on these very important issues, and more research is necessary. Moran's arguments and case studies are quite persuasive. However, this is an area plagued by intellectual uncertainty, and caution should probably be exercised in restricting the range of instruments that might have positive effects for development. On the other hand, disciplining the use of investment incentives is an area where smaller and developing countries stand to gain substantially.

Investment liberalization

The FTAA offers participating countries important win–win opportunities based on achieving investment regime liberalization beyond the important unilateral efforts that LAC countries have undertaken in the last decade. The first win is because increased liberalization and competition may be beneficial for growth and development. The second win is associated with the fact that this liberalization might be in exchange for increased market access in the United States and other trading partners in agriculture and other key sectors, as well as in exchange for other important trade objectives.

Much of this win–win potential in investment liberalization lies in the services sector. Services account for the majority of discriminatory measures maintained by LAC countries, precluding the commercial presence of foreign investors; services receive on average two-thirds of global FDI flows; and services are crucial for international competitiveness. Thus, most of the investment liberalization game in the Americas, as well as globally, is services-centric.[10]

Reasons why some LAC countries have resisted a more open FDI policy include, first, the presumed market power effect of multinational corporations. An open FDI policy, however, should aim at inviting not just one but many investors and should be accompanied by appropriate pro-competitive regulations. Second, concerns have been expressed about crowding out or scaling down domestic entrepreneurship. A number of studies have indeed shown a significant change in ownership patterns associated with investment liberalization. However, it can be argued that downsizing of inefficient domestic firms is positive for development to the extent that it contributes to increased productivity, expands consumer choice and reduces prices. In addition, through mergers and acquisitions, and by transferring new technology, FDI can prevent some domestic industries from being wiped out.[11] The potential of FDI to develop local suppliers and transfer technology is also well documented. Ultimately, FDI is an instrument for growth and development, and since growth strategies vary from country to country FDI policy should allow some flexibility to accommodate country specific conditions and strategies.

Modality of negotiation of investment and services (positive versus negative list approach) and architectural issues such as where to negotiate and place commercial presence (GATS mode 3) in an FTA – whether as part of a services chapter or as part of an investment framework that applies to both goods and services – also have a number of implications in terms of transparency, user-friendliness for the private sector, flexibility and other developmental dimensions. However, it is beyond the scope of this chapter to discuss these issues.

Good governance

Although not part of a trade negotiations agenda, there is a wide range of complementary international cooperation initiatives that could enhance investment climates and good governance and thus promote development. Some of these initiatives can be legally binding while others could be more hortatory in nature. These initiatives involve issues such as: bribery, corruption and money laundering; developing codes of corporate conduct for multinational investors; promoting corporate social responsibility; strengthening standards of corporate governance; exchanging information on best practices in investment and export promotion activities; and so on. All these are areas where international cooperation has produced important results in recent years and where continuing efforts could complement trade agreement-based attempts at addressing the trade–investment interface. In addition to global efforts such as the OECD and others, the Inter-American System and Summit of the Americas process have initiatives on bribery and corruption (The Inter-American Convention Against Corruption), money-laundering, and corporate social responsibility.[12]

Services

There is increasing recognition that services activities are critical for economic dynamism and competitiveness. Services represent on average 60 per cent of the hemispheric GDP. In trade terms, services are even more important to the smaller economies of the Caribbean and Central America. The importance of policy in the service sector goes beyond the sector itself. Services are essential inputs into the production of virtually all other goods and services. Several studies show that on average, 60 per cent of manufacturing value added is represented by services inputs, which means that competitiveness in manufacturing products is strongly dependent on competitiveness in services. Highly priced and inefficient services raise costs for all users, imposing a 'tax' on the whole economy. Thus, service sector policy can have a major influence on economic performance. As a recent report by the World Bank argues, services is one of the most important areas to liberalize for developing country competitiveness.[13]

All this makes the FTAA services negotiations, and the liberalization and competitiveness that they might induce, one of the principal benefits of the FTAA for participating countries.[14] Moreover, as explained above, given that services account for the majority of discriminatory LAC measures precluding commercial presence of foreign investors, most of the investment liberalization game in the Americas, as well as globally, gravitates around services sectors and issues.

Service sector reform is a complex task. Service sector policies need to balance efficiency and competition objectives with the legitimate role for governments to offset market failures and achieve national development objectives such as the universal provision of education or health care services. As the OECD argues: 'For service sector policies – and national commitments on trade and investment in services in the WTO or in regional trade agreements- to contribute to development, liberalization will need in many instances to be accompanied by *strengthened* regulation ... regulation and competition policy may need to be in place to complement trade and investment liberalization' (OECD 2001a, p. 4).

A number of developmental concerns have been expressed: (a) that services negotiations and the GATS pose a threat to rights to regulate the production, sale, distribution or import of service activities; (b) that the GATS and a regional services agreement may restrict room for development policy in sensitive sectors such as education, health, water supply, electricity distribution and other utilities with strong public goods connotations; (c) that services or investment agreements are designed to promote the interests of large multinationals and restrict industrial policies; d) that due to the asymmetric power relations and information asymmetries, most action at the multilateral level has been on sectors of interest to developed countries while there has been little progress in sectors of interest to developing countries such as mode 4, movement of natural persons.

Some of these arguments are based on misunderstandings of how the GATS and services agreements operate. Others are genuine and need to be addressed. Analyses and answers to these and other concerns about the GATS have been provided by OECD (2001). The main points are the following:

Right to regulate

In the GATS context, a number of sovereign rights are recognized as fundamental and preserved. Under the GATS, governments retain the right to: regulate in order to pursue national policy objectives; modify or withdraw commitments undertaken (subject to compensation); designate or maintain monopolies, public or private; choose to which service sectors and modes of supply they wish to grant market access to foreign suppliers, and the conditions of such market access; make no GATS commitments on any particular sector. In short, the GATS explicitly allows member countries to advance at their own pace. It is also important to point out that the objective of GATS is the progressive liberalization of services trade, not deregulation. As pointed out above, to contribute to development, liberalization has to be accompanied in most instances by more (but different), not less, regulation. In light of its flexibility, and its emphasis on the progressive, voluntary, nature of liberalization, it is possible to argue that, in fact, the GATS is the most 'development friendly' of all Uruguay Round Agreements.

Services liberalization, development policy and public services

GATS rules do not dictate any specific roles for the public and private sectors; governments are free to decide what sectors will be reserved for the state or state-owned enterprises. Countries are free to decide whether or not to open sensitive public services to outside competition. Of course, countries will be under pressure to liberalize or provide access in certain public services sectors. However, it is up to them to decide what is best according to their own growth, social and development policies.

Benefiting multinationals or host countries

Whether liberalizing trade in services benefits multinationals or host countries is a false dilemma. Many benefits can accrue to both international investors and national economies provided there is appropriate regulation and an open, competitive environment. The potential host benefits of FDI are well documented. FDI may have multiple benefits well beyond job creation and the provision of capital. Contingent upon the pursuit of appropriate host country policies, the main potential contribution is a bundle of intangible assets including technologies, best management practices, marketing capabilities, human relations policies, labor force skills and other potential spillovers and externalities that are highly beneficial for host-country economic growth and poverty alleviation. In addition, FDI may exert positive influence on environmental performance and social conditions, for instance by transferring 'cleaner' technologies, or promoting more socially responsible corporate policies. As explained above, trade agreements pose the issue of what policy instruments host countries can use to maximize the flows and the benefits from FDI. However, the instruments that are most relevant, such as investment incentives and performance requirements, are covered under investment and subsidies disciplines, not in the services area.

Balanced outcomes

Services negotiations are not a major arena for North–South tensions, or industrial versus developing country divides. In fact, many developing countries are deliberately, and often autonomously, inviting FDI in key services sectors to upgrade their domestic infrastructures in financial services, telecommunications, transportation, and so on. From this point of view services liberalization should not be viewed as a 'concession' to other countries, but as a self-interested national policy for enhancing domestic economic performance. This having been said, there are a number of issues as regards services negotiations that are of particular interest to developing countries, including more progress on the movement of natural persons, improving access to distribution channels and information networks and the liberalization of market access in sectors of particular export interest.

OTHER RULES-RELATED DEVELOPMENTAL ISSUES

Two additional rules-related developmental issues are intellectual property and industrial policy, or as called in 'new paradigm' language, promotion of competitiveness.

Intellectual Property

Intellectual property protection is arguably the area where there has been the greatest and the most heated controversy, in terms of its implications for development. WTO Director General Supachai Panitchpakdi has identified the debate on how the Agreement on Trade Related Aspects of Intellectual Property Rights (TRIPS) can best be applied by developing countries and how the TRIPS Agreement and the international framework can be improved as one of the areas of focus for the WTO in the Doha Development Agenda. (Supachai 2002)

Critics of the TRIPS Agreement and the intellectual property system in general, with special emphasis on patent protection, allege that the existing regime of intellectual property rights (IPR) does not serve the interests of developing countries (particularly less developed countries). There are three main areas where the TRIPS agreement has been criticized as being an obstacle to development: (a) It is claimed that IP protection, as codified in the TRIPS Agreement, has increased the costs of technology transfer, widening the technology gap, and income inequalities. Some consider that it prevents developing countries from catching up and climbing the technological ladder (Chang 2001, Correa 2000). (b) In the area of public health the main critique is that it allows the price of basic medicines to be unduly high. (c) Controversy also surrounds its application to agriculture, where the concern is that it may damage food security for the poor, and threaten the right of poor farmers to save, sell, and exchange seeds.

Defenders of intellectual property protection, while not disputing the increased short-term financial burden of importing new technologies, claim that IPR protection encourages domestic innovation, provides incentives for MNCs to invest in developing countries, and incentives for faster diffusion of new technologies into developing countries (Maskus 2000).

Given the private, territorial and exclusive nature of IPR it may be unrealistic to expect that the TRIPS Agreement (or any national IPR legislation) can provide the solution to public policy issues as complex as access to essential medicines, high cost and lack of technology transfer, and the application of IPR protection to agriculture in developing countries. IPR is an important factor among several that play a role in each of these issues. Moreover, the TRIPS Agreement can not only improve IPR protection but address developing country concerns. However, the WTO cannot constitute the only forum for discussion and TRIPS the only instrument for solutions. Effective responses require a broader agenda and serious cooperation from public and private sectors in developed and developing countries.

Patents, technology transfer and incentives to innovation

This is a very complex debate. Perhaps the most incontrovertible evidence is that patent protection has increased the financial burden for developing countries of importing new technology. The World Bank estimates that the six major industrial countries with significant surpluses on intellectual property trade will see their revenue increase by approximately $40 billion as a result of TRIPS (World Bank 2002). At the same time, overall transfers from developing countries in the form of license payments to patent holders, which are mostly Northern TNCs, will rise almost fourfold from their current levels of $15 billion.[15]

However, to determine whether these increased costs prevent developing countries from closing the 'technology gap', the costs would have to be weighted against the benefits in terms of increased availability and diffusion of technology (for instance, information technology), increased innovation and technological variety induced by patent protection, and positive impacts on developing country productivity associated with importation of capital goods and other technologies.

As with international trade, the relationships between IPR and FDI are subtle and complex. While the weight of theory seems to suggest a positive impact on FDI, overall it is inconclusive. Decisions on FDI depend on a host of complex factors regarding local markets and regulations. IPR clearly play an important role, though their importance varies by industry and market structure. Thus, IPR protection is more likely to be important in industries in which intangible, knowledge-based assets specific to each firm are significant, such as pharmaceuticals, chemicals, food additives and software, as well as firms considering investing in local R&D facilities (Maskus 2000).

Another significant factor is the key role of the private sector. Technology, whether patented or in the form of know-how, is primarily in the possession of industrial companies. To such companies, their technology is a valuable commodity which they have paid for by investment, and which they cannot afford to give away without a reasonable return (Grubb 1999). Even if required to implement international agreements, governments cannot force the transfer of those technologies.

As suggested by a recently issued report Integrating Intellectual Property Rights and Development Policy published by the UK Commission on IPR, 'Technology transfer and the development of a sustainable indigenous technological capability are determined by many factors, including but by no means limited to IPR. Therefore it may be unwise to focus on TRIPS as a principal means of facilitating technology transfer.' The Report highlights that the crucial issue in respect of IP is perhaps not whether it promotes trade or foreign investment but how it helps or hinders developing countries to gain access to sophisticated technologies. They recommend a wider agenda, including serious consideration by developed countries of their policies for encouraging technology transfer and more effective research and cooperation with and among developing countries to strengthen their scientific and technological capabilities (Commission on IPR 2002).

Access to medicines and IPR

The high profile cases of South Africa (1997) and Brazil (2001) in their efforts to ensure availability of affordable medicines to treat HIV/AIDS illustrated the impacts of patent protection on the price of medicines as well as the vulnerability of the public health safeguards of the TRIPS agreement to being trumped by irresponsible pressures based on commercial interest (Oxfam, 2002). These cases, and the contrasting US and Canadian responses to the anthrax spores crisis in 2001, giving immediate priority to the public health interest over the private interest of patent holders, provided important long term lessons about the importance of flexibility, appropriate safeguards, and the need for intellectual property protection agreements, both in multilateral and regional settings, to give precedence to public health priorities over patent claims. The importance of this flexibility was recognized in the Doha Declaration on Public Health. In Doha ministers addressed most of the issues and concerns raised by developing countries at the TRIPS Council during the years following the entry into force of the WTO Agreement. In general, the Declaration sought to highlight the need for balance between protection of IP and flexibility for developing countries while applying and implementing TRIPS.

The end result was a very carefully drafted document that balances the interest and concerns of developed and developing countries. On the one hand, the separate Declaration highlights provisions in the TRIPS Agreement that provide members with the flexibility to address public health emergencies such as HIV/AIDS, tuberculosis, malaria and other epidemics. Thus, each member has the right to grant compulsory licenses and to determine the grounds upon which such licenses are granted, and the freedom to establish a national regime to deal with parallel imports.[16] On the other hand, through the Declaration, members expressed their support for the TRIPS Agreement and the importance of Intellectual Property Protection for the research and development of new medicines.

The impact of patent protection on the price of medicines is a real issue, particularly for developing countries. But this concern must be balanced against the recognition that some degree of protection is necessary to provide incentives to the industry to invest in R&D and develop new drugs. However, stronger patent protection will not solve a very important issue, and this is that the large asymmetries in market size between rich and poor drug consumer markets produce a disincentive to invest in R&D on drugs to combat the diseases of 'the poor' (pneumonia, malaria, typhoid, cholera, tuberculosis, and so on) as opposed to those of 'the rich'. As the WHO Commission on Macroeconomics and Health concluded, this can only be solved by a major international effort, backed by increased aid and facilitated by public–private partnerships.

IPR and agriculture

In Doha, Ministers restated the mandate to review TRIPS Article 27.3b, which allows countries to exclude plants, animals and certain other biological processes from patentability. If countries decide to use this exclusion, they must provide for a *sui generis* system of protection. This may be a UPOV-type Plant Breeder's Right system,[17] another *sui generis* alternative, or some combination of systems.

Assertions have been made that there is a link between the availability and adoption of patent or plant breeders' right protection, and the replacement in many areas of the world of complex, diverse agro-ecosystems containing a wide range of traditional crop varieties with monocultures of single agrochemical-dependent varieties (Dutfield 2000). Some critics maintain that IPR provide perverse incentives which encourage activities that are prejudicial to biodiversity, and cause erosion of indigenous methods for using agrodiversity and of soil diversity (Reyes 1996). Others have also raised concerns regarding the impact of patenting of seeds on the rights of farmers and plant breeders to save seeds from cultivation and replant, sell or exchange them in subsequent seasons.

Even among developed countries, there are different views with respect to the patentability of inventions in areas of innovation at the forefront of scientific endeavor (for instance, life sciences) or where the pace of technological change is very fast. Some variations occur, for example, in the patentability of biological materials: some countries allowing organisms of all kinds (humans excepted) to be patented, others excluding patents on plant and animal varieties, and some rejecting all patents on biological materials. Experts agree that this is a highly complex issue and that an objective evaluation is hard to achieve when there is such a dearth of reliable empirical evidence (as opposed to anecdotal evidence and pure speculation).

IPR enhance incentives to develop seeds that will have a large potential demand. The commercial breeders chain respond to the demands of farmers, market signals from consumers, food retailers or other purchasers or users of their crops. What can be presumed is that it is most unlikely that the erosion of agro-biodiversity can be attributed to a single cause such as IPR (Dutfield 2000). Other factors commonly cited are: government farms' credits and subsidies, policies and programs of international agencies and donor institutions, demographic changes, marketing, research and development programs of TNCs, concentration of pesticide and agro-biotechnology research and distribution, and certification requirements in many countries (Dutfield 2000). A consequence of this trend is that research priorities overall will be increasingly less relevant to the needs of poor farmers in developing countries (Commission on IPR 2002).

On the application of plant breeders' rights according to UPOV, the privilege of breeders to use protected varieties as an initial source of variation for the creation of new varieties and to market these varieties without authorization from the original breeder (the breeder's exemption) is upheld in both versions (1978–1991). Regarding the farmers' privilege, that allows a farmer to re-sow seed harvested from protected varieties for his or her own use, such right is not included in the 1978 Convention. Nevertheless members of this version of UPOV do indeed uphold it. The 1991 version is more specific about this matter and, pursuant to Article 15, governments can use their discretion in deciding whether or not to uphold the farmers' privilege.

A very controversial element has to do with genetically modified crops – creating transgenic plants with built-in resistance either to herbicides or to insect pests, and even more the so-called 'terminator technology' that prevents a variety from being propagated by farmers and makes it impossible to save, replant or sell seed. Allegations are that the widespread application of such technologies would threaten the customary seed saving and exchanging practices of traditional farming communities. Corporations in these technological fields claim that without IPR protection they would have no incentive to invent or innovate. As explained by Dutfield, in this case it is not so much the patent or plant breeders' right that has been criticized but the technology claimed in it. 'The award of a patent is not itself an authorization to commercialize the technology, product or process ... Indeed patent offices are not the right places for such evaluations to be made since decisions on allowing or banning technologies should ideally be made in open and democratic fora' (Dutfield 2000).

Other issues advanced by developing countries: biotechnology, biodiversity and the protection of traditional knowledge

Related to the patentability of plants or the protection of plant varieties through a *sui generis* system, is the nexus of issues relating to biotechnological inventions, biodiversity and traditional knowledge with IPR. The discussion of this issue was included in the WTO agenda in Doha with the support of developing countries, and it is among the pending work of the TRIPS Council. A central part of the debate covers the relationship between the TRIPS Agreement and the Convention on Biological Diversity (CBD).[18]

Increasing commercial interest in plant and animal species in industrializing countries, and in traditional cultural expressions and medicinal remedies, has raised questions of ownership of such resources, previously assumed to be in the public domain. Research-based corporations have recognized the value of biodiversity and the indigenous knowledge of local communities regarding traditional plants and medicines. In some cases, researchers from the developed world have invented novel, patentable products, based on biological materials from the developing world. However, there is a concern that developing countries are not adequately compensated when foreign researchers develop products based on existing material or knowledge once taken out of the public domain of developing countries. This has led to a debate in international fora on the rights of developing nations and local communities to biological resources and traditional knowledge.

Basic questions in this controversy are: Are corporations to be allowed to patent genetic resources from any country irrespective of origin? How can community rights and local knowledge be respected or benefits shared and is the TRIPS agreement the right instrument to ensure this? Should a framework to respect and reward local or community knowledge and folklore be created inside or outside TRIPS? Since developing countries account for around 90 per cent of the world's biological resources these are very important issues.

Views on the relationship between the patent system and the CBD's objectives vary widely. The pro-patent view is that they are compatible with each other, and neither is to be applied in such a way as to undermine the objectives of the other (Grubb 1999). Moreover, defenders of IPR indicate that, in principle, the IPR system can play an important role in stimulating the development of new plant varieties and pharmaceutical products – to the benefit of both developed and developing countries. Specifically, IPR could foster local research or the formation of research joint ventures with foreign companies, for example in the initial screening process of biological material and in the early research stages. On the other hand, concerns have been expressed regarding the extension of IPR to cover life forms or traditional knowledge. Critics in principle oppose the patenting of inventions based closely on genetic resources or traditional knowledge, even if the patent holders have undertaken to share benefits with the communities concerned (Reyes 1996).

A more pragmatic view is that IPR should not be the only means of protecting traditional knowledge and genetic resources. Rights of indigenous people and genetic resources can be protected through a non-IPR instrument that is part of a broader arrangement allowing a pharmaceutical company to patent inventions related to the know-how of an indigenous group or from genetic resources, but with certain agreed restrictions attached to the right to patent or commercially exploit the invention. Others have suggested that trademarks and geographical indications may also be appropriate forms of protection for some products based on traditional knowledge even if they cannot protect the knowledge per se (Dutfield 2000).

As part of the preliminary work in the TRIPS Council on this issue, a group of developing countries introduced a proposal to amend TRIPS seeking to require that entities applying for patents disclose the country of origin of the biological resource and the traditional knowledge used in the invention, provide evidence that the national authorities in the country of origin consented to the extraction of the resource, and give evidence of 'fair and equitable benefit' sharing (*Inside US Trade*, 30 August 2002). These amendments seek to address what some perceive as the increasing risk of 'bio-piracy' (unauthorized commercial exploitation of the knowledge and biological resources of indigenous peoples and/or developing countries). Other countries oppose this amendment, arguing that the TRIPS agreement governs intellectual property rights only and not access to genetic resources, which would be better regulated through contracts between national authorities and entities seeking access to those resources.

Industrial Policy and Competitiveness Promotion

Although most LAC countries have floating foreign exchange rates, and have simplified and liberalized their foreign trade regimes by, for instance, eliminating most export and import quotas and substantially reducing tariffs, many industrial and competitiveness policy instruments are widely used. These include: export subsidies, in agriculture and industrial goods; government procurement policies that give preference to local suppliers; Export processing zones with tariff exemptions but also a host of tax concessions and other incentives; national and sub-national investment incentives and regional assistance; domestic content, joint-venture, majority ownership and other technology-sharing requirements for foreign direct investment; pricing and marketing arrangements; and others. Some of these subsidies and instruments have been used in a targeted, sector-specific fashion, against the principles of non-discrimination and national treatment at the basis of the multilateral trading system.

In the past, conventional wisdom held that many of these policy instruments were important for promoting competitiveness, productivity, growth and development. Many of these instruments were widely used by the Asian high performing countries. However, economic research and experience has shown that some of these instruments are highly inefficient, that they may stifle innovation, discourage state of the art foreign direct investment and associated productivity and technology transfer benefits, as well as being highly vulnerable to protectionist abuse, rent-seeking behavior and corruption. Many are also self-defeating when considered from a general equilibrium and global level, leading to 'subsidy wars', high fiscal costs and global welfare reductions. This is why the uses of a number of these instruments are disciplined, and in some cases prohibited by multilateral trade rules (GATT/WTO) and are being gradually phased out. This paradigm change has led to heated debate. Some are concerned about the extent to which WTO provisions constrain the policy measures developing countries can use to protect domestic suppliers, promote exports and competitiveness and transfer technology and argue in favor of flexibility. Discussions of these issues are important to allow developing countries to make informed choices about policies and institutions that are appropriate for them. Some of these issues were discussed in the previous sections of this chapter. Trade agreement flexibility to use a number of industrial policy instruments, or as called in more modern language, instruments to promote competitiveness, also fall under the rubric of special and differential treatment.

SPECIAL AND DIFFERENTIAL TREATMENT

Much of the discussion about the trade and development relationship in trade negotiations and agreements has been organized around the concept of 'special and differential treatment' (S&D) in the GATT/WTO and around the heading of 'treatment of differences in size and levels of development' in the FTAA.

S&D Treatment in the GATT/WTO[19]

Since the early days of the GATT both developed and developing countries accepted the concept of S&D treatment for developing countries, but its justification, form and content has evolved over time. Before the Uruguay Round this concept was used to give developing countries special rights and privileges based on three major justifications: the infant industry argument, the importance for the growth and diversification of their exports of preferential access to developed-country markets and several asymmetry rationales to justify non-reciprocity in trade negotiations.[20]

The S&D treatment provisions reached their peak during the Tokyo Round with the 1979 decision known as the 'Framework Agreement on Differential and More Favorable Treatment, Reciprocity and Fuller Participation of Developing Countries'. Also known as the Enabling Clause, this framework offers a comprehensive statement and legal cover on core S&D treatment issues in four major areas:

- enhanced market access via preferential tariff treatment for developing countries in accordance with the GSP and similar non-reciprocal schemes;
- exemption or possibility of opting-out from the Tokyo Round codes (technical barriers to trade, government procurement, subsidies and countervailing duties, customs valuation, import licensing and antidumping actions);
- a waiver to developing countries to engage in Regional Trade Agreements among themselves; and
- special treatment or flexibility to least developed countries identified as a distinct group as defined by the UN classification, in making concessions and contributions in view of their special development, financial and trade needs.
- In addition, the 1979 Enabling Clause codified a graduation principle by which developing countries would be expected to take on more obligations as their economies grow stronger.

However, this concept of S&D treatment received a number of strong criticisms as a way to promote trade and development before and during the Uruguay Round:

- First, the infant industry argument for protection of domestic industries was substantially discredited, and during the 1980s and 1990s many developing countries pursued aggressive liberalization above and beyond multilateral commitments.
- Second, non-reciprocity has a serious disadvantage, it means that developing countries cannot participate fully on a reciprocal basis in market access negotiations, which in practice means reduced leverage and missed opportunities to gain effective market access in developed country markets.
- Non-reciprocal arrangements have two additional disadvantages: they limit the potential use of the GATT/WTO framework as a mechanism to restrain unilateral actions by developed countries; and they also have limited value in providing a stable and reliable framework for investment.
- The other main component of S&D treatment, derogation or exemptions from full discipline, has also been criticized as counterproductive to the extent that the market distorting measures so allowed would impose a self-inflicted cost on developing economies.

These and other assessments led to quite a drastic change in the form and content of S&D provisions that resulted from the Uruguay Round. The adoption of the principle of 'single undertaking' that required all members to adhere to the full family of WTO agreements, significantly reduced flexibility for exemptions and derogations. And many S&D provisions were reformulated in terms of longer transition periods and differences in threshold levels. Thus the general orientation of the Uruguay Round outcome was that developing countries should eventually meet virtually the same set of standards as developed countries on a broad range of both market access and rules issues, implying an eventual convergence in standards of behavior between developing and developed countries. However, there is still a variety of S&D provisions incorporated in the WTO agreements.

The difficulties of implementing of Uruguay Round commitments and new evidence about the costs of adjustment as well as the costs of institutional capacity building, led to deep dissatisfaction by many countries and experts with what were perceived as deficiencies with post-Uruguay Round S&D treatment provisions. These issues were subject to heated debates in the preparation of the Doha Ministerial Meeting. Many developing countries insisted on the need for more flexibility; longer transition periods than those agreed in the Uruguay Round; more technical assistance for capacity building; a revisit of the issue of full or partial derogation from certain disciplines; a revisit of the issue of classification of WTO member countries; in short, on the need for a careful rethinking of the concept of S&D treatment – of its justification, form and content. Some of these issues were subject to specific mandates in the Doha

Development Agenda (DDA), in particular those related to capacity building, implementation and S&D provisions.[21]

Treatment of the Differences in Size and Levels of Development in the FTAA

The issue of treatment of the differences in size and levels of development was present from the start in the FTAA process. It was highlighted as a special concern when the FTAA project was launched in the Summit of the Americas in December 1994 and then again when formal negotiations were launched in the next Summit in April, 1998. There are also a number of instructions on this issue in successive ministerial declarations. However, the concept of special and differential treatment has not entered the language of the FTAA talks.

The San Jose Declaration of March 1998, that provides the blueprint for the negotiations, states the following principles:

- Special attention should be given to the needs, economic conditions (including transition costs and possible internal dislocations) and opportunities of smaller economies, to ensure their full participation in the FTAA process.
- The rights and obligations of the FTAA will be shared by all countries. In the negotiation of the various thematic areas, measures such as technical assistance in specific areas and longer periods for implementing the obligations could be included on a case by case basis, in order to facilitate the adjustment of smaller economies and the full participation of all countries in the FTAA.
- The measures agreed upon to facilitate the integration of smaller economies in the FTAA process shall be transparent, simple and easily applicable, recognizing the degree of heterogeneity among them.
- In order to ensure the full participation of all countries in the FTAA, the differences in their level of development should be taken into account.

There are several reasons why S&D language never entered the FTAA talks:

- One is that this is clearly a reciprocal arrangement, so a non-reciprocity rationale for S&D will have no place in the architecture of the FTAA.
- Another is that the objective is to create a free trade area, so an infant industry argument rationale for S&D will also have no place in this framework. And besides, LAC countries already tried to promote infant industries for several decades under the import substitution strategy of industrialization.

- Third, the FTAA talks were launched in the post-Uruguay Round environment where, as stated above, the general orientation was towards an eventual convergence in standards of behavior between developing and developed countries.

Given the simultaneous nature of multilateral and regional negotiations, including target completion date, it would not be surprising if some developments in the Doha Development Agenda negotiations influence the FTAA content in this area. However, these are two different processes. The FTAA objective is quite clear: it is to create a free trade area where tariffs will go down to zero and all tariffs are under negotiation, without exceptions. In practice, what degree of market access will be achieved in agriculture, services, investment and government procurement, what will be the path to get there and what differentiated treatment during the transition some countries will get, are open questions that will be defined by the negotiations. In the rules area it will also be up to the negotiating process to define how the principles stated above on treatment of the differences in size and level of development will materialize and receive legal expression.

TRADE-RELATED CAPACITY BUILDING

Lessons from Experience

Another set of very important developmental issues posed by trade negotiations and agreements relates to trade-related capacity building. During the last seven to eight years there has been significant learning from experience in the multilateral system and in regional and bilateral practice on Trade Related Capacity Building (TRCB).

One field of learning has been the multilateral system. There have been two waves of responses to the need for TRCB by the least developed and developing countries. The 'first-wave' response occurred in the second half of the 1990s and focused on three initiatives: (a) the Joint Integrated Technical Assistance Programme for Selected Least Developed and Other African Countries (JITAP) launched in May 1996 at UNCTAD IX; (b) the Integrated Framework for Technical-Related Assistance, Including Human and Institutional Capacity Building to Support Least Developed Countries in their Trade and Trade-Related Activities (the Integrated Framework or IF), launched as a result of decisions taken at the Singapore WTO Ministerial Meeting; and (c) the 'positive agenda' program of UNCTAD. The 'second-wave' response dates from around mid-2000, following reviews from JITAP and the IF, and is concerned with 'mainstreaming trade' as an integral part of the overall development and poverty reduction effort by countries.[22] This latter response is particularly focused on assisting countries in analysing the impacts of trade policy reforms on poverty reduction.[23]

A second field of learning has been the rich experience by various donors, both bilateral and multilateral. Many lessons from this experience are reviewed by the OECD Development Assistance Committee on best practices for donors.[24]

A third field of learning for the countries of the Americas has been the FTAA. The FTAA process has contributed to a significant additional mobilization of resources for trade-related capacity building, and has been a tremendous learning exercise for many countries.[25] However, much more needs to be done. Countries have been working on the design of a Hemispheric Cooperation Program.

Drawing from these different experiences of trade-related capacity building a number of points need to be stressed. First, when discussing the rationale for the priority of trade capacity one of the first issues is what could be called the *paradigm issue*. This refers to the key question of the role of trade in achieving growth, development and poverty reduction. Different answers to fundamental issues in the links between trade and growth, growth and poverty and growth and income distribution will give different answers to the priority and modalities of TRTA and TRCB in the development programs of countries and in the cooperation programs of donors. Most developing countries are generally convinced of the importance of trade and trade-related capacities for wealth creation and poverty reduction. The Doha Development Agenda has clearly been a turning point, and constitutes a victory for this view and for a reassertion of the role of trade in development.

A second key question is how to define, articulate and prioritize trade related capacity building needs into national development strategies and in international cooperation programs. This has been called 'mainstreaming trade' in the context of the WTO. To do this, there has to be minimum agreement among governments and donors about the scope of TRCB. Is TRCB to include only issues close to trade negotiations and trade agreement implementation? Or should it also include assistance to strengthen supply-side response capacities, such as export promotion, investment attraction and policies to promote competitiveness (particularly of small and medium-sized enterprises), or even issues of basic infrastructure development, macroeconomic stability and financial issues? One of the lessons from the first five years of the Integrated Framework is that lack of agreement on the definition of trade-related capacity building can affect policy coherence, coordination among donor agencies and delivery of technical assistance.

Different definitions of TRTA are also at the heart of differences between the development community and the trade community. What these two communities have traditionally understood by cooperation is very different. Trade negotiators are used to deliver courses and training on trade rules, agreements and other issues close to negotiations. More recently their agenda has expanded with a concern for trade agreement implementation particularly in behind the border issues. The development community is used to a much broader spectrum of policy areas where in many cases trade, market institutions or private sector development might not even appear or have only secondary importance.

One of the major challenges is then to bridge these differences between the development community and institutions and the trade community and institutions, a difference that is sometimes expressed not only at the international level but also between different national agencies and institutions.

Towards a Trade Related Capacity Building Framework for the Americas

The establishment of a sound trade related capacity building framework has to be based, first, on solid understanding of the types of costs involved in trade and of the different capacities countries must develop to engage significantly and beneficially in the global and regional trading systems. It is possible to distinguish between trade policy making and negotiation costs; implementation costs; adjustment costs; and costs of developing international competitiveness.

Trade policy-making and trade negotiation costs

Trade policy-making and trade negotiation costs involve aspects such as training a world class trade negotiating team; investment in internal consultation mechanisms with the private sector and other civil society sectors; general economic and sectoral impact studies; trade education and outreach; and, of course, the costs of appropriate expert participation and follow up in the numerous meetings that the different negotiating processes entail.

The costs of a bad negotiation resulting from incapacity to invest in these items could be very high indeed in terms of development and business interests. Limited capacity to participate in any specific trade negotiation for a particular country or group of countries can have serious costs also for the rest of the participating countries. The post-Uruguay Round problems with implementation of obligations were related in part to the fact that many developing countries did not engage significantly, and this led to insufficient sense of ownership, perceptions that a number of obligations were imposed on them and lack of political will to implement obligations. In summary, trade negotiations require significant investment. Only if each one of the participating countries makes the required investment can they maximize the benefits of a good negotiation and generate the 'ownership' by all relevant stakeholders and the appropriate political conditions to implement obligations.

Implementation costs

Implementation costs break down into costs of complying with the obligations and costs of administering the agreements to the benefit of the country. The former could be relatively low in some cases (tariff reduction, putting in place some new procedures). However, in most areas of behind-the-border or domestic regulation they can be very substantial and imply major investment decisions. This is the case in areas such as technical standards, sanitary and phytosanitary standards (SPS), competition policy, customs valuation, and intellectual property among others.

Michael Finger and Philip Schuler (2001) estimated the costs of implementation in three areas covered by WTO agreements (customs valuation, SPS and intellectual property) using World Bank project data. They showed that these investments require purchasing of equipment and software, hiring and training of specialized personnel, systems development and other items to upgrade developing country institutions and systems to industrial country standards, which means that, depending on each country's existing capacities, the required investment may be of the order of dozens of millions of dollars.

The development dimension of the behind-the-border issues negotiated in trade agreements needs more research and increased understanding, in order to avoid in the FTAA frustrations and implementation problems of the type that arose after the Uruguay Round.

Adjustment costs

Adjustment costs are those associated with the productive reestructuring, job dislocations and fiscal impacts of the transition to freer trade. Some of these dislocations are a necessary part of adjusting the economy to higher levels of productivity and competitiveness. The economic and social costs of these dislocations can be minimized with appropriately designed and financed adjustment programs and social safety nets. Even a developed country such as the United States has implemented Trade Adjustment Assistance Programs (TAA). TAA in the United States was significantly strengthened as part of the Trade Act of 2002 that also included Trade Promotion Authority.

Costs of developing international competitiveness

While adjustment costs and the required investments can be seen as defensive, investments to develop international competitiveness can be seen as proactive in a pro-growth and developmental sense. These may involve a wide variety of policies in areas such as support for small and medium-sized enterprises; policies to develop competitive advantages in specific clusters à la Michael Porter; credit policies; infrastructure development and upgrading; technical and vocational training; general education policy; even some aspects of health and housing policies are key to have the type of workforce that can make a real contribution to global value added and further help in making the country attractive as a production and sourcing base for international investors.

It is important to note that multilateral rules, and most likely regional rules in the context of the FTAA, imply that, increasingly, member countries will have to shift the focus of their export and investment promotion policies as well as industrial transformation and competitiveness policies from discriminatory, sector specific policies to a comprehensive, non-distorting, non-discriminatory approach. In this sense, the effect of the new WTO and FTAA rules is not to eliminate the role of government but to transform it. The emphasis of policies to promote competitiveness under the 'new paradigm' is shifted toward enhancing the efficiency of infrastructure, regulatory reform and liberalization of services sectors, including business services, improving human capital formation, trade and business facilitation, promoting Internet readiness and information technology services, and creating an environment conducive to investment and innovation.

POSITIVE IMPACTS ON INSTITUTIONS AND THE POLITICAL PROCESS

The final set of developmental issues posed by the FTAA selected for this chapter has to do with national and international governance: as a comprehensive agreement, the FTAA will have a major impact in influencing the economic policies, institutions, regulatory frameworks and traditional market governance practices of LAC countries. The FTAA will be a major force to promote transparency, predictability, competition, non-discrimination, and rule-bound behavior in many areas, reducing the scope for discretion, corruption, collusion, rent-seeking and arbitrariness. It is not just that markets will be more open, but that their institutional and legal fundamentals will also be stronger as a result of FTAA rules and commitments.

For instance, the impact of NAFTA in locking in not only a broad range of economic reforms but democracy has been widely recognized. NAFTA was instrumental in determining the policy response of both the Mexican and the US governments to the 1995 peso crisis. Mexico maintained the reforms and increased its credibility as a location for international investment, and the US response demonstrated that NAFTA meant more than just trade policy.[26]

How precisely the FTAA would help the members integrate into the world economy, and benefit in terms of growth and development, will depend on how the agreement is designed, and the availability of additional development assistance induced by the agreement, by mechanisms internal or external to the agreement.

TOWARDS AN FTAA DEVELOPMENT AGENDA

The WTO Doha Ministerial Meeting produced a Doha Development Agenda, characterized by an unprecedented mix of trade and development priorities. In order to maximize benefits for the participants, induce higher standards of living in Latin America and the Caribbean, and accelerate economic convergence the FTAA also faces the challenge of blending trade and development issues. There is a unique opportunity in the inter-American system to do this, given the smaller number of countries, their geographical proximity and the existence of important inter-American and regional institutions. Parallel trade-related capacity building efforts can facilitate the transition and upgrade the countries' public sector and market institutions to meet the development challenge.

The initiation of a Hemispheric Cooperation Program as part of the FTAA process is a major positive step in this direction. However, important questions remain unanswered. A number of distinguished economists think that, for economic convergence, integration arrangements, or parallel efforts, have to incorporate substantial transfers of resources from the richer countries and regions to the poorer ones to close infrastructure, education, institutional and other gaps.[27] This raises a number of important issues for the FTAA:

- Will the trade–cooperation nexus established in the FTAA be sufficient to mobilize the necessary resource transfer particularly to the smaller economies to finance the trade and development challenges outlined in the section on TCRB?
- What will be the proportion of resources mobilized by the United States, as a partner in this agreement, versus the resources mobilized by other bilateral donors and multilateral agencies?
- What institutions would it be appropriate to create, or what kind of strengthening of existing institutions, to sustain aid, resource transfers and capacity building efforts to the smaller economies?
- Are the smaller economies themselves under-estimating the challenge of financing the domestic tasks required by hemispheric free trade?

Given the asymmetries in size and level of economic development, the foundations for a win–win outcome from hemispheric free trade must include both a world-class trade agreement and a no less impressive capacity building component.

NOTES

1. Director, Trade Unit, Organization of American States, (jsalazar@oas.org). The views expressed in this chapter are those of the author and should not be taken to represent those

of the OAS General Secretariat nor those of any of the OAS member countries. The author is grateful to Cesar Parga and Theresa Wetter for their discussions and input in the section on intellectual property.

2. For Brazilian positions on the FTAA see Lafer (2001), Barbosa (2001) and Soares de Lima (1999).
3. Argentina, Brazil, Chile, Colombia, Mexico, and Venezuela.
4. However, non-FTAA countries would benefit from the non-discriminatory effects of this measure: the United States expands imports of all grains, oilseeds and bovine meat by more than 15 per cent from the rest of the world.
5. The index measures each country*'s faced tariffs* from its partners weighted by its *total exports* in the numerator, and each country's *imposed tariffs* weighted by the *total exports* of all its partners in the denominator, calculated one by one based on a potential regional integration agreement. The index can be used to gauge the concessions that each country makes relative to those it receives.
6. For an analysis of the implications for agriculture of NAFTA and the adjustment challenges particularly as regards Mexico, see Veeman, Veeman and Hoskins (2002), Yunes-Naude (2002), Appendini (2003) and Lustig (2001).
7. For analysis of the spread and impacts of what some call 'the antidumping epidemic' see: Prusa (1999), Lindsey and Ikenson (2001), Finger and Schuknecht (2001), Neufeld (2001), Finger (2002).
8. The stakes for beneficiaries increased in 2000 with the enactment of an obscure new law that is transferring lots of money to certain US manufacturers. Under the Continued Dumping Offset Act (CDO) of 2000, also known as the Byrd Amendment, an account is set up into which duties liquidated by the Customs Service from each AD and subsidy case are placed. Those funds are then transferred to domestic producers that were the petitioners to cases at the end of the year. The Byrd Amendment was found by the WTO Appellate Body to violate WTO rules on 16 January 2003. At present the US Congress and executive are considering options to bring the Byrd law into conformity with WTO obligations see *Inside US Trade*, 17 January 2003.
9. Some degree of discipline on investment incentives is contained in the WTO Agreement of Subsidies and Countervailing Measures (ASCM). However, such disciplines are largely indirect when applied to investment, apply only to goods-related transactions (no equivalent disciplines exist for services under GATS); and can be invoked only in rather restrictive circumstances.
10. For multilateral negotiations this argument is made by Sauve (2002).
11. Hoekman and Saggi (2002).
12. For further information on these initiatives see the OAS website www.oas.org.
13. World Bank (2002).
14. For a collection of analyses on the role of services in hemispheric integration see Stephenson (2000).
15. According to different experts these figures should be treated with caution. According to the UK Commission on IPR's report, these figures depend on a number of debatable assumptions (Commission on IPR 2002); Maskus points out that there are several reasons why published data on royalties and licensing fees (RLF) may not capture adequately the amount of technology being traded. Licensing fees are determined through complex contracting procedures, which attempt to price the implicit value of information. Further, fees paid may be influenced by tax laws, accounting rules, and management decisions regarding the extent and form of income repatriation. Finally joint ventures, business alliances, and cross-licensing agreements may encompass different volumes of licensing than would be suggested by straightforward licensing fees (Maskus 2000). Additionally, the importance of IPR for trade has gained more significance as the share of knowledge-intensive or high technology products in total trade has doubled between 1980 and 1994 from 12 per cent to 24 per cent (Primo Braga and Fink, 1999). Ryan (1988) states that exports, as measured by RLF, amounted to about $27 billion in 1995, while imports amounted to only $6.3 billion. At least $20 billion of the exports are transactions between US firms and their foreign affiliates.

16. Compulsory licensing – a permission to use intellectual property, compelled by the government in order to accomplish some political or social objective. Compulsory licensing forces an IPR owner to allow others to use that property at a fee set by the government.

    Parallel imports (grey market goods). A foreign manufactured genuine product that is imported by a third party without the consent of the right holder. The legal status of parallel imports is a matter of national decision and is related to the issue of the exhaustion of rights.
17. The International Convention for the Protection of New Varieties of Plants (UPOV convention) was signed in Paris in 1961 and entered into force in 1968. It was revised in Geneva in 1972, 1978 and 1991. The 1991 Act entered into force in April 1998. UPOV provides a framework for intellectual property protection of plant varieties. These rights are most often referred to as plant variety rights or plant breeders' rights. Fourteen FTAA countries have joined UPOV. Most of them adhered to the 1978 Act. The US ratified the 1991 Act. New members can only sign on to the 1991 Act.
18. The 1992 Convention on Biological Diversity (CBD) is an international agreement which has as its objectives the conservation of biological diversity, the sustainable use of its components, and the fair and equitable sharing of the benefits arising out of the utilization of genetic resources, including by appropriate access to genetic resources and by appropriate transfer of relevant technologies. Pursuant to Article 15 of the CBD nation states have sovereign rights over their own biological resources. This principle gives each country the right to control access to genetic resources within its territory, and to determine the conditions under which this will be allowed.
19. This section draws heavily from Oyejide (2002) and Fukasaku (2000).
20. A recent paper by the WTO Secretariat contains an inventory of S&D provisions introduced in the GATT and then WTO agreements since the 1950s grouping them in three categories: (a) those allowing fewer obligations or the easing of rules for developing countries (right to protect infant industries, right to use trade measures to address balance of payments difficulties, right to establish RTAs among developing countries, principle of non-reciprocity); (b) those requiring positive actions in favor of developing countries (preferential access to developed country markets under the legal cover of the 1979 Enabling Clause such as GSP and other non-reciprocal trade preferences); and, c) those meeting the special needs of the LDCs.
21. As regards the latter, in DDA paragraph 44 ministers 'agreed to examine all provisions on special and differential treatment with a view to reinforce them and making them more precise, effective and operative'.
22. For a description and assessment of experience with these initiatives see Luke (2002).
23. See Hoekman et al. (2002).
24. OECD (2001b).
25. See Weintraub (2000).
26. This is also why some analysts consider the US government response to the crisis in Argentina an important test of Washington's interest and commitment to a hemispheric vision. See Hakim (2002).
27. See Lopez-Calva and Lustig (2002) and literature therein. Of course, aid and international resource transfers will not do much good if the internal redistributive mechanisms (tax policy, social policy) are not working, and no social safety nets are in place.

REFERENCES

Appendini, Kirsten (2003), 'The challenges to rural Mexico in an open economy', in Joseph Tulchin and Andrew Selee (eds), *Mexico's Politics and Society in Transition*, Boulder, CO and London: Lynne Rienner Publishers.

Barbosa, Rubens (2001), 'The FTAA that is in Brazil's interest', *Gazeta Mercantil*, 5 November.

Berries, M., J. Granados, M. Jank, J. Monteagudo, and M. Watanuki (2002), 'Prospects and challenges for the liberalization of agricultural trade in the western hemisphere', prepared for lADB/Harvard University forum, FTAA and Beyond: Prospects for Integration in the Americas, December.

Burfisher, Mary E., Sherman Robinson, and Karen Thierfelder (2001), 'The impact of NAFTA on the United States', *Journal of Economic Perspectives*, **15**, 1 (winter), 125–44.

Burfisher, Mary E., S. Robinson, and K. Thierfelder (2002), 'The Effect of an FTAA on agricultural trade in the Western Hemisphere', mimeo.

Chang, HJ. (2001), 'Intellectual property rights and economic development – historical lessons and emerging issues', background paper for 2001 *Human Development Report*, New York: UNDP.

Commission on Intellectual Property Rights (2002), Integrating intellectual property rights and development policy, London, September, available at http://www.iprcommission.org

Correa, Carlos M. (2000), *Intellectual Property Rights, the WTO and Developing Countries: The TRIPS Agreement and Policy Options*, London and New York: Zed Books Ltd.

Decreux, Yvan, and J.L. Guérin. 2001. 'MERCOSUR: free trade area with the EU or with the Americas? Some lessons from the model MIRAGE', paper presented at the Conference on Impacts of Trade Liberalization Agreements on Latin America and the Caribbean, Inter-American Development Bank and Centre d'Etudes Prospectives et d'Information Internationales, Washington, DC 5–6 November.

Diao, Xinshen, E. Díaz-Bonilla, and S. Robinson (2001), 'Scenarios for trade integration in the Americas', paper presented at the Conference on Impacts of Trade Liberalization Agreements on Latin America and the Caribbean, Inter-American Development Bank and Centre d'Etudes Prospectives et d'Information Internationales, Washington, DC, November 5–6.

Doha Development Agenda 2001, ministerial declaration.

Dutfield, Graham (2000), *Intellectual Property Rights, Trade and Biodiversity*, London: Earthscan Publications Ltd.

Finger (2002) 'Safeguards: making sense of GATT/WTO provisions allowing for import restrictions', in B. Hoekman, A. Matoo and P. English, *Development, Trade and the WTO. A Handbook*, Washington, DC: The World Bank.

Finger, M. and L. Schuknecht (2001), 'Market access advances and retreat: the Uruguay Round and beyond', in B. Hoekmam and W. Martin, *Developing Countries and the WTO. A Proactive Agenda*, Oxford: Blackwell Publishers.

Finger, M and P. Schuler (2002) 'Implementation of WTO commitments: the development challenge', in B. Hoekman, A. Matoo, and P. English, *Development, Trade and the WTO. A Handbook*, Washington, DC: The World Bank.

Fukasaku, Kiichiro (2000), 'Special and differential treatment for developing countries: does it help those who help themselves?', The United Nations University WIDER working papers no. 197, September.

Grubb, Philip W. (1999), *Patents for Chemicals, Pharmaceuticals and Biotechnology. Fundamentals of Global Law, Practice and Strategy*, Oxford: Oxford University Press.

Hakim, Peter (2002), 'Aid to Argentina: strings attached', *Washington Post*, 5 March.

Hoekman, Bernard, and Michel Kostecki (2001), *The Political Economy of the World Trading System*, 2nd edn. Oxford: Oxford University Press.

Hoekman, B. and K. Saggi (2002), 'Multilateral disciplines and national investment policies', in B. Hoekman, A. Matoo and P. English, *Development, Trade and the WTO. A Handbook*, Washington, DC: The World Bank.

Hoekman, B., C. Michalopoulos, M. Schiff, and D. Tarr (2002), 'Trade policy', ch. 13 in, *A Sourcebook for Poverty Reduction Strategies*, vol. 2 Washington, DC: World Bank.

Jank, M., I. Fuschsloch, and G. Kutas (2002), 'Agricultural liberalization in multilateral and regional trade negotiations', Paper presented at the IADB Seminar 'Agricultural Liberalization and Integration: What to expect from the FTAA and the WTO?', Washington, DC, October.

Lafer, Celso (2001), 'Brazil at the inter-American dialogue', speech by Ambassador Celso Lafer, Minister of Foreign Affairs of Brazil, Washington, DC, 1 March.

Lindsey, Brink, and Dan Ikenson (2001), 'Coming home to roost: proliferating antidumping laws and the growing threat to US Exports', Center for Trade Policy Studies, CATO Institute paper, no. 14, July.

Lopez-Calva, Luis and Nora Lustig (forthcoming), 'Inclusive trade: strengthening the sources of convergence within the FTAA', in Antoni Estevadeordal, Dani Rodrik, Alan Taylor, and Andres Velasco (eds), *The FTAA and Beyond: Prospects for Integration in the Americas*.

Luke, David (2002), 'Trade-related capacity building for enhanced African participation in the global economy', in B. Hoekman, A. Matoo, and P. English, *Development, Trade and the WTO. A Handbook*, Washington, DC: The World Bank.

Lustig, Nora (2001), 'Life is not easy: Mexico's quest for stability and growth', *The Journal of Economic Perspectives*, **15**, 1 (winter).

Maskus, Keith E. (2000), *Intellectual Property Rights in the Global Economy*, Washington, DC: Institute for International Economics.

Messerlin, Patrick A. (1989), 'EC antidumping regulations: a first economic appraisal, 1980–85', *Weltwirtschaftliches Archiv, Review of World Economics*, 125.

Monteagudo, Josefina, and M. Watanuki (2001), 'Regional trade agreements for MERCOSUR: the FTAA and the FTA with the European Union', paper presented at the Conference on Impacts of Trade Liberalization Agreements on Latin America and the Caribbean, Inter-American Development Bank and Centre d'Etudes Prospectives et d'Information Internationales, Washington, DC, 5–6 November.

Monteagudo, J. and M. Watanuki (2002), 'Evaluating agricultural reform under the FTAA and MERCOSUR-EU FTA for Latin America. A quantitative CGE assessment', paper presented at the IADB seminar 'Agricultural Liberalization and Integration: What to Expect from the FTAA and the WTO?', Washington, DC, October.

Moran, Theodore H. (1999), *Foreign Direct Investment and Development*, Washington, DC: Institute for International Economics.

Moran, Theodore H. (2001), *Parental Supervision: The New Paradigm for Foreign Direct Investment and Development*, Washington, DC: Institute for International Economics.

Moran, Theodore H. (2002), *Beyond Sweatshops. Foreign Direct Investment and Globalization in Developing Countries*, Washington, DC: Brookings Institution Press.

Neufeld, Inge Nora (2001), 'Antidumping and countervailing procedures – use of abuse? implications for developing countries', Policy Issues in International Trade and Commodities, Study Series no. 9, UNCTAD, Geneva.

OECD (2001a), 'Open services markets matter' policy brief, October.

OECD (2001b), *The DAC Guidelines: Strengthening Trade Capacity for Development*, Paris: Organization for Economic Cooperation and Development.

Oxfam (2002), 'Rigged rules and double standards. trade, globalization and the fight against poverty', accessed at www.maketradefair.com

Oyejide, A. (2002), 'Special and differential treatment', in B. Hoekman, A. Matoo, and P. English, *Development, Trade and the WTO. A Handbook*, Washington, DC: The World Bank.

Primo-Braga, Carlos, and Fink, Carsten (1999), 'How stronger protection of intellectual property rights affect international trade flows', World Bank, February.

Prusa, Thomas J. (1999), ' On the Spread and impact of antidumping', National Bureau of Economic Research working paper series no. 7404, Cambridge, MA, October.

Reyes V. (1996), 'The value of Sangre deDrago', *Seedling*, **13** 1, March, 6–21.

Roland-Hoist, David, and D. van der Mensbrugghe (2001), 'Regionalism versus globalization in the Americas: empirical evidence on opportunities and challenges', paper presented at the Conference on Impacts of Trade Liberalization Agreements on Latin America and the Caribbean, Inter- American Development Bank and Centre d'Etudes Prospectives et d'Information Internationales, Washington, DC, 5–6 November.

Ryan M.P. (1988), *Knowledge Diplomacy: Global Competition and the Politics of Intellectual Property*, Washington, DC: Brookings Institution Press.

Sauve, Pierre (2002), 'Multilateral Rules on Investment: Lessons from the Periphery', paper prepared for conference on The Evolving WTO Regime and Regional Economic Cooperation: Implications for Northeast Asia, Seoul, September.

Soares de Lima, Maria Regina (1999), 'Brazil's alternative vision', in Gordon Mace, Louis Bélanger et al. (eds), *The Americas in Transition. The Contours of Regionalism*, (Boulder, CO: Lynne Rienner Publishers).

Stephenson, Sherry, (ed.) (2000), *Services Trade in the Western Hemisphere: Liberalization, Integration and Reform*, Washington, DC: Brookings Institution-OAS.

Supachai (2002), *Commission Report is Food for Thought on Intellectual Property*, accessed at http://www.wto.org/english/news e/news02 e/com report intel prop 17sep02 e.htm, 17 September 2002.

Tavares de Araujo Jr., José, Carla Macario, and Karsten Steinfatt (2001), 'Antidumping in the Americas', OAS Trade Unit studies no. 10. Washington, DC, March, accessed at <http://www.sice.oas.org/tuni t/pubinfoe.asp#tustudies>.

Veeman, Michele, T. Veeman and R. Hoskins (2002), 'NAFTA and agriculture: challenges for trade and policy', in Edward Chambers and Peter Smith (eds), *NAFTA in the New Millennium*, San Diego: Center for US–Mexican Studies, University of California, Edmonton: The University of Alberta Press.

Weintraub, Sidney (2000), *Technical Cooperation Needs for Hemispheric Trade Negotiations*, Washington, DC: Organization of American States and Inter-American Council for Integral Development.

World Bank (2002), *Global Economic Prospects and the Developing Countries. Making Trade Work for the Poor*, Washington, DC: The World Bank.

Yunez-Naude, Antonio (2002), 'Lessons from NAFTA: the case of Mexico's agricultural sector', The World Bank, accessed at www.worldbank.org.

12. The hemisphere in the international political economy

Sidney Weintraub and Gavin Boyd

A free trade area of the Americas that is not slimmed down in substance will have a great potential to complement the role of the European Union as a large advanced regional system in the international political economy. The USA and the European Union (EU) dominate the world trading system, and the prominence of this Atlantic relationship, based on large scale structural interdependencies, will be increased as countries in the Southern Hemisphere become more closely linked, economically and politically, with the USA. Industrializing countries in East Asia, South Asia, the Middle East and Africa have been unable to form viable systems of regional economic cooperation. Of the major transnational economies, Russia is still recovering from acute recent macromanagement failures, and China, developing a system of national socialism with the support of substantial foreign direct investment, is forming economic ties with nearby states, but shows ambivalence about cultivating closer relationships, and this is reciprocated.

As a free trade area, the Western Hemispheric system will be an elementary form of regional economic integration in which rising levels of structural interdependence will tend to motivate consultations for the harmonization of policies conducive to further market integration, subject to the effects of cultural and political differences that will restrain initiatives for collective management. The elementary level of integration will entail a weaker capacity than that of the EU for coordinated involvement in the world economy, and the contrast will become sharper if the EU continues advances toward the formation of a stronger system of centralized authority, with more complete market integration. Moreover, while the EU draws peripheral countries into closer association because of its large internal market and the benefits of its system of collective management, geographic factors will not be conducive to the expansion of the Western Hemispheric free trade area.

The prospective expansion of structural links between the USA and Latin American countries will be internationally less significant than the continued growth of large scale investment and trade flows between the USA and the EU, which are forming an extensive pattern of interregional integration. This has asymmetries, due to weaker growth in Europe and the greater dynamism of US international corporations which have a strong presence in Europe, but there is more stability under the macromanagement pattern in the EU, while there are stresses in the Western Hemisphere macroeconomic cooperation.

Outside the Atlantic context, the USA is more extensively involved than Europe in the world economy, because of the larger scale operations of its international firms, and the vigorous management of trade and investment policies which facilitate their activities. The more active US corporate presence that is developing in Latin America will gradually add to the revenues supporting the growth of transnational production systems linked with that presence. European investment and trade is a moderate challenge for US firms in the Southern Hemisphere, and history suggests that initiatives to expand it will be relatively weak, despite the effect of hemispheric trade liberalization on Latin American policy orientations: the attraction of the US market will have become stronger.

The main area of US economic involvement outside Atlantic relations is East Asia, where structural interdependencies are seen to be more challenging than in the Southern Hemisphere, and these have to be managed under exceptional constraints because of large East Asian dollar reserves that are used to sustain upward pressures on the US dollar, in conjunction with investment flows to the USA.[1] Issues in this regional context demand more immediate policy level attention in the USA than problems of hemispheric trade liberalization which can be managed with greater bargaining leverage. Longer term considerations, however, necessitate that the USA focus on the formation of a hemispheric free trade area.

A Free Trade Area of the Americas (FTAA) can prepare the way for transformation of the hemisphere into a large zone of stability and growth. Successions of macromanagement failures by incompetent and poorly motivated administrations have caused decades of lost growth in Latin America, with heavy accumulations of debt, prolonged dependence on primary industries, general discouragement of entrepreneurship, acute vulnerabilities to volatility in global markets for primary products, and persistent failures to overcome problems of institutional development. Overall technological lags behind the USA have become larger, and attempts at sub-regional integration have been unsuccessful. The USA, meanwhile, has experienced a recession after a speculative boom in the 1990s which evidenced serious weaknesses in macromanagement, despite clear dangers of destabilization. Very large current account deficits threaten to force currency depreciation, fiscal deficits are pushing up high levels of government debt, and yet increases in exports that could aid growth have been hindered by upward pressures on the currency until recently, due in large measure to investment inflows. Altogether, serious problems will have to be overcome as hemispheric commerce is liberalized, but the basic logic of regional market integration will remain valid. Moreover learning experiences resulting from the challenges of rising and often unequal interdependencies may well develop through spontaneous expansions of cross border consultative networks.

If there is progress towards collaborative hemispheric management, through endeavors to develop and harmonize trade, investment, competition, and infrastructure policies, functioning in the common interest, an FTAA could become a highly constructive partner of the EU in the international political economy. A key consideration is that the dynamics of US macromanagement, through intensified sensitivities to multilevel interdependencies, could become more oriented toward integrative cooperation with Latin American countries, while enhancing their capacities for productive responses.

CONVERGING PERSPECTIVES

Assessment of the significance of an FTAA for the world economy has to focus on a complex pattern of reciprocal causality in which extensive cross border structural change is activated by transnational enterprises operating in macromanagement patterns that have varying degrees of openness. Rivalries and forms of cooperation between the transnational enterprises affect and are affected by the macroeconomic and microeconomic policies of governments relating to each other on the basis of interests in trade and investment liberalization, but also on concerns with enhancing structural competitiveness and with using or resisting leverage for policy changes that may alter spreads of gains from world commerce. The transnational enterprises operate with increasing autonomy, advantaged by the investment bidding of governments, and in rivalries for world market shares drive weaker firms into decline. International concentration trends result, but there is little cooperation between governments, except in Atlantic relations, where US antitrust authorities interact with those in the EU. Governments, meanwhile, lose elements of economic sovereignty, as corporations expand international production systems, but they can exert greater influence on corporate activities by forming regional economic integration systems.

The formation of a regional integration system tends to alter the terms of interaction between policy levels and firms, depending on the degrees of integration attained and the extent to which a liberal or coordinated regional market economy becomes established. In a free trade area, the absence of institutionalized collective management leaves wide scope for independent corporate activity, and will in effect widen that for enterprises based in the larger members, while tending to reduce the scope for structural initiatives in the smaller members. A major extraregional consequence is likely to be that use of the opportunities for expansion by firms based in the larger member or members will facilitate gains elsewhere in the world economy. A further probability is that a free trade area, to the extent that cohesion develops between its members, will be a concentration of relative bargaining strengths in multilateral trade liberalization negotiations. Finally, of possible significance for policy learning and corporate learning, a free trade area may have demonstration effects, indicating potentials for productive collaboration that may influence outside states, while attracting some of them to associate with its actual or projected dynamism.

Trends and issues in the international political economy, meanwhile, can be challenges for the management of interdependencies in a free trade area. This is especially evident in the operations of international financial markets. Comparative regional systems theory has to take note of work in behavioral finance that raises questions about efficiencies and also to consider the destabilizing effects of international financial flows, while indicating requirements for more effective regulation of those flows.[2] Problems of institutionalizing the necessary regulatory arrangements also have to be recognized, with insights drawn from institutional economics.

Macromanagement theory, adapting to governance imperatives as advanced economies become more knowledge based and structurally more interdependent, with asymmetries, while recognizing also problems of advanced political development, has to become integrated with regional systems theory.[3] In a free trade area, macromanagement capabilities tend to be exposed more directly to competitive pressures, with consequences that affect the extraregional trade and investment of member countries. Macromanagement difficulties, moreover, can motivate efforts by larger members to impose adjustment costs on smaller countries that may in a sense be locked into a free trade area.

NEW ECONOMIES AND NEW REGIONALISM

In an FTAA the USA's status as a *new economy* will have special significance because of the dynamic effect which it will tend to have on the evolution of knowledge based economies in Latin America, through direct investment, trade, communication flows, and contributions to infrastructure development. Meanwhile the further development of the US new economy in the context of hemispheric market integration will strengthen the US role in Atlantic economic relations, the main area of interregional interdependence in world commerce.

Technology based growth in the USA is sustained through continuing frontier innovations, with advances in European and Japanese research being drawn upon as US firms and research institutes develop international linkages. Financing the development and application of frontier technologies is more and more feasible for large US enterprises gaining stronger positions in world markets, and enables them to increase leads in the building of advanced production capabilities, notably in rivalries with European and Japanese firms. Problems of entrepreneurial coordination persist in the USA, but in a changing context in which technology based alliances are formed, leading however to mergers and acquisitions which increase concentration trends, and these can restrict opportunities for new entrants. The overall dynamism of knowledge based growth tends to attract investment from slower growing areas, including the EU, while encouraging quests in those areas for preferential trading relations with the USA. The most important opportunities for US responses to those quests are in East Asia. As noted, political difficulties hindering East Asia regional cooperation allow the USA wide scope for choice in expanding forms of liberalized bilateral commerce.[4]

While the USA is a new economy in the sense of being highly knowledge intensive, generating increases in total factor productivity with multiplying applications of frontier research, it has also been considered new in terms of the financing of growth. Appreciations of stocks during the 1990s boom facilitated speculative funding of new technologies which, through productivity advances, were expected to sustain the asset appreciations. Much of the wealth effect however went into consumption, while the stock appreciations rose faster than the productivity increases, which were mainly the consequences of new information and communication technologies that lowered transaction costs and facilitated larger scale entrepreneurial coordination, notably in the management of transnational production systems.[5] A major feature of this process was the attraction of high volume investment inflows from the rest of the world, contributing to the asset appreciations and to their consumption and production effects. A long standing problem of external imbalance became more serious as related currency appreciation and increases in domestic demand, in excess of domestic output, caused very large current account imbalances to approach unsustainable levels.

The new economy has thus been challenged to institute more functional knowledge intensive macromanagement, through regulatory restraint on speculative stock appreciations, monetary policy measures to reduce overvaluation of the currency, and engagement with the problem of external imbalance through initiatives to increase domestic output substantially. Extensive corporate cooperation has clearly been required, because strong combinations of incentives to produce at foreign locations have in effect been strengthened by the growth philosophy of the new economy. Macroeconomic cooperation by other governments has become functionally more imperative, but a further effect of the liberal orientation has been to limit interest in regional economic collaboration.

Yet interest in an FTAA, in conjunction with the enlargement of the EU, can be considered indicative of a new regionalism. Large internal markets with substantial technology based growth potentials attract smaller and less developed outside economies. For those economies there are also incentives to combine with others in similar circumstances for purposes of market integration and to build coalitions for the representation, of interests in multilateral trade negotiations. The perceived opportunities depend on geographic and cultural factors. It must be stressed, however, that geography has severely limited Latin American options in this regard, while in contrast the EU's immediate neighbors are responsive to its attraction and also have incentives to collaborate with each other, although these are not as substantial as those motivating the development of closer ties with the Union.

The new regionalism, then, is primarily a European trend, but its logic is given some expression in the growth of trade and investment links between EU members, especially in Spain and Portugal, with Latin America.[6] These links tend to encourage market led use of the Euro on a modest scale, which may diminish with hemispheric trade liberalization, as that will make the attraction of the US market more potent. Latin American countries can cultivate ties with Europe to diversify their foreign economic relations, but have to reckon with the EU's status as a lower growth area compared with the USA, and as a regional integration system with decisional problems that could hinder management of economic cooperation ventures in the Southern Hemisphere.

The functional logic of the new regionalism, for the USA and Latin American countries, can be seen as an imperative to devote much energy to the formation of a dynamic hemispheric integrated market. The motivating vision, however, has to recognize that the functional logic will tend to increase general awareness that economic policy cooperation on a widening scale would assist orderly and dynamic development of the hemisphere's rising structural linkages. Plans for integrated regional infrastructure development could thus be considered more and more appropriate. The formation of a system of regional financial regulation could also be recognized as a functional imperative. A rationale for hemispheric competition policy cooperation could also be seen. Policy level inclination in the USA and Latin America may be to wait upon events, in view of all the uncertainties of initial evolution in a free trade area, but the hoped for growth effects of hemispheric market integration clearly will depend on planning for engagement with the collective management issues to be anticipated in view of the production and marketing linkages that will expand with wider ranging entrepreneurship.

INTER-REGIONAL INTEGRATION

A hemispheric free trade area will become associated with the Atlantic pattern of deepening integration formed by cross investment and trade between the

USA and the EU. Structural asymmetries in this pattern are becoming more pronounced because of overall disparities between US and European enterprise in terms of organizational strengths, financial resources, technological levels, international market positions, and entrepreneurial vigor. Because of the magnitude and complexity of issues affecting the evolution of the structural interdependencies, however, numerous consultative networks of official and corporate representatives operate to aggregate interests and contribute to a rather functional pattern of multilevel Atlantic governance. This is knowledge based and is conducive to interregional community formation.[7]

The formation of consultative networks that seems likely on a smaller scale in a hemispheric free trade area would initially have few links with the Atlantic pattern but would tend to develop closer connections with it, because of the growth of European economic ties with the Southern Hemisphere. European and Latin American interests in the expansion of those ties would no doubt become more active in response to the challenges of hemispheric market integration.

For the USA, however, the very large dimensions of the Atlantic interdependencies will continue to demand high priority attention, because of the EU's enlargement, the importance of joint management of the world trading system and of collaborative regulation of international finance, as well as the wide range of global security issues on which European cooperation has to be sought. The EU, moreover, is being challenged to be much more active in Atlantic relations than in its links with the Southern Hemisphere, and in particular has to cope with the problem of large investment outflows to the USA, which limit prospects for regionally based growth in Europe.

Stresses in Atlantic economic relations, affecting potentials for collaborative management of the rising interdependencies between the USA and the EU, are tending to increase, despite the consultative activities in the networks of multilevel governance, because of US compulsions to expand exports on a large scale, so that unsustainable current account deficits will be reduced. The EU is under pressure to make its market more open and to adopt expansionary macroeconomic policies that will increase demand for imports. With enlargement, however, European bargaining capabilities have been strengthened, and meanwhile European assessments of the relationship have had to take account of problems of stability in the US economy that have been persisting since the onset of its post-1990s recession.

The potential for increased regionally based growth that can be seen in a hemispheric free trade area has long term significance for the USA's Atlantic relations, but it must be stressed that the magnitude of the issues in those relations tends to force vigorous self-reliance for the achievement of short term results. Politically, demands for European cooperation can be domestically advantageous, because of protectionist demands roused by high volume trade deficits. While this means that hemispheric market integration may well have low priority it also means that trade policy activism responsive to protectionist demands in Atlantic relations will tend to be evident also in commercial negotiations with Latin American countries.

In advance of further EU enlargement, and of the possible formation of a stronger and more centralized system of governance in the EU, US trade policy activism may attempt very strong leverage against the EU, for greater market access. This could be intended to have the side effect of discouraging European initiatives to strengthen economic ties with Latin America, and Latin American efforts to develop such bonds. These possibilities deserve consideration by Latin American administrations, especially because their interests in diversifying their foreign economic relations will become stronger while hemispheric trade liberalization continues, and while the EU further expands.

NEW EAST ASIAN BILATERALISM

Outside Atlantic relations the main area of US foreign economic relations is East Asia, and for this area the prospect of hemispheric trade liberalization is significant, primarily because there may be shifts of outward oriented manufacturing from industrializing Southeast Asian countries to Latin America, following increases in US direct investment and the growth of manufacturing export capabilities by Southern Hemisphere firms. US interest in East Asia is responding to trade deficit problems that have been accumulating for decades, and that, as noted, have awkward linkages with the pressures on the US dollar in world currency markets.

Market integration logic is being expressed in East Asian bilateral trade ventures. The most important has been a commitment by China and members of the Association of Southeast Asian Nations (ASEAN) to liberalize their trade over a ten-year period. Evaluation of this has had to take account of long standing problems of economic cooperation within that Association, and of their interests in commerce with the USA, very much as competitors against China,[8] Japan has been much less active in East Asian bilateral trade diplomacy, but structurally has been very significant because of investment in outward oriented manufacturing throughout the area.

East Asian tendencies to see trade liberalization opportunities in bilateral contexts have been consequences of problems of collective action in the Asia Pacific Economic Cooperation forum (APEC). In this large association the failures of collaboration in ASEAN[9] have contributed to US emphasis on bilateral dealings with Japan, made difficult by that country's financial crisis, and on separate interactions with China. In the latter there has been little scope for leverage to secure balanced trade liberalization, and interactions have been complicated by East Asian security problems. In relations with Japan imperatives for a different type of trade balance, based on intra-industry commerce, have been seen to require direct engagement more comprehensive than that possible with China.

Latin American economic links with East Asia are small, and accordingly hemispheric trade liberalization will have little effect on the major forms of bilateralism in the USA's East Asian relations. Beyond the short term, however, the Southern Hemisphere will tend to attract considerable Japanese foreign direct investment, especially in manufacturing for the US market. If US interest in Asia-Pacific trade liberalization becomes more active, the formation of an FTAA will facilitate more vigorous engagement with issues in commerce with Japan and China. Recognition of this probability could well motivate US efforts to conclude agreements for hemispheric trade liberalization without delay, and in a spirit of liberality conducive to community building, and, thus, to spontaneous initiatives for cooperation in trade related policy areas. The recently concluded US–Singapore free trade area may be a harbinger of what is to come.

GLOBAL GOVERNANCE

Larger scale development of international production systems by US, and, to some extent, European multinationals will be aided, in moderate but increasing degrees, by hemispheric trade liberalization. Global concentration trends in which these firms are involved will also be strengthened. Major challenges will thus be evident for Japan and industrializing East Asian states, especially if there is a US drive for Asia-Pacific market integration. Such a drive, it must be stressed, would require careful management of the monetary interdependence with Japan and industrializing East Asian states that have been achieving export led growth while restraining appreciation of their currencies and acquiring large dollar reserves.

Subject to uncertainties about balances of competitive strengths in Atlantic corporate rivalries, the combined structural effects of hemispheric market integration and the enlargement of the EU will tend to increase investment bidding by industrializing countries in the rest of the world, thus facilitating the expansion of international production systems by US and European transnational enterprises. Increased geographic dispersals of manufacturing processes will be probable, with limitations on technology transfers to host country firms, and restricted opportunities for the development of linkages between those firms and transnational enterprises.

Meanwhile, the internationalization of financial markets, in which concentration trends dominated by US and European firms are continuing, will further interact with the development of international production systems, affecting in particular speculative and productive flows to Latin America. Issues of financial market regulation will demand attention in a hemispheric free trade system, that is, in conjunction with problems of Atlantic and global financial regulation. The USA will have more and more vital interests in these policy areas because of the difficulties of extending the external reach of necessary regulatory tightening at home while transnational production expands and while financial market linkages become stronger,[10] Latin American administrations will have parallel interests and, although these will be on a smaller scale, they will be increasingly significant in the development of hemispheric interdependencies.

The prospect of increasing complementarities of hemispheric interests in the regulation of external as well as regional financial markets may well motivate US and Latin American efforts to form hemispheric policy networks, for knowledge based collaboration. The regulatory interdependencies that will increase with regional market integration demand recognition, and the goodwill that could be generated through constructive engagement with these would help to resolve issues arising directly out of trade liberalization as well as the related expansion of direct investment. The USA's scope for initiative could be used with positive effects to sponsor long range planning for hemispheric regulatory cooperation, in conjunction with regional infrastructure development.

In the policy priorities of US foreign economic relations, however, an immediate requirement is to combine solidarity building for hemispheric market integration with Atlantic coalition building for further multilateral trade liberalization. That coalition building has become very absorbing, because of the difficulties of securing EU trade concessions of vital interest for US export promotion.[11] Negotiations for hemispheric trade liberalization can be managed apart from the Atlantic diplomacy, but it would be highly advantageous to complete them in advance, with timing to suit the US electoral cycle. Multilateral trade liberalization, in the Doha Round under the World Trade Organization, is likely to be a slow process, with US involvement predicated on achievements in renewed diplomacy for reductions of Asian and Pacific trade barriers.

In the Atlantic coalition building, an urgent task for the USA, and of special interest for Latin America, is to extend domestic financial regulatory tightening in harmony with EU reform while enhancing efficiencies in the funding of productive ventures. US status, for European investors and policymakers, has to be raised because of the numerous cases of corporate fraud during 2001–2003, and the necessary improvements in financial regulation on each side of the Atlantic are needed to reduce flows of investment into high risk speculation that is likely to involve undetected fraud. Increased funding of productive ventures is the objective to be hoped for, in the interests of passive investors and of overall growth in Europe and the USA.

Atlantic financial market reform and regulatory tightening will help to sustain Atlantic monetary cooperation, by contributing to more dynamic and more stable interdependent growth, and to the development of more productive interactions in policy communities shaping consensual assessments of issues of inflation, growth, and exchange rate stability confronting the Federal Reserve and the European Central Bank. Active Atlantic monetary cooperation will be essential while US macroeconomic policies work for renewed and more stable growth, and for the urgent objective of external balance.[12] Latin American association with the USA in the major areas of Atlantic cooperation, while informal, would have bargaining advantages, or mutual benefit, and could also help to make the interactions more knowledge intensive, especially with the aid of specialists in the Organization of American States, the Inter-American Development Bank, and the Economic Commission for Latin America and the Caribbean.

Latin American administrations, it must be stressed, will have to collaborate with US regulatory authorities to ensure sound development of emerging financial markets in the Southern Hemisphere, that is, to improve conditions for domestically and regionally based growth and to attract foreign direct investment. European involvement in these emerging markets will have to be brought under the necessary new regulatory arrangements, and this may well require special US efforts to secure Brazilian cooperation, and to allay Brazilian concerns about possible elements of regulatory protectionism in US policy, directed against Europe and also Japan.[13]

The development of numerous multilevel consultative links between US and Latin American policy communities in a hemispheric free trade area will increase the challenges of knowledge intensive external accountability for administrations in the Southern Hemisphere. The diffuse effects on problems of political development could be very beneficial. Meanwhile US involvement in the major areas of global economic governance would gradually assume more representative status, with demonstrable effects that could encourage responsiveness in parts of the world where regional collaboration has been difficult, including especially East Asia. A hemispheric free trade area could prove to be a vital learning experience, for each participating government, and for corporate associations. This will be all the more likely if there is intensive concerted collaboration, with visions of fairness and reciprocity derived from new thinking in behavioral macroeconomics,[14] with new understandings of linkages between efficiencies and social justice, and of imperatives to generate knowledge intensive and highly motivated social capital.

A revised Washington Consensus,[15] sensitive to issues of interdependent governance, can prepare the way for a hemispheric consensus, more broadly knowledge based, and more oriented toward comprehensive micromanagement, with collegial capitalism. This consensus could well become linked with an Atlantic consensus on the formation of a coordinated interregional market economy, distinguished by collaborative liberal administrative guidance and entrepreneurial dynamism.

NOTES

1. See Ronald I. McKinnon (2001), 'Euroland and East Asia in a dollar-based international monetary system: Mundell revisited', in Guillermo A. Calvo, Rudiger Dornbusch and Maurice Obstfeld (eds), *Money, Capital Mobility and Trade*, Cambridge, MA: MIT Press, ch. 12.
2. See John Grieve Smith (2003), 'Agenda for Global Financial Reform', *International Review of Applied Economics*, **17**, 1 (January), 115–20; and Wendy Dobson and Gary Clyde Hufbauer (2001), *World Capital Markets*, Washington, DC: Institute for International Economics.
3. Growth becomes less domestically based as structural interdependences increase and, with these, regional market integration offers prospects of higher growth through production specializations. Regional economic cooperation can thus become more necessary for macromanagement. Hence it must also become more knowledge intensive, especially because the structural linkages develop with more and more applications of advanced technologies. See discussions of the knowledge based economy in Daniele Archibugi and Bengt-Ake Lundvall (eds) (2001), *The Globalizing Learning Economy*, Oxford: Oxford University Press; and 'Symposium on the new economy', *Oxford Review of Economic Policy*, **18**, 3 (September) 2002. On new trends in regional cooperation see Mario Telo (ed.) (2001), *European Union and New Regionalism*, Aldershot: Ashgate.
4. See Zainal-Abidin Mahani (2002), 'ASEAN integration: at risk of going in different directions', *The World Economy*, **25**, 9 (September); 1263–78 and Peter Lloyd 'New bilateralism in the Asia-Pacific', in ibid., 1279–96.
5. See Symposium on the New Economy.
6. See Alvaro Vasconcelos (2001), 'European Union and MERCOSUR', in M. Telo, *European Union and New Regionalism*, ch. 7.
7. See references to consultative networks in Mark A. Pollack and Gregory C. Shaffer (eds) (2001), *TransAtlantic Governance in the Global Economy*, Lanham: Rowman & Littlefield.
8. See Lloyd, 'New Bilateralism in the Asia-Pacific'.
9. See Mahani, 'ASEAN Integration'.
10. The regulatory tightening has to cope with European reluctance to cooperate as well as with resistance by US investment and auditing groups, while the scale of international corporate activities is enormous compared with the surveillance capabilities of US regulators. See coverage in *The Financial Times*, 9 January 2003, 24 January 2003, and 10 January 2003.
11. For a US perspective on the Atlantic trade problems see Robert Zoellick and Ann Veneman (2003), 'No half measures in the quest for free trade', *Financial Times*, 7 April.
12. See Pier Carlo Padoan (ed.) (2001), *Monetary Union, Employment and Growth*, Cheltenham: Edward Elgar.
13. See references to regulatory protectionism in Benn Steil (2003), *Building a Transatlantic Securities Market*, New York: Council on Foreign Relations.
14. See Joseph E. Stiglitz 'Information and the change in the paradigm in economics', *American Economic Review*, **92**, 3 (June), 460–501.
15. See Pedro-Pablo Kuczynski and John Williamson (eds) (2003), *After the Washington Consensus*, Washington, DC: Institute for International Economics.

Index